A FURLONG TO GO...

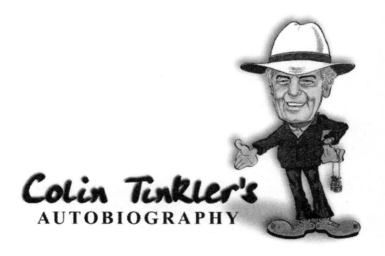

Colin Tinkler's
AUTOBIOGRAPHY

GREENWATER
PUBLISHING

First published in Great Britain in 2001
by Greenwater Publishing
A division of Crystalsight Limited

A CIP catalogue record for this book is available
from the British Library

ISBN 1-903267-06-4

Printed and bound in Great Britain by Mackays of Chatham PLC

Contents

Introduction

I'm Colin Howson Tinkler, the senior member of the Tinkler Racing Clan. From the outset it was always my intention to complete this autobiography by the time I reached my seventy fifth year. This has been done and all that occurs from now on is another story in which no doubt the younger elements of the Tinkler Clan will predominate. I suppose, other than my gambling escapades, I'm best known for being responsible for introducing group ownership (in its present form) to racing and for my part in, what was, the immensely successful 'Full Circle'. But there has been so much more, to describe events as unique would be putting it mildly; in fact at times my life has been totally bizarre. Yes, it would have been easy to have done little, then life would have been so boring!

In the following pages I've tried to give a true insight of how things have been for me and how I have perceived them over the years, whether it be with humour or differently. At the same time I've refrained from entering into controversy and sensationalism, no matter how intriguing it would have been to have done so. I'm also aware that some readers might find certain passages of limited interest, but they have had to be included to give support to some sort of continuity to the autobiography.

I'm generally known as GEEGA; the name originated when I was in my mid thirties. I'd helped to organise a mini Grand National, for ponies, being held at a riding school. I'd built the course with a miniature Bechers Brook, a Canal Turn - the lot and I also acted as the starter. There was one small pony in the race, being ridden by a girl of about ten, which refused to start until I gave it a bit of vocal. The pony then bolted across the field and deposited the rider into a slimy smelly manure heap! Crawling out of the sludge and pointing in my direction, 'The little stinker' screamed "It's that old Geega in the flat cap's f*****g fault - he shouldn't have bawled at me!" though I'm sure she meant to say old geezer!

Appreciation

I wish to say how much I appreciate Margaret Pawson, for all the work she has done in transferring my scribble into type and for her cheerful tolerance. I also thank all those at C. & E. Rowsby for their similar assistance.

Photographs

Chapter one

The early years

In the early days of racing, before there were commentaries, a bell would sound the Off at most of the courses. In fact they still use one at Ascot as the runners turn into the straight - a lovely exciting sound.

Well I'm going to give the bell a ring for the start of my autobiography and I hope you don't find the going too heavy!

I was born on the 26th June, 1926 in rather an expensive nursing home in Darlington, which is just over the border from Yorkshire. My mother, who I always referred to as Mumso, had the fact that it was expensive tattooed on my bum - you know - like Made in Hong Kong but, in my case, Made in expensive nursing home! I don't know whether I was born with a silver spoon in my mouth but, if I was, I'd bet it wouldn't have been paid for. You see, my parents, no matter what their own financial position was at any given time, seemed to have the notion that people didn't require being paid for things; consequently very few got paid for anything! Apparently the 26th of June that year was a glorious day - well of course it was! But there was one little cloud in the blue sky, just one, my two year old brother called Peter. He kept on poking me to see if I would cry and I did incessantly; in fact I howled and I've had a big gob ever since! They do say it was because of me the expression 'what a howler' came into being. I have already hinted that my parents had a yo-yo existence with money; however, they were rather flush at the time of my arrival. I understand my nanny got the sack for stealing a couple of large solid gold nappy pins - yes, gold nappy pins!

Mumso (called Winifred) was born just before the end of the nineteenth century - was rather small and tubby and definitely in the Queen Mother mould. She was continually worrying about her figure, but not the one in the bank! A delightful person, and I liked her a lot, but what an utter snob - mind you I always found her terribly amusing. Mumso was permanently on stage. She would have murdered for a title - an unbelievable character. When she hit the thick pile in a five star hotel's foyer or the lounge of an exclusive coffee house she would change gait. I once asked her how she was going to vote in the election, she replied "With a cross and stop insulting my intelligence!" One of her phrases, and she used it with dignified grace, was "I'm in reduced circumstances at the moment." meaning, when translated, that she was flat f*****g broke. Another of her humdingers was "I'm monied you know, I've got independent means" which was somewhat of a contradiction of terms. She missed many a bus she was waiting for because she wouldn't stand at a bus stop, fearing someone might see her and assume that she hadn't got a car! When a bus did appear Mumso, who would be standing some distance away, would suddenly make a bee line for the stop but unfortunately quite often got there too late and would be left puffing and panting and straightening her hat! Another of her idiosyncrasies was, she wouldn't use a public phone box - yes you have it - as if anyone could ever imagine she didn't have a phone at home! A 'Harrods' green carrier bag with the gold lettering was always on hand for the occasional shopping excursion, though, of course, she had most goods delivered!

I don't recall her ever doing very much, though I suppose she must have done. Actually she did like making bread and considered it to be her forte. Probably that's why we had so many bread and butter puddings!

I can't remember her parents (my grandparents) all that well. They used to live in Darlington but both died when I was quite young. I do however recall my grandfather being a nice old boy, with a pipe and a walking stick and before he retired I understand he was an engineer. Mumso would say "He was something on the railway - in a high position of course". I suppose he would have been if he was constructing bridges! Honestly, Mumso was the original, the forerunner of Mrs. Bouquet, the television character. As to my grandmother, I vaguely recall her rocking away in front of the fire - no, not to music, I'm talking about in a rocking chair!

I will now introduce you to my father, whose name was Harold, and then a few more of my ancestors. When we were very young we used to call my father Daddy then, as my brother and I got a little older, we would have to address him as Sir, when in public. Please don't get the idea he was strict or severe with us, for he wasn't. I only ever got a couple of smacks from him in the whole of my childhood and they were administered with a slipper on a trousered backside, but never a twank from Mumso. I am always a first name person, so my father will throughout be known as Harold. He would be a couple of years younger than Mumso, therefore just missing the First World War (thank goodness he did). I spoke to my brother recently and, on learning I was to write this book, he said "Don't say too much about Daddy will you." Obviously Peter is ashamed and hurt by many of our father's actions during his short yet hectic life. Harold would be five feet ten inches tall and very slim, dark haired with skin like a shammy leather and was a bundle of nervous energy. He always dressed immaculately, totally in fashion, and would go racing in

3

lounge suit and natty bowler, put on at a jaunty angle. He had the features of the legendary Gary Cooper but, if I were to liken him to anyone, it would be that brilliant trainer Ryan Price. Harold had style and an abundance of charm but was unbelievably selfish, in so much as he cared only about his own pleasures. He lived at a hundred miles per hour and drove at the same speed, even in those days. On one occasion, it was a Sunday morning, he had a wager of a 'packet of gaspers' that he could drive up Sutton Bank (a mile long road with hairpin bends and a 1 in 4 gradient) in some impossible time - which he made possible. That was when the road was an ordinary grit surface and there were sheep strolling about! The passenger in the car, a Riley Sports, was Amy Johnson, the airwoman. She was teaching at the local glider school at the time. Actually I wondered how close their friendship was. Anyhow, to celebrate, he threw a party at the Hambleton Hotel.

Harold had many affairs and Mumso knew about most of them. It was a shame for her, she was so loyal and never stopped loving him. I could not understand why at the time but, of course, I do now - love is very powerful. I'm not talking about infatuation, I mean love. Harold would smoke over a hundred cigarettes and drink a couple of bottles of whisky a day, yet I never saw him the slightest bit tipsy. As for eating, it would be scrambled eggs on toast and he had a liking for tomato soup. He would hang his trousers over the bannisters at night to keep them in shape and I can remember on one occasion Mumso getting awfully cross, because one morning a maid had seen him on the landing in his underpants - how times have changed. Another thing he used to do was iron his money (that's where I've got it from!), though it never took him as long as it takes me!! Harold was very well educated, having been to public school at Barnard Castle and was a star pupil. He had a brother Roy, who was a lot younger than he but, apart from a couple of incidents, important as they were, he didn't really come into my life. On leaving 'Barny', as his school was known, Harold got a job in a bank and was soon put in charge of a branch at Stokesley. He apparently took some samples home and the 'higher ups' didn't like that; well, they wouldn't would they! Thankfully his mother's influence smoothed matters over.

He was still in his early twenties when he first met Mumso and he also started to help his mother extensively with her political work. As for his own aspirations, he next went into partnership with Curly Turton, a Middlesbrough bookmaker, and began operating a football pool. That would be in 1923, the same year that Littlewoods commenced and a couple of years prior to Vernons starting. Things went well for a time with more and more people doing their coupon; apparently it was just a straight ten results in those early days. Gradually, as time went on, the dividends being paid out to winners became less and less as more participants appeared to be forecasting correctly. This was not the case, in fact it was Harold putting in coupons after he knew the results that was causing all the damage. Absolutely ludicrous - doing the correct thing was just not in his make up. From that venture, which obviously collapsed, Harold set up business as an insurance broker but he took far too many chances, didn't stop to calculate the risks and there was one fire too many. He was a very heavy gambler; he would not face up to realities and would continually take chances with all aspects of life. He would be selfish one moment then over generous the next; most of what he did was doomed to failure because of his inconsistencies, though his brain kept churning out marvellous ideas. When his insurance firm went into liquidation (I would be three at the time) the Tinkler family moved from Eaumont - our extremely nice home in Darlington - to Stockton to live in one of Harold's mother's houses. I have been back to see the place a couple of times, once about twenty years ago, and got a terrible shock. It had become an utter slum, as had my grandparents' home which was in the adjoining road. This used to have a black marble front door step, which I certainly remember and being ordered not to put a foot on it. My little legs couldn't stretch across so I had to take a running jump; consequently getting from the outside to the inside of the house was like negotiating 'Bechers Brook' and I often slipped up when landing on the polished parquet flooring. The once elegant terraced town house had become a graffiti mess. The marble step was still there but, criminally, it had been painted white. On my second visit only recently it was entirely different; there had been a complete renovation to my old home. It had been transformed into a nice little mews type place and the cobbled street was a picture with its window boxes and hanging baskets. I'm glad I went back for a second look.

Now to tell you something about my grandparents on the Tinkler side. My grandfather died from a heart attack when he was in his early sixties. I recall him picking me up in his arms and saying "Look I am as fit as a fiddle." I find it extraordinary that I can remember word for word what someone actually said all those years ago. He had a large store in Stockton, just off the High Street, which sold furniture, linen and all manner of such things. It was a real old fashioned business but I believe it must have been sold on because when the shop closed some years later it wasn't much of a talking point in our household.

Tinkler is not a name shared by a great many people compared with the majority of other surnames, though it is more likely to be found in the North East than elsewhere. My grandfather's family had always been farmers from away back; that, of course, was before the area became industrialised. I understand that one of my enterprising ancestors went to India and returned with some elephants to work the land. As they were smaller than the African he thought they would be ideal. The concept was alright but in principle I believe it was a non starter; probably they ate too much!

I will now introduce you to another grandparent and by far the most interesting and controversial of all - that was my father's mother, Jessie. Jessie Tinkler, nee Howson, was always referred to as the grand mater. It stemmed from and was a natural transition from Harold calling his mother the mater. She was born in the late eighteen seventies and, like her husband to be, came from a farming background though one of her forebears was Dr. Howson, the first resident surgeon when the new hospital at Stockton was built at the turn of the nineteenth century. It's extraordinary how little one really knows about one's ancestors and I'm not going to dig too deeply or I might discover that one of the rogues hung alongside Dick Turpin on York Racecourse was either a Tinkler or a Howson!

The grand mater was a real live wire; she stooped badly as time wore on but I understand that in her younger days she was an attractive and immensely bright young lady, at a time when mainly men were to the fore. She only had the two sons and undoubtedly my father Harold was the favourite - unfortunately I was similarly favoured as far as her grandchildren were concerned. I say unfortunately because, in the circumstances, I was expected to go and stay with her from time to time. I was used as a sort of peace offering, when Harold went over to borrow money from her. No matter how much he earned he would always spend more than was affordable; he was not only a workaholic but also a spendaholic. I hated those 'holidays' - they were so boring; she would show me off as her little prince; God, I felt so bloody stupid. I used to divide the days into hours and the hours into minutes and the minutes into seconds, to estimate how long it would be before I was returning home; no wonder I became good at mathematics.

Actually she married a second time; it was later in life and only for companionship for I am sure there was no love there. Her second husband was retired, I believe from the army, and died after a year living with Jessie! Personally I hadn't expected him to last that long and I'm convinced he died from mothball poisoning. You see the grand mater had a thing about moths - she disliked them intensely - consequently there were mothballs everywhere and I mean everywhere. I once ate one thinking it was a mint! The grand mater was greatly respected around Stockton and did an awful lot for the poor people of the town, especially the children. She was very much into politics and helped Macmillan, who eventually became Prime Minister, when he stood for the Conservatives in the Labour stronghold of Stockton in 1926. In fact she was the first political woman agent in the country. Apparently Harold (my father) used to drive her about with blue posters stuck all over her very smart little yellow Austin Seven. Without a doubt it was because of her campaigning that Macmillan won the seat and was returned to Westminster but there were ructions in the camp. The grand mater once told me that she and Macmillan had been lovers and that his wife, Lady Dorothy, had got to know of it. Apparently matters became awkward, in fact very difficult, and Jessie did not receive the recognition she deserved for all the work she had done. The grand mater was so upset that at the next election she changed her alliance and Macmillan lost the seat. He did however get elected a couple of years later but a woman's scorn can be very damaging.

Apart from politics her other main interests were horse racing and the 'dogs'. She was a regular visitor to the greyhound track at Middlesbrough which opened in 1928 and Stockton had a racecourse in those days which unfortunately is now an industrial estate. I didn't go racing more than a couple of times with her though on one of those occasions, when I was about eight or nine, I remember Willy Nevett having a double and the name stuck in my mind. I don't suppose I gave it a thought that one day he would train for me.

The following happened during the last time I stayed over at the grand mater's. She had moved house a couple of times over the previous ten years and was by then living in a quiet cul-de-sac near to the park in Stockton. It was a summer evening and I was doing nothing in particular when my Uncle Roy arrived. He was extremely agitated and wanted to have a talk with his mother, so I agreed to go and see a film and mentioned that I would be back soon after nine o'clock. When I did return the road was cordoned off by the police, who asked who I was and, after I explained, they let me go into the house. The grand mater was in bed and, on seeing her, I got a terrible shock, she had aged twenty years and had a lot of black bruising about the neck. Apparently there had been a row - nobody ever knew what about - and Roy had tried to strangle her. It seems he ran out of the house and, bumping into a neighbour, shouted "I have killed her, she is dead." It was the neighbour who called the police and the ambulance but Jessie refused to go to hospital or press charges and, as the police knew her well, they respected her wishes. Roy was not seen for several days and I know he and his mother never spoke again. Hanging was the order of the day at the time and just how near was Roy to that end.

When Jessie died many years later, in her mid eighties, there were only five people at her funeral; very few people knew she had died - or cared. I thought, what a shame, because she had done so much for the town of Stockton. I went and Roy was one of the others but he made it plain that he would rather not have been there. As for my father, he had already died by that time. The grand mater always seemed to be bearing a grudge, which made her not a nice person - she appeared to be so unhappy and disillusioned; probably she had a lot to be disillusioned about.

The first thing I can remember in my life was a ghastly nightmare. I would have been three at the time. I was going to nursery school so it wouldn't have been any earlier than that. Someone very stupidly had sent my brother Peter a book of Hans Andersen's Fairy Tales. I had been looking at the drawings on some of the pages and it was that which had triggered off the nightmare. Rows of hideously ugly, smashed guillotined heads, slowly went past me; they were covered in blood and I was screaming. Mumso came into my room; I told her I was dreaming and what I was seeing. I was sobbing "Please waken me, I'm still dreaming." I was so full of fear. Mumso said I could not be dreaming if I was talking to her. I screamed "Here come the heads again and they are falling on to the bed." I don't know if the bedroom light was on or not but I was not awake. I was having a nightmare the whole time. If only Mumso could have understood. The horror of it all left a lasting and cruel impression on my mind.

The taxi business Harold had ventured into, along with other enterprises, was not doing well, so it was bye bye to the private school with its little black shoes and grey uniform, the coloured cards to play with and the glass of mid-morning milk with ginger snaps. Oh yes, and the good conduct stars. I got some of those but I never knew what the hell for. It was then on to a council school; in fact I went to two such schools in the short time we remained in the town. It's strange but I don't recall Peter, my brother, being at either. Home for me was always a happy place, though not a secure one; even at that early age I was aware of the problems. My parents didn't show any real affection towards me and I always knew Mumso preferred Peter. There must have been a difference of opinion with the grand mater regarding the house, because we suddenly moved to Darlington and stayed with Mumso's people for a while, which of course meant yet another school. I would be six by then and had already been to four. This one wasn't too bad actually, though nobody liked the way I spoke. I had a couple of fights - well I had to stamp my authority! I'm not sure what Harold was doing for a living during this time but the taxi business was no more. I'm not saying much about Peter but we must have got on very well because I would have remembered otherwise. By the way, he was always three or four inches taller than me and still is and I don't think I will be catching him up now! After a few months in Darlington, the Tinklers moved to a newly built house in Kirkby Overblow, a village a few miles south of Harrogate. My parents rented the property and by certain standards it was not great, though naturally Peter and I were very pleased about the move into the country.

Kirkby Overblow was and still is a lovely little village though today most of the properties have been beautifully renovated and are now very expensive homes. Harold had got a new job, a very responsible position with the West Yorkshire Bus Company; he had to handle and be accountable for large sums of money. I thought - "Please, don't get your money mixed up with theirs or, what is rather more important, don't get their money mixed up with yours!" We moved to the village in the spring of 1933. I reached my seventh birthday in the June and I started at the little school after the summer break. It was a very relaxed and easy going place, where happiness seemed to be the main criteria and this I found very much to my liking. There would only be about forty pupils, with ages ranging to school leaving age. The oldest boy there frequently used to be kept back after lessons, as a sort of punishment for misbehaving. The headmistress would remove his pants and put him across her lap for a twanking. The boy told me "I get naughty on purpose like, it's right good fun and it don't hurt but don't tell anyone about it cos I don't want me dad to find out". Of course, he didn't want his dad to find out; if dad found out, dad would be first in the queue to be naughty! I didn't become much of a scholar whilst I was there; in fact nobody did.

Living in the village was really exciting; Peter and I would go exploring through the woods and across the fields. The things I remember most were the bluebells, there seemed to be so many, the birds nests which were like little treasure troves and the perpetual smell of horse manure in the air - what a combination! Whenever the fox hounds came through the village, Peter and I would follow them for miles and miles. It would not matter if it were a school day or not - we would be off. The hunt was such a colourful spectacle. There seemed to be so much activity, the sound of the horn, all the hollering and the noise of the hounds. Then there was the steam rising from the gleaming horses, the ladies riding side saddle wearing black and the bright red coats of the huntsmen and others. It always seemed to be misty or pouring with rain but nobody cared, least of all Peter and I, but I did care about the cruelty that seemed to be in the air. I know I always wanted the fox to get away - and it usually did.

I was passing through the village recently - the leaves were coming off the trees, it was misty and raining, the same mist, the same rain. I got out of the car - it was over sixty five years since I ran down that road and clambered over the gate, the same gate. In my mind I could hear the sound of the hunting horn and over a hundred horses cantering by; it was ghostly and very emotional and I felt rather sad - I don't know why - perhaps it was a touch of nostalgia.

We had been at Kirkby Overblow about six months when my sister Ann was born, on October the twenty eighth; it was early evening and Harold had not arrived home from work. Mumso asked Peter or I to go and get the district nurse, who lived in the village, to come as quickly as possible. She was West Indian, which was unusual in those times, and I remember her being a very kind person. Ann arrived and all was well but Mumso was not happy living in a village; she felt cut off from civilisation, particularly with Harold being away so much, so the Tinklers upped sticks and moved to 'Green Lane', Knaresborough. At the time there were fields between the new houses, which were being constructed, and the town but, of course, it has been built up since. I took the move in my stride; I suppose I had no option. I was only seven yet had a delightful crush on a girl back at Kirkby Overblow. She was twice my age, tall and thin with blonde hair and dark eyebrows - without a doubt the prettiest girl in the school. Have I ever wondered what happened to her? Well, not until now!

An amazing incident occurred just before we left. There was a cart horse that had foaled at the neighbouring farm and Mumso thought it would be a good idea if Peter and I could be photographed with them both. Just before she clicked the camera a scruffy boy jumped over the wall and said "Missus can I av me phota tuk wiff em?" With that he stood between Peter and myself, Mumso took the snap and then the boy must have run off, because he disappeared. None of us saw where he went and we had not seen him before in the village. Amazingly, he didn't come out on the photo - just the mare, the foal, Peter and myself and the space where he had stood between us was filled by the grass in the field and the hedge that was behind us. We discovered later that a boy had died at the farm a few years before. Extraordinary and most decidedly unexplainable!

We all liked our new home on the outskirts of Knaresborough and settled in well. It was a nicer place than the one we had left in the village and, of course, we were more or less still in the country. Again, my parents had not bought our new home but that was no problem. We had jolly nice neighbours, especially on one side, and I would like to give them a mention. Fred Eshelby was a bouncy little fellow, a brilliant cricketer who worked for an insurance company; his wife Bessie was a nice girl and they remained good friends with Mumso throughout their lives. Fred must have had a touch of shell shock during the war because he returned a different person and a trifle unbalanced; he became a scruffy recluse and just rotted away. They had two boys who were a real credit to them. One joined the Navy and became Commander of a nuclear submarine; then later was promoted to Admiral.

I went to school number six and was pretty hopeless apart from maths. On one occasion a teacher asked me to add sixteen twice then twice again. She said it very fast and I realised she was trying to confuse me. I replied "Sixty four and when I grow up I won't be a teacher trying to catch out little boys!" I got caned for insolence but it was worth it. We did the usual things that families did, though Harold was always on the go and didn't spend a lot of time at home; however at weekends he would take us onto the moors or to the seaside. On one occasion we all went to the Bramham Moor Point-to-Point; it was my very first race meeting and I was enthralled. Amazingly, half a century later, whilst going through some old books I unearthed a photograph of me being there. I was very young, nevertheless I felt for my parents for I realised there was a general shortage of money in the Tinkler household, though I suppose in general I was happy enough. However there was a sad note; a young girl who lived a few houses away from us died after having an operation. That disturbed me, just as it had when one of Peter's little friends got knocked down and killed when we were at nursery school. I'm not suggesting anything in particular triggered it off, but I had a nervous breakdown. I continually nodded my head and this went on for months and months. I was ordered to have a complete rest and went to the seaside for a holiday but to no avail and naturally school was out of the question. It was during this time that Harold lost some of his firm's money. He said it had been stolen from the car while parked in Doncaster - it happened to be St. Leger week, enough said and, of course, he lost his job. I suppose one could say it was a blessing in disguise because he had two or three really good things going for him - charm, ambition and he was a workaholic. He went over to Leeds and called in at Pointings. Most of the car showrooms were in Albion Street before the war and this firm were not only distributors for the Nuffield Group but also main agents for other makes. Harold told them he didn't require a salary but would work on commission only and assured them he would boost their sales. He must have impressed, because he started work immediately and went house hunting around Leeds. Without Mumso having seen it, he bought a property on a new development in Moortown, again with fields all around. Once again, the house had just been built and Mumso was delighted. They fitted the place out with new carpets and curtains and a lot of new furniture. I was now ten and had completely recovered from the illness - matters seemed to be improving for the Tinklers and I'm sure that helped me a great deal. Now for school number seven, which was within walking distance of our home. On my first day there I was jumped on by some older boys but I gave them hell; I was small but I was tough. The message went through the school like quicksilver - "Don't tamper with the new kid, he's dynamite." It's funny what one remembers but a little girl came up to me and said "Are you going to be a boxer when you grow up?" I told her I was, so she said I could have a look at her knickers! I don't see the connection actually. Do I wonder what happened to her? No, but I have a good idea!

Harold set Pointings alight. The Manufacturers wanted him on their stands at the Motor Show and Mumso was walking on air and back with the snob routine. My little sister was growing up all the time and Peter and I had been booked into Leeds Grammar School, which along with Manchester Grammar were, I believe, the only two totally non boarding schools which had the public school tab.

The day came when Peter and I had to take the common entrance examination. My brother just managed to scrape through but I could hardly read some of the questions, never mind answer them, though apparently my maths marks were exceptional. There was a post mortem at the Tinklers as to why I had failed so miserably. Harold was extremely angry and considered I had been lazy. He said learning is all in the mind; I thought, that's an obvious statement and Mumso informed me in her upmarket voice that I would never become a doctor. A doctor! This was a new one to me; besides, if our family was anything to go by, doctors never got paid! I suggested that as I was only eleven years old, at my seventh school and had missed a year's education due to the nervous breakdown, these facts might collectively have been responsible for my academic shortcomings. No - it was decided that I was just plain bloody lazy and that I should yet again change schools to one that just might not tolerate my attitude!

School number eight was run by the council but it was not a large place and consequently there were not many pupils. I had to take a tram ride to get there; yes, we used to have trams in those days. They would go glang, glang up and down the middle of the roads. The headmaster was very keen on sport and encouraged my boxing - I had taken it up as I realised there were certain perks to be had! He also put me in the school football team. However he did have a chat with me regarding lessons and made it clear that his reputation was on the line and wanted me to try hard and learn enough to get a place at 'Leeds' the following year.

Harold was working very hard and going great guns. He would sell on average three or four new cars every day, and was never still; time was always at a premium. Having said that, he was actually spending more time with us. We would go to the rugby and cricket at Headingley and would also go quite often to the boxing in Leeds on a Sunday afternoon. I enjoyed that more than anything and found the whole atmosphere so fascinating. It was held in a large, old, rough wooden building; there was the cheering, the stamping feet, the smoke, the gambling, the lights over the ring, all the toughs, the hangers on, the sawdust and the chicks looking for clients. I might not have passed the common entrance but, at that young age, I was bright enough to know what the hookers, and I don't mean the ones with the gloves on, were doing.

When we didn't go to the boxing on a Sunday we would all go off in the car somewhere. This was not a new thing but seemed to be happening more often than it had in the past. Harold had also started to take us racing. I can remember having a nice day at Pontefract and Wetherby was always on the agenda; in fact, we hardly missed a meeting there around that time. In those days the queue of cars used to stretch for miles on all the roads into the little town and then down to the racecourse. The bookmakers would allow me to bet in sixpences, saying "We will need you when you grow up". Little did they know it was me who was going to need them! I hardly ever lost. It was great. Some of Harold's friends would ask me which I was backing and give me some money when they won. I kept scrap books from the racing papers and, after all these years, still have them.

Peter was also very keen, though he was probably a little apprehensive about his future, but I knew where I was going - into racing in some capacity or other. I remember sending away to a saddlers in London for one of their glossy catalogues. That was another time my parents were furious with me. I didn't understand why, because I thought it was rather enterprising. I found it more stimulating than 'Beano' or 'Film Fun'. I just liked looking at the photos of bridles, saddles and horse rugs; crazy may be, but I was dreaming of the future.

Harold was always in a hurry. He drove around as if the accelerator pedal was stuck and thought he had the exclusive rights to the roads. There was the occasion when he had some business in Huddersfield and took me along for the run, promising we would do the magical 'ton'. On the way back we reached twenty miles an hour plus that; it was some speed in those days. The car was an M.G. Tourer - not the midget, but a larger model. Talking about those M.G. Midgets, the Leeds Police used them on patrol duty and Harold would lend them cars for the weekend in return for not being stopped for speeding. He had many accidents and unfortunately was involved in one when a person was killed. Admittedly he was not at fault but had a girl with him at the time; they were on their way to her place. What made it worse was that she was the wife of a good friend but, it appears, not as good a friend as she was! She lived at Harewood with her husband in a lovely house; he was very keen on polo and kept a string of ponies. His business was in Leeds, producing dripping for the trade such as hotels and fish and chip shops. I remember the Tinkler family going to their home one Sunday and thinking something was afoot with Harold and the wife. As I have said earlier, Mumso knew of the affairs but preferred to believe they didn't exist.

During the summer of '37 it was decided that we should tour the highlands of Scotland. Harold was to do all the driving because Mumso couldn't drive, that is apart from the back seat, and she did that incredibly well, especially on that Scottish run. "Mind the sheep." "There's a bridge ahead." "There is a car coming towards us." "Are the lights on?" "I can hear a chattering noise." - "So can we Mumso, so shut up." Actually we did the whole excursion in four days, but it was still enjoyable. I liked the hotels, particularly The Queen's in Perth where I have stayed many times since and where I bought some Scotch rock from a sweet shop close by. According to Mumso we were all correctly attired for Scotland - she and my little sister wore Fair Isle - "The best, you know" - and had kilts made from some "Very good quality cloth in Tinkler tartan you know." I was able to laugh in spite of the fact that Peter and I were rigged out in Plus Fours in heavy tweed and it was August and bloody hot. With my little legs I felt a right twit togged up like a gun dog's dinner. I'm surprised Mumso didn't get Harold a 'crook', at least it would have been in keeping. Back to those Plus Fours; it was definitely Mumso's idea, it had to be, and I haven't mentioned the little green tabs on the socks - well I have now! I suppose she must have seen a photo in The Tatler of some Lord Pratt's son wearing a pair and thought - my boys would look just perfect, dressed so. By the way, we toured Scotland with a copy of Country Life on the rear window ledge of the Wolseley; and to use more of Mumso's delightful dialogue "One of the large models you know"!

When Harold was doing the taxiing he used to chauffeur parties to Blackpool illuminations and was always saying how marvellous they were and promising that one day he would take the family. The day arrived, it was in the autumn after the Scottish gallop round. We set off in the evening and were half way across the moors when

Harold decided to stop. We were miles from any civilisation, it was pitch black and, as we got out of the car, Mumso said to me "Colin, a car might be coming soon, one never knows, so if you require a little 'wee wee' go over the other side of the wall and undo your fly buttons (no zips in those days) - don't just roll up your trouser leg". Chance would have been a fine thing, I was in those bloody stupid Plus Fours again, wasn't I! Actually there was very nearly a disastrous outcome to that stop. I did as I was told, jumped over the wall and rolled and rolled down what was a steep bank. Had I clambered over a couple of yards further along I would have been into a deep quarry and undoubtedly killed. I have flown over the place many times since, on my way to Haydock Park, and always think of what might have occurred.

We had not been at Street Lane all that long - in fact the road had only recently been tarmacadamed - when Harold and Mumso came home one afternoon and announced they had bought another house, it was in Adel and just off the Leeds - Otley road. I thought, Crikey, not again! As I write I can hear Mumso saying "A much more refined area. It's a larger house, we will be able to have servants again and I must get the Tatler every week from now on." I replied "But Mumso, I believe it's only published monthly and, by the way, have you thought about school number nine for me?" Actually it was a nice house, detached, mock tudor with four or five bedrooms. Adel was basically a village which had become sort of suburban but had retained the village school, next to the church and close to the most picturesque little golf course.

The decorators came and went, as did the carpet and curtain fitters and some of the servants stayed longer than others, though I preferred just to call them girls. It was a case of Madam for Mumso, Sir for Harold and Master Peter and Master Colin and, naturally,

Miss Ann! I thought, what have I done to deserve this! Mind you, I thought the same when one of the girls, she was only fourteen and had come from one of the mining villages in Durham, said "When I'm at home I always bath my brother; would you like me to bath you." I was not all that partial to baths but I suddenly had a distinct change of mind! I asked her how old was her brother and she told me he was nearly a year! We agreed not to tell Peter about the 'spongings', because we thought he might be envious and mention it to Mumso. She wasn't with us all that long, though long enough to give me several 'spongings'; unfortunately she had to return home to look after her mother who was ill. Most of the girls who left home to work in houses were too young to be away; they were like little lost kittens but, as you have gathered, not all of them!

We have come to the spring of 1938 - I was eleven years old and nobody was worrying about a war that, most people believed, just couldn't happen - Bradman and Hutton were smashing balls to the boundary - Donald Campbell and others were going faster and faster - footballers got a rise to £8 a week and Tommy Farr was the heavyweight to admire. One could buy an exceptionally nice house for under a thousand and Fords had introduced a car, licensed and ready to drive away, for less than £100. Good farmland was changing hands for £25 an acre and for a penny I could gobble down a bag of chips - but I never said anything about the chips to Mumso! It cost me only fourpence to go to the cinema but I invariably sneaked in for nothing! Two pence would buy five Woodbines; I know because I bought a packet of the ghastly things, smoked one, was violently sick and haven't had another cigarette since. There is just one other comparison with today that I will mention. Windsor Lad who had won the Derby in 1934 was insured for a then incredible £30,000 for his stud career. Across the card, most things now cost a hundred times more than they did then, though earning comparisons show some well below that ratio and others far in excess.

Peter, of course, was by now a cog in the wheel at the Leeds Grammar and I was swotting away at The Adel School. My little sister, whom we all loved, had commenced private school which was "Well worth the expense", according to Mumso. Harold had formed a partnership with the sales manager at Pointings. He was also called Harold and they certainly made a formidable team. Basically, they were using Pointings' facilities, the name and the company's capital. It was far better than having a business of their own, which would have incurred overheads. Harold was not yet forty but was burning himself out. Apart from that leathery skin he looked fit and well, but he was like a coiled spring waiting to be released. He wasn't aggressive with the family but was with others; people either liked him or loathed him but it was mainly the former. He would swear a great deal but no more than "damn" and "blast" with a few bloody hells, which was mild by today's 'language' and delightful amusing Mumso was still in her element, swanning around with an air of superiority and living a pretence when reality would have been enough. Both Harold and she liked partying; I'm not talking about high flying rave ups, but just nicely socialising. If they had not arranged for people to call round for the evening they would go out somewhere themselves. I can't remember when we, as a family, had a quiet few hours at home. They both hated gardening; never in a million years can I imagine them doing any. In fact Peter and I took over the work of cutting the lawns and that sort of thing, though Peter did the majority of the work.

I took my common entrance for Leeds again in the June and passed with flying colours this time. Peter thought it was only because he was already there. That might have been the case, but who cared - it was going to be school number ten for me. Had I ever gone on Mastermind my chosen subject would have been 'architecture of English schools'; I had seen the inside of so many of them!

During the summer my interest in racing developed further. Harold became my bookmaker. I would make out a list of my day's bets and he would have them before he left for the showroom in the mornings. He had a sixpenny limit as my stake on each individual wager; apparently it was to protect his liabilities! I thought, what liabilities? - when I win I don't get paid out! Peter and I were not given pocket money as such but would not be refused money if we asked for some but, of course, I am only talking about small amounts, enough to go to the cinema or buy sweets and that sort of thing. However I was also building up quite a nice little bank from the days I actually went racing and backed with the bookmakers on the course. There was one occasion when Peter was invited to go to York races with a friend called Michael Hope and his parents. I gave Peter a shilling to put on Catch Penny and it won at 20/1; that would be equivalent to winning more than £100 today.

The next twelve months came and went with matters staying pretty well the same with the Tinklers. But life wasn't boring as so much was happening all the time. There was no change in the house staff; we had Freda, who had stayed longer than any of her predecessors. She was in her late teens and her boyfriend used to come and see her quite often. When war broke out they married but tragically he was killed, I only hope things turned out well for her eventually. For a prank I once put a toy mouse attached to a string in her bed which I pulled from another room. You can imagine the screams when she got into bed and I gave the string a tug. I was a nasty little sod at times - some say I still am!

23

I didn't like Leeds Grammar School because I found the work so difficult but enjoyed the sports, though they didn't have boxing. I played rugger and cricket for the Colts and was Captain of my form yet bottom academically. Having said that I was jolly good at two subjects, maths and cribbing! Talking about bottom, I received six on mine from a cane for not knowing some Latin. All I can say is I deserved it, for I shouldn't have been so stupid as to lose my cribbing card! The lack of tuition from the previous nine schools had undoubtedly left its mark just as the Latin Master had! To get to school we had to go by bus; some of the boys had bus passes which their parents had bought but Peter and I would just buy a daily ticket from the money Mumso gave us. I soon realised I could make a bit of spare cash here, so I bought an old pass from one of the boys, altered the date and covered the whole thing with sticky jam. The reason for the jam was two fold, to make the date even more illegible, and which conductor would want to inspect a grubby pass covered in sticky jam? I was prepared to do one for Peter, but he declined the offer saying he didn't want anything to do with the 'sticky business' - he just wasn't adventurous. Half way through the summer term I caught flu or something. It was just before my thirteenth birthday, consequently I didn't go back to school again that term. In fact I never attended school again. War broke out in September and the school was dispersed all over the place but Peter and I, along with many others, didn't take up the option of evacuation, so I actually left school when I was twelve!

During the August of 1939 the international situation looked very black and most people at last realised war was imminent. We had booked a holiday on the Norfolk Broads for the last week of the month and it was decided that, in spite of the impending trouble, we would still go.

On the way down to Norwich, where the boat was kept, we

stopped overnight at Newmarket and watched the horses gallop on the heath the following morning. It was exceptionally misty but that made it all the more magical and exciting - this was going to be my life but I still hadn't thought how I was going to enter into it. The gallop watchers and touts knew every horse by name but what they didn't know was that the little boy on the heath that morning was going to bring about a radical change to racing with the introduction of group ownership. Yes, agreed, someone else would eventually have thought of the idea but it was I that first approached The Jockey Club with the concept and had it approved. The touts would have been even more surprised if they had been told that the same little fellow would introduce racing information by a premium rate service and receive literally millions of phone calls. We stayed on the heath for about an hour and then took the Bury road heading for the Norfolk Broads and it had certainly been a very impressionable hour for me. Luckily it was a brand new cruiser; that really was the icing on the cake and what a marvellous time we had. It was fantastic but, true to form and par for the course, Harold had the throttle full on all the way, up and down the rivers flat out; everyone else was relaxing but not the Tinklers and I thought it was supposed to be a Leisure Cruiser! I don't think the small dinghy we were towing ever touched the water! We did stop occasionally, when Harold spotted a really nice riverside pub - then he would shout "Fenders down - get ready to tie up". Also, of course, in the evenings, we used to 'drop anchor' near a riverside village, do some shopping and have a meal. The weather was gorgeous; I remember it being very hot indeed and none of us wanted the holiday to end.

There was an amusing scenario to the holiday, which was pure Mumso at her 18 carat snobbery best. Additional to the Tinkler family on board was Freda who, as I have already mentioned, helped

Mumso in the house. Freda would usually be referred to by Mumso as the maid but had now suddenly become the nanny to little Miss Ann, who was by now nearly six. To make the role more authentic Mumso bought Freda a nannies uniform, in fact two such uniforms. One was for mornings - even this had starched cuffs - and another, even more formal, for the afternoons and evenings. Freda was encouraged to 'go on deck' as it was no use having a nanny people couldn't see and she might as well get a suntan on her hands and face; what's more the Broads holiday was considered to be Freda's annual leave - only Mumso could play those cards and keep a straight face!

Chapter two

The war begins

As with most people the war completely changed my life. We had only been back home a few days, from our holiday on the Broads, when hostilities with Germany broke out on September 3rd. There are no words to describe the appalling suffering millions and millions of people were going to endure over the coming years, the stupidity and horror of it all. Words cannot describe the utter barbarism that took place; such acts should never be forgotten or forgiven, but I fear they will be.

The first few days of the war were comparatively quiet though there was an air raid warning on the first night. It was however a false alarm but that didn't prevent fifty powerful searchlights scanning the skies over Leeds, supposedly looking for enemy aircraft. They were play-acting, doing one night stands; Manchester got the lights on the following evening, then Liverpool the next. It was to boost morale and confuse the enemy but I shouldn't think it did either; it was farcical really.

Harold, in his wisdom, decided the best way to combat the German U boats was to get a store of food in as an emergency. We went down to the grocery store but Peter and I stayed in the car; nevertheless we could see, through the large shop window, Harold pacing up and down, indicating he required this and showing interest in that. I thought - 'we will never get it all in the car, we will have to make two or three journeys'. He eventually came out of the shop, followed by one of the assistants carrying a medium sized cardboard box and it wasn't even full - some sugar, half a dozen tins of tomato soup, a tin of ham, two tins of apricots, one tin of cream, and a couple of lettuce - yes, lettuce! When we got back home Harold proudly carried the box into the kitchen and announced "That shopping has made me ravenous." So we all sat down to a meal, the five Tinklers in the dining room and Freda in the kitchen, but only after she had served us, of course! What did we have? Tomato soup for starters, followed by ham salad, with apricots and cream as a sweet. After the meal, which was most enjoyable, I said, in not too loud a voice "Well, we have got something left for the siege, even if it's only two tins of tomato soup!"

Pointings had come to a standstill; most things were going to be rationed, including petrol, and nobody was in a buying mood for a car. Harold's reaction to the situation was to join the army; most of his friends were going to wait to be conscripted, but not he. I don't know the exact connection but Harold knew Walter Easterby, uncle of the brothers Peter and Mick, and it was Walter who introduced him to a high ranking officer at Northern Command in York. The fact that while at school at Barnard Castle Harold had been in the OTC and obtained a 'Cert A' which made him, along with other attributes, officer material. But to come out of the interview a Staff Captain, red tabs and all, in the Service Corps showed his persuasive personality.

His appointment was immediate and he used to travel to York each day to the offices of Northern Command. After a couple of weeks he was told he was to be posted to Derby, where a contingent of the Indian Army was stationed, and it was to be his responsibility to buy all the food for the men and the horses. One's mind boggles at the possibilities for Harold!!

Out of the blue came Harold's decision to sell our home, much against Mumso's wishes; "It's going to get bombed in any case," was his senseless reasoning. He said Freda could get a job in Leeds, making munitions, and live in lodgings and then mentioned that he was right about never letting us keep a dog - I thought, what the hell has that got to do with anything. I asked where were we going to live and was told we would be renting a house in Derby, because there was no Officers' Mess where he was going. No one said anything about education, Peter's, mine or my sister's; it just didn't come into our parents' calculations.

The house sold straight away at a give away price; I remember Mumso was really upset and entitled to be so. I felt so utterly, utterly sorry for her and how things had changed in a couple of months. We moved down to Littleover on the outskirts of Derby; we realised our new home was only temporary but that didn't make the house any more endearing. It was, however, only a few hundred yards from the mansion the army had commandeered as their headquarters. We were only there a few months, but I remember discovering a piece of scrub land not more than half a mile from where we lived. There was quite a lot of gorse about and Peter and I made a miniature steeplechase course; it would be a couple of hundred yards round with a dozen fences. As we had no ponies we had to make do with our own legs but still it was a lot of fun. We had races and, using horses' names, I'd give a running commentary; it was exactly that, a running commentary. I'm not going to say which of us won most of the races, as you would only think I'm a show off! Twenty five years on my two boys did exactly the same thing - even to the commentary - but they had ponies to bring the game nearer to reality and now their children have followed suit. They have horses in the blood; I just got gorse in mine, particularly when I didn't jump high enough at the pretend 'Bechers Brook' fence!

Harold was soon re-posted, this time to Nottingham, which was not such a haul. A Midland Command was being put into operation, answerable to Northern Command but basically a separate entity. Initially there wasn't a mess for the officers, so Harold again lived at home. Mumso found our new place in West Bridgford, a suburb of Nottingham. The property was typical of the district in which every house seemed to have a tarmac drive, a privet hedge, mini iron gates and some crazy paving. No, I didn't like West Bridgford. Besides there were far too many people asking me why I wasn't at school 'number eleven'!

As to the war, the Germans were advancing through France and on to the English Channel and, of course, Dunkirk. It was hard to imagine that the boat we had on the Broads was now under gunfire. It was one of many holiday cruisers, used to bring back to this country the troops stranded on the beaches of France. Racing was still taking place, albeit in a curtailed fashion, The Jockey Club had moved the Derby to Newmarket and, while the race was being run, Dunkirk was happening a few miles away. What a ludicrous situation and how absurd man can be. After Dunkirk we had the threat of the Germans invading and, throughout that summer, the Battle of Britain.

Mumso and Harold, I suppose, were contented enough; we had been at Nottingham six months but everything seemed to be so futile. What the hell were we doing other than wasting our lives away. By the autumn of 1940 the lease we had on the house had expired and this coincided with the Officers Mess being established. Harold was no longer going to live at home and, as we didn't like where we were, it was decided we should have another move. I don't know how it came about but we discovered a farmhouse to let in a village called

Stathern, which was about fourteen miles from Nottingham and in the Vale of Belvoir. Harold had recently bought a car; it was an Austin with no personality at all but it enabled us all to go over and have a look at the newly found property. I liked the village, it had a pub, a garage and a small shop that sold literally everything. It was a quiet place and, apart from market day at Melton Mowbray on a Tuesday, only one bus left Stathern each morning and that was to Nottingham and it returned in the evenings. The village also sported a station about a mile away, which was unmanned and on very much a secondary line. The whole area was open farmland, mostly grass, with a back cloth of the Belvoir Woods on the rising ground. The property we went to view was an old brick farmhouse with a new bathroom fitted. There was a small barn and a couple of cow sheds, the garden being quite large and entirely surrounded by a high brick wall but everywhere was completely overgrown. The place was in the village itself but in no way crammed. I felt it had so many possibilities - we could do so much there. Mumso wondered what it would be like in the winter but, in spite of everything, we moved in. She had been rather quiet over the past twelve months and understandably so, again, there was a serious shortage of money within the Tinkler household. However with the change of air she seemed to take on a new lease of life. She started playing a new role of the privileged Staff Officer's wife who had been evacuated with the children to the country. "I don't mind forfeiting comforts if it's for the children's sake you know but I must have a woman to do the rough - I let my maids go and work in munitions - well, I have got to do my bit you know - We have just brought the bare essentials with us, most of our things are in storage you know." But of course they weren't. She found a woman to do the rough, I believe her name was Tilly but it should have been spelt with an S, as I don't believe she got paid all that often. Her first job in the morning was to clean out the grates and make up the fires and, of course, it was back to the Master Colin and Master Peter routine.

We got through the winter alright and by the spring of 1941 we had things looking pretty tidy. Peter and I had worked very hard since we moved to 'Woodland View' and had transformed the place; amazing really because practically the only money we had spent was on paint. There had been what we thought was a yard made from rubble but, after thoroughly weeding, we discovered the surface was of closely knit, hand made, rust coloured bricks. That was in front of the house and leading onto the road through a pair of large iron gates.

The war was really brought home to all at Stathern, as there was a newly built airfield a couple of miles away across the fields. A dozen planes would set off in the evening to raid Germany and sometimes only three or four would return home the next morning, like tired lame ducks, just skimming the trees. On one occasion an aircraft just skimmed the roof of our home and failed to make base; there was a loud explosion, a ball of fire, then black smoke darkened the sky. The sky would also have been darkened for those close to the airmen that were killed. Later that day we listened to the news on the radio and it said "Last night the RAF bombed Germany with the loss of no aircraft." It was difficult to believe anything one heard on the radio or read in the papers after that.

I remember being asked by one or two who were in the home guard if I would like to join. I would have been fifteen at the time and there would be about a dozen in the outfit altogether. It was all very reminiscent of Dad's Army, though we hadn't any uniforms and only one rifle. We would meet in the evenings at one of the houses and spend hours learning how to clean the rifle after firing - considering we didn't have any ammunition I couldn't see the point. Correction, the old boy with the rifle did have one highly polished bullet - a souvenir from the First World War. He said he was saving it specially for Hitler. I wasn't very popular when I asked, "If Hitler is going to come and land by parachute, which I very much doubt - what guarantee is there that he will land at Stathern?" I was even less in harmony with the others when I was told to bring a pitch fork so I could learn how to us it in battle and I turned up with a spade. I said that I didn't fancy taking on a machine gun-nest with such a primitive weapon and felt the spade would be far more useful, even if only to dig a hole in which to hide! I don't remember whether I was kicked out of the unit or resigned. Most likely both!

Mumso received practically no money from Harold, forcing her to become an artist at getting things without paying for them. Mind you, that had always been the case with Mumso. She didn't know what a settling day was; quite amusing really, but not for everyone! Groceries would be delivered from one first class shop in Nottingham, then from another in Melton Mowbray, then back to Nottingham. Mumso would always give the delivery driver a tip and I would think, they're cheap groceries! I remember her taking Peter and I to a gentlemen's outfitters in Melton Mowbray for some trousers and telling the shop assistant "My husband is a Staff Officer and I have an account here". We bought, though to be more truthful acquired, several items of clothing other than just the trousers. As we left the shop, carrying numerous parcels, Mumso said "Colin, I'm so upset, you should not have asked the assistant, would he consider taking a pair of plus fours in part exchange". I replied "Not as upset as he is going to be when he discovers you don't have an account there". I suggested we make a beeline for the bus station though Mumso was not happy; in her put on 22 carat voice she asked "Must we really go home in a bus?" I said "Yes", then explained why my answer was in the affirmative; we only had ten pence between us and it was going to be a lot easier to dodge paying on a bus than it would be in a taxi". Exactly! Harold would come over to see us periodically and started getting cheques cashed at the village butchers. I'm talking about £60 or £70 at a time and in those days that was not 'Mickey Mouse' money. I thought it would just be a matter of time before one bounced and it was! In fact it was never honoured.

One of the farms in the village, of about two hundred acres, was owned by the Clamp family and was just around the corner from our place. The father had died a few years previously leaving a Mrs. Clamp, her twin boys Tommy and Morris, in their mid twenties, and her daughter Vie, who was a couple of years older than her brothers. We struck up a friendship with them and Peter and I would go and help about the farm. The brothers were very keen on racing and had done a fair bit of point to point riding before the war and still kept one or two horses about the place. Peter and I would earn six shillings a day when the threshing machine came to the farm; it would be our job to take the chaff away. I remember on such days the threshing would disturb the rats that were living in the stacks and they would make a bolt for it. There was a young fellow, a casual helper, who would dive full length to catch them. Everyone knew him as 'terrier'. I also got paid when I chain harrowed the grass fields. I would walk behind a couple of horses that pulled the harrows but we were not generally employed. Of the two brothers Tommy had the more character, but they could both knock back the booze and chase the girls. Tommy used to say "I like them married, it's a lot safer." Actually Morris did marry a very nice girl and got a farm of his own but Tommy and Vie stayed single. Tommy died two or three years ago, leaving quite a lot of money, I was surprised really for he was a heavy gambler and, by seeing him at the races regularly through the years, we had kept in touch. The Clamp boys would take me to 'Melton' market on a Tuesday and to the farm sales where there was always a pub close by. I would pop in for a sandwich and a glass of beer, young as I was, and on one such occasion, this 'old codger' in the corner of the bar kept buying Tommy drink after drink, so I said to Tom "Who is he?" Tommy came back with "I don't know, but if he keeps buying I'll keep supping!"

I remember Mumso spending an evening round at the Clamps and, Tommy being the perfect gentleman for once, escorted her home. When she got back she stormed into the house and announced "I've never been so insulted in all my life". I said to her "Don't get upset Mumso, what happened?" She replied "Absolutely nothing!"

Peter and I had no friends of our own age at Stathern but I secretly adored a gipsy girl; she would be a little younger than me and was so lovely. She lived with her parents and grandparents in a tiny cottage on the outskirts of the village. The whole family used to do odd jobs and on one occasion her uncle was putting a new water supply into the village. He dug the trench and laid the pipes but at one point he deliberately cracked the cast iron before covering it over with soil. I was watching him working at the time; he called everybody 'Surry' and said to me "Surry, I know where the leak will be, but I might just forget; it will be a nice little job for me looking for it!" Actually the grandfather taught me how to be a water diviner. In fact, I can still locate the presence of water underground; not only water but also electric cables.

Chapter three

I go to the dogs

The Clamp family had a couple of greyhounds at the White City, Nottingham. I might be wrong but I believe throughout the war years greyhound racing only took place on Saturday afternoons. Anyway the boys took Peter and me down to the track to see the action. I was amazed at the size of the crowd - literally thousands, including Harold who didn't seem all that surprised to see us. While there I was introduced to Len Harker - he would be in his fifties and had been with greyhounds since the start of track racing in the mid-twenties. As well as breeding greyhounds he also had a pig farm and lived at Clipstone, a village about half a dozen miles from Nottingham. The two businesses worked well together, because he collected swill from hotels and restaurants in and around Nottingham and sorted the most suitable food for the greyhounds and the rest was cooked for the pigs. Len suggested I look after a couple of young dogs for him back at Stathern, give them plenty of exercise and get them fit for the track. He would pay me and Peter was also to be involved. This would be in the spring of 1942 and, looking back, it's rather amazing that it was never in anybody's mind that Peter or I should get a job, even though money was still very tight at the Tinklers. I was backing horses by post with a firm in Glasgow; they would accept bets so long as the envelope was time stamped prior to the time of the race and the stake enclosed by way of a postal order.

At that time there was only one trainer, a young Irishman called Savage, and there were half a dozen kennel staff. In order to ensure the public kept going to the track, Jolly liked to make certain several favourites won at each meeting and Len knew that certain greyhounds got preferential treatment the week prior to a meeting to ensure this would happen. He told me that if I could discover which dogs they were, or even just one a meeting, he would pay me between £15 and £20 a week, depending on how much he won punting and, of course, I was not to tell anyone else. £20 a week on top of the £2 wage I would be getting was fantastic money in those days; it doesn't take much imagination to work out what it would mean in today's figures. Greyhound racing was booming, there was so much money about and one could appreciate the logic of the stadium's owner. As long as the punters kept going through the turnstiles, there was the gate money, revenue from the tote and, in the long term, the bookmakers would also gain.

I asked Len if it had always been his intention, since we first met, for me to work at the White City. Apparently it had and he was convinced that I could do the job properly and make a lot of money. I rang for an interview and saw the racing manager, who asked if I knew Mr. Harker; I said that I did and that he had sent me dogs to look after. I believe being open and above board helped me to get the job, though he was rather curious and I think it was touch and go. Mumso was rather upset at what I was going to do and thought it was so degrading and wanted to know "How many staff officers' sons would be working with greyhounds or whippets or whatever they are!" Mumso also mentioned the word 'Doctor' again and that I could have gone to night school. I had to remind her of the fact that I didn't even go to day school!

I used to catch the bus each morning at about 7.30 and get back

I was winning money but not that much; definitely not enough to make a living.

Len Harker brought the greyhounds over and one of the cowsheds made a perfect kennel. We built some traps and had an old upturned bicycle, using the back wheel to haul two hundred yards of string with a rabbit skin on the end. It was about this time that Harold came over - he seemed extremely agitated and was pacing up and down. Then he suddenly said "We will go for a run in the car, take the road through the woods and shoot a pheasant for dinner." I couldn't understand what it was all about but went along with his wishes. Harold insisted he went into the wood on his own; after a few minutes we heard a couple of revolver shots and when he emerged he was ashen and there was no need to ask what had happened. He had gone into the wood to shoot himself but changed his mind at the last moment and fired the revolver to get rid of the bullets. Apparently, though we didn't know at the time, Harold had set up house with a girl in Nottingham, telling her that Mumso existed but they were separated and that she had money of her own. At the time Harold was in the wood contemplating suicide the girl was having the first of their children. What an appalling situation he had created and Mumso did not know of the terrible state of affairs for some time; his mind must have been in complete turmoil. One could never reason with him, making it impossible to get close enough to help.

Len Harker was pleased with the way we looked after his dogs and replaced them with a couple more. Then out of the blue he came over to see me and mentioned that there was a vacancy at the White City in Nottingham for a kennel boy. He explained the set up - the track was owned by a person called Jolly, who also ran a large taxi business in the town. All the dogs were trained at the track, which was nearer Trent Bridge than the location of the present White City.

home to Stathern early in the evening. There would be about eighty dogs in the entire kennels and I had a dozen in my row to look after. It was amazing, but I soon got to recognise every dog in the place and after only a couple of weeks I had the whole caboodle sussed; by the time I had been there a month I saw a couple of dogs I was sure would go well on the Saturday. Along with others they both had a trial on the Thursday finishing first and second. They looked a million dollars and, if my memory serves me right, I believe one of them was called Maesyoo Maroya. I phoned Len that evening and mentioned that I hadn't contacted earlier because I wanted to be sure about things; actually he was surprised I was in touch so soon and I felt he was not all that confident in what I was saying - but he should have been; both dogs were favourites and both dogs won their races. Looking after those that Len had sent me had certainly taught me a great deal. Len was a very quiet and unassuming person and didn't say much when he came over to Stathern on the Monday evening and handed me a little bundle of £1 notes; there were twenty two of them and I was suddenly rich. I wasn't greedy but decided I would also do some punting, though I would have to be very discreet. I suppose the good thing was that the dogs would be a short price, making it easy for anyone to get on comparatively unnoticed, - or so I thought. Of course, I personally was not going to do the actual betting; Peter could do it to start with. I realised the whole thing would not last - well I didn't imagine it could possibly do so. The following Thursday it was the same routine at the White City but I only managed to see one trial and obviously didn't want to fuel suspicion by being too 'quizzy'. There was a dog from my row which won the trial easily and during the past couple of weeks had been sparkling; Len and I agreed I should phone him from Stathern when I got back on Friday evenings. On this particular Friday lunchtime however I went down to the shops for something to eat and get an early edition evening paper with the tomorrow dog card in - we were on the front in a handicap. I knew the starter and the hare controller would be 'sympathetic' which is something that would not be tolerated today.

On the way back to the track I had to pass a factory or it might have been a laundry; there was a low brick wall in front of the building where four or five girls were sitting in the sunshine. As I was passing they started to chat and said they wanted to show me something in the store - what they should have said was they wanted me to show them something in the store! They jumped on me and you can imagine what they did! I thought my birthday had come two weeks early! They seemed a bit concerned afterwards but I assured them that I would forget all about it; though obviously I haven't!

I phoned Len when I got back to Stathern and mentioned that Peter was going to the track to punt for me; I told him because I wished to be totally straight about things and he appreciated that. The dog duly won; I can't remember the exact figures involved but it was something in the region of £50 in bets and a score from Len Hawker. As the weeks progressed we increased the stakes and I had not given Len one single loser - incredible I know, but these are the facts. They had all been favourites and his payments to me had stayed the same, between £16 and £23 a week; which nowadays is similar to receiving £1,000 a week and remember I was barely sixteen. It was certain that not only Harker and ourselves knew about and were backing the 'good things'; I was not so naive as to think otherwise.

On one of the Saturdays I decided to give Peter a break, solely to allay any suspicions there might be, and I called in an uncle of ours called Bernard. He was Mumso's brother-in-law, a rather negative and insignificant person really, who drove a three wheeled Reliant and sported a little Hitler moustache which, in the circumstances of what was happening in the world, showed his stupidity. Now Bernard had never been to a race meeting in his life, neither dogs nor horses, nor had he ever felt a lovely crisp white fiver. I don't think he had a job at the time and lived just north of Wolverhampton. He came over to Nottingham by train and I booked him in at the Black Boy Hotel and told him the 'birds' might be a nuisance. He said "Yes, I have noticed a lot of pigeons in the square, so will keep the windows shut!" - Crikey, he was thick! To illustrate proceedings to him I used matchboxes for the bookmakers' boards, little lead cowboys for punters and Red Indians for the bookmakers, which I thought was rather appropriate really! I went through the whole rigmarole of what he had to do and gave him twenty white fivers - that was £5 for each bookmaker on dog number 5 in the fourth race. I didn't say this to him but I thought he would have difficulty, because of the time factor, to get the lot on. The greyhound was a recent arrival at the track and there had been a lot of hype in the press about her. I'm sure she would have won without any help and she certainly had plenty of that. But please understand I'm not suggesting any drugs were being used, it was just a question of certain dogs having matters in their favour. Bernard was to get a taxi to the track and, as soon as the race was over, he was to go back to the Black Boy, have some tea sent up to his room and wait for me there.

In the fourth race I was leading round one of the runners but also watching the line of bookmakers and they were shouting evens the field. The tote indicator was showing about the same, but there was no activity from Uncle Bernard - what the hell was he doing, or rather not doing? We put the dogs in the traps, the hare swished past and thirty seconds later the big, brindled bitch flew past the post well clear. I was soon to know what had happened - Bernard had got the wrong bloody race; as I was leading round for the next, I saw the little Mustachio bobbing in and out between the bookmakers, placing bets. Trap 5 was showing 3/1; of course there was always a chance it could win, but it didn't. I realised it was entirely my fault. I should not have asked a complete novice to do a difficult job such as remembering in which race to do the punting! I was not only thinking about the £100 I could have won but also the £100 plus expenses I had lost. On arriving at the Black Boy after racing I was told Uncle B was in his room so they called him down and, as he stepped out of the lift and before I could say anything, he called out "We did it" and handed me a brown paper bag containing one bookmaker's ticket and £610. He had backed number 4 in the fifth race, completely the wrong way round, and miraculously the dog had won at 6/1 - utterly - utterly incredible. He managed to get all the money on though one bookmaker said he had not pointed to number 4 and wouldn't pay him, hence the bookmaker's ticket and some of the prices he received varied slightly. Bernard didn't think it strange that the bookmakers gave him so much money when I had mentioned the previous evening that it would be far less. I don't believe he really grasped what had happened. Anyhow I gave him £25 and his expenses and he was over the moon. I never saw him again for he died from a heart attack the following year, which is something I nearly did - that Saturday afternoon!

Jack Hardy, a bookmaker who later also became a racehorse trainer, made a book at the White City at the time I was there. Jack is not alive now but a few years ago we were reminiscing and I mentioned the 'Uncle Bernard' episode and the circumstances behind what had happened. Jack could remember the whole affair which had mystified all the bookmakers. They wondered who was this 'cheese' that knew nothing about betting and who went down the line, bang, bang, bang, won all that money and was never seen again. They were wondering who was behind him? Well, Jack finally found out even though it took him fifty years to do so.

I had been at the track just short of four months when Len mentioned that there was a rumour going round that I had made thousands since I'd been working there. I suppose people were bound to put two and two together though it appears they hadn't connected Len in any way. In the circumstances I was not surprised when, a couple of weeks later, on a Friday afternoon, the racing manager called me into his office and handed me an envelope. I guessed what was in it and guessed right; my activities had decidedly not been to his liking! Even if the Tinklers had kept a lower profile and done less punting or even none at all, it would still have been just a question of time. To me the most amazing thing was that the bonanza had lasted as long as it had. Len was obviously disappointed but philosophical; I suppose he had to be, besides he must have won an awful lot of money. We remained good friends over the years and had been one hundred per cent with each other. I mentioned it was a Friday when I left the job but I still had a good thing for the Saturday - it was a dog called 'Whirlspring'; his sister was in the same race and I decided I would go for a forecast. I went down myself to do the punting but on reflection it was not the most sensible thing to have done; nothing was said but there might have been, though at no time had I done anything untowards. Anyhow Whirlspring won and the forecast was also successful making me over £500. The perfect end to what had been a nice little earner but fortunes can change as I was to find out.

We had just short of £4,000 in the kitty and had not backed a loser; with the value of money as it was then, the figure was staggering. I can't recall Mumso's reaction to what had happened but obviously she must have been pleased and, as for Harold, he wasn't coming over to see us as often as he had been doing and he never knew. Had he known, I'm sure he would have asked me to cash a cheque!!

The main issue was what to do. The house was kept going without any aggravation but we certainly didn't spend, spend, spend. Peter and I had worked well together and all the money had gone into a pool, so we decided to invest some of it by going into business breeding greyhounds. We altered the place to provide for this and bought a couple of bitches. The better of the two we acquired from Aldridges sales in London for £60, the other we received as a gift from Len Hawker. Over the next couple of years everything seemed to be going satisfactorily; we bought two more bitches to breed from and sold a number of youngsters. They had not exactly set the world on fire but had made reasonable prices. Some were sent down to Aldridges and others were bought by the greyhound track at Middlesbrough. Len had introduced me to Burns, their racing manager, who had a fixed price of £60 each; they had to be dogs, not bitches, neither had they to be too big but their breeding was immaterial- a very useful outlet.

Looking back we had no definite plans for the future but nobody had; the war was still raging and, until things got back to normal, people were in limbo. As Peter was eighteen he was required to register for National Service. This he did but somehow his papers got mislaid at the Enrolment Office which, one must say, was a sort of bonus for him. The greyhounds required a lot of milk but it was against the law to give them any unless from one's own cow, so I bought a rather old, but newly calved, Friesian from Melton Market. I used to tether her in a wide grass lane on the outskirts of the village and made a small trailer which I pulled by a bicycle; this was used to take her water and, of course, to bring back the milk! She started by giving six gallons a day and was the purchase of a lifetime, as she cost only £18. The Clamp boys had taught me how to milk and it certainly proved very useful. We got the bread we required from a baker who used to deliver by horse and trap and never got round to Stathern until midnight; he was very ghostly and costly! As for the meat, I would buy dead sheep and calves from farmers in the area, skin them and cook the carcass in a large washing boiler. The niff was a little overpowering at times especially for Mumso's nose! She would say "Oh what a terrible smell, I hope the neighbours don't think I'm preparing dinner." Actually there was a very unfortunate incident connected with the dog meat; once cooked, I used to put it through a giant mincer. On one occasion, while doing this, I stretched for a knife and was not looking at what I was doing. Peter picked it up at precisely the same moment, with the result that the tendons on three of my fingers on the right hand were badly cut. The injury has been permanent and the stupidity of not having it attended to when it first happened has caused me many problems.

Although it was not required by the Middlesbrough track we always used top class stud dogs and the difference in the people who owned them and how the dogs were kept was unbelievable. With not having a car we went everywhere by bus or train. I remember going over to Manchester and from the station I took a taxi to this old farm dwelling which had become surrounded by new houses. They were nice people, but rather eccentric; greyhounds were everywhere; there was a bitch and her pups in the bath and every door in the house was eaten away. Of course there were no carpets - they just swilled the floors. The stud dog slept on their bed and ducks wandered in and out of the kitchen. What did they offer me for tea? Duck eggs - no bread, just two duck eggs and a cup of goats milk! Another place I went to which was entirely different was the Dewar's near East Grinstead. They bred and raced horses and were also keen on coursing. The greyhounds were trained by a person called Steel, who also looked after the breeding side and all the dogs were kept in a range of kennels at the stud. The whole property was in a most beautiful setting. I arrived early evening with my bitch, the mating was accomplished and I said I would return for her the next morning, having booked in at the Felbridge a couple of miles away. I decided to walk back to the hotel and to take a short cut across some fields. Suddenly a blanket of fog came down and I couldn't see a thing. I was utterly stranded but did eventually reach some post and rails; unfortunately these only led me to a pond! Despite difficulties I made my way back along the fence to a gate where I realised my safest option was to stay put until the fog cleared but it didn't until seven the next morning! It was early spring, had been very frosty and I was bitterly cold and hungry. When I got to the kennels I apologised for arriving sooner than I said I would, but didn't mention my ordeal - no way was I going to advertise my stupidity!

Peter and I were kept reasonably busy and any hint of a girlfriend Mumso would make some uncalled for sarcastic remark. Basically I am, and always have been, far too sensitive, an attribute which has done me no favours over the years. I was doing a fair amount of punting; I remember having a very large bet on Dante when he won the Derby and an even larger punt on Tudor Minstrel when he didn't a couple of years later.

By the spring of 1945 the war in Europe was finally coming to a close and in the Far East the Americans were to drop the atom bomb that also ended the conflict out there. I was then eighteen and my sister Ann was eleven and growing up; She was a lovely girl, totally unspoilt and managed remarkably well to cope with all the trials and tribulations the Tinkler family went through during her young life. Peter and Mumso decided the local school Ann was attending was no longer suitable and she should go to boarding school at Stamford Bridge. To me it was crazy. For financial reasons it was obvious there was no guarantee that she would be able to stay there until her education was completed. We had got through a fair amount of money one way and another. The greyhounds were not, as yet, paying their way and prices were falling, which was not a healthy state of affairs; what is more Mumso was receiving zero money from Harold. The authorities eventually decided that they were happy that Peter was doing farm work as against standing guard outside Buckingham Palace! Actually he did little of one and nothing of the other! As for myself, I was awaiting developments from the Conscription Board. There was an inkling they wanted to send me down the mines - not the Siberian salt mines but the British coal ones, which I wasn't all that pleased about! As you can see, the Tinklers situation was not that stable.

Over the next few years we suffered many reverses, some of monumental importance. Harold came over one morning to have a talk with us, or rather with Mumso, but Peter and I were present. It had been ages since we had seen him and he arrived with no buttons on his military tunic; they had been removed, as he had been cashiered from the Army. I don't know the full reasons but one was that he had a number of call girls on the Army payroll as civilian typists. Many years later I had a runner at Towcester where the late Mr. Schilizzi was a steward. He came up to me and said "Had you a father called Harold?" He told me he'd been Harold's Senior Officer in the war when they were on the staff at Derby and Nottingham. He talked about Harold being cashiered and considered he had been used as a scapegoat. He confirmed that everybody knew what was going on, even though not all approved, and apparently the crunch came when some legitimate typists were called in to type! Harold's reason for coming over to see Mumso was to tell her that the army had fired him and now had a position with Moss Empires, the theatre people, and was going to be their manager in Leeds. But then he dropped a real bombshell; he was going to set up home with the new person in his life and their little girl. Mumso was devastated; it came completely out of the blue. It was the old story of the wife being the last to know. Mumso, under pressure from Peter and I, which we had no right to impose, reluctantly put in for a separation. Harold didn't stay long in his new job and I don't know the circumstances of his leaving but I could guess! I did make one excursion up to Leeds to see him while he was there. My intention was to try and convince him of his responsibilities as far as Mumso and Ann were concerned, but it was to no avail. The girl in the ticket kiosk at the Leeds Empire commented on how much alike my elder brother Harold and I were; it was obvious what he had been saying. Actually that was the last time I ever saw him. His next appointment was manager at a chemical works in Lancashire; I understand that was a very good post indeed but, unfortunately, he soon became alarmingly ill and was admitted to hospital, where he was placed in intensive care. Mumso went over to see him and was so terribly unhappy when she got back. She realised Harold's condition was extremely serious and told us that he was just a grey skeleton. A couple of days later he died. The disease was a form of meningitis, but I personally believe his nervous system, his highly strung emotions and the turmoil that went on inside him played a big part towards causing his death. He was only in his forties; what a terrible waste and what had it all been about. I am appalled to say I had no feelings. I did not build the wall between us, made from selfish bricks; it should have been, and could have been, so different. I know Peter felt the same but, of course, Ann was upset because she didn't know him all that well and Mumso would not hear a word against him. At the funeral, which neither Peter, Ann nor myself went, Mumso pretended to be just a relative, as there already was a Mrs. Tinkler there with her little girl. Mumso did many silly things in her life as we all do, but that piece of devotion was the silliest, yet most unselfish, thing she ever did. The grand mater never got over the tragedy and she also died shortly afterwards. I will close the paragraph with another piece of sadness to add to the Harold saga, something I didn't know until quite recently; Harold and his girlfriend also had a baby boy during their relationship and apparently they had him adopted; my thoughts are not very charitable, not very charitable at all.

During this time I had an idea to develop a new greyhound track and as I knew the Knaresborough district quite well I chose that town. I did an awful lot of research and managed to interest a local solicitor in the enterprise. He was sure we would get a licence to operate and was prepared to back me with some of the finance that was going to be required. The council had some land near the river which would have been ideal, if I could have leased it, and it was on the cards that I could. Of course, there would have been some opposition to the scheme from some of the towns people but that was only to be expected. I was not proposing to build some magnificent stadium but just a small, tidy little track for summer racing. Len Harker had one or two people interested, who wanted to talk to me. The trouble wasn't that I lacked sufficient confidence to have a crack but rather that I felt too many people were going to become involved. On reflection I was pleased I hadn't persevered with that particular venture but all the time I was continually thinking about other projects. Every decision in life is similar to being at a crossroads with no sign posts; it is so easy to go in the wrong direction, but rather futile just to stay put.

By the autumn of 1945 the war was over but the country had not got back to normal; there was rationing and a great shortage of some foods, in particular pet foods. One or two national names were still in business but only in a limited capacity. I weighed up the situation, talked it over with Peter and decided to investigate whether we could start manufacturing dog food. I visited several wholesalers in the area and I came to the conclusion we could sell all that we could produce. It would mean taking over a run down knacker yard with a licence and it so happened there was one for sale in Melton Mowbray. Hygiene laws were not so stringent in those days; I'm not referring to cleanliness as such but there were not so many regulations. My idea was to put the dog food in jars with screw tops. The reason for this was threefold - jars were easier to obtain than tin, the cost of bottling against canning limited quantities wouldn't bear comparison and, apart from anything else, the capital outlay would be less. I had arranged to go to Bristol to have talks with people who were connected with a food preserving company, but had to cancel because all our greyhounds suddenly contracted a mystery illness. They would take a couple of strides and fall down; some started gnawing at the muscles of their legs, all were continually shaking. It was an appalling sight and the sound of them whining with pain was just too ghastly. A couple of vets were called in and they diagnosed the disease called Chorea, a viral infection of the nervous system. There was no possible way we could save any of them and the buildings would not be free from the infection for years. We had no alternative other than putting all the dogs to sleep; there were more than twenty altogether, with the youngest being six months. The only consoling factor was that the greyhounds were no longer in pain - but we were. It had been a nightmare of an experience and burying them in the garden was something we should not have done, for it made forgetting less easy. All in all, the venture had lost us a fair amount of money but that seemed of little importance; we liked the dogs and selling them had always been a wrench.

It was at that time I bought a hundred day old chicks, reared them to about ten weeks then sold them on to a butcher. It took him five minutes to kill the lot and I have been a strict vegetarian ever since. I never eat anything that's had a face.

Chapter four

Behind bars

We were forced to shelve the proposed dog food business we had contemplated starting because I'd received further word from the Conscription Board; the war was over but conscription wasn't. I was ordered to report for training at a colliery as I would be working down the mines as opposed to going in to the army; they had eventually come to that firm decision, which I ignored. I was also having a brush with authority because, technically, it had been wrong that I had been feeding the greyhounds milk, even though it was from our own cow. Both matters lingered on through to the beginning of 1946, when a court hearing was arranged, for February and to be held in Leicester. It was a formality that I would be found guilty, on both counts; in fact I was fined £25 or 76 days in prison for the more serious charge and a £1 fine or 7 days in prison for the other. I told the bench I would not be paying but they still gave me a week in which to change my mind, but I didn't.

I should have waited at home to be arrested; instead I popped on the bus to Leicester and literally knocked on the prison door. It caused rather a lot of confusion, because they weren't expecting me! There was no warrant out for my arrest as yet and the wardens told me to go home but I stayed put. I thought the sooner I commenced the sentence, the quicker I would be released. After waiting a couple of hours in an unlocked cell one of the administrators at the prison came to see me; he told me that he had pulled some strings and that I could stay! He also gave me some advice for the future, as if I was going to make a habit of this "Come late in the evening as it still counts as a day." I liked the bit about he pulled some strings, so that I could stay! I should have had my lunch at noon; it was now evening, so naturally the boiled potatoes in their skins plus some soil and the semolina pudding were cold and decidedly uneatable. I had a bath and was given some rough prison clothes and taken to a cell on the top floor. There were 250 prisoners in total, about 50 being Italian prisoners of war who lived in a separate block; they were there for committing sex offences, while working unsupervised on farms. They were a horrible, dirty, scruffy crowd; I'm not inferring that Italians in general are, but this bunch certainly were. I remember once I was going on an errand and had to pass their exercise yard, when they called out "Me jigy jig with you". That was the only time I encountered anything approaching homosexuality whilst in jail. The remainder of the prisoners each had a cell to themselves, identical to those that we have seen many times on television, and there would be about 30 wardens working in shifts.

On day one, as on all days, a bell rang at 6.30 a.m., then the cell doors opened and all the prisoners shuffled along the landings, carrying chamber pots, then queued to 'slop out'; the stench was overpowering and I was violently sick. I couldn't tackle any food for days and, when we did eat, we had all the meals on our own in our cells. During my first morning behind bars, a warder unlocked the cell door and said "Colin, the Governor wants to see you." It was amazing - I was the only inmate the wardens referred to by his first name, but it has always been like that. I am known as Colin or Geega to everyone and very rarely do people say Mr. Tinkler; but I like it

Dr.Howson *(Ancestor).* *(p7)*

I attend my first race meeting at the age of eight - it was the Bramham point to point. *(p14)*

Above:
Stratford race card for my
first ride. *(p67)*

Above:
The race in which I
rode. *(p67)*

Below:
Nothing changes! *(p84)*

Left:
I lead in Foglight after winning at Doncaster (Bob Turnell up). *(p81)*

Above:
Queen Elizabeth presents Marie with the trophy. *(p102)*

Above:
Marie jumping the last on Fanny Rosa to win the Queen Elizabeth Cup (1953). *(p102)*

Above:
Marie with 'Jockey' (young Col). *(p109)*

Above:
'Jockey' wins a leading rein class when only15 months old. *(p112)*

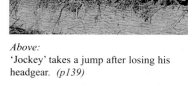

Above:
'Jockey' takes a jump after losing his headgear. *(p139)*

Below:
'The Dog Men' wearing their natty jodhpurs with 'Mr. Chad' on the left. *(p139)*

Left:
Jockey feeding grass to his first pony.

Below:
Nigel on his first pony. *(p161)*

Below:
Nigel with Little Zaneavar. *(p162)*

Left:
Marie going to weigh-in.

Above:
'Word of Honour' after winning the Staintondale Ladies Open Point to Point. *(p154)*

Below:
Marie and Too Dear jump the last at the Middleton. *(p163)*

Above:
Young Col leads in Marie and Too Dear after winning at the Sinnington. *(p163)*

Above:
Marie winning the Ladies Open at Cottenham on
Zangavar. *(p187)*

Below:
Marie and Flexodus capturing the Ladies Open at
the Holderness. (p187)

Above:
Marie on Pin Harbough winning the Ladies Open
Point at the Bramham Moor. *(p199)*

Above:
Our home at lower Dunsforth. (p.127)

Above & Right:
Our home at Boltby. *(p180)*

that way.

The Governor was a pleasant enough person. I was informed that the minimum sentence to qualify for good remission was three months so basically I was going to do a couple of weeks longer by having a shorter sentence! He continued by telling me that as I was educated I would normally have worked in the library but I wasn't going to be there long enough for that. I thought, educated! Some of the others can't have gone to school at all - come to think of it - they most likely hadn't! Actually my duties weren't bad considering; I cleaned windows and had my own ladder! Also, as a trusted person, I cleaned the prison offices in the mornings, including the Governor's. Thank goodness most of them smoked because taking the tab ends back was worth a good supply of duff (fruit pudding) and the newspapers I took out of the waste paper baskets made life easier! Prisoners in those days had no television, no radio nor newspapers; they were kept rather ignorant of what was happening in the world outside. I don't want you to get the idea it was cushy - it wasn't - it was sheer hell. The lack of freedom is what hurt most and everything was so grey, the clothes we wore, the buildings and that bloody high wall. I met a couple of murderers who were doing life, one a young fellow with permanent tears in his eyes. He had been in the Army in India, had deserted, then joined a tribe and married one of the girls; he had killed a British soldier when raiding a convoy of lorries. The other murderer was just a numskull, a thug, but most of the inmates were there for doing petty crimes. Being a vegetarian was a bonus; it meant I was on invalid diet, extra cheese and all that sort of thing. During my last couple of weeks there I was put on food orderly duties, which meant I dished out the food, including the porridge. One or two of the 'guests' would stand in their cell doorways holding out their chamber pots for their cereal, as they held more than the plates! I also did a brisk trade in chocolate bars, from which the cocoa drinks were made. The only drawback to the consumer was they contained an excess of bromide which made them even more dozey than they normally were! Each prisoner was allowed one bath a week - that's when he would be issued with clean clothing and, for a read of my newspapers, I would take over another prisoner's turn on the rota; that way, apart from the extra baths, I always had a clean shirt.

I asked Mumso and Peter not to come and see me but I shouldn't think there was any need for my request. I can't imagine either of them relishing the experience of visiting a member of the family that's 'doing time'! Outside my cell was a card with the date of my release; it was 76 days in total, so I assumed the two sentences were to run concurrently, as against consecutively. The last few days certainly passed slowly and, on the evening before the final day, I got a real blow; I was told I had the other seven days to do or pay the £1 fine. I was dogmatic to the end and told the Governor I would be there for another week. Next morning when my cell was opened I was told "Pack your things, someone has paid your fine." I didn't ask who and I wasn't going to embarrass anyone because I knew the fine had not been paid; they just wanted to get rid of me. Prison routine had been a boring repetition; day after day it was a couple of half hour walks round and round the exercise yard, four hours of work of some description and some actually did sew mail bags; in fact I had a short spell doing so. The rest of the time was spent locked up in the cell. Let's put it this way, it had been an experience, an unpleasant one, but nevertheless, an experience and I can now always recognise an old lag. I have just got to mention the word Duff; it is like a Freemason sign! As soon as I got away from those high walls I took a bus back to Melton Mowbray and then on to Stathern and the thing that struck me most was all the green, all that lovely green. The grass, the trees, the hedges, what a glorious colour. Had I any regrets? Yes, just one - that I didn't use the ladder to escape; it would have added a bit of spice!

Once back home I realized I was going to have to spend the next couple of years down the pits or go back to prison. There was no point fighting a losing battle with the powers that be. The dog food business was still very much in my mind but I realised that, by the time I got out of the mines, the established manufacturers would most likely be back in full production, making starting for the Tinklers very difficult. It wasn't long before I heard from the Coal Board asking me to report for training at their centre at Eastwood, between Derby and Nottingham. We were now approaching summer and the weather was too nice to be going underground like a mole but I was not alone in the farcical situation. There were other Bevin Boys, so called because it was Ernest Bevin, the Minister of Labour, who thought up the crazy scheme, also being trained at Eastwood. We lived in a hostel alongside a couple of hundred other miners, mostly immigrants, including some Irish. An amusing incident occurred during my time there; I was in the dining room when one of the Irish 'lodgers' was kicking up a hell of a fuss, complaining that he couldn't eat his dinner. He was shouting that the meat was cold and that the greens weren't cooked. "It's a bloody disgrace it is for sure and you with your fancy white top hats and all" - actually he had been served a ham salad! Mumso asked me about the food and said "Of course, they won't cook like me." I thought, No, thank God! Most of the staff at the hostel were young Irish girls, very mischievous they were too; I believe that is the nicest way I can put it! When the training was completed I was sent to a colliery in the same area but after a couple of months I was dismissed. The reason

57

being my insistence that the half dozen ponies they had should be treated a lot better in every way. They were in appalling condition, sores on their bodies where the old and ill fitting harness had chaffed. They often worked many consecutive shifts, admittedly only three or four hours a shift but it meant them being out of their stall all the time and hardly ever getting a drink of water. I went to the manager complaining; his response was "I don't care a toss about the ponies, the men, or you; my job is to get the coal out and you are sacked." I'd caused trouble and the ponies were brought up soon after and some were destroyed. Other managers in the vicinity were reluctant to employ me but eventually one did. The mines had recently been nationalised; what the Labour Government had done was to pay millions for a lot of holes in the ground. What is more, many of the mine owners had then been given plum jobs to boot. I was assigned only mundane work such as moving timber, coupling tubs, controlling conveyor belts, all that sort of thing. Some of those jobs took me on to the coal face, which would in some places be a mile or so from the pit shaft but no more than a hundred yards underground. This was not a great distance when one considers all that was happening on the surface. Often the seams were not more than two feet thick with working conditions of about three feet but, of course, the roadways would be higher. As you can imagine, it was not the most pleasant way to spend one's time; the ground was always rough and often there was practically no light. Coal seams naturally go parallel to the ground above and the area where I worked was rather hilly, consequently everywhere had steep inclines making for difficult and dangerous working conditions.

I wasn't bothered about claustrophobia but I was about the dust - it was terrible. Basically I put the miners into two categories, though they all intensely disliked anyone in authority. Firstly there were those that worked on the coal face in various capacities and really grafted. Then we had those that hated work, did as little as they could, and earned a lot less money. There was a distinct dividing line.

I used to work five days a week for less than £1 a day but always got home for the weekends. Peter was keeping 'Woodland View' tidy, Ann was still away at school and seemed to like being there whilst Mumso, on the other hand, was not happy and the whole Harold saga had taken its toll. By the end of 1946 I'd been in the pits eight months and wondered what the hell was I doing there; obviously we were spending more than I was earning, which wasn't very difficult. I was doing some boxing at the time and Peter wanted me to turn professional but I knew I wasn't good enough. Besides, in those days, there was no real money in being a welterweight.

Chapter five

I venture into racing

The next few pages will make incredible reading but the events happened as they are told. The utter stupidity of it all defies all logic but it is not fiction - it was reality.

Peter and I had a board meeting and decided we would go into horse racing and wondered why we had not done so sooner for it was always really what we wanted to do. Peter was to become an owner and a trainer, as for myself, I was to be a jump jockey. What Peter knew about horses was zero and I knew less about riding. In fact I had only been on a horse once in my life and that was for ten seconds! The Clamp boys had some horses in a field and, when they were away, I put a saddle and bridle on the smallest of them, led it to the gate, clambered up and away I went! Ten seconds later I was tasting grass. The bridle had come off and the saddle had slipped underneath the horse as it went galloping round the field; obviously the girth had not been tight enough. One of the farm workers saw what was going on and came to my rescue. I was alright. I just wanted the saddle off the grey and to forget it ever happened. He did manage to catch the horse and remove the saddle but he told me that I had it on the wrong way round. Now, how did I manage that! It was even money and unluckily I'd got it wrong - no wonder I fell off! In fact it's rather amazing how I ever got on in the first place!

As I have said, it was towards the end of 1946 and Peter noticed an advert in the Horse and Hound for an assistant at Harry Kitchen's yard at Stokesley. Peter thought if he went there for a few months he would learn how to ride and pick up a few hints on training. He got the job but unfortunately, whilst there, had a nasty bicycle accident, making a hell of a mess of his face. Harry Kitchen was rather a shrewd trainer and brought off one or two gambles during Peter's time with him, notably Hurgill Lad and Scottish Command at Hamilton Park and Mesena at Redcar. Peter was now doing what I had been doing at The White City, keeping his eyes open, consequently we had some nice little 'touches'. Going back two or three months, that 46-47 winter was a shocker. The worst there had been for a long time and apart from the weekends when I went home, Mumso was at Stathern by herself. Spring came and Caughoo won that memorable Grand National and by the end of June I'd had my twenty first birthday - which went pretty well unnoticed.

While Peter was at Stokesley I did a fair amount of punting which helped with the day to day expenses. The Coal Board had become rather shirty about people taking days off. Because of this and other factors I had delayed learning to ride but I thought, no hassle, I will soon get cracking when we get the horse! At the weekends most of the time was taken up gardening, though I did alter what were originally the cow bays into a couple of stables. I also did a conversion job on a military saddle I'd bought, turning it into a racing exercise job! I was told it had once been used in the Charge of the Light Brigade - I wonder what the word 'Light' referred to. Exactly! Peter had also done some buying from the saddlers up at Stokesley; rugs, bridles, blinkers - I mustn't forget the blinkers - oh, yes, and some tail bandages and that sort of thing. Actually I've mentioned earlier that I had difficulties gripping, because of damaged tendons in the fingers; to counter the problem with the reins, I had some loops of leather sewn on.

We learnt there was a bloodstock sale to be held at Stockton Race Course in August, so sent away for a catalogue. It contained an entry from Bobby Renton's stables at Wetherby; it was a six year old bay gelding called Brave Boy by Fearless Boy out of Lucky Girl. He was still a maiden over jumps and Bobby Renton, who was in his sixties, had ridden the horse in a hurdle race the previous season. This surely meant it was a decent ride and very much a plus. We discovered that Brave Boy had a bit of a reputation as a thinker but we would soon alter that! As we would his maiden tag, or so we thought! Peter gave his notice to Harry Kitchen and I took a day off work, then to Stockton Sales we went. He was a hell of a nice looking horse and it was all so exciting, Brave Boy came into the sale ring, then five minutes later the auctioneer's hammer hit the top of the rostrum, Bang! - sold for 300 guineas - "Your name, please, Sir?" "Colin Tinkler." I had bought my first racehorse and not spent all that much though years later I was to give over £100,000 for one. In anticipation we had booked a horse box on the train from Stockton to Stathern which was quite a haul, and we didn't get back until very late that night. In fact they had to leave the station open for us and laid on a special train just to pull the one wagon! We had already bought some hay, oats and straw from Tommy Clamp, who had been most helpful. Mumso didn't show a great deal of interest other than saying "Well, you always wanted a racehorse, didn't you!" Next morning it was a question of who should have the first ride as we had both bagged the leg up. Peter said "I'll ride to start with and quieten him, then you can take over." That seemed sensible enough and that's what happened; the one thing I did notice was the ground appeared to be a long way away! We again swapped over and Peter gave Brave Boy a canter - we were in business - I don't really know what kind of business but that didn't seem to matter!

I had got permission to work Brave Boy in a fifty acre grass field at Plungar, which was a couple of miles away and the grass lane where I used to keep the cow made an excellent canter so we were alright for facilities. Had Peter had his way there would have been another place to do a bit of fast work - the local canal tow path! Admittedly it was overgrown with grass but I didn't fancy being pissed off with along there and having to duck my head every time we came to a bridge. I'd had a couple of days away from my job so it was imperative that I got back to work. I was home again at the weekend but I had started working the afternoon shift which meant that I didn't get home until mid morning on the Saturday and this was going to be the norm for the conceivable future. I mention this because I could have ridden out then but Peter was a stickler for routine - he thought it too late, so I only had the Sundays for my riding. A month went by which of course was only four riding days and I was having trouble with the trotting; I couldn't get the bounce right. I wasn't too bothered about it really - I could always stand in the stirrups; in fact, I had seen jockeys doing exactly that when going on to the racecourse - I thought, probably they couldn't bounce at the trot either!

In those days, as now, a trainer had to have a licence but, if one trained one's own horses, not even a permit was necessary. The wording, 'privately trained' was used and, as for amateur riders over jumps, no sanction was required. Only a limited number of amateur flat races took place and they were for 'Gentlemen' only but permission had to be sought to ride in those - work that one out because I can't! Owners, of course, had to be registered along with their colours and Peter, remembering his school colours, chose old gold, dark blue hoop and white cap. Personally they would have been the last I would have had; something like Khaki camouflage would have been more my preference. Exactly!

Even entries for the mundane races used to be made six weeks prior to the meeting and Peter reckoned it about time we got Brave Boy into a race. Mind you, we had only had him about a month and my riding, as you have gathered, wasn't progressing that well. Having said that, Peter was keen and Brave Boy was entered in a two and a half mile novice hurdle at Stratford on Saturday, November the fifteenth. As far as I was concerned it was five hours riding time away and I wasn't even cantering yet. Peter tried to console me by saying many people have never been behind a steering wheel yet pass their test after only half a dozen lessons - Help! Have I got to have a test!! Two or three weeks on and I was eventually cantering but still could not do that stupid bouncing at the trot - oh yes, I would bounce but not in harmony with the saddle! I had only been unshipped once and that was when Brave Boy whipped round but I wasn't at all perturbed for I'd seen jockeys get unseated on such occasions. A couple of weeks before the race I did a gallop - the speed, the power was breathtaking and what a perfect gentleman of a horse. By now Peter had rigged up a row of sheep hurdles with no gorse and nondescript wings and we tried to give the horse a pop but to no avail; in other words he stopped! Peter always had a tail bandage on Brave Boy but I just couldn't understand why; I suppose it might have been to protect the horse against me falling off backwards! After the schooling fiasco we spent the whole of the Sunday afternoon building a miniature chase fence in the grass lane. There was no way we were going to be able to run out - besides the jump was so inviting. I suggested I could get home mid week for a schooling session but Peter thought it would not be necessary and the following weekend would do. When all was said and done he was the trainer, though I felt time was becoming rather important and I didn't want to go to Stratford, never having been over a jump of some description! The following weekend I was back home again and ready for my first 'pop'. Mumso came down to watch though she didn't seem that interested really. I let Brave Boy have a good look at the fence, then took him back a couple of furlongs, turned, then full throttle and over we went. I bumped my nose on the horse's neck, but thought 'not a bad effort'. Peter called out "And again" as he moved some of the jump to let me return. Same procedure and I was full of confidence; this time it was perfect and I got a real buzz. I would have liked to have given myself a bit more schooling but Peter considered it "best to quit while on top!" I didn't know exactly how to interpret that remark! I now realise Brave Boy was unquestionably the most economical jumper I've ever had anything to do with for how else would I have stayed in the saddle. Peter called out to Mumso "The kids riding quite well". So I'd suddenly become the offspring of a nanny goat - thank you very much Peter!

We had arranged to go to Stratford by rail, leaving Stathern on the Friday and hopefully returning on the Sunday - with the emphasis on hopefully! It meant two nights away, the first of which we had booked in at The White Swan. The journey took ages and we didn't arrive at the raccourse stables until quite late, having walked from the station to the course. On the Saturday morning my intention was to give the horse a canter but he was so strong I thought it best to leave well alone and just walk. I had got quite used to the cut down military saddle but for the race I would be supplied with everything by the valet - boots, breeches, racing saddle, crash helmet, the lot.

After breakfast Peter spent half an hour attending to Brave Boy, while I walked the course and the impression I got was that the hurdles were big, rather upright, and very firm in the ground; it was also a hell of a long way round. There was no overnight declaration of jockeys, not even runners, in those days but the press used to get it amazingly correct by just talking to people. I understood there were going to be twenty five runners in my race and I was down as the rider claiming 5lbs (the maximum allowance at that time). I was thinking it a pity it's not the other way round - five runners and 25lbs! The day was passing pretty quickly and 3.30 p.m., the time of the race, was approaching. I can recall the changing room being very crowded and rather a hostile place - nobody seemed to want to talk; well not to me and that was even before the race. I weighed out and then took the saddle over to the saddling boxes where my brother was waiting with Brave Boy. He asked me to hold the horse whilst he gave him a quick 'dust over' and finished the operation by sponging Brave Boy's arse and nostrils (in that order). Peter suddenly stopped and looked extremely upset, he said "I've done that the wrong way round, do you think he noticed?" I tried to console him by saying "I'm sure he didn't" but Peter was not convinced. He said "Brave Boy is pulling a face". My answer to that was "Of course he is; seeing me in the colours he's just realised who's riding him this afternoon and I don't think he would appreciate any cracks about who's a Brave Boy then!" After saddling and double checking that the saddle was facing the correct way, I did this by taking a quick look at some of the other runners, I returned to the weighing room where the valet tied the silks on to my crasher - I nearly took him with me to the paddock so he could tie me on to the horse! Peter was leading round so I asked someone else, who had a runner in the race, if he would leg me up. He was friendly and wished me all the luck in the world, but I wondered if that was going to be enough! In 1947 Stratford had no rails on the far side of the course, just poles every fifty yards or so, and the start of the two and a half mile hurdle race was adjacent to one of the chase fences opposite the stands. This meant the twenty five runners had to start in two rows. It was a very warm, sunny afternoon, surprisingly so for the middle of November, and the low sun was going to make some of the hurdles difficult to see and just another hazard to overcome. With the start being where it was it had been my intention to walk there but Brave Boy had other ideas, he started to trot! "What the f*****g hell is he doing". The saddle I had from the valets felt very slippery and the leathers were cutting through the thin racing boots into my legs. I should have been better prepared, but it was too late to bother about that. We milled around at the start as the jockeys' names were being called; "Tinkler" "Here, Sir" and I should have added "But not all there, Sir!" We duly lined up in the two rows with Brave Boy in the middle of the front one. I wanted him to get a good view of the jumps but it wasn't going to make much difference to me, as I would have my eyes closed anyway. I was ready - I shouted "Now, Sir". The starter obviously heard me for there was suddenly the sound of the tape being catapulted across the course; someone shouted "They're off" and I nearly was as Brave Boy bounded forward.

There were two complete circuits and ten hurdles to negotiate, the first of those was only fifty yards from the start and, as we cleared it, there was a hell of a clatter, a lot of shouting and so much bumping but we had got over in one piece. Round the first bend I was on the rails - how the hell did I get there, no wonder there was so much shouting behind me! Over the second hurdle I was lying third, about a length down, but one of those in front went a 'purler' and I could see the jockey get mangled by the following cavalry charge. Three or four passed me as we went down the far side and I was mighty close to the poles which marked out the course at that point. We must have jumped a couple more hurdles for suddenly we were in the home straight for the first time; at the next Brave Boy took off outside the wings and just made it - bloody hell I thought, that was close. He was more sensible at the next and the next, by then we were on the final circuit. Everything was happening so fast it seemed like a dream, or should I say nightmare! As we went down the back straight for the second and final time there were horses all around but still only half a dozen in front of me and that's how it stayed over two more flights and on to the finish. I should have been overjoyed that I'd got round safely but actually I was just a little disappointed that we had not done better; I hadn't thought winning was a complete impossibility. That was the absurdity of it all and I hadn't appreciated, because of my ignorance, what an absolute super fellow Brave Boy had been. He carried 11 stone 5 lbs, but with me in the saddle bouncing about, it would have seemed a hell of a lot more than that. I can't remember Peter's reactions but I do remember a humorous note to the occasion; after unsaddling I hurried through the weighing room tossing my number cloth into a corner as the other jockeys were doing, when a very officious looking tweed suit - the material was reminiscent of my old plus fours - came up to me and said "I say, tell me, have you been riding long?" I replied "Yes, I have, but I will ride shorter next time!!"

As we had to start our journey home rather early next morning, we slept that night in one of the stables at the racecourse and eventually got back home late on Sunday. Apparently Tommy Clamp had laid 50/1 about me getting round, though that price had not been a true reflection of the situation - it should have been 500/1!

Brave Boy's next race was at Wetherby a couple of weeks later; Peter had kept him ticking over and I gave him a gallop but no more schooling. A cattle truck was hired for the Wetherby run and we arrived a couple of hours before the race, which gave me plenty of time to walk the course. The hurdle track used to cut across the present circuit which meant the home straight was that much shorter. It's strange but I can't remember much about the lead up to the race, although I do remember the race itself. There was not the hurly burly of the Stratford run and I felt I had ridden a lot better. Brave Boy jumped immaculately again, which put me in the firing line most of the way. I took up the running turning into the straight and thought we had the race won but he suddenly petered out and finished in the middle of the pack. I saw Bobby Renton, his previous trainer, later in the afternoon; he thought I'd come too soon and advised me to hold him up next time but for me there would be no next time. When we got Brave Boy home he was lame. It didn't look too serious but, with our lack of experience, it was very difficult for us to judge correctly. No wonder he shut up shop in the race for he had obviously been in pain. Brave Boy had not necessarily sustained the injury at Wetherby; a slight strain could have developed at Stratford or even in training, in fact at any time, but I now believe he actually had the tendon trouble when we bought him.

Peter decided to give the horse a rest and try and get him back for one of the Easter meetings at the end of March but, of course, now we would know a much longer holiday was necessary. We had in any case been looking for another horse for some time but, with the situation which had developed, adding a second string to the bow had become even more important. Someone had mentioned they had seen a good looking little thoroughbred out hunting that was very fast. The owner, a Mr. Wright, had a farm near Newark and apparently was prepared to sell, as the horse was not really up to his son's weight. Peter and I went over to have a 'look-see' and give the little fellow a bit of a spin. Spin was the operative word because he continually kept whipping round but I managed to stay on top and yes, he seemed to be very fast in the work we did. The Wrights thought that he had raced at some time but, after much research, we found nothing to verify this and there was a complete mix up with the horse's pedigree. In spite of everything we went ahead and acquired him; no money actually changed hands but it would if he managed to win a race for us and there was the added proviso that he could be returned whenever we wished. Rather appropriately we named and registered him as 'Misinformed', a bay gelding, age and pedigree unknown. Once we had got him back to Stathern we soon realised he was just plain bloody crackers and not really the sort of horse I should be riding. As he was pretty fit from hunting it was not going to take a lot of work to get him ready and a novice hurdle at Southwell was his target. It was going to be on Thursday, March 25th, a couple of days before Brave Boy's come back race, also at Southwell. We did work the two horses together and the 'little terror' could take a real hold; I'm sure we must have schooled him over jumps, but I can't remember doing so.

Easter was looming and I was taking more time off from the pits because I'd developed a problem with my knees which was caused by crawling about at the coal face. I wore pads for protection but still got the tissues around the joints damaged. It was arranged I should go to the University Hospital at Nottingham to have an operation to try and rectify matters. I booked in on the Monday before Easter, assuming I would be out by Wednesday and ready to ride on the following day. When I mentioned this to the surgeon, and he realised I wasn't joking, he hit the roof - which was better than him hitting me! I was told the effect of the anaesthetic would take a few days to wear off completely; then there was always the risk of infection and, because of the bandaging, I would be unable to bend my knees for some time. In fact, I was told I would definitely be in hospital for a couple of weeks - how right he was! Nevertheless, as planned, the surgery was carried out on the Monday and on the Tuesday morning I had a marvellous piece of luck, or so it seemed at the time. I discovered the fellow who brought round the papers to the wards was friendly with the driver of the spare ambulance used at Southwell racecourse. This came to light during general conversation when I ordered 'The Sporting Life'. I told him that I was going to be discharged on the Thursday morning which, of course, was not true, and I asked if he could arrange to get me a lift to the races. He agreed and we discussed a place to meet the ambulance; fortunately my clothes were in a cupboard next to the bed and I'd already obtained a roll of plaster to take the place of the bulky bandages. At the appropriate time on the Thursday, I hobbled to the cloakroom, changed and swapped the bandage for the plaster, then tottered off down the corridor and out of the hospital. The doctor had done his morning round and I was hoping I wouldn't be missed for some time. The ambulance driver was a decent sort of chap and very helpful; it didn't take all that long to get to Southwell and I had a snooze on the stretcher bed in the back. I'd contacted Peter and said I would meet him in the weighing room and naturally I wouldn't be walking the course! Peter duly arrived, we had a chat and I was surprised he was going to declare blinkers. We were in the first race so I changed into my colours and weighed out. As I made my way to the parade ring, twenty minutes later, I could hardly walk and felt really groggy; I thought, why the blazes am I doing this. It was a boiling hot day, there was not a cloud in the sky and thousands of people were milling around; it was a real holiday crowd. Southwell as we know it today is nothing like the intimate Southwell of old, with its wooden buildings and little wooden stands; the place was unique and full of history. It was soon 'jockeys up'; in those days, when the signal was given, the horses didn't turn in and stay put as now but would be led about looking for their connections. It was utter mayhem when there were large fields! Eventually, and with difficulty, Peter helped me into the saddle. Misinformed was bouncing all over the place; he bolted with me going down to the start and was very excitable as we waited for the off. Jockeys' names were called, we were then asked to make a line behind the tape, then suddenly we were away. There were eight hurdles and two miles in front of me, but I didn't get very far. Misinformed shot to the front a couple of lengths clear and running very free - round a slight bend and on to the first. The little horse started to steady, so I gave him a slap down the neck. Now that's where I went wrong - remember he was wearing blinkers and he turned his head to see what the hell I was playing at - CRASH! CRASH! CRASH! he never really took off, he hadn't seen the hurdle with any clarity and came one almighty f*****g purler. I was catapulted to the ground, my crasher came off, there were horses and jockeys falling all around me - what a shambles. I received a terrible crack on the head; I felt nothing but certainly heard it. I lost consciousness, but came to for a couple of seconds as the depleted field went thundering past on the final circuit. The next I knew I was on a bed with red blankets which I assumed was in the first aid room. There were quite a number of other jockeys lying on the floor; I thought "Surely I'm not getting preferential treatment just because I'm an amateur!" No, it must be that I'm in worse shape than they are and some of them were groaning. Everything seemed very quiet and I tried but couldn't move a muscle, couldn't even speak, yet could hear someone say "We can't move him because he's too badly injured". I knew they were referring to me; Peter was there looking shattered and I came to the conclusion there would be no tomorrow for me, no more green fields, just darkness. I felt so utterly sad. The doctors hadn't realised I'd regained consciousness for a while but I was soon out again.

Apparently seven horses had fallen at that first hurdle, most had tripped over me and I'm ashamed to say several of the jockeys were badly injured. A decision was eventually made to move me to the University Hospital at Nottingham! Whilst in the ambulance I again came to for a short time and, of course, it was the same vehicle that had taken me to Southwell several hours earlier. For a second or two I thought it had all been a horrible nightmare and I was really on my way to the races but was brought back to reality when I discovered I was paralysed, though that turned out to be only temporary. I don't know what happened to the administration when I arrived at the hospital but I imagine it was in turmoil. I regained consciousness later in the evening and found myself in the same bed I had left that morning. The nurses on night duty couldn't understand what had happened; because of the mess I was in one thought I must have jumped out of the window - I was on the third floor! Actually I had fractured my skull, broken some bones in my back and in one of my hands, cracked some ribs and was generally badly knocked about. Some time later I learnt no one had missed me on that Thursday because the nurses thought I'd gone to another ward for some physio!

For several days I was far too poorly to have any visitors but, when Peter did come to see me, he brought some devastating news. He had run Brave Boy on the Saturday and had actually ridden the horse himself; it was his first ride ever and his last! Apparently the new aluminium bit he had in the bridle came apart as they approached the second hurdle, causing Brave Boy to duck out. He then galloped loose round the course and broke his neck when colliding into another horse after the race. Both died instantly but thankfully Peter was unhurt. Brave Boy's vision was naturally restricted by wearing the blinkers but accidents happen, full stop. It was goodbye to a very nice horse and what a cracker he would have been had he been sound.

I can't remember how long I was in hospital; I know I had difficulty persuading the staff to allow me to have enough pillows to enable me to sleep sitting upright. This I had to do for many years afterwards; if my head became horizontal, particularly in those early days, I would lose consciousness. For me, hospital was like being in prison again and, after a while, I decided to get out but do so more conventionally than previously. I simply asked if I could return home. The doctors were not that happy with the request, but agreed so long as I signed a 'not officially discharged' statement. On hearing from the hospital the Coal Board released me from any further duties. I suppose it was automatic really as I had not much time left to serve anyway. On my twenty second birthday I kept an appointment with the specialist who saw me on my arrival from Southwell; he was extremely efficient and very sincere. It had only been three months since the fall and I thought I was progressing satisfactorily but he told me it was going to take a long, long time for things to adjust and for me to make a full recovery. The big dipper sensations that were depressing me would eventually go but take years to do so. At least I knew what I was in for and it could have been so much worse.

Autumn came and everything was about the same, apart from the Tinkler finances which were dwindling. Ann was still away at school and must be excluded but we other members of the family might as well have been watching paint dry. A board meeting was necessary - over the past few years it had not been a question of bad luck all the time but mainly bad decisions. I had to take the brunt of the blame but surely others had contributed to the adversities. I am ashamed at what we decided to do but the eventual outcome proved the decision correct. We literally sold up. The house we lived in at Stathern was only rented; it should have been bought when we had the money but it wasn't and that was just another bad decision. Basically it was the contents that were disposed of and the fact that it forced us to go and do something different was important. There was no hassle and we saw the winter through before arranging our future. As a family we had been happy together and splitting up was going to be a wrench but, as things were, I could not see an alternative.

Chapter six

Mumso

The following is a short piece about Mumso and what developed over the later years for her. I will restrict its length but that does not minimise its importance.

We all moved from Stathern in the spring of 1949 and Mumso took up a position of housekeeper for a person in Nottingham and had Ann with her. Because of the lack of finances my sister had left the school at Stamford and went to one close to where they lived. She was so likeable that everyone got on well with her, which made the change of schools more tolerable. Over the next couple of years I am sure Mumso was not at all happy; it must have been a very worrying time for her - all the spark had gone. She was only in her very early fifties, yet seemed older. I didn't see Ann or her as often as I would have liked because I felt I was intruding, with it not being their own home but in no way was that ever inferred. One afternoon Ann got a dreadful shock when she came home and found Mumso collapsed on the floor; she was rushed into hospital and apparently had suffered a minor stroke. The events of the past few years can't have helped matters; however, she soon recovered and thankfully there were no after-effects. I don't exactly know the circumstances but, to recuperate, Mumso went to live with a doctor and his wife, whose son was friendly with Ann. The doctor had a Caribbean background, but was not entirely West Indian. They were a marvellous family and unbelievably kind to Mumso and Ann. They had been comparative strangers yet had opened the doors of their home to them. The doctor then helped Mumso to secure another housekeeping appointment with a retired widower who had been head of accounts with the Stag Furnishing Company and had a very nice house in Nottingham. Both Mumso and Ann seemed more contented there than they had been for a long time. There were further developments when Len asked Mumso to marry him and start a new life by moving down to Eastbourne on the Sussex coast; they moved into a very nice flat near the sea front and the old sparkle came back to Mumso. She learnt to play Bridge and Bridge has never been the same since; she gave a new dimension to the game! She also invaded the coffee houses of Brighton and they would go to the theatre every week; shopping excursions to London were also a frequent occurrence. "I do my shopping at Harrods, you know." Mumso could also often be heard saying "We haven't brought the car down to Eastbourne, well, taxis are so convenient you know." Yes, Mumso was treading on the thick pile again - good for her. Ann married but, disappointingly for me, not to the doctor's son who, incidentally, was best man at Peter's wedding when he married. For some reason Len became tired of living in the south and they came back to Nottingham; but, of course, his roots were there and that could have been the factor. I can remember Mumso saying "We are having our new place re-carpeted throughout you know." I'd heard those words before - away, away back. Eventually Len died and the Stag Company were good to Mumso in so much as they continued to pay her a part of his pension.

There was an amusing incident at Len's funeral or rather at the ham tea that followed. Len had one arm shorter than the other; he was born with the slight disability but never tried to disguise the deformity. Apparently, just before he died, he had a suit made which he never wore and Peter knew of this; as we were all chatting the conversation between Mumso and Peter went something like the following:

Peter - "Len's new suit would fit me, may I have it?"

Mumso - "Yes, darling but one sleeve is shorter than the other."

Peter - "But there are two pairs of trousers, I could use a leg from one of those for the alterations."

Mumso - "Yes, I suppose so but surely the sleeve in the jacket made from the trouser leg would be too long and wide, but you know best darling."

I thought, what marvellous humour, though it was not meant to be.

After Len died Mumso moved to a small bungalow near Lowdham in Nottinghamshire and I used to call in and see her when going to Nottingham races but Peter would visit more often than I whilst Ann, who lived locally, would see her every day. She was over 90 when she died in 1989 and was buried in a small churchyard in a village near where she last lived. Without her I would not be here and I thank her for that and for so many other things, not least for all the merriment that surrounded her 'superior social status!' Mumso was very fond of Peter and Ann but I'm not sure whether she really liked me or not; she was always very critical, probably with good cause but no hassle - I certainly liked her and I only wish she had been able to tread the thick pile more frequently during her life. Mumso was reasonably religious, though I'm not, but when a person dies it makes one ponder and ask, "What has it all been about?"

Chapter seven

I meet Marie

I will now revert to the spring of 1949 and in a couple of months or so I would be twenty three and going nowhere very fast. Tom Bailey had agreed for me to have a spell with him; he farmed in a limited fashion and trained a few horses though his head man, Ron Hodgkinson, held the licence. There were never more than half a dozen horses in the yard and most would be his own; in fact the whole operation was run mainly so he could ride them in races, though other jockeys were used on occasions. The Baileys lived in a lovely old house near Scarrington, a village which was not all that far from Newark and I assumed they were reasonably wealthy people. Tom Bailey was aware that my riding ability was not up to much, but I kept from him the fact that my head injury was causing problems. He was brother-in-law to Rip Bissill who trained a large string close by at Aslockton and it was there that Peter got a job 'doing his two'. As we both had to find somewhere to live, we bought a new caravan and fortunately Tom Bailey was a very generous person; not only did he allow us to park it behind his stables, but also had the caravan connected to the water and electricity mains. Both Peter and I settled in well with our new jobs, though I didn't ride any fast work and very rarely even cantered. One of the horses I looked after was Fog Light, who won at Doncaster at 100/6 and was ridden that day by Bob Turnell, Andy Turnell's father.

After the Southwell fiasco, Misinformed went back to the Wrights and never in a million years would one have expected the Tinkler brothers to repeat the lunacy that had occurred; but that is exactly what we did. Old man Wright, Peter and myself did a further deal. Tom Bailey said he would train the horse but, because of our financial position, which was flat bloody broke, we decided Peter should do so in his spare time. I have scanned the dictionary to try and find words to describe the folly but can't discover any adequate enough! We rented a stable at the local rectory - I think Peter hoped God would be on our side! Misinformed was entered for a couple of novice hurdles, one at Market Rasen and the other the following week at Nottingham. I didn't sit on him at all leading up to the first of the two races. Peter did all the exercising including a couple of pieces of fast work on Bissills gallops. I know you can't believe what you are reading; I can hardly believe what I am writing but it's true. The day of the Market Rasen race arrived and Tom Bailey was again most helpful, lending us his horse box and driver. At Market Rasen we didn't jump a flight but just followed those in front who were flattening the hurdles. Misinformed got rather tired and pulled himself up two out. For Nottingham we again borrowed the horse box and Tom Bailey came into the paddock to give me support and a leg up. In the race itself the little horse pulled like a train going to the first, put in an almighty leap and I simply fell off, bringing down Tim Molony who was not overpleased. Many years later when Tim was training at Waltham, near Melton Mowbray, I called in to look at a horse that was for sale; he diplomatically said he couldn't remember that day at Nottingham but I knew he could. Mumso came to watch the race and, as I walked in off the course, I was greeted by her saying "It is so silly of you Colin, you are such an exhibitionist. Why had you to jump off like that?" I tried to explain the jumping off, as she put it, was not exactly intentional - but to no avail! Misinformed returned to Wright's and spent the remainder of his years hunting. Peter returned to reality and, hopefully, I returned to sanity, knowing I was an extremely lucky person to be about at all. I did, however, have a few rides in the mid sixties, when a lot more capable and, in fact, rode a winner at Sedgefield; it was only a two horse race but it was a winner and an ambition fulfilled. More about that later on.

During the summer of 1949 the few horses Tom Bailey had in training went out to grass and, as there was no more work for me to do, I was forced to take a holiday but was told I would be welcome back in the autumn. Tom Bailey's generosity continued, for he allowed our living arrangements to stay as they were. I was thankful because the elastic band around the wad of notes I possessed was not over stretched, though matters looked a little brighter after an excursion I made to Nottingham. I had a couple of punters from the greyhound era, to whom I gave racing information; one was a butcher and the other had recently had his transport business nationalised. Both were very heavy gamblers and the object of my going over to see them was to do some collecting. The butcher was rather busy when I called but said he would definitely pay me if I were to call back later. I'm afraid the other fellow was a complete loss. He'd got through all the money he received for his business, re-mortgaged his house to the hilt, was having an affair with his ex-secretary and had just crashed his car - all-in-all was in a hell of a mess. I had arranged to meet him for a sandwich at the Black Boy Hotel where he took me up to a suite. It was like a bookies in an American movie; a large black board covered one of the walls, a ticker tape was pouring out information, phones were ringing and people were milling around. I was introduced to the bookmaker who, without hesitation, accepted from my punter a £5,000 bet on the last race favourite at Lincoln. I imagine he owed the bookmaker so much it just didn't matter anymore. The bet was made five hours before the race, the utter nonsense of it all and we mustn't forget what £5,000 was then worth in purchasing power. Every time I mentioned the money he owed me he became evasive. Realising I was fighting a losing battle I left and never saw the fellow again. In all probability no one else did - certainly not the bookmaker because, needless to say, the last race favourite at Lincoln lost! The butcher, on the other hand, kept his word; I went back to the shop and he gave me £300, all in one pound notes stuffed into a carrier bag, along with some pork chops - no, I didn't tell him I was a vegetarian, I wasn't that stupid! I caught a train back to Aslockton, having collected more than I could have earned working in stables for a couple of years.

Peter and I must have been winning a fair amount with our punting because Lyons, a London firm of bookmakers, closed our account but, of course, we soon found another bookmaker. I learnt there was some hoeing to be done on a nearby farm so I took the temporary job and one of the fields I worked in was adjacent to the main road into Newark. At that time new cars were coming on to the market again and I could see them gliding up and down the highway. This really rubbed salt into the wounds and I realised I had to pull myself together as quickly as I possibly could, and alter the position I was in.

I had done about a month of 'killing docks' when George Flinders, the local blacksmith, mentioned there was a job available in show jumping with a person called Toynbee Clarke. The stables were at Bottesford, about half a dozen miles away, and his business was making and selling show jumpers in addition to doing a limited amount of horse transport with his horse box. It transpired that his horse dealings were also very limited. I went over to see him;

actually he knew a great deal about me as he had obviously been asking around. He suggested I start immediately, which I did and stayed there for three and a half years.

Toynbee was in his fifties and looked the spitting image of Tweedle Dee or was it Tweedle Dum? He was no more than five feet three inches tall, usually wore tight jodphurs, highly polished, laced brown boots, a bowler hat and always a spotted bow tie. We got on brilliantly because I never took him seriously but he was not a likeable person. He had the most nasty eyes and they used to talk - they would say exactly what he was thinking. He was a good horseman of the old school and rarely took a fall but, when he did, he would roll on the ground kicking like a naughty child as he was so terribly bad tempered. His wife was a tall thin person and rather severe; they just didn't seem to suit at all and she certainly had a lot to put up with.

I gave Tom Bailey the news that I would not be going back there in the Autumn and I'd be moving the caravan straight away. He said there was no need to do that as things might not work out at Toynbee's and he would keep my old job open for me; in fact I didn't move the caravan over to Bottesford until the following spring. Tom Bailey had been very good to me; tragically he was killed in a car accident some years later.

There were never more than three or four horses on the place at Toynbee's with a young mare called Susan 'C' the mainstay. We would do most of the county shows, all the principal horse shows and take in the local Saturday 'pop overs'. To me it was like a holiday and in those days there would be a couple of dozen teams doing 'the circuit' and a great crowd they were too. We would live in the horse boxes on the showgrounds and the horses would be stabled in makeshift portables, though I would more often than not build our 'de luxe accommodation' with straw bales. I became intensely interested in the whole business but didn't imagine it would ever reach the dizzy financial heights that it has done. It took no time at all for me to know everyone and everyone to know me; I called the riders 'jockeys' and the phrase soon caught on. The introduction of betting was also my idea; it was kept very low key but I did manage to put my prices up on the official notice board at the 'International', when it was held at The White City. The punting didn't become as popular as I thought it would but the sweepstakes I operated were a huge success, particularly at the holiday venues such as the Southport Flower Show. I always sold a fantastic number of tickets and the money I made was considerable.

When I first went to Toynbee's I was, as you know, still living at Bailey's and would bicycle the dozen miles each day. When the weather was fine it was quite enjoyable but not so during the winter months. I would set off in the morning at about six o'clock and return in the evening, somewhere around seven. I didn't see much of Peter because he had become very friendly with a girl from Bingham, a nearby village. She was rather plain and uninteresting with starchy parents, I just couldn't see what the attraction was. It lasted for quite some time, in fact until the joke Peter conjured up at the girl's brother's wedding; as a present he sent them a baby's potty; it would not have been so bad if it hadn't been opened at the reception in front of all the guests! As soon as he realised he had boobed Peter went on the defensive and said the present was from me but his intended future in-laws guessed otherwise and bang went the relationship. He left racing soon afterwards and had a short period with an insurance company before moving on to the Milk Marketing Board. When Peter was living with me and I was travelling to and from Bottesford he would always prepare my evening meal; it was a rice pudding, which he would leave in the oven before going out. It never varied, it was always the same, a rice pudding. That was until one particularly bitterly cold night, with frost hanging from my eyebrows and fingers frozen, I was greeted by a blancmange jelly!! and a note saying "I've noticed your eyes have started to slant so I've made you something different". I left a reply for him which read "Thank you very bloody much!"

I wish to make a special mention of Anne, a lovely girl I used to take dancing. Tragically, she contracted cancer and died when quite young. She married Don Cobling who was a friend of mine and still is. Don loves his racing and is one hell of a decent fellow. He hasn't married again and now lives in a bungalow that was built in the paddock of Toynbee Clarke's old home. I told him the other day I must have cantered many times through his kitchen!

I haven't mentioned much about girlfriends but, up to the time we have reached, I didn't have anyone I considered special. Of course, I liked pretty faces - I still do! - and would take girls to dances, ice hockey matches and that sort of thing. I had fun but not as much as the more flighty ones would have liked. Having said that, girls at that time were in the main not as promiscuous as the majority are today and one wasn't called a wimp just because you didn't make love at every conceivable opportunity. I'm not moralizing; to me it was never a moral issue but I was rather allergic to shotguns! I knew nothing about drugs; I still don't, but they were then non-existent in normal society. The very few bum boys that existed were just a bloody nuisance and, as for lesbians, I believe there were a couple who lived together in the village but they didn't bother me - well they wouldn't would they! From the time I was at Scarrington I got a real kick out of dancing and, in those days, there were village 'hops' every week in the area, summer and winter alike. Peter and I would do the rounds and certainly set things alight - The Old Time, The Waltz, Fox Trot and Quick Step were not in our routine; we simply danced jungle rhythm, just as most do today, but it was often met with disapproval in the late forties; I was barred from some of the village halls, though others gave me a good reception. During my first year at Toynbee's, I had the 'distinction' of being asked to leave the Tower Ballroom, Blackpool and the Winter Gardens, Southport, on consecutive nights! I was, however, in good company - with me were several international show jumping riders including Wilf White, the then captain of the British team! We all got the boot because of the style of my dancing. At one of the first Horse of the Year Shows, which was held indoors at the old Harringay Arena, I gave an impromptu 'Performance' on live television to the sound of the Vancouver Boys dance band. They were playing during an interlude between competitions; not many people knew but I did the dance in the middle of the arena to win a £5 bet I had with Shamus Hayes, who was one of the best show jumping riders at that time. For years after, wherever I went, I was remembered for my dancing at the Horse of the Year Show and was never again asked to leave another dance hall!

I learnt a terrific amount during my years at Toynbee's, mainly by being observant because, apart from teaching me how to ride efficiently, he was unnecessarily secretive about things. He didn't win very often at the larger events - his horses just weren't good enough; he did, however, mop up at the smaller shows. We were always experimenting with different ways to school the jumpers. When I first went there it was just the crude hedgehog skins on rapping poles which were used. This manner of schooling, along with other rough methods, had been in existence ever since show jumping began. I didn't consider it cruel because horses are a lot tougher than most people imagine. That is not a fallacy - look at the way they can demolish a chase fence. However, I wanted something more sophisticated, so I developed a rather complicated device. On one occasion when I was setting it up the powerful catapult elastic, which was part of the mechanism, brought down the heavy jumping pole on to my head! - I went out like a light. I was unconscious for some time, for it was late in the evening when I came to and, unfortunately, the Clarkes had been away and hadn't noticed me lying on the ground when they returned. I had no noticeable after effects, though some might disagree!

My next creation was 'Humfrey'; the concept of the device came from the time I was in hospital and had noticed the 'high frequency' machine used for the treatment of all manner of ailments requiring heat to hasten recovery. What intrigued me about the appliance was the sharp tingling sensation caused by a harmless repetitive spark, if a certain attachment was fitted. The buzzing sound it made also gave me an idea; the whole machine was no larger than a portable radio and worked from an electric wall socket. After much searching I eventually found the makers and bought one for something in the region of £30, which was no small sum in those days. I was also lucky enough to find an electrical engineer who managed to alter Humfrey so it could operate from a car battery; the conversion meant that it could be used anywhere. It was now a question of adapting a means of getting the high frequency to a horse's legs as it was jumping but I must emphasise it was not an electric shock as such. The sensation being similar to that now used in the more up-to-date horse walkers. I constructed a device consisting of two slender telescopic uprights, secured to the ground by giant 'corkscrews'. A length of fuse-like wire was stretched between springs on the uprights and an elastic band was inserted at one end of the wire to make for easy braking. At the other end the wire was joined to the box of tricks and a car battery. The wire carrying the 'sensation', which the horse felt on contact, was placed behind a fence and released upwards as the horse was jumping. I anticipated a horse would soon associate the buzzing sound with the feel of the spark. The electrician also made me a small buzzer, about the size of a packet of cigarettes, which I could carry in my pocket and use it in the practice area before a competition. It was all a question of auto-suggestion and it proved very successful.

The schooling of show jumpers is all about appreciating the obvious; horses can't jump higher than they are capable of doing. It is no good trying to get a horse to jump six foot if his maximum is only five foot - actually one should do it the other way round; if a horse can jump five foot, school at a much lesser height.

I will continue on from the spring of 1952, when I had been at Toynbee's three years. We took Susan 'C' to the Windsor Horse Show; it was held then, as it is now, in the shadow of Windsor Castle and has always been a prestigious event. It was at this show that I first saw Marie; she was riding her newly acquired Fanny Rosa. I noticed she rode her with shorter stirrups than other riders and got a perfect stride at every jump, then kick-kick and over. They did a marvellous round but unfortunately just touched one of the poles. Her Land Rover and trailer were parked quite close to our horsebox and, as she rode past after competing, I said "Hello". Her response was friendly, as most people would be if one spoke to them but I knew at that moment my life would change; she was GORGEOUS and her face showed so much character. Marie is a lot older now, aren't we all, but she still possesses those same precious qualities.

Before Marie left the showground I went over to have a chat and asked her where she was going next and learnt it was the Oxford

County in a couple of weeks time. Her elder sister was helping and seemed rather cool towards me though I didn't take much notice of that. They were soon away but I had Oxford to look forward to, as I knew Toynbee had entered. Later in the day I was chatting with Ted Williams, who was an arch enemy of Toynbee; they had been at loggerheads for years. I'm sure Ted had gypsy ancestors; he was a brilliant rider and one of the few real professionals at that time. When talking to me he said "I saw you with the Delfosse sisters this afternoon; if I were you Colin I would change stables - that Marie is a hell of a nice girl."

At the Oxford show Marie and her sister were rather late arriving, only just in time to go into the ring. As they weren't in the jump off and just doing the one day they stayed no time at all. However, I managed to have a short conversation with Marie and learnt she was going up to the Blackpool Show on her own as her sister, who incidentally was called Martha, was playing in a golf tournament. I mentioned that Toynbee Clarke wasn't entered but I would be pleased to go and look after her horses there - so this was agreed. Toynbee was most reluctant to give me the time off, even though it was the first holiday I'd had in the three years I had been with him; in fact I'd worked on over a thousand consecutive days. I kept in touch with Marie and it was arranged that we would meet up at a garage some 50 miles from Blackpool which meant with her Land Rover and trailer, a couple of hours journey; certainly plenty of time in which to talk. I learnt Marie was a year older than myself and that both she and the sister that I had encountered were veterinary surgeons though didn't practice other than the odd locum. Marie told me she had four sisters altogether but no brothers, that her mother was German and her father, of whom she seemed very proud, was half Belgian and the Delfosses lived at Moor Park, adjacent to the golf course. Marie also mentioned that she played a lot of golf. I gathered her father was a screw manufacturer and had a factory in London. He used to have quite a number of horses in training at one time, but none recently, the reason being his utter disappointment when he missed buying Lovely Cottage, winner of the Grand National half a dozen years previously. The horse had been for sale over in Ireland and Marie's father had made up his mind to buy him but couldn't get through on the phone. Apparently the Post Office controlling the lines had closed for the evening - it could only happen in Ireland! I suppose he thought what has to be has to be and didn't try again the following morning. He was interested in Marie's show jumping but didn't go to watch very often because she had broken her neck some years previously when galloping a pointer and he was fearful of another fall.

Eventually we arrived at Blackpool where the show was on a bleak disused airfield and was to commence the following day. We got the horses bedded down for the night, then found Marie's hotel, went to a show, had a meal and a very pleasant evening. Had the horses jumped a little better it would have been preferable but as it was we had a nice couple of days. I felt so comfortable with her. Love is a strange thing; how does one define it without using a string of adjectives; besides, I am an emotional person and love is rather a personal thing. That was a long time ago and a lot has happened between us since then, some fantastic days and some unhappy ones but, in our sphere, we achieved much together. We married and, for no real logical reason, divorced. My feelings for Marie now are the same as they have always been; she is such a genuine and generous person - eighteen carat.

Whilst at Blackpool we arranged to join forces for the beginning of the following season. Marie said that telling Martha would not be difficult because she was playing more and more golf and wouldn't mind not doing the shows. We discussed schooling and 'Humfrey' in particular, though Marie seemed a little apprehensive about the box of tricks. I promised that in the meantime I would learn to drive and, of course, I told her why I had not done so previously. I saw her another couple of times during the rest of the season and also kept in touch by phone. I gave Toynbee Clarke an incredible six months notice and he rewarded me by being exceedingly nasty and very aggressive.

After half a dozen driving lessons in Nottingham my instructor advised me to put in for a test straight away; this I did and got a mid January date. Toynbee gave me no help whatsoever; in fact he did his best to undermine my confidence by having a bet that I wouldn't pass at the first attempt. Christmas arrived and Marie sent me a jolly nice calendar but the envelope had been opened, the card torn and the envelope sealed again. There was only one person who could have done that - Exactly!

I was due to go down South at the beginning of February as Marie was going to Switzerland on a skiing holiday and I wanted to be there to look after the horses whilst she was away. Even though I had given Toynbee that lengthy notice, after five months he said I had to leave, as he had someone coming to replace me. It so happened I learnt about a Mrs. Pollard whose groom had gone into hospital and she required help with looking after her couple of hunters for a few weeks. It suited me perfectly as she only lived a dozen miles away. She was an extremely wealthy poultry farmer, in her mid forties, and her husband owned a large ball bearing factory in Newark. I believe it has since been taken over by the Japanese - what hasn't! Toynbee Clarke did very little showjumping after I left and, rather amazingly, I never saw him again but I did once meet the girl who was my replacement. I don't think she stayed that long and was certainly too nice to be working for the little tyrant. She laughed as she recalled him kicking the car as he went past because he was cross about something. Toynbee is no longer about; in fact he would have been a hundred if he had been alive today. What a terrible thought!

There were many amusing incidents whilst I was at Toynbee's. One was when I'd left my set of keys to the horsebox back at Bottesford, when we had gone down to a Horse of the Year Show. I didn't mention it to Toynbee who, of course, had his. I was managing quite nicely by climbing in and out through the window above the rear door, that was until one evening when I had taken a pretty girl back for coffee - and Tweedle Dee arrived back much earlier than expected. On hearing us he shouted "Open the door", which, of course, I couldn't for it was locked. "You have a girl in there, haven't you? - God knows what you are up to". With that he started to unlock the door with his own key and, getting extremely cross, shouted "I'm coming in". This was met by the girl saying "That is one thing I can guarantee you are not going to do, Toynbee!" It was all so very funny but the most hilarious incident must have been the one which occurred at the Richmond horse show. Toynbee and I were on a stand watching a Hackney Class being judged, with Toynbee sitting next to the gangway steps. Then up trudged the formidable and very much overweight Dorothy Paget. She was making her way to the entourage of young ladies sitting directly behind us. They had already opened the impressive display of food hampers, with the initials D.P. on the lids and, as she passed Toynbee, she accidentally knocked his bowler hat off with her shooting stick. Then, in temper, immediately kicked it into the arena. Any premiership striker would have been proud of the lob and the bevy of delightful young ladies started to giggle as Toynbee, recognising who she was, apologised for him being there.

Then, turning to me, he said "Go and get my bowler hat." At that 'Dorothy P.' gave him a poke in the belly, at the same time ordering him to "Go and get your own f*****g hat you stupid little man." Not waiting for any more abuse 'Tweedle Dee' bolted down the steps, retrieved his battered possession and went storming off. I took the opportunity to chat up the prettiest of the girls, not realising it was an utter waste of time - well, how was I to know! When I got back to the horsebox Toynbee was caressing his beloved bowler, I'm sure it was even more dented than when it landed in the show ring, well, I've already mentioned what he was inclined to do when he got cross.

The reason for Dorothy Paget of Golden Miller fame being at the Richmond Show was to see one of her show jumpers in action, though it was not generally known that she was interested in the sport. She employed a succession of leading riders including Dorothy (Pug) Whitehead whose daughter was Sue Armytage, mother of Gee, the celebrated jump jockey. Actually, having known me over the years, it was Sue who persuaded me to write this autobiography. When young she was one of the more accomplished girl riders doing the circuit and was always so bright and breezy; unfortunately she had a nasty fall in one of the earlier ladies flat races and never completely recovered, Sue sadly died a few years ago.

I passed my driving test at the first attempt, thereby winning my wager with Toynbee which, incidentally, I didn't bother to collect. Fortunately I had been able to transfer the examination from Nottingham to Newark which in those days was a quiet market town apart from the main road through. To give me a bit of an advantage, I chose a half day closing for the ordeal and, to help even further, I borrowed a short wheel based Land Rover and took the hood off, to give me better all-round vision. Actually the Land Rover belonged to Mrs. Pollard who had lent it to me over the past couple of days in order that I could have a 'refresher course' and she very kindly drove me over for the test. It was a freezing January afternoon, with snow in the air and blowing a bitterly cold wind. To combat the elements (remember I had taken the hood off the Land Rover) Mrs.' P.' wore what seemed like half a dozen pullovers, a sheepskin coat, thick tweed skirt, fur-lined boots and a woolly hat and I was similarly dressed - I said similarly, not exactly! I met the examiner at the appropriate time; he was rather a pale thin character. In fact he didn't look all that well and that was before the test! Surprisingly, he was not wearing a coat. I was going to offer him my windcheater but didn't want to do anything that might look like a bribe. The examiner got into the passenger seat and away we went. He had introduced himself as Mr. Snowballs - actually I think it might have been singular rather than plural. In the circumstances, I thought it a most appropriate name. After only ten minutes we were back at our starting point and I was asked to pull in. Mr. Snowball got out of the vehicle and paced up and down the pavement banging his arms to his sides and blowing into his hands. Then out of the blue - yes, literally out of the blue - he informed me, through a bout of sneezing "You have passed". I was utterly amazed at the shortness of the run and I had not even been asked any questions about the Highway Code. Naturally I was delighted with the outcome, yet a little disappointed I had not shown off my reverse into a side road routine; I had been practicing that manoeuvre and found it specially easy with the transport I had! In fact the examiner was writing something on a pad, when I asked would he indeed like to see my party piece? His reply was most precise "No, I don't, I'm f*****g freezing and I wouldn't push your luck if I were you Mr. Tinkler!" I somehow don't believe he was exactly enchanted with the vehicle I'd brought; anyhow I apologised and, showing some decorum, thanked him and quietly slipped away. Mrs. P. preferred to take a warm taxi home so I drove smugly back to the farm on my own, blissfully unaware of all the trials and tribulations that lay in store for me behind a steering wheel.

I stayed exactly a month at the poultry farm yet didn't see a hen the whole time I was there. They were all isolated because there was a real fear of fowl pest but I certainly saw plenty of eggs - I lived on them, mostly scrambled. It had been an extremely cold four weeks with the temperatures at freezing point and my accommodation was again a caravan. Nevertheless, Mrs. P. had been most helpful throughout my time there and was kind enough to see me on to the train going south with all my luggage - destination, a new life and a new era. Mumso had remarried by then and Peter and Ann also seemed contented with the way life was treating them, which, of course, was good for my peace of mind.

It was mid-afternoon when I arrived at Moor Park Station. The weather was glorious, utterly fabulous for February, and I hoped it was an omen for the future. There were not that many people about as it was far too early for the commuters to be returning from London; however, Marie was there to meet me. It was great to see her and I remember we piled all my luggage into the Land Rover and then went for a sandwich at a nice little coffee shop, just outside the station. I never visualised when I started writing this autobiography that it could be anything else but fun. I hadn't realised that at times I would get torn to pieces by my emotions because I'm not just remembering the past but, in fact, reliving it.

Moor Park was, and still is, a very prestigious and private estate with tree lined roads and very expensive detached houses, many with gardens large enough to require a full time gardener and it was with Ted, one of the Delfosse's gardeners, I was to stay. I didn't know really what to expect, I knew Marie was indulging in an expensive sport but so were others whom I would not consider wealthy and she had not given the impression of being financially privileged. We hadn't discussed the matter of wages and I didn't really want to. Marie knew my main interest was to help make the coming season a huge success, nevertheless she had been thinking about the money situation and felt it only correct that I should go on the payroll; so a figure was agreed. After the coffee the next stop was the gardener's home to unload my things. This was at Rickmansworth which was a couple of miles or so from Moor Park. Ted lived with his wife, who was affectionately called Doll, and their two daughters. They were a nice enough family but I had very little in common with them; saying that is uncharitable of me for I was a guest and they certainly made me welcome, in fact embarrassingly so - all rather overpowering.

We next went to the stables, which were at the other side of a golf course from Marie's home. To reach them by road one had to go on a stretch which was used in the making of that classic comedy film, Genevieve, with its endearing harmonica theme tune - the whole area was so peaceful and quiet in those days. The charming stable block was constructed of wood with a pantiled roof but as the light was deteriorating it wasn't possible to give them too much attention, though I was there long enough to notice that the horses looked exceptionally well.

We then motored round to the Delfosse house called 'Chivilcoy', which was a beautiful place, very imposing and built some twenty five years previously, on land backing on to the golf course. It had a large garden with massive oak trees and a couple of paddocks of about four acres. The interior possessed a lot of oak panelling and a very wide staircase; I mention this now as it's relevant to something that was to happen some years later. I found the furniture very masculine and rather depressing and unfriendly but probably I shouldn't be making such comments. One sister who had married a doctor, who became medical officer at Windsor Racecourse, was not there but the rest of the family were. They kept arriving home at varying intervals and wandering about from room to room. They all seemed very individual and not that interested in each other nor in why I was even there.

Marie's father 'Edward D' was of a similar build to myself and in his sixties. I never really got to know him fully, yet well enough to respect him. Over the years which were to follow he, indirectly through Marie, made life easier for us financially; it was not asked for, nevertheless it came and I feel I should make it known. He had various business interests including owning the Ormond Engineering Company which, from a factory in central London, manufactured screws mainly for the motor industry. He had built the business from scratch and I imagine one of the main reasons for his success was his integrity. He was pleasant to me that evening on our first meeting but it was obvious he was most possessive of his daughters. He was a very matter of fact and unpretentious sort of person and would drive down to business in a little Ford Anglia, leaving far more luxurious cars in the garage.

Marie's mother, as I have already mentioned, was German and, after thirty years in this country, had not mastered the English language all that well, which certainly had its drawbacks. When I arrived at Chivilcoy I noticed two rather magnificent lead lions guarding the entrance but there was something just not quite right about them! Apparently Marie's mother had mentioned to Ted, referring to the dirty washing lines, "Please gardener go and make the lions white." And that's exactly what he did, giving the two enchanting sculptures a thick coat of white gloss but kept the paint away from the noses and eyes, making them look like a couple of bloody poodles!

I have already 'introduced' you to Martha, who I'd met the previous year and the next sister I saw was Hilda. She was half a dozen years younger than Marie, a tall dark haired girl who worked in the offices at 'The Ormond' but did everything independently from 'Edward D'. She loved being one of the commuters; it was just one whacking big game to her. She was a strange girl but I liked her and immediately felt there was a sort of affinity between us. The last of the home based sisters to come on the scene was Elsie who, as a hobby, kept a few Jersey cows, one or two calves, some chickens and more than a few rabbits, which were housed in some buildings in one of the paddocks. She asked me "Do you like rabbit? if so come to dinner tomorrow because it's Harry's turn for the pot." All the animals had names and if I hadn't been a vegetarian, I certainly would have become one!

Over the next couple of days I got to know the area and Marie was preparing for the Swiss holiday. I was surprised that only three of the family were going, 'Edward D', Marie and Martha but apparently that was 'par for the course'. I mentioned to Marie that I would be giving the stables a spring clean but didn't say to what extent as I wished to keep it a nice surprise for when she returned. The Land Rover was a year old and similar to the one in which I passed my driving test - they were smaller than the later models and a lot nicer to drive. I steam cleaned the entire vehicle and highly polished the paint work, something I had not seen before on a Land Rover and it looked fantastic. When she did return Marie was absolutely delighted with the transformations; even 'Edward D' went to have a look at the stables, something which, apparently, he very rarely did.

So much happened over the coming months; we had a very busy yet marvellous time doing the shows and for relaxation Marie played golf; I was caddying for her one day at Moor Park when she holed in one, it being the third time she'd managed the feat. However the 'highs' were marred by the legacy left from the Southwell fall. The disturbing sensations I had to endure were still prevalent and any sudden movement of the head would activate them.

Marie and I became close, we laughed a great deal and were very happy. Just to spend time with her was such a pleasure - I absolutely adored her. It seemed we had known each other for ages, though it was only the previous spring that I first saw her at Windsor and, before even speaking to her, knew that we would become partners. The wedding took place at the Watford Registry Office, not the most romantic of places and the event proved rather amusing. No one was told beforehand because neither of us wanted all the commotion and hype a conventional wedding would have entailed. As witnesses, we brought in a couple of old codgers from the street. They said their names were Olly and Wally and apparently being witnesses was their full-time occupation! The smaller of the two could not write so he put a cross where his signature should have been. Marie jokingly suggested to him that he could command a higher fee than the ten shillings we gave them, if only he would learn to write his signature correctly! Our reception breakfast was coffee and a sandwich; actually that should be plural as we had more than one sandwich and several coffees - then off to a horse show in the afternoon. People there noticed we were wearing pink carnations and asked had we been to a wedding. But our reply of "Yes, ours" was not taken seriously.

Marie had concentrated on just the one horse, Fanny Rosa, which was owned by her father; she was a beautiful robust mare with bags of courage. Marie would always get the mare on to her hocks like a coiled spring ready to be released, then kick, kick and over. Fanny

Rosa had tremendous scope and I'm sure she loved jumping the big fences as much as her rider did. Throughout the season the combination hardly touched a pole, a wall, or anything else. It was success all the way - apart from winning the Queen Elizabeth Cup at The White City they won many other prestigious competitions during that very hot summer; these included the pairs with Pat Smyth at the International, the Six Bars at Brighton, divided the high jump there when clearing over seven feet and the Coronation Cup at Rhyl. The excursion to North Wales was a bundle of fun and took place after The White City success. We stayed over a couple of days and the promoter of the show also owned the resort's main theatre, where he introduced us to the audience as brother and sister, obviously thinking we were. On the way back home we called in at a small unaffiliated affair in Cheshire, giving the mare the name of 'Hot Toddy', a tune of the day which all the leading dance bands were playing. The jumps were rather flimsy, nevertheless 'Hot Toddy' put in a couple of perfect rounds.

Obviously winning the Queen Elizabeth Cup was really special for all concerned and I believe it was the first 'Ladies Championship' to be televised. I originally had the contest on film but managed to get it transferred onto a videotape and even now play it often, with a fair amount of emotion. Fanny Rosa was exceptionally cautious over the first two or three jumps but Marie soon instilled confidence and they jumped the most brilliant clear round. There had been half a dozen altogether and the jump off was on time. This Marie and Fanny Rosa won by a fifth of a second - it was a magnificent round, par excellence, but no superlatives could really do it justice. Other jumping events would be forgotten but not the Queen Elizabeth Cup. A rather extraordinary party was held at 'Chivilcoy' to celebrate the win, with the cup being held aloft. I say extraordinary because neither Fanny Rosa's jockey nor trainer were invited. I suspected Martha had something to do with that; I was not exactly the apple of her eye and matters have not improved over the years. We didn't know at the time that Marie was carrying young Col, thereby making him the only male that has ever won the pinnacle of ladies show jumping! When I told his two sons, Nicky and Andrew recently, they thought it "absolutely brill, super, super, what an achievement." I don't know whether they meant on Marie's part or Col's! There wasn't a more accomplished rider than Marie in the country, apart from her all round ability she possessed such confidence and certainly deserved the success she had.

Marie's sister, Hilda, rode the mare the following season but without any success. Marie and I had moved up north by then but went down to stay at 'Chivilcoy' for The White City week, though it was rather sad to see Fanny Rosa jump so flat. She later developed leg trouble and was retired to stud, though didn't pass on any of her great attributes to any of her offspring.

During the summer Marie was introduced to my brother for the first time; it was when he was running in the mile race at the Milk Marketing Board's annual sports at Thames Dutton. We met Peter off the train at Kings Cross, drove him down to the sports ground and, of course, stayed to give some moral support. I was surprised he thought he might be in the minority wearing 'spikes', as it turned out he was about the only one without the full regalia. In general they seemed a pretty hyped up lot, doing short ten yard sprints all afternoon and I don't know what the hand flapping and the rolling of the head was all about! Peter said he had trained hard for the run so I was pleased that he didn't finish last - in fact he was followed home by a very tall, thin, middle aged fellow, who was bald and had a well trimmed thick black moustache, with matching socks, held up by red suspenders! He in turn was followed home by a rather scruffy terrier, which took up the chase on the last lap, yapping all the way round. Mind you, he had stopped to 'cock a leg' at one of the small flags marking the final bend!

It eventually became known that Marie and I were married and 'Edward D' was not all that pleased but accepted it. I could understand his point of view as, on the face of it, I had little to offer materially. He knew I was a hell of a grafter but he probably also knew that Timeform would give my pedigree a couple of squiggles! By now the show jumping season had ended and Marie and I had decisions to make. For financial reasons a move away from showjumping was a must, at least for the foreseeable future. I was not offered a job at the Ormond; there was no reason why I should have been nor even expected to. Actually Hilda's future husband was given a position with the company when they married but neither lasted that long, the job or the marriage.

My Uncle Roy (my father's brother) had risen to the top with Hardy's furniture store and was at their Head Offices in London. I contacted him with a view to working in one of the shops. He was only too pleased to help and, with Slough being comparatively close to Moor Park, that's where I chose. We moved into a small hotel in the town, which turned out to be a ghastly place and we only stayed there a few days; it was then on to a nice little coffee house in Eton. Marie would come into Slough every lunch time and we would meet up for a sandwich. One might consider that not really of particular interest but for me it was most important. I only stayed six weeks at Hardy's, much to Roy's annoyance. Selling the furniture was not a problem - in fact I was selling more than the other three salesmen at the store all put together. It was a strange world, so far removed from anything I'd ever done and I didn't particularly like it, although it had been educational.

I don't know why but we spent Christmas Day in London; the place was utterly deserted apart from a few eccentrics standing on soap boxes at Hyde Park Corner and a few more eccentrics listening to them! I felt so close to Marie and I knew we would make good; it was not a question of 'I hope we do', I was far more positive than that. My next move was to get in touch with Harold Lander, my father's colleague when they were both at Pointings before the war. We met up and it was arranged I should join his motor firm, Box of Dewsbury, on the car sales side. Harold Lander made a lot of money during the war 'buying and selling' anything and everything and had invested in the Dewsbury firm. Ironically he had also bought Pointings in Leeds, which had become just a shadow of its former self.

One of the last things we did before moving north was to buy the most beautiful piece of furniture we had ever seen, a small refectory table in oak which had a lovely golden colour. We bought it from Toller, an antique dealer in Eton. It cost £30 though its value today would be in excess of £5,000. Incidentally, it was that piece of furniture that first kindled our enthusiasm for antiques.

Chapter eight

We head for Yorkshire
Col is born

Towards the end of January 1954 Marie said goodbye to all at Chivilcoy and we headed North in the Land Rover. Once in Yorkshire we immediately started house hunting, concentrating in the area north of Leeds, as I knew it would be more preferable to live there. After not too much searching Marie came across Scarcroft Grange, a large country house on the edge of the golf course belt, between Leeds and Wetherby. It was in the process of being converted into half a dozen luxury flats, most of the work had been completed and they were about to be decorated. The smallest was at the end of the building on the second floor, yet had a private ground floor entrance. It also had a stone stable on its own piece of garden. All the flats were very individual and this one was exactly what we were looking for as our first home. One of the others had already been sold to George Yates, a leading racecourse bookmaker, for £6,000 and we were more than happy with the price we gave for ours which, after some gazumping, was £2,850. We were told we could be in by the middle of March which was important for our baby was due at the beginning of April. Buying for the house, even though we had not a lot of money to spend, was rather exciting. Marie did a marvellous job putting everything together and, of course, we had that gorgeous antique table sent up from Eton.

Between first arriving in the north and moving into the flat we stayed in a guest house in the centre of Leeds; it wasn't that bad a place though a little austere. All the residents were permanent, one being a university lecturer in Economics. I thought from his standard of living he should be taking lessons, not giving them! - it was rather like having a bankrupt as a financial adviser! The proprietor was an absolute 'hoot'. Every morning when we came down for breakfast he would call through the hatch into the kitchen "Keep Mr and Mrs Tinkler's eggs shelled, they haven't started their cornflakes yet." He should have had a parrot doing the job! After a couple of months of that we were pleased to move into Scarcroft Grange - into our very cosy little flat.

On April 7th 1954, the day young Col was born, I awoke very early with the sun shining through the windows. Marie had been admitted to the nursing home in Chapel Allerton the previous evening and I was anxious when I rang through to enquire about her, I asked "Have there been any developments?" I was told "Yes, and all is well." Both Marie and the little boy who we affectionately called 'Jockey', had arrived a few hours earlier. They were asleep and yes, the little fellow had the correct number of fingers and toes. I put the phone down and gave the loudest "Yippee" of all time. I ran down the stairs and passed the newly acquired, so superb and so expensive, Silver Cross pram with the extra large wheels. Then into the Land Rover all shining and bright. The hood was off and the windscreen flat on the bonnet and away I went. It was a glorious morning in every sense. The weather was just as it was the day I arrived at Moor Park a little over a year ago - brilliant - everything was brilliant. The tyres hummed away on the surface of the road, playing a tune on the tarmac; even 'Fanny Rosa', for that is what we had named the Land Rover, was going well. Marie had not wanted me to pace the nursing home floor, which was the reason that I returned home on the previous evening. 'Jockey' was absolutely great and I was pleased Marie seemed relaxed. It goes without saying she was thrilled with the little fellow. I stayed for about an hour then left, as I realised they both required some rest. My thoughts as I drove over to Dewsbury were of the past as well as the future; where was I ten years ago and where will I be in ten years' time? As I was contemplating the pros and cons a police car passed with flashing lights - I was doing 75 m.p.h. in a 30 m.p.h. limit area but was let off with a "Watch how you go in future". It definitely was my lucky day!

During the afternoon I went to pick up a car for servicing and passed a junk shop where, hanging outside, was some kind of candle lamp. It was obviously very old and I could see the potential for a really nice lantern - it would require converting to electric, some antique glass fitted and a wall bracket made. I bought it for six shillings, had the work done and have had it ever since. It's unique and is now hanging next to the front door here at Huttons Ambo and I'm not even going to guess its present value. I mention the lamp because of its association with that very special day. I left Dewsbury early, made my way back to the nursing home and spent the evening there. Jockey had changed colour to a lovely brown and Marie looked really well and as pretty as always. I used to call to see them twice a day until they returned home to Scarcroft Grange after about a week.

Marie was marvellous with Jockey, nothing was too much trouble and she would walk for miles every day, pushing the pram; it certainly wasn't long before the tyres on the Silver Cross needed changing! Officially we named the little fellow Colin Harwin Tinkler and, not believing in all the Mumbo-Jumbo of a christening, he wasn't put through all the rigmarole. His middle name is the same as a very good racehorse, which belonged to a friend of Marie's father.

There is no real connection, it's just that we thought the tag rather nice. It was not until years later that it was pointed out to us that it bore splits from my parents' names - Harold and Winifred; I can assure you this was sheer coincidence! The summer went by and we had our second Christmas together but, of course, the first for the three of us. I made the 'little rascal', who had become exceptionally strong, a 'spring horse' made from a large coil spring; it didn't rock but went up and down and how he enjoyed the rides. Marie and I were very happy and I loved her a great deal; it was always in my thoughts, though not in hers, that she had given up so much. We took Jockey down to Moor Park a couple of times during the summer and it was an eight hour journey in those days. There were always long delays getting through Doncaster, Newark, Grantham and Stamford but that was before the arrival of the bypasses and motorways. It wasn't a hum drum existence for us though it might seem that way compared with what was to come, but, to be perfectly truthful, every day was an adventure.

I couldn't get 'acclimatised' to the car showroom in Dewsbury because there was absolutely nothing to do. New cars were in very short supply, consequently there was little to sell, so I went to the auctions and it wasn't long before I could value any car to a tenner - values would change from day to day but it was a matter of having a certain aptitude for the job. I realised by the time I built up sufficient capital I would be proficient enough to commence on my own and to work mainly within the trade.

To help accumulate funds we were careful in what we spent, not to the point of meanness, but certainly we were not extravagant. Having the time to give to punting was also a bonus and I kept winning money, though it was immensely difficult compared with now. Today one can go to a meeting, come home and replay the S.I.S.

video recordings again and again - time consuming it is but very informative. After six months at Dewsbury I asked to be transferred to their branch in Leeds, which went under the Pointings banner and dealt solely in used vehicles. In fact they were those taken in part exchange at Dewsbury and always over-priced, making them terribly difficult to sell. However, there was always a steady turnover. I remember on one occasion a young man wanted to trade in his motor bike for an exceptionally clean small van we had. I did the deal and six months later he was back wanting to sell the van back to us, saying he required the cash, as he was having to get married. I looked inside the back of the van and noticed a couple of rugs and one or two cushions! He would have been far better off not parting with the motor bike in the first place!

I next went from Pointings in the centre of Leeds to manage the firm's newly opened petrol station, in Street Lane, which was on the northern outskirts of the city and quite close to a house I lived in for a while when I was a boy. The idea was to develop car sales there but I had no sooner started doing this than the Suez crisis occurred. Petrol then became rationed and car sales came to a halt but, in spite of rationing, the station's petrol turnover quadrupled, with long queues at the pumps; it's easy to explain. Basically it was a vicious circle but, for me, not so vicious! If I sold 5,000 gallons of petrol and received the required coupons the petrol company would deliver a further 5,000 gallons, so on and so on. You might ask, where did the customers get the extra coupons? - from a Good Samaritan. Everybody was happy - the customers, for they had all the petrol they required, be it a little bit over the odds! - Harold Lander, although he couldn't understand what was going on - the petrol companies, because obviously they were selling more petrol - and, of course, the Good Samaritan who was the happiest of them all. Exactly!

When the Suez disturbance ended after several months I decided it was time to commence trading on my own account, as I now had the necessary capital! The crunch came when Lander wanted Marie to sell one or two of his firm's cars from our home, advertising them as a private sale, lady owned, low mileage; that would have been three lies for a start! The farcical thing was he wasn't going to give her any commission for her trouble, saying "It will help Colin in his job" - stuff it, I was away.

The spring of 1955 arrived and for Jockey's first birthday we bought him a pony which cost only £32; he was a two year old, very small, narrow and looked like a miniature thoroughbred. Marie got to work making jodhpurs and some tiny riding boots and I built a container with a ramp which fitted into the back of the short wheel based Land Rover. Jockey shaped jolly well and had fantastic balance which he must have inherited though not from me! He couldn't walk, yet would bounce at the trot - amazing really. We entered them in a leading rein class at the Harewood Show; Jockey was just thirteen months at the time but we arrived too late to compete. However we made no such mistake at the Boroughbridge Show a couple of months later and they won first prize. I had chromed one of the tiny shoes the pony had on that day and I have it in front of me now, as I write. We toured all the local shows during the summer, winning more times than losing; we had enormous fun. It was at about that time that Anthony Makin, who was a stalwart of showjumping over the years, asked me to commentate at some of the shows. One was at Roundhay Park, where a skinny lad in baggy jodhpurs arrived with a couple of horses in a converted bread van. His name - Harvey Smith and one of the horses was Foxhunter; both became prolific winners in the show jumping arenas around the world and, of course, Harvey and his wife Sue are now successfully training racehorses.

As Scarcroft Grange was adjacent to the main road into Leeds we realised that, before Jockey became old enough to be running about, we would have to move to somewhere less hazardous to live. Having a joint entrance meant the gates were invariably open, making it rather dangerous for children. Towards the end of September, when scanning through the local papers, Marie saw advertised for sale a dilapidated cottage in the village of Sicklinghall, which was between Wetherby and Kirby Overblow. It was in the latter of those two places that my sister was born and where I lived for a while when I was seven. We piled into the Land Rover to go over and have a look and, apart from a couple of places that had been modernised, Sicklinghall was, I imagine, the same as it had been for ages. We were terribly disappointed to find the cottage too small and crammed between other dwellings, with no garden. However, on leaving the village, we noticed an unoccupied detached cottage with a reasonably sized garden, though it was overgrown with nettles five feet high. The place looked hideous, having been pebble dashed, but I chipped off a corner and it revealed some lovely sandstone in various colours and the interior had some very nice beams. We enquired as to the owner and bought it the following day for £600. The flat at Scarcroft Grange took no selling at all, in fact we made a small profit and, until the renovation work was completed on the cottage, we stayed at the village pub named The Scotts Arms. Our new acquisition was called Rose Cottage and we retained the name. It had three bedrooms and we built on a stable and a garage and when everything was finished, including the garden, it looked really pretty. Passing cars would skid to a standstill to enable the drivers to have a better look; in fact there were a couple of crashes while we were there, with cars following too close to the one in front.

I must mention a rather amusing incident whilst doing the renovations. The builders required a new vice as the one they had been using had broken. They also needed to fasten a couple of beams together and, as I was going down to Wetherby, I said I would call in at the hardware store and see what they could come up with. I told the pretty girl behind the counter "I'm looking for a vice and a long screw." With eyes sparkling she quipped "I can supply both but I will want some help with the long screw."! Such delightful humour.

During the year my brother Peter, who had been engaged for some time, married Kathleen and my sister Ann was also married by then, her husband being connected in some way with agriculture. As for Peter, he was living at Louth in Lincolnshire and had joined Boots as a field representative. Marie and I had been to both weddings though, having lost our way, coincidentally on both occasions, we missed the actual church services; though did get there for the receptions. We were always so busy that we didn't see much of either side of the family but, over the years, various members would come and stay with us from time to time. We did however, during 1956, take Jockey on a 'whistle stop' visiting everyone, and made Mumso's the final call. She and her husband had, by then, moved to the flat in Eastbourne. Whilst there we toured the area and bought some fabulous antique furniture, all small pieces, tables, chairs and that sort of thing. We filled the Land Rover and for safe keeping wanted Mumso to house them overnight but no way did she wish to do so and informed us "Sorry, but I don't want that Second hand junk in our luxurious flat; what would the neighbours say if they saw it!" Ah, well! One of the bits of junk was an exquisite Windsor backed armchair in yew! We also visited a commercial art gallery whilst in Eastbourne and were utterly enthralled by the early Dutch paintings we saw. Marie and I didn't buy on that first encounter with Koek, but we did do so a few years later.

Chapter nine

Our time at Sickling Hall.
Marie joins the Ministry of Agriculture
and I commence motor trading.

Marie decided she would put to good use her veterinary degree so joined the Ministry of Agriculture carrying out testing for Tuberculosis and commenced during our first summer at Sicklinghall. She drove two or three hundred miles a week and tested a similar number of cattle; the admiration the farmers had for her was tremendous. It was not a question of Marie being bored with looking after Jockey, far from it, besides she still managed to do that as well. No, it was a question of helping with the finances. I'm sure I showed appreciation but I didn't help matters by my objection to every nanny she employed. There wasn't one that lasted for more than a week; they were all so damn lazy. I don't know why Marie kept employing girls with beauty and not brains. Most husbands would have had a field day, particularly with one of them, who could not understand her sole role was to look after The little fellow and not my little fellow! Marie stayed testing practically the whole time we were at Sicklinghall, which was almost a couple of years, and later did a further period after moving to Lower Dunsforth.

We didn't have a lot of time to go racing though never missed a local Wetherby meeting, the bonus there being we could take the Land Rover into the paddock, which meant it was somewhere that Jockey could rest. His riding was progressing but, of course, he was still very young and what a lovely happy boy he was growing into and so independent. We bought a litter of pedigree piglets and kept them in the stable under heat lamps - they looked like balls of butter. Jockey would shriek with delight as he chased them about - yes, just the one litter and then back to sanity.

It was a 'hot little village' with rather too much extra shagging going on; one such 'naughty' was taking place a couple of houses away from us. Every morning at about nine o'clock this fellow, who worked on a local farm, would crawl along the side of the hedge separating our garden from a field at the rear and on to a gap in the fence at his 'port of call'. Half an hour later he would make the return journey but travelling much slower! Yes, every morning other than Sundays, obviously his day of rest - or perhaps he reserved that day for someone else!

That reminds me of the encounter I had with the local hermit-cum-tramp, a giant of a man, who lived in a shed on a rubbish dump in Wetherby. He would come into the village for his lunch and anything else he could get at the small nunnery! The first time I ever saw him it was pouring with rain and I was driving over to Harrogate and he was trudging along the road. Not realising he was so scruffy and disgustingly dirty I stopped and enquired where he was heading and did he want a lift. He replied "I have no immediate plans, is the answer to the first question, so I can't answer the second one!" and thankfully he went on his way. Now to the real point in discussing him. Marie and I had been in the village about six months when one of the farmers remarked that the tramp had told him that he'd seen me on the job down the lane with this posh married bit and mentioned her name. It so happened that I often spoke to her so I thought it best to put a stop to the totally false rumour. I arranged for my informant and the tramp to come and see me the following Sunday, not telling the reason why nor that the other would also be present - the day arrived and both duly came. They soon realised what it was all about and, after a short three way conversation, I told the tramp that if he had said those things I was going to knock his ruddy head off and likewise the farmer told him that if he denied saying them, he, the farmer, was going to knock his ruddy head off. The tramp was, by then, in rather a predicament, especially after Marie came in the room and handed him a towel with the curt remark "I don't want blood all over the carpet." The tramp took one look at the farmer, who was a lot bigger than me and stuttered, as he turned in my direction "Yes, I reckon it was you I saw." Now the tramp was a tramp because obviously he'd made wrong decisions all his life! Well, he had just made another one, BANG, BANG, BANG, and thank goodness for Marie's foresight! I didn't kill the tramp but I did the rumour!

I had started motor trading on my own not long after moving to Sicklinghall. The first vehicle I bought was a Land Rover at one of the auctions which, after extensive cleaning, I re-sold the following week at a farm sale. It made a fantastic profit, something equivalent to ten weeks wages at the job I had left. This transaction was followed by a couple of Jowett Javelin deals - I developed a good trade outlet for the unusual looking car and they became a speciality for me. I would attend three or four auctions a week, mainly at Leeds, Bridlington and Glasgow - buying at one - cleaning - then selling at another. During the first couple of years I would never have more than three cars at any one time and never more than one at home, yet moved a tremendous number of vehicles. Very few mechanical repairs were ever undertaken, though I would give the odd oil warning light a tap with a hammer! I'd hardly ever buy privately or directly from other traders because of the risk factor. At least if one bought at auction there was protection, one knew the vehicles had not been stolen and were guaranteed to be free from hire purchase. However, risks were sometimes taken and, fantastic as it may seem, not once did I get my fingers burnt. Selling privately was a different matter as there were no risks whatsoever; sometimes a bit of hassle but that was all. My first private sale was when a young fellow, who lived near Wetherby, turned up one Sunday morning and explained exactly what he wanted - a shooting brake for not more than £200 and he would leave it to me to get him the right vehicle. Now, I wasn't entirely sure how genuine a buyer he was so consequently was a bit apprehensive. However, he kept calling round - and became a little impatient. A few days after one of his visits I found myself at Leeds Auction with no transport home - I had sold a couple of cars and had not managed to buy one - when in came the last lot, a green hand painted Bedford van with windows and curtains! I thought, this is my transport home; the old van was knocked down to me for £15. As soon as I arrived back at Sicklinghall I put it into the garage - out of sight. As I was leaving for the sales the following afternoon who should arrive on the scene but the fellow wanting the shooting brake - his eyes lit up when he saw the monstrosity I was sitting in. "Is this for me? - just what I want but I can't afford more than £200." He was so excited at seeing the shooting brake, for that's what it had suddenly become; I just stood there in disbelief - dare I ask him "Would you like a test run?" No, I thought I'd better not appear too pushy or test providence - in no way did I sell him the vehicle, he bought it, literally! I don't know what the hell he wanted it for but he said he liked the curtains! I only hoped he wasn't going to put too much stress on the springs!

Another vehicle I bought for very little money about that time, making a similar amount of profit, was a red 1930 M.G. two seater sports - not quite vintage but certainly looked so, with its brass headlights and trimmings. It would go round in circles without a driver and there was a switch on the wooden steering wheel which regulated the speed - did I say speed? Its top would be about 15 mph. The longest journey it did while in my ownership was from Sicklinghall to Wetherby and back for a spot of shopping and that took all morning! I bought it at auction for the unbelievable figure of £8 and had a lot of fun driving it about the village. Unfortunately the inevitable happened - it broke down and spare parts were difficult to obtain, yet I managed to swap it on for a car which I sold for £200; though the little M.G. would be worth a few thousand pounds today.

When I went to the car auctions in Glasgow I would catch an early train, arriving up there at about 8.00 a.m., have some breakfast and then to work and, if I happened to buy a couple, there were always drivers around. It was on one of these excursions that I had the first of my many crashes on the roads. I was not more than a dozen miles from home when I fell asleep at the wheel, apparently I went into the back of a ten ton lorry completely writing off my vehicle. I was taken to Northallerton Hospital, put on a trolley and the doctor said to a nurse "Give him an A.T.S." - which, apart from a medical term, is also an abbreviation used meaning a girl soldier. Still unconscious I managed to say "What, on this narrow bed!" At one stage a nurse asked whether or not I had a donor card, which I thought was rather insensitive of her! All's well that ends well and I was back home the following day.

During the Suez crisis, when I was with Pointings, I was able to supply 'Remoco', a retail vacuum cleaner firm, with petrol for their dozen transits. The vehicles were working from Leeds and covering the whole of the North of England. It looked a fantastic business from the outside but proved to be very volatile. Calling at the offices as often as I did, gave me an insight into things and I fancied a crack myself. I felt that if I went low-key the business could work alongside the motor trading. I'm not going into the whole rigmarole of how I set it up but a firm in Hendon agreed to manufacture a vacuum cleaner for me. They were already producing similar machines for other retail outlets but, to make it personal to me, there were slight variations and it also carried my own name plate - Harwin. 'Lombard' the finance company at Reading were to finance the sales and with no recourse if a customer failed to pay the instalments. I bought a low mileage Mercedes Transit, 'borrowed' a supervisor from 'Remoco', along with three or four of their salesmen. The vacuum cleaners cost me roughly £8 each and we sold them for £30 plus the hire purchase charges - yet I only made £2 a sale profit. The part exchanges were not an issue as any losses on those were deducted from the salesmen's commissions. They weren't paid a wage but the transport costs were astronomical; I'm sure the driver thought he was in Formula One! To obtain sales it was tap, tap on the doors, I went out with them one evening to the Hunslet area of Leeds and the first door I knocked on was in fact the only door I knocked on! The householder, who was an extremely thin and ill looking woman, said "Come in, Luv, and sit down while I go and get my teeth in." Judging by the ages of all her filthy looking children that were about, she could not have been that old but certainly looked it. There was a naked light bulb hanging from the cracked ceiling and I couldn't sit down because the two chairs that were in the room were already occupied by a scruffy old cat in one and a mongrel dog in the other. As you can imagine, the floor hadn't a carpet but was littered with dirty old newspapers. I thought, what the hell am I doing here, she doesn't need a vacuum cleaner. Now if I was selling a high powered jet hose, yes, but not a vacuum cleaner. I was soon out of the house and away home - I quickly realised selling vacuum cleaners was not my forte.

Lombard suffered an awful lot of bad debts, resulting from forced selling by my team, and after about twelve months they scrapped the original agreement and asked me to take recourse on future sales. In no way was I prepared to do that on a long term basis - I was not in cuckoo land. However, I had to get rid of the stock I had, some twenty machines. I soon realised it would have been better to have given them away for seventeen of the sales bounced, the customers just not making any monthly payments whatsoever. It was no use trying to repossess the cleaners for I could buy new ones for very little money. I just closed down the whole business, sold the Merc Transit, reimbursed Lombard and that was that. Financially I came out on the right side but only just. The enterprise, though I think that is the wrong word to use, had not taken a great deal of my time and had not hindered the motor trading in any way.

We had one or two scary times with Jockey in his early years, the first being when he became very ill one evening. The local doctor was called in but failed to make a positive diagnosis and rushed him to an isolation hospital in Leeds. He feared it was meningitis but those at the infirmary were sure that it wasn't and said if he didn't improve in a couple of days they would take some tests. We returned to Sickinghall but we both went over to the hospital the following morning and again got negative replies to our questions. Jockey wanted to come home and, as we considered he was more likely to attract a disease there than get rid of what ever was wrong with him, particularly as he wasn't receiving treatment, we decided it was 'Home James' for the little fellow. I wrapped him in a blanket, carried him to the car and we were away, but not before the Matron had received a first class bollocking from Marie! After two or three days he had completely recovered and we never did discover what had been wrong; the attitude we had encountered at the hospital had been appalling.

Another time was when we spent an agonising afternoon at Saltburn, a small Yorkshire seaside resort. It was during the same summer as the hospital episode. We had gone there to take Jockey for an afternoon's fun; the first thing he spotted was the kiddies roundabouts and I'm sure he would have been quite happy staying on those all afternoon but eventually we persuaded him to leave them. We ate ice creams, did some paddling, then played on the sands, then suddenly he wasn't there; we hadn't taken our eyes off him for a minute, yet he had gone. It was mid-week and there were not a great number of people about; many had noticed him, but hadn't seen him wander away. Saltburn has a high cliff the full length of the pedestrian promenade so there was no point looking in that direction. We ran back to the roundabouts but he wasn't there; we started calling his name louder and louder but all to no avail. By the time we had run up and down the promenade and the sands several times, looking in every beach hut, the toilets, in fact everywhere, half an hour had flown by. We talked to the police and the coastguards but nobody seemed to be treating it with any urgency - they would a similar situation today, but not then. Marie and I were panicking as we believed someone had taken him and he could be miles away, that gorgeous little boy with the blonde curly hair. An hour went by and still no sight of him, then Marie suddenly saw a red spot, more than half a mile away, near some large rocks down by the south cliff. The tide was coming in fast, Marie was crying and said "It must be Jockey because just before he disappeared I put him a red cardigan on". Neither of us can remember running down to where the red dot was seen; our minds must have been a total blank. We searched around then saw him behind a large boulder, paddling in a pool left there when the tide had gone out but was soon going to be part of the sea again. He was oblivious to what had been happening, thank goodness he was. We just picked him up and cuddled and cuddled him. We hadn't looked as far away as that because we assumed we would have seen him on the wide open sands. All that mattered now was that he was safe - no recriminations. I just loved him and I loved Marie and, as we drove back home, I daren't think of what might have been if it weren't for that little red cardigan.

Ever since Marie and I had been in the North we had felt it was a sort of intermediate period until we went on to do other things. We had planned that Marie would take up point to point racing, something she had always wanted to do. The Newmarket Town Plate was also on the agenda as, at that time, ladies riding under rules was still some way off. We also intended to take up training eventually but we needed to move on and the change came one Sunday afternoon in October 1957. We were in the garden when a car pulled up and an elderly couple got out and said "We just love your cottage, please let us know if it ever comes on the market." They looked round the place, gave us their telephone number and we said we would be in touch. Marie and I discussed the matter that evening and decided to sell; we got on the phone and the deal was done, in principle, at £3,850.

After only a couple of weeks we found a cottage that required modernising at Lower Dunsforth, a hamlet some three miles south of Boroughbridge. It was constructed of hand made bricks and had a reasonable sized garden and a small paddock. We also understood that a six acre field close by was soon to come on the market. We went ahead and bought the place, coincidentally for the same price as we had originally paid for Rose Cottage - £600. There was a great deal of work to be done but it would be exciting, though even more exciting was the fact that Marie was going to have another child which was due in the following February. We packed everything and left Sicklinghall richer in every sphere than when arriving there two years earlier and many lessons had been well learnt.

Chapter ten

Our ten years at Lower Dunsforth. Nigel is born. We commence training and I ride a winner. Marie back in the saddle. The boys.

By the time we had done the demolishing in the cottage at Lower Dunsforth there was literally only the shell left. Marie thought White Gates would be an appropriate name as we intended to have two such gates on the short drive, as a safety measure, with one gate always closed. The cottage was situated in the centre of the village and all the six farms and the dozen other dwellings were set back, away from the road. All had comparatively large gardens, consequently the buildings were not too close together. There are always pluses and minuses with every place and Lower Dunsforth was no exception. On the plus side was the peace and quiet, with not much traffic passing through and the small market town of Boroughbridge only three miles away was an added attraction. On the minus side we had the most ugly and uninviting building for a pub, which had only recently been constructed to cater for all the anglers who converged there on a Sunday; the river being only a few hundred yards away was something we hadn't realised before we moved there. It also meant the land was low lying and prone to flooding; though White Gates never suffered any damage. Another 'thumbs down' was the draining system; the main ditch had not enough slope to take away all the cesspit overflows. Often in the dry summer months the open drain remained stagnant and it took me back to the smells I endured whilst in prison. I'm certainly not a hypochondriac but eventually, after years living there, I became allergic to the stench. Looking back, I don't know why I didn't try to obtain some sort of medical help, nor do I understand why I was not more fearful of what the consequences might have been. There was a period of three or four months one year when I couldn't walk for more than a hundred yards before collapsing with exhaustion and literally gasping for air. As soon as the main drainage was installed in the village I recovered completely. It was only then that I was entirely certain the allergy was triggered by the unhygienic conditions. Actually, at one stage, Marie suggested I should go to Switzerland to recover and she would hold the fort at home. Kind thoughts, but I couldn't see me doing that.

Our time at Lower Dunsforth was, without a doubt, an eventful ten years. As with Rose Cottage, we decided to get all the building work done as quickly as possible and, so that we could be on hand, we hired a caravan to live in for a while, it was nothing special, but sufficed. We parked it close to the cottage to make it easier for the electricity and water to be installed and you can imagine how much fun the mischievous 'Little Imp' found in the whole escapade! Everything was completed by the end of January 1958 including landscaping the garden; we'd had a double garage and three stables built on to the cottage. The small paddock adjacent to the garden had been post and railed and re-seeded. I had curtailed my activities at the motor auctions whilst doing the renovations but had not entirely ceased operating. We were well installed by the time Jockey's brother arrived. It was great to have a nice home again, especially for Marie who had weathered things remarkably well in the circumstances.

I must tell you about the amusing time I had when the local policeman called on a courtesy visit. It was some time in early

December when Marie had taken the opportunity to go down to Moor Park and naturally took Jockey along. It would be mid-morning when he wandered into the garden - the whole place was a hive of activity - the cement mixer was rattling away and I had just commenced filling in an old well, starting with a couple of bags of lime, which I'd found in the outside toilet we'd demolished. After introducing himself and finding me edgy (which was an act) and noticing the lime down the well, Policeman 'Plod' said in a commanding voice,

"Your wife not about, Sir?"

"No she, no she has gone away."

"Where to, might I ask, Sir?"

"London."

"That was a quick reply, Sir."

"Was it?"

"Yes, Sir, and London is a very big place."

Then, suddenly, one of the 'builder boys' tipped a wheelbarrow load of concrete down the well from the mixer and said "Two more loads should do it but I think it's a waste of good concrete, rubble would do, but if it's concrete you want, you're paying." The policeman then went over to talk to the plumber, then suddenly away in his van without coming back to see me. The plumber was laughing and apparently had told the policeman something or other, all to wind Mr. 'Ploddy' up. The 'builder boys' filled the well, gravelled over the top and, as expected, a couple of police cars arrived shortly afterwards, plus our 'local' in his van. When the two detectives 'wanted' to have a word with me, I thought it was time the flippancy stopped. I told them I couldn't understand what the fuss was all about; we called Marie on the phone and they all went away apologising profusely. "Sorry for the misunderstanding, Sir." It had been good fun! - and please don't reproach me for wasting police time, I know I shouldn't have done so.

I nearly had my come-uppances over the coming weeks - yes, plural, as there were two separate instances. The first was when mending an electric cable. Two lengths were joined together and covered with tape and, as no current was flowing through, obviously they must have come apart. I was just about to mend it when the phone rang, distracting me from taking the plug out of the socket. After the call I commenced the repair job by biting off some rubber, which was covering one of the lengths of wire. Then suddenly I realised the power was not turned off - it could so easily have been the length of cable going to the mains that I'd put in my mouth, talk about Russian Roulette!

On the second occasion I had an even greater stroke of good fortune. I was still having trouble resulting from the racing fall and it was never possible for me to lie on my back without the roller coaster sensation occurring. I'm mentioning this for, in a bizarre sort of way, the fact that I had to sleep actually sitting up most likely saved my life. I'd have several pillows between my back and the bed head. Usually I would sleep alone but the lack of space in the caravan meant Marie and I sharing the double bed. This particular night it was blowing a gale and someone had left a ladder propped up against the cottage wall. It was about two in the morning when an extra gust brought the ladder crashing down, smashing the large window above the bed we were in. One piece of jagged glass the size of a large dinner plate sliced one of the pillows behind me and through into the one underneath. It was just where my head would have been in normal circumstances. There was glass everywhere but incredibly neither Marie nor I received a single cut. It was certainly rather a miraculous escape for us both.

Jockey's little brother was born on February 28th, 1958. There was nearly four years difference in their ages but it wasn't a problem after a while for they got on so well together. Obviously there had not been quite the same tension and concern that there was the first time round. Marie phoned me from the nursing home in Harrogate, soon after Nigel arrived - that is the name we decided to call the little fellow (Nigel Delfosse) - and she assured me all was well with them both and that he was a lovely baby with laughing eyes. I went over straight away to see them and naturally took Jockey along. The nursing home was in a quiet and very peaceful area of Harrogate; Marie and little Nigel looked a million dollars. We were very lucky people to have two such lovely healthy children. I remember a tune called Magic Moments was being played on the radio and yes, they were rather Magic Moments. Jockey's expression when he saw his future playmate was really something - a mixture of curiosity, pleasure, humour, and utter amazement; I can see his face even now. Marie brought Nigel home after a few days and I can't remember him ever crying.

We had been at Lower Dunsforth nine months when there was another near catastrophe with Jockey. As I have mentioned, a river was comparatively close to our cottage but we thought the two sets of high gates that were on the short drive made things safe enough. On the occasion I'm relating he was not confined to our garden; a young couple named Turner, who farmed in the village, had invited Jockey over to play. They had a couple of boys themselves and a little girl visiting, she wouldn't have been more than three years old, and there were also some other children about. We left Jockey there and returned home to do some gardening. The summer's afternoon wore on then, suddenly, panic stations. Yes, again! just as it had been at Saltburn twelve months previously. A neighbour called in to say she had seen an older boy of about fourteen pied piping a group of small children down the path to the river and Jockey was among them. I had often seen a boy of that age, who looked a little on 'the slow side', walking about the village and I assumed it would be he. To say I was concerned is a gross understatement. I asked Marie to dash over to the farm just in case he was still there. I then ran down to the river. I found all the children sitting in a rowing boat which was moored some two or three feet from the bank of the swiftly flowing Ouse. The children were soaking; apparently they had waded through the water and then been pulled into the boat by the older boy. Jockey and the little girl, the two smallest that were there, must have had the water whirling around their shoulders and how they hadn't drowned we will never know. It would not have been possible, once their game was over, to have got back on to dry land, unless the boat had been pulled to the bank. The horror was too dreadful to contemplate and I was too relieved to be cross with anyone and I never knew what the reactions of the other parents were. Jockey had not been disobedient in any way for we hadn't told him about the river because we considered it more prudent not to promote any curiosity. The buckets of water I threw over him when we returned home were not meant as a scolding but as a reminder not to visit the river again. I didn't like what I did, neither did Marie as she thought it totally unnecessary but I felt, with him being so young, words would soon have been forgotten. So ended another day of bringing up children but not a nice day to reflect upon. In general, both boys were super kids and never, ever did we need to say anything twice; it wasn't that Marie or I were strict disciplinarians - they were just very happy children and a delight to have around. I did twank Colin once for something or other - it just shows we are not all perfect. I'm talking about me not him!

I used to take Jockey down to the car auctions - he loved that, it was such an adventure and everybody made a great fuss of him. I was turning over a lot of vehicles but not in the literal sense; my bout of crashes came later and, as the years progressed, the numbers I bought and sold increased but the actual number of cars I brought home for cleaning became less. Mostly they went straight from one auction to the next as there were always drivers available to do the shunting. You might ask why would a trader give more for a car than it had made at a previous sale? The answer is simply that different sales attracted different dealers; besides not many of them could value a car with any degree of accuracy. I also catered for Saturdays when there were more private buyers present. I enjoyed all the banter with the auctioneers and would always put a reserve on my motors. If they didn't reach the figure I would bid myself to way above the price I wanted, in the hope that someone would step in; with all the chatter this invariably happened. It was my livelihood yet also a game and every auction a challenge. I soon became a force and I'm sure was respected. I didn't build an empire of distributorships - I didn't even build a showroom but was more successful than many that did. Of course, there were some that took chances, borrowed heavily, invested in bricks and mortar and came out on top but there were many others that took the same paths but the overheads bankrupted them.

Whilst on the subject of the motor trade I will relate some interesting stories connected with the business. On one occasion I called in to see a trader I knew who had premises in Wetherby. He was making an appalling job of spraying a perfectly clean and comparatively new Rolls Royce, which didn't appear to be requiring a paint job at all. Shortly after that he fled to South Africa, having fraudulently pocketed over a couple of million, at today's values, by numerous crooked dealings - then conveniently lost it all at the casinos. After a while he voluntarily returned, got eighteen months and when released opened a large garage down south. Nice one!

Another time I'd bought an immaculate A30 rather cheaply from a trader I didn't know too much about; as I was somewhat suspicious because he wanted cash for the transaction, I checked the car immediately with H.P.I. to find out if it carried any hire purchase - H.P.I. being an organisation that keeps track on such things - and it came back negative. However, I was still a little apprehensive and made another enquiry the following day - this time it was different. The person from whom I had bought the car had put it on hire purchase after selling to me, it goes without saying a very serious criminal offence. I went over to Morley, near Leeds, where he had a petrol station and kept a few cars on the forecourt; it was dark by the time I got there and the place looked deserted apart from a girl in the kiosk. I dumped the 'questionable' A30 and asked where was her boss. "He's gone abroad - went this morning" was the answer I got. I thought, I've lost this one and went to a phone box a couple of hundred yards down the road, to call Marie and put her in the picture but our conversation was interrupted by a crossed line. It was the petrol girl talking to her boss who, it appeared, was also her boyfriend and what's more he hadn't gone abroad, yet. She was saying "He wanted his money back - yes, he has gone back home". But, of course, I hadn't and didn't until I got the matter squared. I returned to the petrol station and once the girl realised I'd heard the telephone conversation she cracked and told me where I could find her boss. He was shocked to see me but paid out in full, plus a little extra for expenses! I think that is the best way to phrase it; but it had been a close call.

Shortly after that incident I nearly lost out on a Sunbeam Talbot

Sports. A dealer from Scarborough asked if he could show the car to some guys who ran a mock auction on the front. I agreed and told him that as it was not licensed he should bring his trade plates along. When he left my place all was in order but that was the last I saw of the car. I eventually discovered it had been in a crash and was a complete write-off; it was not insured as no trade plates were on at the time. I came to the conclusion that the dealer had in fact sold the car to the mock auction people, before it crashed and before they had insured it, but between themselves they agreed to say otherwise, thereby leaving me with a pile of scrap. The police said it was not in their jurisdiction and it would have to be a civil action but suggested I take a couple of heavies and "Beat the money out of them". Now that seemed sound advice to me! Actually one was enough and I think the large scar on his face helped matters. I was paid with a hire purchase company's cheque, so obviously I had been correct - he had sold the car.

Another close shave I had that could have been really serious had I not been so vigilant was when I lent half a dozen nice cars to a firm in York, on a sale or return basis. The 'sextet' had been there for some time but weren't playing a profitable tune so I decided to pop over and have a look see. On arriving I parked up and, as I walked past a Volvo, I noticed, lying on the back seat, the log books belonging to my cars. I assumed they had been shown to a hire purchase company and used to borrow money, with the hire purchase company not realising the cars in question didn't belong to the garage. I retrieved the log books and whistled up some drivers and had my cars removed before evening. By the way, it was not long before the firm I've been discussing went bust. I wasn't in the least bit surprised.

Once we had settled in at Lower Dunsforth I again started to take more interest in punting. Most of my fellow traders knew of this but not many were that interested in racing. The same could not be said for Harry Crawshaw; he had a small showroom in Leeds but also did a lot of buying and selling within the trade and consequently spent a great deal of time at the auctions. He was always asking me which horses he should back, which leads me to the following amusing story.

Marie and I bought a greyhound bitch for breeding; apart from anything else we thought the boys would think it a lot of fun. Actually she only had the one pup with her first litter and it grew into a massive dog. We kept him until he was about fifteen months old then took him down for a trial at a track that existed in Leeds at that time. The dog was put into the traps and as the hare set off I'm sure he put his paws over his ears to deaden the sound. The traps opened and 'Mr. Dogy' walked nonchalantly out then, noticing a fur hat being worn by one of the onlookers, ran across, jumped a wall and snatched it from her head. He then bounded over to where we were, still with the fur hat in his mouth, and sat down on his backside with a f*****g stupid expression on his face. After several further 'no go' trials we gave the dog away to Harry Crawshaw who thought he might have a potential world beater. Now, why would I do a nasty thing like that, for I quite liked Harry? - it was because I owed him a bad turn! He had sold me a Standard 8 which slipped out of third gear when he had been adamant that the car was straight. Time elapsed and I still felt I had not repaid him sufficiently, so one day with tongue in cheek I told him that Denys Smith had a horse running at Doncaster that afternoon, it was its first outing and would definitely win. The horse's name was 'Too Slow' and I thought my choice rather amusing with a name like that. I said "Don't have more than a tenner on it Harry because I don't want you to shorten the price", chuckle, chuckle! The joke was most decidedly on me for

'Too Slow' won at 20/1; after that I was more than ever bombarded for information but no way was I going to risk giving him another 'dud' - Exactly.

Bridlington Auction on a Thursday evening was my favourite sales venue. It was a small family business and there were never many vehicles for sale but I found it virtually impossible not to make a profit, whether I bought or sold there. One of my best buys was a Standard Vanguard pickup, a very clean vehicle sent in by a garage, and had no reserve. I bought it for the incredibly low figure of £60 but I had a suicidal journey home in the dark. The brakes failed totally as I went down Garrowby Hill, a notorious place for the number of people killed in runaway vehicles! The fact I had it in bottom gear made no difference whatsoever; it soon jumped out of that, careered down the hill, round the bends - sixty - seventy - eighty - ninety miles per hour - we didn't pull up until we got to York! Someone said to me later "I don't suppose you had time to be frightened." My reply was "Oh, yes, I bloody well had". Apparently a seal or something had leaked and a fiver put it right. It didn't require too much of a clean and made £220 on the Saturday at the Leeds Motor Auction. To compare figures - a new 'Mini' cost less than £500 in those days.

Two or three years later I had the most embarrassing encounter at the Bridlington Sales, not for me necessarily but for the young lady in question. She was very smartly dressed and in her thirties. Lot 26 came into the ring, an immaculate little Morris Minor that was eventually knocked down to me but the girl, who was standing close by, thought it was her bid. A genuine misunderstanding on the part of the auctioneer and he asked if he should offer the car up again but I said "No, we will sort it out between ourselves." The girl then said to me "I'll toss you off for it" but, of course, meant to say "I'll toss you for it". She went scarlet; some humour might have eased the situation but with her very stern looking parents standing close by, who thankfully had not heard her gaff, I decided to give such thoughts a body-swerve. To conclude, I took a tenner profit and sincerely hope she had as much fun with the little car as I would have liked to have had with her!

I was seventeen years 'playing the motors' but the more we became involved in racing the more restricted I was for time to spend at the sales. The business peaked in the middle sixties and, apart from anything else, by the early seventies it had become extremely difficult to operate the way I had been doing. The trade had changed and maybe I was looking for an excuse to finish, I don't know, but the end came on a Saturday afternoon at Leeds Central Auctions. I'd bought a car with a defect which had been sold as straight and I refused to accept the motor but was informed that I had to as there was nothing wrong with it. I responded by taking their man out for a test run to show him the fault and crashed into a brick wall on my return. Needless to say I didn't take the car, for one thing it was no longer mobile and for another I hadn't intended to. I never went to another motor auction. What was the defect with the car? Oh, yes! Bad brakes! It was the end of another era for me - it had been my occupation for so long. I'm not going to say I made a vast amount of money though I suppose I hadn't done too badly. Things must have been a grind at times but I mainly remember all the fun I had.

Now that I've put my time in motor trading to bed, I can focus on other matters. During our first two or three years at Lower Dunsforth, Marie and I spent most of our time working and bringing up the boys but there was still time for other things. Marie joined a couple of golf clubs and took up the game again. I must just mention a scrumptious bakery at Boroughbridge to which we would pop down for the most delicious ice buns; I was also very partial to crumpets with lashings of butter - no wonder I put on a few pounds! We spent many happy times in the kitchen eating, drinking coffee and chatting away but most important of all, laughing. A day never passed by without young Colin wanting to be in the saddle though we had decided not to rush with Nigel. To be perfectly truthful we realised we'd been a little premature with Jockey; he was riding brilliantly, even before he commenced school, but we had been lucky for there were some scary moments. One was when he was 'trying out' a new pony, a lovely grey and very sensible. I don't know exactly what happened but suddenly Jockey, who had been cantering, was being dragged across the field with a foot hanging in the safety stirrup; luckily his head gear stayed in place but the thick rubber band had not released the foot and fortunately the pony came to a halt after about 100 yards. Jockey suffered no ill effects and there wasn't even a whimper from him. It could have been nasty; I'm not saying it wasn't, but it could have been worse. Ever after that near calamity I dispensed with the traditional safety rubber band and used ordinary elastic ones, these being far safer as they would snap if necessary. It might appear by reading all about the little fellow's 'escapades' that he spent his time courting disaster. This was not so and, to use an expression usually associated with an older person, he was very 'laid back' in all he did. As to Jockey's schooling, he didn't start until he was five and the school was some distance away, on the other side of Boroughbridge at Marton-le-Moor. As Mumso would have said "It was a private school, you know, very expensive!"

The photo of the two boys in their bespoke jodhpurs tailored by Marie was taken about Christmastime 1960, and don't they look mischievous? For Marie's present that year I got her an MGA Coupe in powder blue. That was some lovely car and if cars can be feminine that car certainly was - it was beautiful - a hard top and just out of this world. It had been registered for January 1st, yet I got it delivered on Christmas Eve. It absolutely reeked of new leather and I put it in the garage and wrapped it up in a sheet with a blue ribbon on top. The whole thing came as a total surprise for her and to have it gift wrapped was something special.

The following Spring Marie arranged to have a couple of weeks holiday with her parents and two of her sisters over in Switzerland. To help me with the boys she thought it would be a good idea if we borrowed the German 'au pair', who was staying at Moor Park at the time. Actually she came up a few days prior to Marie leaving to get 'acclimatized' to the place and on our first night with Marie away, I discovered two hot water bottles in my bed, one on either side! I got tackled next morning in broken English with "Colins, do you like to insult - can't you take a hint when you see I put the two bottles in your bed - it was not what I expected". It certainly wasn't what I expected either! Marie's sister, Elsie, hadn't gone on holiday and phoned me later that morning, saying she required the au pair back as there was so much work to do. Or did I imagine she phoned! Anyhow, I put Olga on the afternoon bus back to London; I didn't want the hassle and thought "out of sight out of reach" was the best policy. I'm sure I could have escaped from Colditz - in fact I just had!

We got on very well with the people in the village until, for no apparent reason, the thirty year old son of our immediate neighbour started to get aggressive. We had a couple of large stones outside the gates to the cottage and he would keep throwing them into the garden and making an awful mess. As he always moved the boulders at night, he didn't notice the thick black printers paste I spread on to them one evening - well not until it was all over his hands and clothing. Next day he came round wanting a fight and he got one. It wasn't a question of bang, bang, bang, as with the tramp, this was a real scrap. Once on the ground I kept banging his face into the gravel and the thing I remember most vividly was Jockey jumping up and down with excitement, shouting "Come on, Colin." The boys have always called me by my Christian name - I find it far less stuffy than Dad. Eventually I marched my neighbours' son out of the garden and we had no more trouble after that. We never spoke again, which was an added bonus. I recently mentioned the scrap to Col and he remembered it well.

Time progressed and we were getting 'itchy feet'. There were the facilities to train a couple of horses, so why not do so. I applied for a permit from The Jockey Club and we decided to get a horse for hurdling and a point-to-pointer for Marie to ride. Before doing so, we bought a couple of fresh ponies for the boys; though Nigel had reached three he was not showing any inclination that he actually wanted to ride, nevertheless he thought the world of his new friend, even though it was no 'Munnings'. We had the paddock next to the cottage but bought a further six acres of grass on the outskirts of the village for £600. This was the piece of land we knew was available when we moved to Dunsforth. Marie and I constructed a large shelter with a corral there, post and railed the entire boundary, built a couple of fences and put down a circular tan canter. That field was one of the best buys we ever made. Later, the boys would spend whole days there, having a marvellous time with their ponies and, once we started training the field, became indispensable plus, of course, there was also the grazing. The fact that the land was lower than the river did sometimes cause flooding but it also proved beneficial because all the fertilisers that were being put on the surrounding land seemingly got washed onto ours!

Our next acquisition was Hoy but he turned out to be one of the worst buys we ever made. He had won the Chester Cup and we bought him at Tattersalls 'Horses in Training Sale' at Newmarket in the October of '61. Hoy came into the ring and was knocked down to us for 2,600 gns, which would be about the figure one would have expected to pay for a horse with his form at that time. We were full of anticipation for it was our first step back into horses. However, the pleasure was very short lived because we soon became suspicious that we'd bought trouble. The reasons for our fears were the jubilant expressions on the faces of the owner of Hoy and Sid Dale, his trainer, as they made their way to the bar! The horse was entered for the Manchester November Handicap, actually run at Manchester in those days, so we decided to leave Hoy with Dale and let it take its chance. At least we would learn something even if it were to have our fears confirmed. Geoff Lewis was a young apprentice at the time, a fact that certainly ages me, and it was he that rode the horse for us. It was a deplorable run - Hoy was never seen with any sort of chance - yes, our fears were confirmed.

I'm not being flippant but there was a very amusing story connected to Hoy's run and well worth telling. Marie and I, with the two boys, drove over to Manchester on that very cold, wet and foggy day, in fact typical November handicap weather. When we arrived at the course Jockey, who was only seven and dressed in a natty overcoat and smart tweed flat cap, wanted to carry the racing colours over to the weighing room. They had been registered in Marie's name and were then scarlet with yellow striped sleeves and cap; the unusual thinness of the stripes, plus the shortness in length of those on the cap made them rather distinctive. We tied the colours in a bundle and the little fellow tucked them under his arm and away he went. On entering the weighing room he wandered about, seemingly a trifle lost. Seeing this and noticing the colours, the very tall official standing by the door into the changing room called out "Jockey?" meaning, of course, was he one. The answer, obviously because of how he was known, came back "Yes". Then the next question "Which race are you in?" Now that is where the misunderstanding really started for Jockey said "The November Handicap" and, without waiting to be asked anything further, volunteered "And the horse is called Hoy". The very tall man took a quick scan at his race card as he opened the door and called out to one of the valets - "Apprentice Geoff Lewis here" - and then to Jockey "Hang your coat on one of the pegs lad and all the best with your ride". Marie and I had been watching the whole incident from half a dozen yards away and thought it about time we should intervene. I wish now Jockey had ridden the horse; at least we would then have had some enjoyment from the run!

After the race Hoy came straight back to our place, where Marie's examination showed he was wrong in the wind. The horse had been bought as seen and with no warranty as to soundness. Obviously certain questions were asked prior to the sale but some of the answers had been misleading to say the least. It was entirely my idea that we should buy the horse and I had not only been made to look like a nincompoop - I had been one. I can't tolerate fools, especially if I'm the fool. Exactly! We sent Hoy down to the veterinary research station at Newmarket to try and rectify his troubles but to no avail and, as a last resort, Marie decided to have him tubed. The operation was commonplace in those days but not seen so often in present times. Once the tube had been inserted Hoy went back into full work and seemed to be going well but, of course, a race would be the real test.

It was early in 1962 when we entered Hoy for a novice hurdle at Wetherby and put schooling next on the agenda. Johnny Gorman was contacted and came over to ride; I wasn't decrying Marie at all for it goes without saying there was nobody better than her to teach a horse to jump but, as Johnny was going to be on board in the race, I felt he should get to know the horse. I had noticed him once or twice and considered he was a very underrated jockey. Regarding my own riding, even though I was still experiencing frequent rides on the roller-coaster I did intend pursuing that elusive winner but hadn't contemplated doing so on Hoy. There were no hiccups with the schooling session but the exhilarating feature of the morning's work was the lead horse and rider, which was Jockey and his grey pony. The little fellow really gave it a crack; he rode very short, was perfectly balanced and flew. Johnny Gorman couldn't believe what he'd seen and said "He is certainly a chip off the old block". As I realised he wasn't referring to me I had to remind him that Marie was not an old block!

After a couple more schools Hoy ran at Wetherby. Marie had been working him quite hard at home but his dismal performance was half expected. We gave him a couple more outings but his wind trouble was deteriorating; the tubing had obviously not been a success so we moved him on as a hack. The whole Hoy business had been a very disappointing and expensive venture and it was something to digest and learn from but not to dwell upon.

There was no question of attaching any blame for the poor runs on to Johnny Gorman's riding, nevertheless I felt I had rather over estimated him, to say the least. After the Wetherby outing Marie remarked with her usual humour "Johnny was just like a baby in a pram - he was waving his arms about, had lost his bottle and didn't do as he was bloody told!" He was riding a novice chaser at Catterick one day, not, I must add, one of ours; it shot to the front and was soon twenty lengths clear of the field until it came to the open ditch, where it slammed on all the brakes. The manoeuvre shot Johnny into orbit, where he did a loop the loop and landed on top of the fence facing the oncoming twenty novice chasers. Johnny just sat there, again waving his arms about as the runners thundered past him on either side - a daunting experience for Johnny but even more so for those who were paying him!

He became quite a tubby little fellow and often wore racing colours of yellow and black hoops, making him look just like a bumble bee in full flight. He really was a character and when he started training his stables were in a pub yard in a village near Doncaster which he reckoned was really handy; I don't know whether he meant being near Doncaster or being in the pub yard but I can take a calculated guess! There was a complete change round of jockeys by then; it was young Col, who was riding for him! The last I heard of 'JG' he was working for a builder but that was a hell of a long time ago.

I had been granted a permit to train the family horses which throughout our time at Dunsforth didn't exceed a dozen in total. Our training there was a partnership just as it was years later when I had a full licence. Marie took charge of the exercising and, with only ever having a limited number in training at any one time, it meant she could keep varying the horses' work, so they never became bored. They could go to the beach and work on the sands or canter through the woods or maybe go to one of the various gallops we used. I'm being rather discreet about where the grass gallops were for I understand they are still putting the divots back! For my part, I would influence everything that occurred in the stables other than, of course, the veterinary. The feed bills were always massive owing to the quality of the food we used but at no time did we employ staff. The boys rode work from a very early age which was a fantastic help and, after Marie bought me a set of farrier's tools one Christmas, I did all the shoeing, the first time taking six hours though I soon got the hang of things. We never lost a shoe on a racecourse with many running in surgical plates of some sort. I would spend hours making such shoes. It wasn't always a question of the feet being actually wrong but, when a horse has thin soles and the ground is firm, it is preferrable to shoe with something different to the ordinary. Marie would get the horses so hard they would have backs like butchers chopping blocks and when the Tinklers had one ready it was definitely Ready; it was a combination of hard graft, know how and nothing being left to chance. The stables were always immaculate and with every comfort. They had infra-red heating for when the weather was cold and cooling fans when it was warm. There was much to learn but we learnt fast and the dreams of the little boy who enjoyed just looking through the saddler's brochure, all those years ago, had come true though I never aspired to being a public trainer with dozens of horses. I realised staff and owners would be a headache I could well do without. Admittedly we did eventually have partners in one or two instances, but none were a success. The horses in question won races - it was the owners that weren't a success!

I'm not going to mention every horse that I have been connected with over the years, nor every winner, though I will devote a few lines to Hot Night. He wasn't much and cost likewise but he was the first ride I had since the day I got unseated or, to be more precise, fell off at Nottingham a dozen or so years previously. Hopefully I had become a far more proficient rider since then, despite my balance and bottle being not that great. My first ride back was at Wetherby in the spring of '63. The going was heavy and it was a selling hurdle with about a dozen runners. I led over the first four or five flights but eventually finished in the middle of the pack. We went back to

Wetherby a couple of weeks later and the run was a repetition in every way of the former outing. In our next at Uttoxeter I was ten lengths clear into the home straight but then petered out and again finished the race on top of the horse and not under him! Actually I had a dozen further rides, a couple of them in points, on various horses and always managed to survive; though very nearly didn't do so, when riding in a point at Charm Park. My horse jumped so big at the second last that I became entangled with some branches of an overhanging tree. Had it not been for the elastic band which I used to place over my foot and the stirrup iron I would have gone into orbit. What with loops on reins, elastic bands round irons and sticky tape to help hold the whip - I wonder how many more innovations I would have conjured up if I hadn't stopped riding when I did. Once when I was due to ride at Sedgefield the meeting was fortunately abandoned just prior to racing because of snow. I say fortunately, for apparently young Jockey had been chatting with one of the stewards in the weighing room. The little fellow had been saying that "Colin, my daddy, is the best rider in the whole world but he wouldn't be winning today because he's not off!"

Throughout I've tried to put together my story in a way that is easy to follow and not necessarily in strict order of happening or significance. I find some things can be said with very little explanation and others, not so important, sometimes require more. I will continue with the hurdle scene while we were at Dunsforth before progressing to other matters during the sixties.

Towards the end of the '64-'65 jumping season we decided to give 'Too Dear' a run in a hurdle race at Hexham's Whitsuntide meeting; it was for amateur riders over 3 miles. He was a pointer of Marie's who will be discussed in more depth later. There were seven runners and, because of his good point form, was made third favourite at 5/1. The little horse didn't jump that brilliantly, booting the low hurdles out of the ground as he went merrily on his way and unfortunately was just touched off by a couple of lengths. I didn't give him a slap - there was no need to as I knew he was doing his best. There was a controversy immediately after the race which was most mysterious to say the least. It was extraordinary that the winner was not required to go into the winners enclosure. The race was won by a horse called Top Link ridden by a Mr. Kane and trained by Jack Fawcus; it was heavily backed and consequently went off favourite at 5/4. With the jockey's allowance deducted the horse was down as having carried the same as my mount - twelve stone. As soon as Top Link passed the winning post he was dismounted and unsaddled on the course itself and then led away to the stables. The horse was said to be lame but the racecourse vet disputed this. Mr. Kane seemed to find the saddle and weight cloth too heavy to carry to the scales for the weighing in, so Fawcus gave a most willing hand and jostled through the crowd. I was asked by an official in the weighing room not to object "We don't want any fuss, do we?" Do I think there was a ring of Dick Francis about the whole thing? Of course, but I have been diplomatically careful not to point a finger at anyone though I do believe two fingers were gestured at me. Too Dear returned home sound and had thoroughly enjoyed the sports and would have undoubtedly chalked up another win had girls been allowed to ride in such races in those days. Marie was delighted that we managed to get placed, but there was a question mark which left a nasty taste. I didn't have a bet; in fact the only time I ever had the confidence for a punt when I was riding was when I won at Sedgefield the following season.

During that summer we bought Sapere for £250. He was an 8 year old grey gelding and tubed, definitely not a long term proposition.

Our first race was at Market Rasen at the beginning of the '65-'66 season where we finished fourth. He was then taken to Hexham for a slightly warmer contest and finished in the middle of the pack but I was pleased enough with the run. The next stop was Sedgefield in a 2 mile selling hurdle on October the 2nd. There were only two runners and the other horse, which was trained by Dennis Yeoman, had won and been placed in its last four races. This was better form than our horse who, incidentally, was still a maiden. The day came, the race came, and they bet 4/5 and evens; I had an even £500, and a nought on the end of that figure wouldn't cover today's value of the wager. We led all the way and won by 4 lengths - at last I had ridden a winner. As we were pulling up E. Campbell, who was riding the other horse, shouted across to me "I backed you". I thought, bollocks, because all I had heard behind me was his whip working overtime and he certainly wasn't smacking my horse! With it being a seller Sapere was put up for sale and we bought him back for £240, then sold him a few days later for £350 to Jeremy Fawcett. Jeremy was an amateur rider and I believe he thought if 'Mickey Mouse' Colin can win on the horse I will be able to - but he didn't. In fact Sapere never won another race. I was 39 years old but decided to retire on a winner, albeit the only one I ever had. Toynbee had obviously taught me something, even if it was only to stay on top of the saddle!

Mick Naughton, Jack Berry and Jimmy Fitzgerald all rode for us whilst at Dunsforth, Jimmy just the once and it might not have been the last horse he ever rode but it was in his last season. The animal's name was Laughing Cheese - the horse did the laughing and I was the cheese. He had ability but refused to use it; his 'get out' was to hang towards the rails and if there weren't any he would go looking for some! I had intended to ride him but thought better of it so booked Jimmy instead. It was a handicap hurdle at Wetherby and how did the race go? Well, let's put it this way, they were so far behind that I reported them missing!

Jack Berry was reminding me recently of the time when he finished third for us on a hurdler at Sedgefield and I overtook him on the run in. I told Jack I couldn't remember the race and asked him what was I riding. He replied that I wasn't riding anything; I'd gone down to the second last to watch and as the field went by I set off after them on foot and passed all but the first two! Jack was quick to point out the ground was heavy and that's why they weren't finishing fast. I concede but I wonder why it didn't stop me! Exactly!

Jack jogged my memory about another incident, this time when I bought a horse from a man who lived in Barnsley. It had a little bit of form away back but, after a couple of days, I realised it was absolutely useless. I'd heard that Mr. 'Smart R's' was jubilant that he'd put one over on me, so I let it be known in a certain quarter that apparently the horse was photogenic. I really spread the jam on thick. I said how a film director from Denham, called Goldberg, was touring the north looking for horses which were photogenic, for a film he was making about Robin Hood. I continued by saying Mr. Goldberg had taken some shots of the chestnut with the scruffy mane - "Don't worry about da mane, I'll give the nag a toupee, but I've got to have him, name your price" is what I quoted him as saying. I also let it be known that I wouldn't sell him the horse because his chauffeur had clipped the edge of my lawn with his Bentley. I waited for the phone to ring from Barnsley and it did "Mr. Smart R's here" or words to that effect "Hello, Colin, I hope you haven't fallen in love with the wife's horse, she says I should not have sold him and if she doesn't get him back she's going to leave me". I said "Lucky fellow, to be able to get rid of the wife and the horse in one clean sweep"! Then I started to sort of sympathise and concluded by

Left:
Young Col and Montabel being led in by Nigel after riding his first winner. *(p192)*

Above:
The Tinklers bring off a gamble with Montabel at Sedgefield with Colin in the saddle. (p.192)

Right:
Nigel leads in Ocean Sailor after his brother had won on him at Cartmel. *(p203)*

Above:
Nigel *(when 12 years old)* takes the ride on Philip in the Town Plate. *(p204)*

Above:
Col on Moley Faye brings off a gamble for connections at Wetherby. *(p214)*

All Below:
Four of Col's Many Big Race Successes. *(p219, 220)*

Above:
Connaught Ranger: Irish Champion Hurdle.

Right:
Autumn Rain - Great Yorkshire Cup.

Above:
Canit: Aintree's Topham Trophy.

Above:
Park House: Sandown's Stone Ginger.

Left:
Nigel's first winner
(Nimble Joe at Sedgefield) and below
in the winners enclosure. (p221)

Left:
Nigel leads in 'Charlie B' after what should have
been a £50,000 touch at Newcastle and below,
jumping the last. (p223)

Left:
Marie leads in young Col and Wild Hawk after landing a gamble at Market Rasen. My Colours were later used by Full Circle. (p227)

Right:
The Tinkler Brothers going out to ride at Market Rasen.

Below:
El Magnifico and Marie winning at
Newbury *(p252)*

Above:
Three Happy Bunnies *(p252)*

Below:
Marie and La Bambola lead the field at Chester
(p254)

Above:
Marie and Atoka winning at
Thirsk *(p258)*

Above:
I lead in La Bambola and Marie after
their Redcar triumph *(p260)*

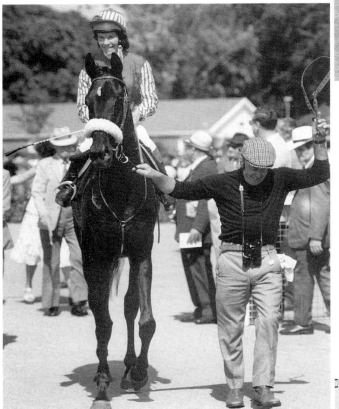

Above:
The Kempton gamble landed
(p262)

Belo
Marie brings Atoka home by
lengths at Kempton *(p26*

Above:
Marie weighs in after winning the Ladies'
Championship and collecting her weight in
champagne *(p265)*

Right:
Fifty five year old 'Peter Pan' relaxing
at home at the end of the '78 season
(p271)

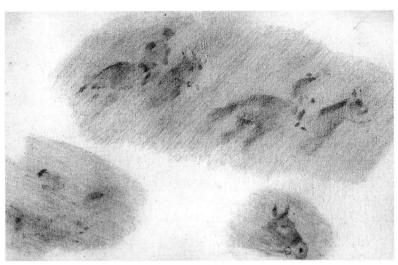

Left:
'*Early Morning Ghosts*' I drew these impressions I had of Newmarket Heath more than sixty years ago *(p26)*

Below:
Flexodus eyes the fences at The 'Holderness' *(p187)*

saying "I will sell the horse back to you but will want a bit of profit" and back went the horse! Funny, but Mr. Smart R's was never able to find Mr. Goldberg of Denham Studios! Well, he wouldn't, would he!

Actually Mick Naughton rode a nice winner for us; it was on a mare called Enchanted at Uttoxeter - I remember it well. It was in the last race on their Whit Saturday card in 1966. I know I had a jolly good bet, a monkey (£500) at 5/1 and it was backed down from that price to 4/1 and won quite easily. The following week I saw Arthur Stephenson, the leading jump trainer in the north at that time, who asked why I hadn't ridden Enchanted myself and that I should have done so; I responded light heartedly by saying "Arthur, I know your game, you are doing a spot of buttering - you want to sell me a horse but I can't buy one from you because you're too clever". He wanted to know how I had come to that conclusion and I told him "Because you have more winners than I do". Now that was the most obvious statement imaginable but it didn't stop 'W.A.', as he was known, from retorting "Well! I have more triers than you!" No comment! Prior to the Uttoxeter race we ran the filly at Wetherby in a novice hurdle and Mick was reminiscing the other day about the schooling session he had at Dunsforth, in preparation for that initial outing. He recalled how he got the shock of his life when he saw the chase fence he was expected to jump and received an even bigger surprise when he discovered his lead horse was to be little Nigel, with one arm in a sling, riding his pony - though I can't recollect his arm being in a sling. Mick said following Nigel was like watching a 'cow jump over the moon'. Mick also jogged my memory about the Wetherby race, when the filly lashed out in the parade ring, catching an onlooker in the back. The poor unfortunate fellow was rushed to Harrogate Hospital in what was thought a critical condition. Actually, the ambulance made a couple of journeys for Mick was dumped in the race itself and coincidentally finished up in the next bed to the person who had been kicked! Both patients recovered quite quickly considering, Mick in a couple of days and the other in a couple of weeks.

The next few lines are about a pair of racing boots I had specially made but, as I never felt comfortable in them, they were discarded. I put them in the wardrobe in my bedroom, as I was rather reluctant to throw them away. Nevertheless, when we moved to Boltby four or five years later, I decided not to harbour them any longer but cut off the tops to use as padding, as I often placed leather between the sole of the hoof and the plate when shoeing. As I cut the boots I noticed a wad of money stuffed into the foot of one of them - there was £2,500 in the bundle and the elastic band around the money was shrivelled - it had been there for ages. At that time I had a habit of when returning from the races or the motor auctions I would put any cash I had on me into a shoe or boot for the night and to retrieve it the following day but apparently this little bundle had been forgotten! What a discovery and, by the way, I don't do it any more - I'm talking about using shoes as a night safe! I mention this, just in case anyone has any bright ideas!

Now back to the early sixties; we were having difficulty finding the ideal horse with which Marie could start her point to point racing though, as we realised later, we had been looking down the wrong channels. It became known to us that Willie Stephenson, who trained at Royston, had an ex French chaser for sale. We contacted him and he mentioned that he would call in and see us the following week as he had a meeting at Boroughbridge and would kill two birds with one stone. I wasn't sure whether I liked his phraseology! When he did arrive he had with him Ken Oliver, the Scottish trainer and auctioneer; they'd met in order to 'set-up' the Doncaster Bloodstock

Sales. They were full of enthusiasm for the project which incidentally had its first sale, in a giant marquee, a short while later in May 1962. As a matter of interest, I understand approximately five thousand horses now pass through the ring there each year. I can't recall why we didn't buy the French chaser but there would have been a good enough reason. It wasn't until the spring of '64 that Marie bought Word of Honour from Claude Hockley, who ran a small point to point yard in Essex. He had advertised 'Honour' for sale because he had some young horses coming along and I believe the horse cost us in the region of £1,600. However, I have suspicions that Hockley had detected a weakness with one of the tendons for we did have trouble. Word of Honour was a ten year old chestnut gelding and a lovely horse, a perfect gentleman. Over the past couple of seasons he had been running very respectably in open and adjacent races, and for those who are not aware, the point season starts early in the year and continues on for only a few months. We got 'Honour' home and Marie's first race was over on the east coast, near Whitby, in the Staintondale Ladies. In the race card it rightly stated that Word of Honour had been qualified with an Essex pack of hounds, so the majority of the race crowd assumed he was a raider from the south and backed him accordingly. I got £200 on at evens but obviously not all with one bookmaker. Marie's sister, Martha, who was married by that time, had come up with her husband to be there for Marie's first ride. The morning of the race arrived and we left the yard at about ten o'clock because with the Land Rover and trailer it was going to take us at least a couple of hours to drive across the moors to the meeting. The course was mainly over stubble and the fences looked very large, something Martha kept mentioning to Marie as they walked the course. There weren't many runners and, as they left the paddock, it was evident that Marie's riding was far superior to the

153

others; it was the same seat she had for showjumping though, as time progressed over the years, she adapted to riding even shorter and stronger, yet still maintaining perfect balance. The race itself was not exactly a procession but Marie and Word of Honour did lead all the way and went further ahead after a most brilliant jump at the last to win rather comfortably by several lengths.

The boys and I couldn't stop cheering; Marie had thoroughly enjoyed the race and hadn't we all. Word of Honour had the most economical action I have ever seen; his stride was exceptional and, whilst he had no great acceleration, his easy movement made him quite fast. It had been absolutely marvellous but the win must have annoyed a little group of people standing in the car park, some of whom I knew. As I passed them I said "Marie's back in business", using the term loosely because pointing was a sport and not a business for Marie, but my remark was misconstrued - or was it? Even so, the snide reply I received was unnecessary - "You shouldn't make your wife do something so dangerous, particularly with having children to look after". How nasty, but they didn't spoil my day.

Marie went on to win a total of 27 point-to-points, 10 while living at Dunsforth, the rest after we moved to Boltby. She also had success in a couple of Newmarket Town Plates as well as riding 7 other winners on the flat, bringing off some tremendous gambles in the process. She won the Ladies Flat Championship in the '78 season when 53 years of age, but looked and had the attitude and zest of someone twenty years younger.

We had a fantastic time over the years; words can't express the admiration and appreciation I had and still have for her, for all the fun and excitement we had was astronomical. But it wasn't all success; inevitably there were setbacks and some of those reverses were terribly hard to take; no other sport can be so cruel but, thankfully, the highs were more numerous than the lows.

Marie had a natural affinity with the horses she rode but the real key to her success, coupled with a desire to win, was the confidence she had. Also, because of her exceptional balance horses ran for her; they must have felt they were carrying far less weight than they actually were and only very occasionally did I ever see her smack one. We mustn't forget that opportunities in those days were very limited for the girls - they could only ride in the ladies races at the points. The Newmarket Town Plate was also open to them but it wasn't until the early seventies that the girls flat racing came into being and even then in a very limited capacity. Of course, Marie was past fifty when girls were eventually allowed to ride over jumps (other than points) and it was a bone of contention when the Jockey Club, because of her age, refused her permission to join them. It probably was the best decision in the long run because she would have been far too brave, I'm not saying irresponsible, just far too brave, as she was when pointing. Marie liked to bet and it became very much a part of her life at one time and I will be relating some amusing stories further on about her punting.

After that initial win with 'Word of Honour' Marie was forced to give him an easy time and, come the following February, was earnestly looking for another horse as a stop gap. We saw advertised for sale in the 'Horse and Hound' a pointer called Too Dear, a fourteen year old gelding who had run with some distinction in the past. He was in Cornwall so Marie hitched up the trailer to the Land Rover and drove down there through giant snow drifts; it was a mammoth journey taking over twelve hours each way. He was lean and narrow, nearly black and not all that big. Marie gave him one gallop, which he apparently flew, before doing a deal at £300. But Too Dear was not a sound horse, in fact he was a crock; had pin fired legs, was gone in the wind and the way he demolished the fences suggested his eyesight wasn't that clever! Marie also detected a dicky heart but he loved racing, he was so bloody game; never was the saying "He was all heart" more appropriate and when he died it was discovered the organ was much larger than is normal. We first ran him at the Goathland, just three days short of a year since 'Honour' had won a few miles down the coast. The rumour went round that we had given £3,000 for him not £300, though both figures seemed absurd, one too high, the other too low. The rumour was started by Harold Charlton, who was at the time in his early sixties; he and the Tinklers became good friends over the years, until he died comparatively recently. The £3,000 price tag came about from Harold as usual opening his big gob and saying "I know exactly how much Too Dear has cost". He then proceeded to hold up three fingers and continued "That's what the Tinklers paid". Why the hell he had to make it so complicated I don't know but it didn't really matter and was just typical of Harold.

I know I'm digressing but I must just mention the occasion of Harold's ninetieth birthday party at The Green Man Hotel in Malton, with well over a hundred guests, all racing people. He was known far and wide and what he hadn't been or hadn't done was nobody's business! Harold got up and spoke, thanking everyone for coming and also said "The nicest people I have ever met are the Tinklers" - I was quite surprised as it was so unexpected; then he continued "Colin doesn't know this but long before he ever met Marie I could have married her", I called out spontaneously "Why the F.....g hell didn't you". Marie wasn't there but, had she been, I know she would have loved the humour and, of course, it wasn't true what he'd said.

Back to the Goathland. Marie and Too Dear went straight into top gear, nought to near forty in three seconds, ploughing through the bottom of every fence. He was loving the fun and so was Marie; how she managed to stay in the saddle - I was going to say "I'll never know", but I do - it was pure acrobatics. They passed the winning post well clear of the rest and the boys and I ran down the course to lead them in. Absolutely brilliant, I would always weigh up the situation and very rarely have a punt when Marie didn't win but usually had a couple of hundred on when she did. The point to point bookmakers in the north in those days were in the main a trifle timid about laying a decent bet; though by spreading my money about I could get on. Brian Dunn was one of the most prominent layers and I suppose still is; incidentally, it was Brian's father from whom we bought Jockey's first pony. If Too Dear's first run had been exciting it had nothing on the next at The Sinnington a month later, which he again won in a flat out gallop. His next whiz round after that was at The Cleveland but unfortunately the fences there were appallingly made, with thick birch all sloping the wrong way and Marie expected trouble. He was even money and won by a couple of lengths but returned home as if he'd done fifteen rounds with the heavyweight champion of the world. As a matter of interest, the Clerk of the Course and commentator at the Cleveland Point in those days was Stan Thomson, father of Derek, the well known and likeable commentator cum television presenter. Too Dear and Marie came second in their next outing, as they did in their last point at The Middleton, in The Roses Cup, the premier ladies race in the north. He was such a tiger, he battled all the way and was beaten a short head by the long odds on Perry Boy - that undoubtedly was his best performance. He just had the one race after that, in the hurdle at Hexham which I have already mentioned. During the summer when he was out at grass he aged so much and suddenly there was no electricity left. He had, in such a short time, given us so much pleasure - it would have been nice if he could have had a long retirement but it wasn't to be. He had given everything to racing including his life for he'd burnt himself out and was without a doubt the gamest horse I have ever known. There are so many words I could use to describe my appreciation of him but none would be adequate enough.

The following year was a blank one for Marie so far as winners were concerned but in '67 Word of Honour was back with a treble. But, on the downside, Marie had a terrible fall at The Hurworth and was ambulanced unconscious to the hospital at Northallerton. Marie hadn't fully 'come round' when I called in there later in the afternoon - all very frightening. However, she was home again the following day and race riding again the following week! Marie had several quite nasty falls over the years but just kept brushing them aside.

Word of Honour was in the main jumping well and we were looking forward to '68; they kicked off with a win at the York and Ainsty, then another second, followed a couple of weeks later by the most horrifying road accident I have ever been involved in. It occurred on the A1 a few miles north of Wetherby, where the road crosses the River Nidd. It was a lovely spring day and we were going to the Bramham Moor Point at Swindon Woods, where Marie was to ride Word of Honour. I was driving the Land Rover with the trailer behind; Marie was in the passenger seat, with Nigel sitting in the back; Col was at school and therefore not with us. We had just remarked on the number of police cars about when suddenly there was an almighty bang, a deafening sound, terrible vibrations and the Land Rover went all over the place. Marie was thrown through the door on to the road, then another BANG and a BUMP. I was convinced the trailer had run over her - the agonizing moments until we stopped and I was able to look back and the utter relief to see

Marie standing in the middle of the road. Police were everywhere, the trailer was on its side but still attached to the Land Rover and, of course, the horse was still inside the trailer. There was also a smashed up car in the road but no driver. By this time the police were shouting to each other but not bothering about us.

Apparently a convict had escaped from Northallerton Prison and had stolen the car for the getaway. On seeing all the police cars waiting on the grass verges he must have panicked and somehow crashed into the back of us. The convict then swam the river and how he did that with all the police about - some even had tracker dogs - I don't know. Incredibly he was never caught and the authorities would not acknowledge liability. Marie and I lost out financially but, thankfully, neither of us nor Nigel were injured. Marie would not even admit to being bruised though her racing colours, which she was wearing, were badly torn. Some people on their way to the Point to Point stopped to help us. We got Word of Honour out of the trailer then managed to get the vehicle the correct way up and on to its wheels. As Marie still wanted to ride we loaded up again and away we went. Unfortunately, or maybe it was for the best, we arrived too late to declare to run. The sad outcome of the episode was not known to us at the time but Word of Honour had damaged his suspect leg in the crash. It was a very severe strain from which he never really recovered.

For the '69 season, Marie had bought Zangavar from the Turners for something in the region of £1,600. The Turners farmed extensively in East Anglia; they were a close-knit family with a large and very successful point to point and hunter chase stable. The son and daughter did the riding and Joe, their father, would say "Every horse in the yard is for sale". After acquiring Zangavar, a lovely chestnut mare, with whom Marie won a couple of races in their first season plus a couple of seconds, I went down and bought Flexodus. He was the most gorgeous of horses, a trifle on the small side but very compact. He was only seven, had won a maiden, had great potential and didn't seem expesnive at £2,500. We bought him towards the end of the '69 season, which was in our last year living at Lower Dunsforth, with just sufficient time to give him a couple of runs, both of which were terribly disappointing. Matters changed the following season when a rubber bit was fitted to his bridle and that was the key to the winners enclosure.

Before progressing with Marie's pointing I'm going back over the years to when Col and Nigel were ten and six and continue with the rest of our time at Lower Dunsforth. They had a tremendous amount of spirit yet never seemed to argue with one another and definitely never with either Marie or myself; the respect we got I know was genuine. We didn't fill their minds with what was, in our opinion, meaningless religion so, from an early age, they knew more about the Arc de Triomphe than Noah's Ark! We treated them very much as equals but didn't let them know it. Apart from the few hairy-scary encounters that Jockey had early on, the boys went through very little for us to worry about. They had measles and that sort of thing, unpleasant at the time but not too serious. We took them for a couple of holidays when they were quite young; on both occasions loud cheers came from the back of the car when we got back home and it wasn't long before they were saying "Hello" to their ponies.

Whereas Jockey had literally hundreds of hours of "Keep your back straight - knees in - hands still" to endure, his mischievous little brother escaped all that. Then one afternoon, he would be six at the time, he decided he would learn to ride without any adult supervision. Jockey however was an enormous help to him and thoroughly relished the thought of his younger brother riding. Marie was playing golf and they said they wanted to give her a surprise when she got back - well they certainly did that. Nigel was on his pony for hours and by early evening had mastered the bouncing at the trot, cantering, and was even popping over small jumps. Incredible really but it all came so easy for him and throughout he has always been a most sympathetic rider which was often misconstrued by certain stewards who lacked understanding! I have been asked many times which of the two boys turned out to be the more accomplished; actually both were naturals yet entirely different - Ken Oliver once described Colin as a pocket battleship. He was immensely strong and always showed great determination, qualities he was to need after the terrible fall that ended his riding career. Both were extremely intelligent riders and I had equal confidence in them, especially when our money was on.

When young, one of the games the boys used to play was 'race meetings'. They built a jumping course in the field, just as I had done when I was their age but the only pony I ever had was 'imaginary'. They would deck themselves out in racing colours and away they would go, each bearing the name of a chaser - all great fun. Marie and I spent many happy hours with them and, of course, their riding was progressing all the time. It wasn't long before we bought them a couple of new ponies; both were fantastic. There was Texas Ranger, a cracking very powerful bay, whom we purchased from the Astons, who now have the Goldford Stud in Cheshire. Jockey would ride him very short and go a real gallop, jumping anything and everything. Nigel's new pony was smaller, rather like a miniature thoroughbred and we named her Little Zangavar. The boys didn't do much hunting or showjumping but were kept busy on the Hunter trial circuit, where they had a fair amount of success, though on one occasion I recall Nigel being rather irate when placed second after obviously doing the fastest clear round over a mile and twenty fences. It was said he was beaten by a tenth of a second (hand timed with a stop watch) and who were the time keepers? - the winning rider's parents! I heard Nigel say something about where they could put the trophy he'd received for being second - and it wasn't on the mantel piece! Marie would occasionally borrow the ponies to compete against horses. That was always something worth seeing for she would go like the clappers. I remember Marie taking 'Little Z' to an unaffiliated show on the wolds where they jumped a four foot six straight up gate to win the class. How the hell it got over I don't know, though I have a suspicion they did the 'Flopsy Flip'! (That is how it was first typed but it should read the Fosbury Flop)!

I also recall the time the boys had gone to a pony club rally; most of the other children were camping out and staying for the week but our boys weren't so adventurous nor, as they put it, so stupid - in fact they didn't even see out the first day. The rally wasn't far away, some half a dozen miles, nevertheless we had taken them there in the trailer and intended to collect them in the evening. Lady Herries was in charge of the rally; she did an awful lot for the district pony club before marrying and moving down to Arundel. Apparently, both boys had been criticised by one of the instructors for wearing crash helmets with black silk covers, which are the norm nowadays, instead of the more traditional hard velvet hunting caps; they had also suffered some criticism for riding with too short a stirrup. With all the hassle they received both young Col and Nigel decided enough was enough and told the instructor that they were "Going to f..k off back home", which was precisely what they did, their logic being "It saved you a journey Mummy". Col did ride for Lady Herries on a couple of occasions when he became a jockey, so all must have been either forgiven or forgotten!! By the way, I hope I don't confuse the issue sometimes by calling young Col, Jockey, and vice versa, but of course as he became older the Jockey tag was dropped entirely.

There was another time when Nigel's choice of words were rather mischievous. He and 'Little Z' were competing in a show class. I suppose we should have insisted that he conform to protocol but, had we done so, I would not now have such delightful memories of that Sunday afternoon. Nigel was adamant that the way he was dressed and the way in which the pony was presented were in order but I presume he thought otherwise after the judges had spoken to him. Because, as he cantered around the ring, Lester Piggott style, he called out to us as he went by "They (I assume he was referring to the judges) don't like my f*****g racing saddle!" If that was all they hadn't approved of they obviously hadn't noticed the red blinkers with bandages to match and I'm not even going to mention Nigel's attire, other than the goggles and the pushed back silks on the crasher, in the manner favoured by most professional chase jockeys! Incidentally, he was placed third; there were a dozen runners and Nigel said "It was a photo finish". He actually wanted to object saying one of the kiddies tried to get up on his inner on the gallop round!! I told him to quit while he was winning and he answered "But I didn't win, I was third!"

Jockey was going great guns on his new purchase, so we decided to take on some decent ponies at a prestigious jumping competition in Sheffield. The boys weren't that keen on show jumping, nevertheless Jockey, who would be twelve or thirteen at the time, certainly entered into the spirit of things and was quietly confident he would go well. I brought 'Humfrey' out of retirement and rigged up a jump on a grass verge in a housing estate in Sheffield. It was - pop, pop, buzz, buzz and a couple of hours later we were returning home with some silverware!

Both boys were always full of fun and very humorous when they were young. I don't know why I've written in the past tense for they still are and great company to be with. This talk about humour reminds me of the time when the landlord of the village pub at Dunsforth used to ride out with the boys. He was rather a pathetic little chap who had aspirations of becoming a steeple chase jockey. His wife, a very slim blonde girl, who I'm sure, under all the heavy 'make up', was quite pretty, gave him no encouragement - but she certainly gave me plenty! I'm talking about encouragement! On this particular morning the publican knocked back his usual couple of gin and tonics before coming round to get on Nigel's spare pony. Actually it was far too small for an adult and Nigel told him rather than put his feet in the stirrups he would be far better with a pair of roller skates! They set off down the road at an agonisingly slow walk but it made no matter, he was soon flat on his back - yes, I am talking about the husband, not the wife! He had fallen off and was rushed to hospital with a suspected broken wrist. He loved the attention he received there and told the nurses he had been doing some fast work, actually the only person capable of doing any fast work in his household was, yes, you have guessed correctly! He returned home from hospital later in the day with his arm in a sling but, apparently, he'd only sprained a thumb. On hearing this, Nigel went round to the pub to take the 'Mickey Mouse' and asked him if he'd strained his cock, would it have been put in a sling! A voice from behind the bar shouted "His what! There's no chance of that ever getting strained!"

Neither of the boys really liked their time at school and both took the same path but, being younger, Nigel followed on four years later. After the pre-prep they both went on to Cundall Manor, a rather nice prep school in a country mansion with its own grounds. It was situated only a few miles from Boroughbridge, on the other side of the river to Dunsforth. Firstly, they went as day boys and then as weekly boarders though, for my part, I would much rather have had them come home each evening for I liked them around. I'm not saying Marie didn't but she was very much educationally minded and considered the course taken was in the boys' best interests. Both however excelled in athletics, with Col representing the East Riding of Yorkshire in cross country and they certainly made use of their natural ability on more than one occasion when running back home. This meant one of two things, either home wasn't that bad or school was deplorable! They were never reprimanded by us for their exploits, neither did we rush them straight back to school; we liked them too much to do that. There was the occasion when Nigel had the bright idea of getting expelled. It was when he was at Cundall Manor, he wrote a letter home, knowing that all mail was unofficially looked at. The head had not the authority to do this but nevertheless did. Apparently Nigel gave him a little help by not sealing the envelope. In the letter which consisted of only two lines, he had called the head 'a c**t' and we learned later it was the only word he'd spelt correctly! As parents we were asked to go to the school and weren't given a clue as to what it was all about but I somehow guessed I wasn't going to be invited to captain the Fathers' cricket eleven. Nigel had not had a chance to talk to us and his little ploy was a temporary success - we were asked to remove him from Cundall. I say a temporary success because he was soon reinstated when the owner of the school became aware of what had happened. I understand he called the head the same four letter word himself and stressed that the school was a business venture and the whole idea was to fill the classes, not empty them! Nigel was always taking the piss; one day the head called him into his study and told him "You don't seem to pick things up very quickly, do you, Tinkler Minor?" At that 'Nige' whipped a book from the Head's desk saying "You couldn't pick up anything faster than that, could you, Sir?"

After Cundall the boys moved on to Scarborough College as weekly boarders; I will stretch events and use this paragraph to conclude their time there. The school were most lenient in allowing them time away from their studies in order to go race riding. I'm sure the school welcomed the attention it received from the media for how many schools would have, as pupils, jockeys at fifteen. Actually both rode winners at that age whilst still at school, which made for even more publicity; however, since those days The Jockey Club have raised the minimum age at which one can ride under Rules to sixteen. Marie realised they weren't going to reach great heights academically so agreed that Colin should leave during his sixteenth year, which he did. Nigel wasn't exactly a rebel but neither did he wear a halo. At one time he was spending rather a lot of time at the local bookmakers in Scarborough instead of in the classroom. Marie recalls how his Housemaster once phoned us to say he was very concerned that Nigel had gone missing and that, after an extensive search, he was nowhere to be found. Marie told him they obviously hadn't looked in the betting shops or the cafe on the front that served double helpings of chips. Nigel was only twelve when he had a fiver on Marie when she won the first of her Newmarket Town Plates at 20/1. Somehow the papers got hold of the story and the headlines read, The Maharajah of Scarborough College - Schoolboy Punter - so on and so on. Then the television people stepped in and you can imagine our surprise when, turning on the set, we saw Nigel talking about his punting and giving his selections for the following day's racing. Those at Scarborough College had taken him over to the studios in Leeds, some sixty miles away, without asking our permission or informing us; it was fortunate for them we didn't mind, in fact we thought it was hilarious. The following year when the Town Plate was run he actually rode in the race and was pacemaker for Marie - consequently more headlines. Just as Col had done, Nigel left school at a younger age than most pupils attending Scarborough College but not before belting one of the masters, for making a most unpleasant suggestion. The master in question died when quite young and how on earth can some people approve of homosexuals. On leaving school Nigel did exactly what Col had done before him, continued to ride as an amateur for a while and then turned professional - more about that later.

I have mentioned earlier that on a visit to Mumso's when she lived in Eastbourne, Marie and I called in at Stacy-Marks Art Gallery and noticed some fantastic paintings though to be correct I believe I should refer to them as pictures. It was pouring with rain and we had only gone into the gallery to keep dry but the visit fired our appreciation of Dutch oils of the seventeenth and eighteenth centuries. It wasn't however until years later that we made our first purchase. It came about when Marie, who loved visiting the antique fair held in Harrogate each autumn, saw a Willem Koek painting. It was of a street scene in Holland and she phoned me to say it was gorgeous and absolutely breath taking. We had seen the same artist's work when in Eastbourne; naturally the quality can vary but Marie assured me the one she had just seen equalled the other. The outcome was she bought it for £800 from Bill Patterson who was working for a London firm. The following year Bill commenced trading on his own with a gallery just off Old Bond Street in London and we bought from him a fabulous 'Liickert', another Dutch artist of the same period; this time it was of a shore scene. It was only half the size of the Koek we had but that was no matter. The quality was superb and it cost only £600. The price was a complete mystery for art dealers are not generally known for their 'generosity', but Bill Patterson must be the exception for we bought a further one rather cheaply - again, early Dutch. Bill loves a gamble and often has a racehorse in training; I see him occasionally and once met his charming wife who was a solicitor. He hasn't altered over the years and is still the same likeable person with the same gallery in Albermarle Street.

Somehow we became known as possible buyers of paintings and several firms sent their representatives to see us. One was from the Eastbourne firm we had once visited and we bought from them an English landscape. I'm not exactly sure of the figure we gave but it was in the region of £1,600. After a short while we came to dislike the painting intensely and were quite prepared to take a substantial loss if Stacy-Marks would buy it back. I'm talking about a very substantial loss but they weren't interested. This meant only one thing - Exactly - we must have overpaid! We bought another painting after that, another Willem Koek, which brought our collection to five pictures in all.

I don't know how it came about but Coulter, a very reputable York dealer, offered us £2,500 for the original 'Koek' when we'd only had it a couple of years and because of the profit angle we accepted but immediately regretted doing so. We tried to buy it back but to no avail as apparently it had already been sold on. A few months later our house was burgled, for the second time whilst at Dunsforth. The first was when we were at a point meeting and, because the ground was so firm, we didn't run and returned home earlier than expected. I guess we very nearly caught him in the act. I say him and in the singular for I believe I know who the burglar was and told the police of my suspicions but they took not the slightest notice. The back door had been smashed and the place ransacked but nothing was taken;

obviously he was looking for cash. We were not so fortunate on the second occasion though there was no damage done to our home. A key was obviously used to open the front door then, after going through several of the rooms, they trod on a security mat, which triggered off the newly fitted burglar alarm. They - I expect there were more than one - must have bolted, for they didn't take all the paintings, leaving the small Liickert hanging on the wall. The nature of the robbery was really rather extraordinary. Marie was in London on business, the boys were away at school and I had decided to go over and have a look at the Zetland point course, to see how much snow there was about. Very rarely would our home be left unoccupied in the evenings but it was on that occasion; I'd called in on some friends and didn't get back until roughly ten o'clock. There was a light covering of snow and any tyre or footmarks there might have been were covered by a recent flurry; in fact it was snowing lightly as I drove down the drive on my return. I always used the back door of the cottage and didn't notice anything unusual until I saw an empty milk bottle on the floor in the kitchen with the milk spilt all over the place. I presume it was knocked over by the thief/thieves as they tried to locate the internal alarm bell. I contacted the police on 999 and within half an hour they had sent over quite a team from Harrogate; there were a couple in plain clothes plus two or three in uniform. I thought I could hear strains of Gilbert and Sullivan as they ran around in circles. The one in charge said, as he sat in the kitchen "I wish you lot would make less bloody noise, you are giving me a f*****g headache". Two of them were discussing the fact that the frames had also been stolen and they thought it would have been easier for the thieves to have cut the paintings out and roll them up - and to think they had been sent to investigate! I told them they had been watching too many films and that one was painted on board and the paint on the others would have disintegrated if what they suggested had been done. One of the officers reported that there were footprints in the snow leading in and out from the front door. The Inspector, rather sarcastically, said "Yes, they are mine, that's one problem solved, we're progressing"! After about three hours and a dozen page statement from me, they decided to push off and "Give Mr. Tinkler some bloody peace - he looks knackered!" and I was. During the next few days there were three other similar robberies in the area, one as close as Helmsley and I asked the police if they could arrange a meeting for all the 'victims', then something might come to light. But nothing came of that suggestion, none of the paintings were ever recovered and the general theory was that they would have been sent abroad. We collected on the insurance, but only what we had paid for them. Admittedly, on one of the pictures that was more than adequate but not on the others. I eventually sold the Liickert many years later, for more than a dozen times the amount it originally cost, though not before having it expertly photographed. The only reason for selling was that I just didn't want the hassle of having thousands of pounds hanging on the wall. I do have some lovely paintings now but they are not at that sort of money.

Whilst living at Dunsforth Mumso, my brother Peter and my sister Ann and their partners visited from time to time. Peter and his wife Kathleen had two girls, Ann likewise plus a boy. Of course, the children are all grown up now with partners and young ones of their own. Regrettably I'm ashamed to say I very rarely see them, it's entirely my fault. In 1963 a terrible tragedy struck Peter's family - Kathleen died of cancer. It was particularly upsetting because of the little girls. Peter was working as a field rep for Boots the Chemist at the time and fortunately he married again. His second wife, Lorna, was a head teacher and they have been together ever since. I've always got on extremely well with her and like her dry sense of humour. She has been good for Peter and the children and a few years back they were breeders and Peter also a show judge, of miniature smooth haired dachshunds. They gave up the business when they moved to a smaller place in Skegness and have now retired. I have always felt Peter should have fashioned his life around racing for, without question, it is something he would have liked to have been involved with.

On Marie's side all four sisters of whom three had married, visited us on occasions, the most frequent being Martha and her husband Gordon, who drowned some years ago in a fishing accident at their farm, near Aylesbury. Marie's youngest sister Hilda and her husband, also called Colin, would sometimes come to stay. He was a few years her junior and at one time was in the army, being a product of Sandhurst. Their marriage was a non-starter, but fortunately there were no children. After her divorce we never saw her again; she joined a religious sect in the north of Scotland and died from heart failure, aggravated by becoming very much overweight. She was only in her forties, reasonably wealthy and could have had a very good life.

Marie was naturally very upset about Hilda's death, just as she was when another of her sisters, Chris, died suddenly a few years later. She and her doctor husband had two girls and two boys, all now married, one of them, George, being a director of Sotheby's who do the auctioning of the racing regalia every year; both brothers are very keen on racing and usually have a horse in training. Marie's parents also died during the late sixties/early seventies and she was very much affected by her father's death; she thought an awful lot of him and was full of pride for what he had achieved. Even though he was in his eighties it was still a shock for her when he died for I don't believe she could imagine him not being about.

After Marie's mother died, 'Edward D' had a slight stroke so Martha decided it would be better for him to move a couple of hundred yards down the road to a smaller place. Elsie was still at home and the move meant her giving up her smallholding; surprisingly she didn't mind and I think she was getting tired of milking, mucking out and creosoting! The new place wasn't so small but was compared to 'Chivilcoy'. The move was going to require some organising and it was not so much a question of what they were going to take but what was to be done with everything else. It was agreed that I should have a week down there and, with Martha's help, sort things out. It must have been a terrible wrench for 'Edward D' because he had been at 'Chivilcoy' for over forty years and had seen so many changes in the area. When he first moved in there were only a dozen or so houses and a sand road to the station but how things had changed. Actually he was going to be no further away from the golf club so could easily be driven the few hundred yards there, see his cronies for a chat, play a couple of holes and open a bottle of wine. The move was not going to take away any of his former comforts; in fact 'Chivilcoy' would have been far too large for Elsie and he and probably held too many memories.

I took a mini van down to transport small items from one house to the other. This went on for several days after the removal people had transferred all the furniture that was required. A quantity of heavy oak pieces were sent over to relatives in Germany and other items of value such as the piano and billiard table were acquired by others. We then systematically went through every room burning everything else on a giant bonfire, carpets, curtains, beds, chairs, everything. After four days all was cleared. There was nothing else Martha or I could have done. A clearance man had been contacted but we were not at all happy with his attitude. Whilst taking down an old curtain from behind one of the stairs, I noticed some marks on the wall, apparently they were measurements of Marie's height and age as she grew up; I thought rather a nice, yet sad, discovery. It brought it home to me that life is so very short.

On the final day of the clearance it was quite late and getting dusk by the time I'd made the fire safe and swept every room thoroughly. I'd just switched the electric off at the mains, then had one more quick look through the house. I went up to the attic rooms when suddenly there was a chilling force in the air. Talk about hairs standing on the back of one's neck, I was petrified. I am now as I recall the incident. I flew down the wide staircase, one flight after another, past all the dark oak panelling and into the garden, locking the front door behind me. Even the giant oak trees standing in the garden, which I had always thought so beautiful, had become menacing. I stood there visibly shaking, looking up at the tall empty house - or was it empty? I felt Marie's mother was in that attic room and she had not approved of what I had done. I never went back into the house again. The place was sold and extensively altered and I believe has been on the market again recently for one and a half million. On my way down to Ascot sales, a few years ago, I did a slight detour to have a further last nostalgic look at 'Chivilcoy'. Again I got the same intense cold feeling as I sat in the car at the bottom of the drive, looking up at the house on the rising ground - disturbingly mysterious.

Now to recall a couple of rather amusing happenings, to take us away from the 'chilly extraordinary'. In the middle of the moving Elsie told me she was going to have two large bed sheets and put everything she wished to keep into one bundle and all the clothes, shoes and anything else she didn't want into another bundle. "Colin, you can take those things I don't require to 'Oxfam'". I don't know how it happened but somehow I took the wrong bundle down to their new home and, as I hadn't time to pop to the Oxfam shop, I put the bundle that should have been kept on to the bonfire. When Elsie discovered the mix up her only comment was "Colin, it's no good you trying to retrieve anything from the Oxfam shop because they will have gone like hot cakes". I thought, well not exactly that but they have certainly gone! Incidentally, because of what occurred, old school uniforms became Elsie's fashion code for quite some years.

There was further humour after I left for home. Marie had asked me to collect the trophies she had won over the years, so I wrapped them in pillow cases, put them in the back of the little van, said goodbye to everybody and headed north. Unknown to me a gardener from one of the houses close to 'Chivilcoy' had noticed I'd been driving past several times and thought I might be casing the district for a likely place to burgle. Apparently he took the registration number of my vehicle and had given it to the police. It seemed that the house moving at 'Chivilcoy' and my journeys up and down the road had not been connected. I'd travelled about fifty miles up the Great North Road when a patrol car slowed me down. It was pitch black by then and had just started to rain as the two policemen approached my van; one said to the other, after checking my van's number plate "Yes, this is it". They then asked me to open the back door. Of course, they found the 'swag' but they weren't in the mood for joking, though I could see the funny side. I told them of the circumstances surrounding the silver and, to verify my story, they asked their Moor Park colleagues to call in at 'Edward D's' to check. His response to their questions was "Did you say Colin Tinkler? oh yes, lock him up - he has just cleaned my house out at Chivilcoy, hasn't left a thing, he has taken the lot - lock him up - my daughter will be better off without him"! I never did get to know whether he had been joking or not - I sincerely hope he was. After eventually contacting Marie, my story was accepted and after what had been an hour's delay I headed north.

Chapter eleven

We move to Boltby

When we were at Lower Dunsforth, training our horses included regular excursions to the Boltby Woods, some twenty miles away. The woods were part of the Hambleton Hills and one could go for miles cantering up and down the slopes, on the grass tracks between the tall pine trees. Over the years all the fallen foliage had made the going perfect, with a cushion to the turf. We would park the trailer in Boltby itself and hack up to the woods and sometimes to the moors beyond. On one occasion, a glorious morning with the bright sunlight shining through the trees, the horses had got rather warm so we decided to walk them for a while on a pathway. As we rounded a bend we saw, in a clearing at the side, a Ford hatchback with the rear door raised. It wasn't the only thing raised, for lying half in the car with her feet outside on the ground was a girl with her little bare bottom stuck in the air. Close by her companion was standing, in more ways than one, his trousers having conveniently slipped down to around his ankles. They both must have got a hell of a shock on seeing us, for I imagine they thought they had found a quiet little haven in the middle of nowhere. Marie and I had the impression we had interrupted something or rather interrupted the start of something! They were only two or three yards away and, as we rode past, the fellow stuttered something about it being a nice day for a ride. Marie called back "Well you obviously think so!" We then broke into a canter and Marie turned to me and said "Did you see the size of it?" I replied "Yes, but it wasn't as big as it looked, it was only a three door hatchback". Marie again quipped "I'm not talking about the car - stupid!" I answered "Oh, that, sorry, Marie, I didn't, I was too busy looking elsewhere!" Naturally.

On another visit in the late Spring of '69 we noticed a For Sale board outside a rather large farmhouse which was actually in the village itself, yet in an elevated position. There were some marvellous buildings, including a barn, a coach house with a granary above and some cow bays. All were built of sand stone with pan tile roofs but the whole place was going to require extensive renovations. Adjoining was a paddock of a couple of acres, sloping very steeply down to a stream and, coincidentally, just as before when buying at Lower Dunsforth, we learnt a fair size field just outside the village could most likely be purchased. Marie and I thought it would be the ideal place in which to start training more extensively so we went to the auction at the Golden Fleece in Thirsk. I can't remember what the bidding started at but we finished it at £5,000, only double the amount I was to find in my old riding boot. As with our former homes, Marie and I were in complete harmony about the purchase; it was going to be another great adventure but there was an enormous amount to do. I was still motor trading, be it not so extensively as in the past; in fact it was gradually winding down and my final day attending a car auction was not far away.

The boys were fifteen and eleven years old by this time, with Col at Scarborough College and Nigel soon to commence there. As they were both weekly boarders the move was not going to affect their schooling. We immediately contacted a couple of estate agents in Boroughbridge regarding selling our Dunsforth place and what complete idiots they proved to be. One valued the house plus the land at £3,000 and the other said he would try for £6,000. In true Irish brogue I will say "Both got the sack before they got the job!" We told the next estate agent we approached the figure we required for the property, namely £10,000 and it was sold in a matter of days.

I was approaching my fortyfourth birthday when we went to live at Boltby and I felt I'd not really progressed fast enough. In no way was I despondent - besides I was well aware that I had much going for me. The unpleasant roller-coaster sensations were still evident at times and always disturbing when they occurred but, thankfully, even they were becoming less frequent. We had been at Lower Dunsforth for a dozen years and I can't say other than the Tinklers were very happy whilst there and we'd had a lot of fun. I could not have wished for two nicer boys, I absolutely adored Marie and was looking forward to the future with all the possibilities it held.

The move itself didn't really take that long; we took a trailer load of belongings over every day until there was nothing left. With regard to the horses, we only had three and a couple of ponies to transport across and they went straight out to grass for the summer. It was farcical how we came to have the grass; about a hundred acres, in various lot sizes, were being auctioned for summer grazing and this particular field was of some two and a half acres. Marie and I couldn't attend the sale because it was on a Saturday afternoon and Marie was busy winning the Ladies Open with Zangavar at the Hurworth point to point. We desperately wanted the field so got a friend to go along and bid for us, with the explicit instructions to get it no matter what the price. The sort of figure one would expect to pay at that time would be up to £15 an acre - £20 an acre wasn't heard of. It so happened that a local farmer, who also couldn't be at the sale, left similar instructions with the auctioneer - with the result that we paid £76 an acre for just a summer's grazing! It was all perfectly genuine and, had the field been offered for sale freehold, I shouldn't imagine it would have made more than £150 an acre. Nevertheless we were still pleased our instructions were carried out and we also had it the following year, but for a lot less money!

Boltby was the fourth home we'd had; again we called the property Whitegates and it wasn't long before we had the place transformed into one of the prettiest stable yards imaginable. It was again a case of plenty of hard graft, and Marie certainly did her share of that. It's crazy really but the more successful people become, the larger the house they wish to live in - they don't need all the rooms but acquire them! We employed a builder but also individual trades, which gave us more control and hastened completion of the renovations. I remember buying lorry load after lorry load of stone slates from a mill that was being demolished in Bradford; they were very reasonably priced in those days and I needed them for all the walling I built. We also bought a large quantity of turf to cover a rough stone yard which was behind the barn. It came direct from Tony Dickinson's new training stables at Harewood where they were constructing an all weather gallop. I was rather surprised when I was told by the supplier that his firm had hoped to get the turf cheaper but Ladbrokes struck a hard bargain - Who? Exactly! - so it was Ladbrokes who owned the stables at Harewood! We had been there a year when we bought the field on the outskirts of the village and, because of the elevated position of our home, it could be seen from the garden. We again did some post and railing, built a corral with stables and put down a rotovated round gallop; also the obsession I had for building chase fences was put to good use.

Whilst the renovation work was being carried out we lived in one of the bedrooms and every evening, before going to bed, I'd take a bath in a tub in what was going to be the kitchen. At the same time I would wash the clothes I'd been wearing, to be ready for the following day. All this is leading up to a rather amusing incident. It was about six in the morning, the sun was shining through a hole in the wall, where the front door was going to be, when in stepped this little old lady called Tiny, all four foot ten of her. She lived in a cottage close by and apparently had come round to bring Marie some flowers - Yes, at that time of the morning, though I suspect she was being bloody inquisitive. I had just reached the hallway and had not as yet collected my clothes, so was absolutely naked. I stood there motionless, hoping she wouldn't see me - well, I didn't want to excite her! - but she obviously noticed me, because she wandered over to the bottom of the stairs and called out "Are you there Mrs. Tinkler? - I like your stuffed gorilla; where are you going to put it?" Marie replied "It's not a stuffed gorilla, it's a stuffed Geega!"

I'm strictly teetotal, not that I'm against alcohol in principle but I would have great difficulty walking in a straight line if I were to have more than a couple of glasses, so I stick to tomato juice (doubles, of course). I'm leading up to a rather hilarious afternoon on a boiling hot day. I was in the paddock at the back of the stables and had just finished erecting a post and rail fence. I was extremely thirsty but there had been some repair work going on in Boltby with the water pipes, making the water a terrible colour and temporarily not fit to drink. I had consumed all the lagers we had and my next move was to open a bottle of champagne but I didn't just open it, I also emptied it and got completely pissed in the process, as well as committing sacrilege by drinking the bubbly through a straw! I couldn't stop laughing and was making Laurel and Hardy faces all the time. I tried to clamber over the fence I'd just built but didn't manage to do so and fell flat on my back. I thought I would soon sort out that little problem and got a saw to the top two rails, making it far easier to climb over! Then I noticed the gate in the fence which I'd forgotten was there! I still couldn't stop laughing. Amazingly I'd sobered up by the time Marie got back from shopping and, what was even more amazing, I didn't get a hangover, neither did the drinking become a habit.

Chapter twelve

*Some dreams come true. Marie wins the Town Plate. It's
bye bye to Pointing. Trouble at the bank. The boys ride
their first winners and launch their careers. My first
£1,000 punt and some other successful gambles. Col's
shattering fall at Newcastle*

In the April of '69 young Col became fifteen and we wasted no
time applying for his amateur rider's licence for both the flat
and over jumps. This the Jockey Club issued without hesitation. The
next thing we did was some scouting around for a suitable horse for
him to ride during the summer months. I had noticed one, a maiden,
coincidentally called "Master Colin". He was a rather gangly, brown,
four year old gelding, trained by Dave Thom at Newmarket. Dave is
a hell of a nice fellow, who's never had a large string of horses but
I've known him bring off some real touches. He actually owned
Master Colin himself and we did a deal at £2,000. It was no use me
applying for a trainer's licence until the stables were ready for
inspection, so it was agreed that Dave should train Master Colin for
his first race for us, which was to be at Ayr at the beginning of May.
We would then send the horse to a trainer nearer home. On the day
of the race the four Tinklers headed for north of the border,
picnicking on the way. As soon as we arrived at Ayr we bumped into
Dave, who suggested young Col walk the course with him. There is
a housing estate bordering the far side of the track and as they passed
one of the houses with washing hanging out to dry Dave's
instructions to Col were "Make your move when you pass that
washing". Col thought, I hope it doesn't rain and they take it in! It
did! And they did! No wonder Master Colin came too late! But,

joking apart, Col rode a cracking race, finishing third - which was marvellous for it gave him so much confidence and the Tinklers en bloc so much pleasure.

We then sent the horse to O'Keefe, who trained near the racecourse at York and used to gallop in the centre of the track. The first time Col went over to ride some work, O'Keefe had not made it plain enough where he should go and the little fellow found himself cantering on the racecourse itself. If it hadn't been for the generosity of John Sanderson, who was Clerk of the Course at the time and who had seen the horse exercising, we would have been in dire trouble. Actually, Master Colin stayed with O'Keefe for a couple of races, in the first of which he was unplaced at Redcar. Then in the next he was third at Thirsk, but there was a mystery about the lead up to that run; in fact it was just another instance, over the years, when I've not been entirely happy about events surrounding horses with which I've been connected. I went over to York on the Friday evening to plate Master Colin for the following day's race, but when I saw him the following day he required shoeing again, because his racing plates had been worn thin. Where the hell had he been. I didn't say anything - we just took the horse away and Jack Calvert, who trained only three or four miles from Boltby, very kindly took him. The horse had three more runs during the month and was again third at Stockton and yet again third at Beverley. By that time Master Colin was over the top. Besides, compared with now, there were nowhere near the number of amateur riders' races and girls weren't even allowed to ride under rules at all, but that was soon to alter. We'd had a jolly nice couple of months racing and young Colin had caught the eye of many good judges.

Mentioning Dave Thom reminds me of the time when there was an on course betting tax in operation. Soon after it was introduced I came to the conclusion that people were giving odds-on shots the cold shoulder. Consequently, to create business the bookmakers were offering better prices about them, than they would otherwise be doing. I decided that I would minimise the tax liability by having accumulators, thus basically only paying tax on the first runner. Surprisingly I got two firms, a local one and Ladbrokes, to accept a standing wager of a £5 accumulator, all the odds-on favourites each day. I say surprisingly, for it was not known until after the off if a horse was going to be odds on or not. I had a marvellous run, until the two firms put a stop to the bet. It was after a day when there were a dozen winners and just the one loser and that one had passed the post first, but lost the race in the steward's room. It meant that if the one at Hamilton had kept the race I would have been £10,000 better off. You might ask, where is the Dave Thom connection - he trained the disqualified horse!

By the beginning of 1970 I had received a full trainer's licence from the Jockey Club, which meant we could, if we so wished, train publicly on the flat and over jumps, giving us a whole new spectrum. Having partners in some of the horses would help financially, both with the buying and the training, though, I believe I've mentioned previously, we would much rather totally own them ourselves. All the work to be done in the field was completed but removing the stones from the oval gallop proved to be a mammoth job. An added bonus to the training facilities at Boltby was when we were permitted to train in the woods as against merely exercising there. The steep up-hill five furlong track we developed was much used over the years.

Now to resume with the Point to Point racing. Marie's two horses, Zangavar and Flexodus, had qualified with the local Bilsdale Hunt and we planned to start the season off at Cottenham in the middle of

February. With the point season being of such a short duration it was imperative to keep the horses sound, but it was inevitable that they would receive some injuries along the way; hopefully, when they occurred, they would be minor ones. We were always ultra careful and would often go to a meeting and, if we considered the going either too firm, rough, heavy or whatever, we wouldn't run. Both Zangavar and Flexodus looked ready quite early on and we were very excited about the months ahead. We met with a setback with Master Colin, who had somehow damaged a joint which was to mean him missing the whole of that year. It also meant we would have to 'step up' our search for some fresh horses, if not for the flat, certainly by the next jumping season. Col was still only sixteen but the Tinklers were in a hurry!

When buying racehorses, either privately or from the sales, one must ask oneself - Why are they being sold? I'm referring specifically to horses in training, but if you are too cautious you can end up empty handed. Over the years I have had many successes with horses bought cheaply but, against that, quite a few have slipped though the net, notably the King George winner, Pendil, and the triple Grand National winner, Red Rum. The former made 3,600 gns when sold at the Ascot Sales in 1969 and Red Rum 6,000 gns a couple of years later at Doncaster. I remember going to see Pendil a few days before the auction, when he was trained at Boston Spa near Wetherby. He was a four year old at the time, a lovely little horse who had won a hurdle race at Catterick but had a suspicion of a weak tendon, so we lost interest. It did cause concern during the whole of his career, but look at what he won despite of it. Pendil became as well known for the photograph (taken by Burns) from the take off side of a chase fence, showing the horse at full stretch, as he did for all the races he won. As for Red Rum, I'd always thought he had poor feet and I had this confirmed prior to him being offered for sale, but again, look what he won despite his trouble. However, I do believe that, had he not gone to be trained by the sea with his daily sessions in the salt water, he would not have become a 'National' hero. We didn't actually toss a coin to determine whether we should buy either horse but it was pretty close. The fact that things turned out as they did has not caused me to cry over spilt milk - only puddy cats should do that! Besides, there was no guarantee they would have stayed sound enough to race had we bought them.

As we drove to Cottenham near Cambridge for the first run of the point season, never could I have imagined what a fabulous year we were about to have. It was winners, winners all the way and we pretty well achieved everything we set out to do, commencing with Zangavar's win there at Cottenham. Marie rode a race full of confidence and hit the front two out from a big field and stayed there, winning quite comfortably. After I'd collected from the bookmakers we headed back home; the sport was then more of a territorial thing than nowadays - horses would sometimes be sent a hundred miles to a meeting but rarely more, whereas our journey that day had been a four hundred mile round trip.

After that first triumph, Marie had a further half a dozen winners during the season, three more with Zangavar and a further three on Flexodus, the first being at the Cleveland. It was then on to the Holderness at Dalton Park, in the most beautiful of settings. The course was and still is in the middle of some lovely parkland, with massive trees all around, and everything always looked so green in the spring sunshine. Flexodus, who reminded me of 'Bambi' the loveable Walt Disney character, ended the campaign in magnificent fashion by winning the Goathland, which was also held at Dalton Park that year. Sandwiched between those wins of Marie's on 'Flexy' was when Col rode him in an Open Point, for men only. It was his first ride in a point and, through lack of experience, he came very late, was literally flying at the finish and just got touched off to finish second. 'Flexy' was not a big horse and the twelve and a half stone he had to carry that day rather put him at a disadvantage. Both horses finished the season sound and, before spending a well earned summer's rest out at grass along with Zangavar, Flexodus had one more race at Hexham, which was to give Col his first ride over hurdles. I was not in the least worried; race riding was to be his profession and he was very proficient. There were ten runners and they finished fourth, again not being beaten that far. I remember 'Flexy' jumped very big and, of course, we were all delighted with the run. Col was, as usual, cool and collected and must have gained further confidence from the outing. Throughout the spring I'd been floating about on cloud nine from one week to the next and the red and yellow colours had become a force to be reckoned with; something the bookmakers had learnt to their cost. Marie's policy of going to the front early and making all had certainly paid dividends though, in doing so, she would very occasionally jump slightly to the right. This was a legacy from the show jumping days, when she purposely guided her horses to jump at an angle. The benefits were two fold in the jumping arena; it not only shortened their stride but when a jump was knocked it was more likely to become wedged between the uprights. Marie left nothing to chance; most point to points are over approximately three miles and twenty fences (twice round a mile and a half circuit) and it was not unusual for her to walk the course twice before racing, just to make sure she was familiar with all the undulations, the bends, the best ground, the fences - in fact everything. Whilst racing was solely fun for her, she was always striving to improve.

During the summer we continued to go racing quite often, with both Marie and myself being very successful with the punting and, with nine racecourses in Yorkshire, travelling was kept down to a minimum. The boys did a fair amount of hunter trialing and we were continually on the look out for more horses. I was obsessed with finding one capable of winning the Newmarket Town Plate, then held on the second Thursday in October, over four and a half miles on the July course. When I was thirteen I'd seen a photograph of Vera Bullock winning the 1940 Town Plate and ever since then I'd had the desire for someone close to me to do the same thing; yes, another boyhood dream - I had so many of them! Marie had a look see ride on a mediocre animal in '69, which actually ran quite well, so we knew what was required.

When looking through Doncaster's September sales catalogue, we noticed a four year old called Blake was entered. He had some good form, having been placed in the spring, and had won the Caledonian at Hamilton the previous year. Blake was trained up at Middleham and was being sold with a sound certificate and supposedly to dissolve a partnership. We took both statements with a pinch of salt and had already learnt that asking questions was an utter waste of time! He was a good looking, dark brown gelding, and a really nice stamp of a horse. Our suspicions seemed to be unfounded at first glance as there was nothing visibly wrong but naturally we were still sceptical regarding his correctness. We went to 1,200 gns for him at the auction but he didn't make his reserve; we did, however, do a deal later in the day at that figure.

The Newmarket Town Plate was in fourteen days time and, on getting him home, Blake did not seem all that fit, though Marie's examination showed his breathing was at least in order. He was a most willing horse in his work and his training routine, over the

189

following fortnight, consisted of cantering through the woods non stop for an hour and a half each day, always carrying a weight cloth, but Marie never galloped him; it was rather amazing how the horse altered physically in such a short time.

Whilst at Doncaster Sales we had a chat with the late Gordon Richards, the Penrith trainer, who mentioned that his old hurdler Montabel was for sale. We arranged to take young Col over the following week to give him a spin and a pop over hurdles, alongside Ron Barry. After the work out Gordon said, in his typical style "Your boy can ride a bit, he will be champion jockey one day". Col never quite made number one but was always high in the list of top riders and in 1975 reached fourth spot. Our journey to the Lake District resulted in buying Montabel for a few hundred and, as he had an entry at Carlisle the following Monday, we decided to leave the horse with Gordon until then. Montabel held another engagement five days later, at the now non existent Stockton racecourse, but we would have him back at Boltby for that. It was certainly going to be a hectic time - hopefully two runs with Montabel over hurdles and one with Blake in the Town Plate, all in less than a week. We got the boys excused from school for a few days and on the Monday we all set off to Carlisle. It's odd but the thing I remember most about the day is Gordon Richards chatting to Col in the paddock prior to being legged up. In the race itself Montabel ran a cracker, especially as he needed the run, and finished second. The Tinklers were again delighted and Col had ridden a lovely little race. We returned to Boltby with Montabel, knowing the run would have brought him on a great deal. It was back to school for the boys and down to work for Marie and I.

Gordon Richards had been a real help throughout and nothing had been too much trouble - well it wouldn't have been, for he was one hell of a nice person and so enthusiastic about all he did.

We took Blake down to Newmarket on the morning of the race. Marie and I had got up exceptionally early in order to get all the work finished, for we didn't want to be late away. Marie weighed less than eight stone and, as runners in the Town Plate are allotted twelve stone, it meant there was going to be a lot of extra weight to carry, so we made a special sheep skin weight cloth. The race was always run at twelve noon in those days and with only Marie and myself with the horse, Marie weighed out before we unloaded; when we did Blake was like a cat on hot bricks; in fact, had I not been so strong he would most definitely have got away from me. He was acting like a crazy horse, which was so uncharacteristic of him; not surprisingly, some thought we'd given him some 'Gee up' pills! Of course, nothing could have been further from the truth. In fact there was no logical explanation for his 'high jinks'. Obviously he hadn't spent all his energy because he went on to win the race by twenty lengths at 20/1; it was unbelievable and as they passed the post I gave out one hell of a "YIPPEE", just as I did the day Col was born, and plenty more were to follow as I motored home. Even now, tears of emotion come into my eyes as I recall the drive back to Yorkshire. Unfortunately, Marie had a Delfosse family meeting in London later that afternoon and went down there by train from Newmarket. Words can't express the utter jubilation I felt; of course, everything is relative - The Town Plate was minor to what Marie was to achieve in winning the Ladies Riders Flat Championship a few years later, but on that lovely Autumn day a dream had come true. Our two boys were as jubilant as I and only wished they could have been there. Nigel had backed Blake with a fiver and had won £100, and, as I have mentioned previously, became known as the Maharajah. Personally, I didn't have a big punt - one couldn't with only a couple of bookmakers standing. The exertion didn't appear to have done Blake any harm and he seemed perfectly sound, which was a great relief. The Town Plate stayed as it was for many years but later was switched to a Sunday, again being the sole race on the card. Nowadays it's still on a Sunday, though run in conjunction with an Arab meeting so, consequently, all the mystique and appeal has gone and is now no more than a very 'Mickey Mouse' event; change is not always for the better.

Marie got back from London on the Friday and we collected Col and Nigel from Scarborough College later in the evening; then on the Saturday it was 'Stockton here we come'. Montabel had been kept on the move since Monday and I gave him a canter on Friday morning. He looked magnificent and had certainly come on since Carlisle. I was pretty confident Col would ride his first winner, which he did by a couple of lengths, at 7/4, having been backed down from 9/4, with a couple of bets of £900 - £400 noted! The 'pocket battleship' had fired his first salvo, the first of many hundreds. Col, like Marie, always had terrific confidence when riding and was always in the right place at the right time. The ride he gave Montabel was perfection, yet it was only his third over hurdles. For Marie and I, October the 10th had been a special day; we always anticipated Col would make the grade and, of course, riding a winner had been important, but we now knew he was going to be good and that was the exciting thing. Over the next three months Montabel had a further half a dozen runs, being beaten half a length at Wetherby in the first of those, but later, in November, brought off a real gamble for us at Sedgefield at 11/2. He was only ever unplaced twice for the Tinklers and certainly taught Col a great deal. Unfortunately he showed signs of wear so we eventually sold him as a hunter.

As for Blake, it was our intention to send him hurdling if his jumping was adequate, so we decided to find out by taking him to Catterick on the Sunday following their Saturday meeting, early in November. Most racecourses provided trainers with those schooling facilities and made a token charge of between £10 and £20 for each horse. We went along planning to give Blake a good gallop over two miles with possibly six flights of hurdles, and hoped to find someone there wanting a similar work-out. I noticed a nice sort of horse being ridden by Brian Fletcher, the Aintree specialist, and he was happy to go with us. As we didn't wish anyone to know it was Blake we had brought, we dressed him up to look like Montabel, with red blinkers and the added ruse of him wearing Montabel's personal rug. However, instead of our horse having a lead as we'd anticipated, it was Brian who requested that privilege; had we said that our horse had only ever been over two flights at home, the masquerade would, of course, have been exposed. The outcome was, Blake led for the whole two miles, jumping brilliantly, with Col asking him at every hurdle and was a distance clear when pulling up. Brian Fletcher came over to us to enthuse about 'Montabel' alias 'Blake' saying "The old horse went bloody well" and asked "When does he next run?" We now knew we had something to bet on and entered for an amateur novice hurdle at Sedgefield's next meeting, towards the end of the month. The horse had responded to Marie's training and had physically altered out of all recognition by the time the Sedgefield race came along. I was a little disappointed to discover there were to be twenty three runners but Marie characteristically said "No matter, once the tape goes up that will be the last Col will see of them!" I'd contacted George Yates, the bookmaker, who was one of our neighbours when we lived at Scarcroft Grange. George didn't stand at Sedgefield but I wanted him to go along to help with the punting and he actually got a monkey on at 6/1 for us, though the starting price was fives. Col slept all the way to the races but he certainly didn't fall asleep in the race itself; by the time they had jumped the first he was five lengths clear, was soon further ahead and won by fifteen lengths, though it looked double that distance. It had been another fantastic effort all round, with Blake jumping splendidly throughout and Col had again ridden with such maturity. Marie had excelled in getting Blake as fit as he was and no way am I going to leave Nigel out of the accolades, as he was always so enthusiastic with his support and did so much about the yard. As for my part, Blake had been the eleventh winner I'd shod since the beginning of the point season, earlier in February. Some might say, that doesn't seem many, but it was compared with the number of runners there had been! Had the race taken place a few years later, when I was betting more heavily, I would have had an extra nought on the wager and it would have been a 'Wellington boot' job. I will explain how the terminology came about, it was many years later in the late eighties; I'd bought the place at Wombleton and was constructing the pond there, I'd bought a pair of Wellington boots but found they were far too big, nevertheless I found a job for one of them - it was to house my collection of £1 coins. All my life I seem to have had a thing about putting money into footwear of one kind or another and the Wellington boot in question didn't escape the obsession! I was racing practically every day, consequently by most evenings I would have some of the said coins and into the Wellington boot they would all go. It took four of five years to fill it up to the top and when counted there was almost £5,000 and I soon made it up to exactly that figure. They were exceptionally heavy and, at a party one evening, no one was able to lift them off the ground without using both hands. I changed the coins into notes and put the lot on one of our horses called Operation Wolf up at Perth. He won at 2/1 on - but, of course, I'd backed it down to that price. So a new terminology came into my betting language - there already was the Monkey, a Thou and now a Wellington boot!

Blake had several more outings over the following months, being placed once or twice, but was running as if something was amiss; then the injury we had suspected, when originally buying him, came to the surface. It had always been on the cards that something was wrong - he had been far too inexpensive. In the short time that Blake had been with us he was another horse that had given tremendous pleasure and won us a lot of money. We kept him for some time but when it was obvious that his legs were not going to stand up to training we sold him on for hacking about. It has always been sad to part with horses that have tried so hard and given so much, but it would be more than just a problem to retain them all, it would be literally impossible, unless one was fabulously wealthy.

We had further injuries to a couple of the horses during the winter, one being Zangavar who succumbed to a tendon problem whilst being trained, consequently Marie went into the next point to point season with just Flexodus, plus a couple of, what we soon discovered, were nonentities. Incidentally, Master Colin had qualified for pointing and it was our intention that Col should ride him.

I must tell you about a Ladies Race, held at Charm Park; it only had two runners, Marie wasn't riding but two of her contemporaries, Pat Mason and Anne Greenwood, were, though neither on their own horses. I took over a bookmakers board for £50 just for the one race and really went to town laying them both (I'm sure I should have worded that differently!). I was giving better prices than the other bookmakers and took hundreds of pounds. Incidentally, Marie had been looking for me to say - "Don't have a bet Colin because both horses look lame". The outcome was, I made myself about £100 and thoroughly enjoyed the experience - but the line of bookmakers were not happy, for I was the only one that had done any business.

Despite a depleted string Marie had another cracking season in '71, all five winners were by courtesy of Flexodus. She raided Anne Greenwood's territory for a couple of her successes, firstly at the 'Pendle Forest' late in March, then the following month at the 'High Peak' where not one of the twenty bookmakers escaped. I systematically went down the line of boards at £20 a throw - some were a little suspicious, because they hadn't seen the new issue before; I believe they thought it was some sort of highway robbery which, I suppose it was! Amazingly, despite my activities, Flexy was always odds against that day, varying between 11/10 and 6/4. I usually led the horses round the parade ring but on that occasion one of the boys did so, for as you can imagine, I was otherwise engaged. I remember it was a dull and bitterly cold afternoon with the odd flurry of snow but all that didn't seem to matter as Marie and Flexodus put another notch on the barrel, winning quite easily and collecting from the bookmakers took a lot longer than it had done putting the cash on. In between the two successes in 'alien' country Flexodus also won at the 'York and Ainsty' and the 'Holderness'; the latter of those was something special as, half an hour after Marie had passed the post, Col also won on Master Colin, making it a Tinkler double. Both won with plenty in hand and Nigel was working overtime with his leading in role.

Master Colin had been difficult to keep sound during his training and regrettably didn't run again. Young Col was in a different league to the other point riders but, of course, he would have to be, young as he was, if he were to make riding his profession. He was being offered quite a number of outside rides (from other pointing stables) and altogether had four winners from less than a dozen mounts. I was rather selective about which he took - it was not a question of how good a horse was but of how safe. I used to recite to him an old 'Geega' proverb "Don't put your neck in a noose if you intend jumping from a tree". In spite of all my so called clever philosophy, young Col suffered a broken ankle riding between the flags. Marie rounded off the season with a win on 'Flexy' at the Bedale meeting, in rather warmish company, and a number of bookmakers there took a real chance by laying me even fifties; I'd never known them so generous. Flexy, as he had become known, was a real favourite with the point followers, he possessed such charisma. Marie's other mounts that year were a complete waste of her time and one gave her quite a nasty fall, but I suppose it was amazing she didn't hit the deck more often, considering her cavalier style.

Zangavar was back for the start of the '72 point season along with Flexodus and, just as in the previous two years, we set off for the first meeting down at Cottenham. But if only there had been snow to prevent us from leaving the village, as there had been the year before, when we slid into the telephone box just fifty yards from our home. On arriving at the course we unloaded 'Flexy' for a leg stretch and the reason Marie chose to run him and not the mare was that he was more forward in condition and looked fabulous - absolutely 'spot on'. The race, however, turned out to be a monumental disaster, because one of the other runners accidentally struck into our horse, knocking the tendon off the point of the hock. Marie immediately dismounted and, as he couldn't walk, I took the trailer onto the course to pick him up. We were well aware of the severity of the injury and rushed him over to the veterinary at Cambridge University. Marie spoke the same 'language' and it was agreed that some very complex surgery was going to be required, but whether the tendon could be made to stay in the correct position was another matter. Were a miracle to occur, Flexy would not be as good as before. We were utterly devastated. I thought I was hardened to horses going wrong but apparently not, for I was so upset and it was a particularly long drive home. The fact that Flexodus was so gorgeous made our misery even more painful and, of course, Marie had lost a fantastic ride on a comparatively young horse. After a couple of months Flexy recovered sufficiently to come home; the operations had not been a success, so he was retired along with our one remaining pony 'Little Z'. The others had been sold, as the boys had advanced on from ponies, even though Nigel was still only twelve. 'Flexy' and 'Little Z' were pals, having spent a summer's grazing together and it was only right they should have each other's company. Actually they went to live on a farm a few miles away, run by the Musgrove family, from whom we bought all our hay and straw; we also used to gallop on their land. I never really knew who was in charge but 'Uncle Jack' seemed to be - he was a bachelor and what a character, with his weather beaten face and attire. He would be in his sixties, was very short and always wore a large floppy hat and leggings - he just couldn't have been anything else but a farmer. Marie and I affectionately called him 'Short-leg'. He never spoke in ordinary tones, literally shouting everything he said. He would bellow "Gallop where you like - snow will put yon footings back and that Flexodus and yon pony can stay here as long as they like" - and they did. In the winter months they lived under cover along with the cattle; it would be nice if all retirements were so comfortable.

The '72 point season had certainly commenced unhappily and concluded in a similar vein with Zangavar breaking down at the Zetland meeting. That was the day I landed Brian Dunn, a leading point to point bookmaker in the north, one on the jaw. The mare had to be pulled up and as I walked past Brian's stand after the race, he called me a twister. I was upset enough about the mare going wrong, without having to endure such remarks, so I lashed out. He has always maintained that I broke his jaw; I'm not too certain about that, though I did break some bones in my hand. I was rather concerned that the stewards would take a dim view of things if they got to know what had been happening, so I thought it best to give one of them a phone call in the evening to apologise. All he said was "Jolly good. I wish I had seen it!" I had no answer to that and was relieved at his attitude. I would like to add that in spite of what had occurred, there has never been any animosity between Brian and myself.

Marie's pointing continued for a few years up until 1976. There were some barren periods but a shortage of suitable horses was the reason. However, we did buy one giant of a horse called Pin Harbour and firstly put Nigel up on him in a hunter chase at Stockton. It didn't tell us much for, unfortunately, they crashed at the first. Marie rode him next in the ladies point at the Bramham Moor held on Wetherby racecourse; he won quite easily and I had rather a large punt. The horse was not a long term proposition and we decided to get rid doing a deal with the likeable Vic Thompson for whom Col was riding. Vic gave us £1,000 plus one of his cast-offs which we sold for a further £1,000 to go eventing. It was all rather amusing for, when we shook hands on the deal, we both thought we had the best of the transaction - let's put it this way, Vic thought he had and I knew I had, Exactly! The following year was a blank one for Marie as far as riding winners was concerned, but, of course, she was immensely busy training the hurdlers. Col had ridden a novice chaser called Shamus for Ken Oliver and we bought him for a little over a thousand when he came up for sale at Doncaster. Marie won a couple of races on him in '76, firstly at the Zetland then, coincidentally, on her last ride pointing at the Staintondale meeting; they had however changed courses since her first ride, when Word of Honour won at the same point twelve years earlier. There had been 27 successes during that time on six different horses. Unfortunately some nasty falls had also occurred, one in particular, but, apart from those, the Tinklers had a marvellous time pointing. But even greater thrills and excitement were to come, as Marie put away the red and yellow pullover and donned the flat race silks.

MARIE'S CAREER - POINT-TO-POINT WINNERS

1964	Word of Honour	Staintondale Ladies Open.
1965	Too Dear	Goathland Ladies Open.
	Too Dear	Sinnington Ladies Open.
	Too Dear	Cleveland Ladies Open.
1967	Word of Honour	Goathland Ladies Open.
	Word of Honour	York and Ainsty Ladies Open.
	Word of Honour	Staintondale Ladies Open.
1968	Word of Honour	York and Ainsty Ladies Open.
1969	Zangavar	York and Ainsty Ladies Open.
	Zangavar	Hurworth Ladies Open.
1970	Zangavar	Cambridge Harriers Ladies Open.
	Zangavar	South Durham Ladies Open.
	Flexodus	Cleveland Ladies Open.
	Zangavar	Staintondale Ladies Open.
	Flexodus	Holderness Ladies Open.

	Zangavar	Sinnington Ladies Open.
	Flexodus	Goathland Ladies Open.
1971	Flexodus	Pendle Forest and Craven Ladies Open.
	Flexodus	York and Ainsty Ladies Open.
	Flexodus	Holderness Ladies Open.
1971	Flexodus	High Peak and North East Ladies Open.
	Flexodus	Bedale and West of York Ladies Open.
1972	Zangavar	York and Ainsty Ladies Open.
	Zangavar	Hurworth Ladies Open.
1974	Pin Harbour	Bramham Moor Ladies Open.
1976	Shamus	Zetland Ladies Open.
	Shamus	Staintondale Ladies Open.

I will end the point scene with an amusing story, it happened at one of the Sinnington Point to Points. The weather was appalling with the rain pelting down. The 'gentlemens' at this location was a tent with a couple of sheep troughs and for obvious reasons a low part of the ground was used. Had it stayed dry that would have been ideal but you can imagine the hazards when the rain came. I certainly would not have risked the perils of being in the area without wearing wellingtons! I had just entered the tent when in came this knickerbockered, deer-stalkered six foot beanpole, a chinless wonder, an absolute ineffectual twit. He called out "Ya! ya! it's not fit for bloody ducks, ya! ya!" Suddenly he slipped and fell full length flat on his back! As he was attempting to get up he somehow slipped again, splash, splosh, flat on his face. What an awful stinking mess, what a prat. As I walked out of the tent I couldn't stop laughing, nor could anyone else. No, I didn't go to his rescue! But I did shorten my stride and walked rather gingerly!

Let me relate a couple more amusing stories on a similar theme. I was at Newcastle Races on a bitterly cold November afternoon; it was also pouring with rain and blowing a gale when I popped into the 'gentlemens' which was situated near the saddling boxes. To call the place primitive would be totally inadequate - the word barbaric comes to mind. It was constructed of four brick walls, one with an opening for entry and exit, the others having gutters to a drain, nothing else, not even a roof. As I entered I saw just one person in there - it was this old codger. He was wearing, along other things, a very flat cap perched at an incredible angle and a couple of overcoats. He had a cigarette hanging from his mouth, was completely sozzled and his one sided conversation, to his willy-nilly, in slurred Geordie went something like this.

"Come oot ye little bugger - I nar ye there."

"Ye nars ye waant a piss - Ye'er a bloody cooard."

"Jast because it's f******g cowld - ye doon't waant ta come oot."

"Ye'd be oot like a bloody shot if there weer a good looking lass aboot."

It was incredibly funny.

Catterick Races also have a similar 'inconvenience', just four walls and a drain, near where the horses come into the paddock. It is in a busy area and consequently used by a lot of people. On this particular occasion the weather was remarkably like that at Newcastle and Sinnington; suddenly in ran this rather tall fellow with a little boy of about three. As he was undoing the small boy's fly zip the youngster said "But dad I want a 'Ar Ar'". The stunned father replied "F*****g Hell, can't you make do with a bloody piss!"

With Blake and Montabel out of the picture, Marie and I went shopping again and bought, among others, Ocean Sailor and Philip, both costing less than four hundred pounds apiece. Philip was bought privately from Bill Haigh, who had only recently moved to Malton to train. The horse hadn't the best of joints, nevertheless, we took a chance as the price was reasonable. He went on to have a dozen outings for us over the following year and, with Col riding, brought off a couple of real gambles, the second of which was only two days after Nigel had, as a thirteen year old, ridden him in the Town Plate alongside Marie. As for Ocean Sailor, we bought him at Ascot Sales; he was a twelve year old liver chestnut gelding, not much bigger than a pony but what a gorgeous horse. I know I use the adjective a great deal but the word says so much.

Ocean Sailor became known as 'Bubbles Bom Bom', a most appropriate name with him having such a nice disposition and such a lively bouncy action. His first run for the Tinklers was at Market Rasen's opening meeting of the '71-'72 season, where he finished second when very much in need of the race. It was then Bang, Bang, Bang, three wins on the trot. We went back to Market Rasen, then over to Cartmel and then down to Folkestone, bringing off some real touches in the process; in fact at Folkestone I'd backed the little horse down to 5/2 on. We returned to the seaside course the following week with our buckets and spades, to dig for some more punting money, though not on Ocean Sailor. This time he finished second to a horse called King Cup which I backed at 7/1. I did so basically because I thought he was the better horse; it was just a question of whether King Cup's dicky legs would see the race through and they did. We were, however, soon back in the winners enclosure when Ocean Sailor trotted up at Fontwell on his next outing. I had £1,000 at 11/8 but, of course, the price immediately tumbled to odds on. Ocean

Sailor's next race was in the Newmarket Town Plate, the race I've just mentioned when discussing Philip, and this he won very easily with Marie in the saddle. The bookmakers weren't so generous on this occasion. As I have mentioned, Nigel was on Philip and thoroughly enjoyed himself making the running for Ocean Sailor and was not in the least daunted by the occasion of his first ride. It goes without saying the Tinklers were delighted with the whole excursion down to Newmarket. However the bookmakers were not so generous about Bubbles Bom Bom as they had been with Blake the previous year; no matter, the win was not about money.

After his Newmarket 'gallop', Ocean Sailor came fourth at Hexham, then second in a good class hurdle race at Nottingham, before his final race at Newcastle where he sadly broke down. We soon found a nice home for his retirement, on a farm, where he spent his remaining years grazing in the summer and hunting, which he loved, during the winter. Between the beginning of August and the end of November he had run ten times in all, winning five races, being second three times and fourth once, all without ever having a serious slap. Of course, the vast majority of racehorses are toys, some very lovable toys, and Bubbles Bom Bom was most decidedly in that category. Col had ridden him in all his races for us, other than the Town Plate, and they became the perfect combination; they were golden days studded with diamonds.

I was at the Newmarket Sales when I overheard a conversation in the bar, between Earl Jones, from whom we purchased Ocean Sailor, and another person. Earl was saying that those Tinklers created a miracle with the horse, for he couldn't keep him sound. He hadn't noticed me standing just behind him until I tapped him on the shoulder and said "That's not what you told me the day we bought him"! There was one very red face and it wasn't mine.

By the end of '71 Col, who was still only seventeen, had ridden about a dozen winners for Marie and I and they had all been well backed. What with that and our other betting activities we soon became known as a successful gambling stable, with suggestions of much skullduggery. I'm certainly not claiming integrity here, but it's my contention that if one stops a horse you learn precisely nothing and the horse learns too much! I've just been looking at some old newspaper cuttings and I quote "Colin Tinkler has trained 17 winners from his last 25 runners"; it doesn't seem there was a lot of skullduggery! Time after time, we won with a horse on its first outing after a long lay off. There have always been people 'away off beam' about my punting. I was talking to a Malton trainer the other day and the conversation got round to betting; he said "Everyone knows what you do Colin, you pop one in a seller that can't lose, have £20,000 on at odds on, win enough to pay for buying the horse back and still make a handsome profit" - If only I did and if only it was as easy as that!

I never wished to have a large string to train and considered four the maximum number we could manage at any one time, but even such a figure required quite a back up team. There were always those recovering from injury in one form or another, plus sound horses that were resting. Of course, in the spring and summer months, when horses could be out at grass, things were much easier but some winters we had as many as fourteen inside. With so much other work to do about the yard I much preferred to ride just the one out each morning, though Marie would ride as many as three lots when the boys were not at home. Col was soon being offered rides from other stables, as was Nigel as soon as he received his jockey's licence, when he became fifteen.

We did eventually bring in some owners and, without mentioning them all, I will just refer to one or two. Gordon Morley quickly comes to mind - he lived locally and was in haulage. It was Gordon who was one of the partners in Blake when we bought the horse; he was rather impressed with the gamble that materialised at Sedgefield and that was the reason he joined forces with us. Another recruit was Ray Quincey, a builder and a lookalike for Kenneth Connor, one of the old Carry On Team. Norman Heslop, a Newcastle bookmaker, was another and then there was Peter Bowker, who had a furniture shop near Cartmel. Peter had a younger brother of eighteen who wanted to be a jump jockey and suggested his brother should stay with us for a while but neither Marie nor I had the time to prat about with pupils. To cut a short story even shorter he nevertheless arrived and was put in the large room above the coach house; it had been renovated and any guests we had staying at that time were given that room. The open wooden lath stairway leading to the old granary had no carpet and after Peter's brother had gone to bed and all the lights were out, I started my 'Alfred Hitchcock lame shuffle' up the stairs and my stick went tap tap tap, and my feet shuffle shuffle shuffle; bloody frightening - even I was scared and I knew it was me! It was most decidedly reminiscent of a horror film. Suddenly the door burst open at the top of the stairs and our lanky guest was down in a couple of leaps. It was pitch black because I'd removed the electric fuse and, as he brushed past me, he let out a scream. We later found him in the village phone box, having phoned his brother to come and collect him. He wouldn't go back to the house and I don't know why but he never came to stay again!

We didn't have a busy social life, and didn't seek one; Marie would play a fair amount of golf and became a member of three clubs. We went racing a great deal, whether we had runners or not, and I always enjoyed the evenings when we took the boys for a meal, usually to the Faulkenburg Arms in Coxwold, a delightful pub in a most picturesque little village near Thirsk. Generally, it was a question of there not being sufficient hours in the day to get through all that had to be done for we didn't have any outside staff whatsoever. Being born a workaholic was not a very clever idea and I didn't always get my priorities right. But at no time do I feel that I ever neglected Marie or the boys; I was always one hundred per cent behind anything they wanted to do.

Amusing incidents were always occurring - there was the time Marie and I were doing a sharp canter on a grass track across the moors. The weather was appalling and worsened as we ran into a blinding hail storm. The pain was unbearable as the icy spikes cut into our faces. At the speed we were travelling it meant there would be fifty strides to the furlong and after I had counted four hundred I called out to Marie through the blizzard "A mile Marie" meaning that we had done the intended distance of the work. What Marie did, instead of pulling up, was to give the most delightful smile from her frozen face - she thought I'd said "Smile Marie" - crikey, what a cracking girl.

One morning, when coming back from exercise, we were crossing the shallow ford which ran through the village and where a whole crowd of red faced Muscovy ducks used to congregate. They were so funny the way they flopped about and were always completely knackered from too much bonking. Suddenly a small coloured beach ball was blown into the stream from somewhere or other and commenced bouncing about on the water; on seeing this one of the ducks got terribly excited and quickly paddled and splashed its way to where the ball was and, without taking much of a look, jumped on top and gave it a good shagging. Marie's expression was absolutely ace as she said "The dopey c**t" - lovely humour!

I must mention the occasion when even Marie's sense of fun was put to the test. It was when an uninvited financial advisor called. Marie and he were having coffee in the kitchen when I entered wearing a wig I'd made from the hair of a horse's tail which I'd trimmed. Actually I didn't think it looked too bad, though probably with the fringe and straggly bits sticking out from under the cap had a touch of the Wurzel Gummidge about it! The fellow kept looking at me and, in a very serious manner, I eventually said to him "You are wondering if it's a topper, aren't you - you are not sure, are you? - Well, yes, it is and what's more I made it". I then asked would he like me to knock him one up as he was going a bit thin on top! I just had to go outside to laugh; I was in stitches and didn't go back into the house until he'd gone. It was the expression of total bewilderment on his face that had been so funny, but Marie didn't find it at all amusing.

On a more serious note - I had what I thought was a brilliant idea that very nearly went disastrously wrong. I decided to prepare for a way in which we could keep the horses exercised during a bad winter. I built, with all the straw that I took out from the stables each day, a hundred yard round canter in the paddock at the back of the stables. The maze like structure had sides of packed straw some eight feet high and the canter inside would be a couple of yards wide and protected from the elements. As it so happened the winter was not that severe, though we did use the 'canter' quite often. Getting rid of the straw was going to be the problem and, as the paddock was going to require re-seeding, I decided to burn it. I poured on the petrol and struck the match before really contemplating what could happen. There was suddenly a change in direction of the strong wind. Hell, I all but panicked as lighted straw sailed over the buildings and into the village; the utter stupidity of what I'd done. For several days, until the fire was completely out, I was ready to release all the horses out into the open field. Naturally the fire brigade was called in and Marie had more than one trip down to the fish and chip shop at Thirsk, asking for "Two fish and a large portion of chips - twenty times, please". All's well that ends well, but it might not have been so.

Not at any stage of my life have I been overdrawn and in general have had good relations with the banks, though not on the occasion of which I'm about to tell. It all began when Marie went to Catterick Races on her own, which was unusual, but I was exceptionally busy that afternoon with things to do in the stables. I have forgotten the exact circumstances but I owed a bookmaker £2,000 and asked Marie to pay him for me; and take the money from my desk to do so - saying there were a couple of £1,000 wads in the top middle drawer. It so happened, Marie wanted to pay into our joint account at Barclays a similar amount of her own money. To do this she cashed a cheque for £2,000 at, what was then, the Westminster, where she kept her personal account. Then, putting the wads she received into her handbag, dashed across the market square in Thirsk to Barclays to pay it in. It would have been far less hassle to pay over a cheque, but Marie wished to do it her way.

She was rather late and wanted to get to the races for the first, so told the cashier this and also said to him "You make the slip out for £2,000, the money is correct because I've just got it out of the Westminster". With that she was out of the bank, in the car, and away. The bookmaker I'd asked Marie to pay was not at the races, so on her return home she put what she thought was my cash back into the desk.

Next day both Marie and I were on our way to Teeside Park

(Marie was driving) when I realised the two wads I'd asked Marie to take the previous day did, in fact, contain £2,500 in each and not £1,000 and, apparently, the ones she put back into the desk were those she had obtained from her private account and were held together by elastic bands. It was plain what had happened - in the rush Marie had got the various wads mixed in her handbag.

I immediately phoned the bank from the car, spoke to the cashier that Marie had dealt with and was utterly astounded at what he had to say. Yes, Marie did give him £5,000 but, as she had said it was £2,000, and there was no need to count it because it had just been obtained from the Westminster, he had put £2,000 into our account and returned the surplus £3,000 to the Westminster. What the Hell - Teeside Races was no longer on the agenda but a visit to the two banks most certainly was; Marie turned the car round and it was full speed to Thirsk.

It looked very much as if there had been some collusion between the girl at the Westminster and the fellow at Barclays. The manager at the former said to us that his staff had told him the books would not have balanced if the money had not been replaced, so in his opinion his cashier had given Marie £3,000 too much which, of course, was a load of popycock. Everyone was in agreement that Marie should have watched the money being counted when handed over at Barclays but this was not the issue for there was no dispute about how much was handed in. We had a war on our hands; Marie and I went backwards and forwards from one bank to the other. At closing time I found myself in an empty manager's office at Barclays and all those I'd had discussions with were nowhere to be found. Of course, the real evidence lay with the wrappers that were around the money paid in, my money, because they had recently come from a bank and would show that the money was not that from the

Westminster; remember, Marie's money was held together by elastic bands. However, we were led to believe that vital evidence had been destroyed, when it went through the shredder. Matters didn't look too promising, well not until one of the bank girls called me to one side just as I was leaving to go home. She said she would be in trouble if it was discovered that she had been talking to me, but the all important wrappers were not shredded immediately. In fact they were put into the bin and only after my phone call had they been located and destroyed. She also revealed that the two cashiers involved, one from each bank, were friendly enough to have been on holiday together. I promised I would not involve her in the matter, which I didn't, but I now knew for certain there had been a conspiracy.

On returning home we telephoned and spoke to the inspectors at both banks Regional Head Offices. A couple of days later we were interviewed and our case was that when Barclays cashier realised £5,000 had been handed over and not £2,000 he could tell by the wrappers the money had not come from the Westminster. So, there was no need to contact anyone at that bank, unless, of course, there was a conspiracy. Also, the fact that we had not been informed on what had happened, nor were we going to be, was a critical point. It showed what the cashier thought, which was that Marie and I would not miss the £3,000 or, if we did, would not realise where it had gone! There was an extensive enquiry, the result of which was Barclays repaid us the £3,000 plus interest and expenses; we also received a letter of apology from them, but nothing from the Westminster, who in fact would not even repay Barclays. Needless to say Marie closed her account with them. The enquiry came down hard on the manager at Barclays and we were told he was transferred to Bridlington. Personally I consider he should have been posted fifty miles further east and, as for the cashier, I never saw him again and would be astounded if the bank had continued to employ him.

During the whole time I held a full trainer's licence (Nigel took it over in 1980) both boys were race riding, but, because of their ages, Col was well established even before Nigel began, though the phrase "well established" wasn't in Col's vocabulary. He would say "No jockey is ever established". Actually Col and Nigel rode the winners of over 400 and 250 races respectively but the figures don't give a true indication of their achievements for, when they were riding, jockeys had not the same opportunities for mounts as their present compatriots. They were in the top flight for over a decade and in the '74-'75 season Col was fourth in the Jockeys Championship, behind Tommy Stack, Graham Thorner and John Francome and ahead of, notably, Ron Barry, Bob Davies, Michael Dickinson and J. J. O'Neill. Nigel achieved third place in the amateur list in the same season, when only seventeen - yet neither really reached the heights their abilities and dedication warranted. So often it was a question of staying clear of injuries and being in the right place at the right time. Marie and I were an enormous help in launching their careers and they were extremely fortunate to inherit from Marie so much ability in the saddle. However, at times, probably my reputation for punting was a drawback for them. I was always aware of the situation so rarely backed a horse they rode, other than our own, but, on such occasions that I did, the horse in question would not have been discussed; their rides for other yards never were. People didn't appreciate how we could have breakfast together yet not mention certain aspects of the day's racing - but that's how it was. In those days racing folk weren't so informative as now; jockeys would not have given television interviews and talked about the chances of their intended rides. It's something I'm completely against, it shows a complete disregard of owners.

Marie and I got great pleasure from their successes, but also suffered at times, by witnessing so many of their crashing falls and sharing the cruel disappointments, which all jockeys have to endure.

They worked exceptionally hard and, even before turning professional, were dashing all over the country, riding work and schooling in the mornings, then on to the races in the afternoons. It was not unusual for them to leave home some mornings at four o'clock, drive up to Scotland or down south, and not get back until late in the evening. I can remember their first cars, Col's a blue mini whilst Nigel chose one of the smaller Fords; it was definitely 'have saddle will travel' and thank goodness the roads weren't so busy in the seventies. Col once went down to Wye when there was a racecourse there, just for one ride, then up to Perth and back the following day - some motoring in a mini!

Right from the very start both were recognised as being very good and much respected and in the main liked by the other jockeys, both professional and amateurs alike. There was one instance though that was decidedly unpleasant. Col was only sixteen at the time and had been riding at Catterick when I noticed, whilst he was taking a bath in the evening, that his back was covered with whip marks. I naturally asked "What has happened?" He told me that he had unavoidably taken 'so and so's' ground and the marks on his back were the result of retaliation. Of course, had the stewards known what had happened it would have been a long suspension for the jockey in question and, as he now has a high administration post abroad, I will refrain from mentioning his name. Col told me he had quietly sorted the matter and they had come to an agreement, that from then on the rail position was Col's! Those weren't the exact words he used but I guess you will have got the drift, Exactly! Col rode all Vic Thompson's horses early on. Vic trained and, in fact, still does, on the coast up in Northumbria. He never had a good class of horse but had a lot of runners, all making for experience. Vic has always been a hell of a nice fellow and very amusing; I remember Col having rather a nasty fall at Market Rasen on one of his horses and received a bollocking for getting some blood on the yellow section of the red and yellow silks. "I will have to have them cleaned now" was Vic's sympathetic conclusion! Another time we were at Cartmel when the Olympic Games were taking place - no, not at Cartmel and I happened to say to Vic there was a new world record for the longest jump - something like nine metres. Vic came back with "Don't you mean nine minutes!"

Ian Vickers was another trainer who admired Col's riding very early on, even when still an amateur. He had a small yard at Sadberge, near Darlington, though it was his father who held the licence. They were very astute and brought off some terrific coups, particularly with a mare called Molly Faye. I distinctly remember a race she won at Wetherby, at one of their May evening meetings; Col somehow conjured up an extra effort in the last few strides, to hang on by a short head at 3/1. Considering the mare was giving the whole field a couple of stone it was a fantastic run, and brought off one almighty gamble for the yard.

Col also rode for Mick Easterby in the early days as he did throughout his years in the saddle. Bumper races had not come into being in this country at that time but Col, as a professional, did have a couple of winners 'on the level' for him - I think it would be more correct to put 'on the flat' for him!

Col had won several races on a very nice horse of Mick's called Royal Roseberry, owned by Bill Jackson, a local farmer; in fact Nigel also rode the horse once or twice when Col was injured and won a valuable race at Wetherby on him by a neck at 10/1. Mick however was not a happy bunny and gave Nigel a real rollicking for not obeying instructions, which were to win by a head! On another occasion, at Hexham, the same horse was to run in a two mile chase with five runners and Col had been booked to ride. Mick phoned me in the morning, asking was Marie going racing because, if she were, he would like her to examine his horse. He continued to tell me it was lame at the moment and if Marie didn't think it should run would she give 'oss a lame certificate. I asked "Why send the horse on a two hour journey if it's not right and why put the onus on Marie; get the course vet to look him over". No - he wanted Marie to do the examination so that, if it was still lame, she could tell Col. You will have gathered Mick wasn't intending going up to Hexham. Half an hour after the first call I got another - "Mick here, a change of plans - 'oss seems all right now; Marie needn't examine him, and I've decided to go up there". Just before the race I distinctly saw Mick and the owner backing another horse in the race but only to small amounts and viewed it as a total sham. Royal Roseberry looked a million dollars in the paddock and sparkled in the race itself, winning by eight lengths. After the race Mick came over to me and said "It's a good thing we ran but it's a pity you must have been put off backing 'oss". I replied "But I wasn't - in fact I had £5,000 to £2,000 about him" away from the course with Ladbrokes!

I received the following story first hand, from a person who bought a horse from Mick, to go flapping up in Scotland. He had paid £1,500 for the little sprinter, when Mick came up with a bright idea. It was that he should also buy the 'oss in the next stable for a couple of hundred. The Scotsman declined but Mick was insistent, saying "You had better take it lad, you will need bugger for spare parts for the one you've bought!"

During the spring of '72, when he was seventeen, Col had a few rides for Ken and Rhona Oliver. Then, on turning professional at the beginning of the following season, he rode many more of the Oliver runners and when Barry Brogan, their stable jockey, left the following year he got his big breakthrough by becoming their number one. Col stayed five years until landing the plum job at Fred Rimell's down in Worcester, in the Autumn of '77. Whilst Col was at the Olivers, Nigel joined him for a time, though, of course, they both actually lived in Yorkshire. Some mornings, in fact most mornings, after they had motored up to Hawick where the Olivers trained, they would school up to fifty horses between them. It seemed rather like hard work to me but Col was riding some marvellous horses, such as Chandigar, Cantastar, Mr Bee, Tom Morgan, Fort Vulgan, Prize Crew and many others, including Treggaron. He won the Greenall Whitley at Haydock as a six year old and was made ante post favourite for the following year's Grand National but unfortunately fell at Bechers Brook. Actually both boys rode in several Nationals without ever completing the course, again it was just how the cookie crumbled and crumbled being very much the operative word, when it comes to the Grand National!

One of Olivers owners was Cyril Young, a bank manager with the Bank of Scotland, at their branch in Coldstream. He actually lived above 'the shop' and, apart from having racehorses, he also kept quite a number of greyhounds, not only in this country but in Australia as well. The best he ever owned was the prolific West Park Mustard, who at one time held the record with the longest winning run of twenty consecutive victories. What made the achievement even more remarkable was that she gained her successes after having surgery to rectify damaged toes. Col has a most lovely porcelain statue of her, given to him by Cyril Young who, incidentally, had quite a reputation of being a heavy gambler. He asked Col to find him a nice young horse off the flat, to go hurdling and gave him a figure of £20,000 to spend. The search found Prince Pepe, a three year old out of Peter Walwyn's yard, for just £12,000. He was a typical Walwyn stamp of a horse and looked cheap at the money. Cyril Young was delighted with the purchase and asked me if I would take charge of the horse for a while so that Col could do some schooling. I was mystified, for had his new acquisition gone straight to Scotland Col still could have done that. It transpired that what Cyril Young really wanted was for the Tinklers to get Prince Pepe ready for a gamble. Not wishing to tread on the Oliver's toes, because of their association with Col, I did as Ken Oliver wished and let him be registered as the trainer. We weren't breaking any rules as my yard was licensed and I wasn't going to charge any fees. I phoned Ken every day to ask for instructions and informed him of the horses progress. Marie reckoned she could get him straight in less than a couple of months so the complex arrangements weren't going to be for long. Everyone was in agreement to the suggestion that he should run at Teeside Park, my happy hunting ground, in a three year old hurdle race there. The big day arrived; it was Autumn, yet a lovely warm sunny afternoon. Prince Pepe had done everything Marie had asked of him in training and I was full of confidence about the outcome. When we arrived at the course we had to wait some time for Oliver's staff to take over because, without an official runner, I was not allowed in the racing stables that day. It was only a minor hiccup but one that shouldn't have occurred. I saw Ken who said that Cyril Young wanted me to put his money on and handed me a very small bundle. Ken also gave me a few hundred of his own to invest but I recall thinking - surely Cyril Young was going to have more on than I'm handling for him. I never got to meet him but we did speak once or twice on the phone and he seemed a most pleasant person.

The outcome of the race was as expected, Col giving 'The Prince' a lovely ride and they beat twenty others by six lengths in an absolute canter. I got 5/2 to all the money though the starting price was 13/8. I never did get to know the whys and wherefores of the Cyril Young punt, so, for me, the mystery has never been solved. Col was second on him in his next race, it being Prince Pepe's first run from the Oliver's yard, but the partnership won quite a few good races after that.

A couple of weeks after the Teeside success, I got a phone call from Ken Oliver. In a very shaky voice he informed me that the Jockey Club were withholding the prize money for Prince Pepe's Teeside Park win because he had not passed the dope test taken after the race. Ken was clearly shaken for he was aware that, being the trainer, he would have to carry the can if I'd been monkeying around; of course, I hadn't, but Ken wasn't to know that. As far as I was concerned no rules had been broken in any way whatsoever and I was quite prepared to attend an Inquiry. It was at a time when the Jockey Club told trainers "Stop using steroids because we can now detect the substance". What the vets had found in Prince Pepe was the tail end of a course of treatment given before we had him. He was tested clear after his next race, therefore the Stewards took no action and the Stockton prize money was paid; Ken had been a worried man and had visualised having his trainer's licence withdrawn.

Col's time at the Rimells was very exciting at first, with yet again some marvellous horses to ride, and the winners kept rolling in. But he became not entirely happy; he was well aware that other jockeys had come and gone before him and realised it would only be a matter of time before he was 'unseated'. The trouble being, Mercy Rimell was far too critical, though Col has never had a bad word for her and recalls what a hell of a nice guy Fred Rimell was.

Of all the horses Col rode whilst at Rimell's, I particularly remember Western Rose winning a Novice Chase at Nottingham in an absolute canter, Monte Christo when he won at the Cheltenham Festival and Connaught Ranger, owned by the very generous Jim McCaughey. Col rode Connaught Ranger to win the Irish Champion Hurdle by five lengths at 5/1. But the one that gave me the most pleasure and received my biggest cheers was Canit, when they won the then named Topham Trophy over two and a half miles of The Grand National course. What made it so special was that Col rode having broken his collar bone the previous day and it was no 'Mickey Mouse' fracture either. Of course, nobody knew about it other than the Tinklers, that is until he tried to dismount in the winners enclosure! It wasn't as if Col had been a passenger, far from it, as he really rode into the big fences and got some terrific leaps from the young horse. Not so many races were televised at that time but that one was, which made it all the more pleasurable.

Even when he was first jockey to the Olivers and later, when filling the same position at Rimell's, Col still rode for many other yards, ours included. He rode Night Nurse for Peter Easterby when he was third in The Champion Hurdle but missed out on 'Peterhof', when that horse won the Triumph Hurdle at 10/1, having won on him previously. Col was unable to take the ride because he had been suspended for four days (the only time in the whole of his career) farcically for not letting a fellow jockey come through on the inside at Kelso. I had a very large wager on Peterhof as insurance against any disappointment I might have to endure but it made no difference - money was no compensation. On a happier note, I was thrilled when he rode Mrs. Eastons great little chaser, Park House, to win the Stones Ginger at Sandown Park, by three lengths at 12/1!

He also took over the reins at Tony Dickinson's powerful stables for a while in the mid seventies, when his son Michael had a nasty fall at Hexham. Michael was out of action for some time and Col rode something like thirty winners from the fifty rides he had for them, which included 'Broncho' when he won the Arkle at the Cheltenham Festival and 'Autuma' in The Great Yorkshire. There was one period when he actually rode eight winners, all chasers, from ten rides.

In spite of all the success, Col left Rimells by the end of the '79 - '80 season and became stable jockey to the voluble and likeable Peter Calver at Ripon. Peter, a veterinary surgeon, never had a large string but I'm sure because of his other commitments working for the bloodstock agencies it was by choice. Col rode a great many winners for the stable, notably Cabar Feidh in a top class chase at Ascot.

It wasn't exactly musical chairs but some of the top jockeys would move around, as they do today, and I'm sure Col would have landed another top job, in a powerful yard, had he not suffered the terrible fall at Newcastle. More on that after I tell you about further successful gambles the boys were involved in for the Tinkler yard. Wild Hawk comes to mind, a tiny four year old we bought privately from John O'Neill, of the O'Neill brothers, in Northern Ireland. We gave him a couple of runs at the commencement of the '73-'74 season, to see exactly what we had and he was second on both occasions. The races brought him to a peak for his third run, which was in a four year old novice hurdle at Market Rasen. I'd made him some special shoes for his uneven feet and we kept very hush hush about the outstanding chance we thought he had of winning. That was the advantage of not employing anyone from outside the family and in Wild Hawk's case we were the sole owners. We poured the money on away from the course at 11/2 and Col and the little chestnut beat Ron Barry on the short priced favorite by a couple of lengths.

Prior to Nigel's first ride under Rules he had been in a couple of Town Plates alongside Marie and had also been in an occasional point to point. However, the serious business commenced a few days after his fifteenth birthday, over hurdles at Wetherby. It wasn't a fairy tale start to our young jockey's career; in fact it was several months before he rode his first winner on a horse called Nimble Joe though, during that time, he didn't have more than half a dozen rides. Nimble Joe was a quirky old fellow, who would remember where the gate was that led on to a course and try to duck out as he passed it during a race. Nigel could cope quite adequately on the first circuit but riding a finish was difficult when the gate was on the run in to the winning post.

We entered him at Sedgefield on Boxing Day with a distinct plan in mind. The gate on to the course there is about a hundred yards before the finish but the gate where the horses leave the course after a race is a similar distance past the winning post. To fox the old boy, on the morning of the race I walked him round the parade ring, then took him on to the course at the exit gate; actually I repeated the ruse several times. To get him on to the course for the race itself I put a hood over his head, which Nigel removed before cantering down to the start. Nimble Joe therefore thought there was only one way off the track and back to the stables and that was through the gate after the winning post. I can remember every yard of the race, there were only half a dozen runners and Nigel kidded the horse along, led at the last and went on to win by a couple of lengths. We brought off quite a gamble punting away down to 7/4 but, far more important, Nigel had ridden his first winner.

Nigel was still at school, consequently there were further

headlines such as "Fifteen year old Maharaja rides winner!" There was a bonus for the Tinklers because as Nigel rode into the winners enclosure Col was doing exactly the same thing, at practically the same time, forty miles away at Wetherby, on a horse called Prize Crew.

Most young and inexperienced jockeys are easily recognisable by the way they sit - they lack a firmness in the saddle - but not Nigel. He had, for one of his age, done a tremendous amount of 'riding work' and it showed. He was a natural and, throughout his career, a very intelligent rider. He used to say "By the time I get down to the start I know what the horse is thinking!" Horses ran for him; they appreciated his gentle handling, he was, and still is for that matter, a horseman. He can go into a field, catch an unbroken yearling which has never had a saddle on its back and, within less than an hour, have it cantering away.

Nimble Joe was the beginning of a whole string of successful gambles Nigel helped to bring off for the stable as he did likewise for others that were recognised as punting yards, notably John Yardley and Jack Hardy. In fact only once did a real gamble of ours go astray when he was in the saddle. It was on a horse called Sandmoor Court at Uttoxeter where Nigel came too early and was caught on the run in. Even in that instance my money was only lent for the same combination won a couple of races the following month at Nottingham and Newcastle, coincidentally on both occasions being backed down from 3/1 to 2/1 and winning very easily. There is rather an interesting little story attached to the Uttoxeter race. At the time I had an arrangement with Colin Miles of Ladbrokes, that the firm would lay me the Sporting Life (a Racing Paper of that time) betting forecast price or akin to it, about any of our horses. On this particular occasion Sandmoor Court was bracketed with the 20/1 others, when a more realistic price would have been a tenth those odds. There had obviously been a cock-up when the paper was put together. I believe Colin Miles thought that I was a party to arranging the false odds for I was never again offered the facility. If I'm correct in my assumption, he was rather insulting my intelligence because no way would I have expected to be layed such a price. In fact I was offered and took 5/2 to serious money.

Now for Charlie Bettyes and the cockup of all time! Back in the early part of '72 we gave him four runs - two at Catterick, one at Wetherby and another at the now non existent Stockton. Even though a seller was amongst the quartet he was never seen with any sort of a chance; in fact he was last at Wetherby and usually started in the 33/1 bracket. 'Charlie B' was a very good looking dark brown gelding and a five year old when we first acquired him but was rather weak and needed time to mature. After those first few runs we turned him away for a couple of years for, apart from anything else, we felt there was a very slight strain to a tendon. As there was no sign of lameness I wasn't too concerned but naturally I'd rather it hadn't been there. Marie brought him back into training during the summer of '74, and he had developed into a nice strong sort; he could really jump and was no slouch. After two or three months he looked absolutely magnificent; I was confident that he would bring off a gamble, in a seller, doing hand stands. We had a board meeting with Gordon Morley who had a half share in the horse; it was all systems go from then on. We found the ideal race for the job, a two mile selling handicap hurdle at Newcastle towards the end of October and it was agreed that I should handle all the punting. Secrecy was going to be at a premium and I stressed that upon Gordon in no uncertain manner. Nigel, who had been looking forward to the ride, was unfortunately injured a few days prior to the race, so Col took over.

Wednesday, the 30th October arrived and I decided 'Charlie' would have to come into the ring late and be well rugged up to hide the stunning condition he was in, at least until some of the money was on! As expected he had been given bottom weight of only ten stone; there were ten runners but it seemed rather an above average seller - but no hassle.

It was a mixed meeting with the first three races being on the flat, which meant there would be a larger crowd than for a usual mid-week all jumping card and, of course, more bookmakers. Our horse was quoted at 33/1 in the racing papers and I promised Gordon, who incidentally only wanted a couple of hundred on, that I would give him first 'pickings'. On arriving at Newcastle I went over to the betting ring and nonchalantly strolled around but immediately sensed something was wrong - too many of the layers were taking a good look at me. Coral's man on the rails called me over and said "Colin, can I have a chat". What he should have said was "Colin, can I hit you on the head with a hammer" because what he had to say was just as devastating. Apparently, Gordon's wife was very ill in a nursing home in Harrogate and Gordon had seen her on the day prior to the race; he'd mentioned that Charlie Bettyes would definitely win the following day and Colin was going to have thousands on. The first part of his statement I considered true and the second part wasn't going to be possible but I did intend to punt away until the bookmakers said "No more".

The inevitable happened - Gordon's wife told the nurses, the nurses told the doctors; they then collected £45 between them and sent the handyman down to Corals to back the horse. He enthusiastically explained to the cashier why the £45 was going on a horse with a string of duck eggs and which had not been seen on a racecourse for nearly a thousand days. The manager at the betting shop was quickly on to Head Office and they, in turn, were soon on to their man at Newcastle. Damage done. Coral's representative told me he'd only mentioned it to a couple of the other bookmakers who, by that time, would have mentioned it to a couple more and so on and so on - Exactly. They are not charitable institutions and I realised it was now going to be most difficult to get on. I'd already said goodbye to the 33/1; in fact a quarter of those odds would not be available and most would knock me back at any price. What an absolute Bollocks! Three years work and literally thousands of pounds down the drain. What a calamity, so much effort and thought had gone into the project - for that's what all major gambles are - projects.

'Charlie B' miraculously opened up at 6/1 and stayed at that price, but only because other horses were being heavily backed. As I had visualised, because there were only a few bookmakers prepared to do business with me, I got about £1,400 on altogether and, of course, a couple of hundred of that was Gordon's. He was rather cross when I paid him out just £1,200 and denied telling his wife; no wonder I didn't want owners. You will have gathered that Col and 'Charlie B' won the race, which they did by a rather easy length but Col reported the horse had hung, which gave us cause for some anxiety; we wondered, had he sprained the leg again. The day had been very much an anti-climax, even though we had won the race and won money, I felt we had really lost out.

To continue the saga, Charlie Bettyes next ran on the following Saturday at Catterick, again in a handicap seller and this time Nigel, who had made a good recovery from his injury, was in the saddle. 'Charlie B' had a 5lb penalty for the win but Nigel's allowance actually countered that. We certainly lumped on, with the bookmakers being not as generous pricewise but more accommodating this time. We backed him down to 6/4 and he won nicely by a couple of lengths. Wetherby was the horse's next outing, though Nigel considered the track wouldn't be suitable and so it proved, with them finishing fourth. It was decided to take 'Charlie B' back to Catterick for his next run, where he again won, this time Nigel getting him home by five lengths and we unexpectedly got 5/1 about our money, probably due to a combination of a couple of other horses being heavily backed and the fact that 'Charlie B' was beaten at Wetherby. The horse had won three sellers and there hadn't been a bid for him at any of the subsequent auctions. We next ran him in a big field, again at Catterick, but this time our horse was beaten a short head, after being badly hampered in a rather rough race. Nigel lodged an objection but to no avail. Admittedly we again backed him but not to a great amount because we felt 'Charlie B' was going off the boil. He had one more outing for us after that, when he finished lame and, unfortunately, slightly strained the leg about which we had suspicions.

I gave my share in him to some people, on the understanding that he was not to race again and be kept solely for hacking about. Gordon Morley wasn't so generous and charged them £200 for his half share, which the new owners thought entitled them to break their undertaking with me. I was very sad when they sold him on to run in hunter chases and it wasn't long before he broke down more severely. He was a lovely horse and deserved better but I could do nothing about it. We won a lot of money backing him but it should have been considerably more; both Gordon and his wife died some years ago but their daughter Liz keeps the family interest in racing alive.

Col brought off another gamble for us when he rode Milesian Star, owned by Norman Grainger, who had a riding school on the

East Coast and gave pony rides on the sands. He trained under permit and when I first saw Milesian Star running at Hexham I immediately thought that if I could get hold of him, we could bring off a real 'touch' in a seller! Norman and I did a deal over the training fees and a plan of action was put into operation. We gave Milesian Star half a dozen runs in handicap hurdles, which produced a couple of placed efforts, which was far better than he had been accomplishing. A few months complete rest was next on his agenda and, when he went back into training, his work consisted entirely of being lunged at the canter. He would do three miles every day, which was basically a hundred times round a 'circus ring', carrying a saddle and weight cloth but wasn't ridden. In fact the first time anyone got on his back in months was in the paddock at Thirsk, before going down to the start for an amateur riders flat race there. I was hoping the Thirsk run, plus a couple of gallops, would put him right for the seller I had in mind. All my plans went up in smoke when Marie finished third on the little fellow at 50/1; surely a good enough reason for divorce! Incidentally, it was Marie's first ride on the flat under Rules and it would have been folly to take in a selling hurdle shortly after that run. In the circumstances we kept him to the level for the rest of the season, with Marie notching up a couple more places. Milesian Star was given the whole of the following jumping term off and brought back at the beginning of the 77-78 season for one almighty gamble in a seller at Market Rasen. He won unchallenged by twenty lengths at 3/1. It was an off course punt with the money being spread about between a dozen bookmakers and obviously one can see by the starting price very little came back. We were also fortunate with the bidding for it only cost a few hundred to retain him at the subsequent auction. The following week at Southwell we again went for another seller, this time with Nigel on board, which they won at 6/5. We'd not had the same sort of bet as the previous week - nevertheless, nice enough. After the race there was definitely some heat in one of his legs so when the auction for him commenced we refrained from bidding. The new owners ran him a few times over the following years but he never won again.

Incidentally, there is a very amusing story attached to Milesian Star or, to be more precise, about the set of colours he carried on his first run for us. They were home made, with the crash helmet cover being a tea cosy, with an extra large cardboard peak sewn on. As Nigel walked into the parade ring the piece of cardboard flipped down and over his eyes; he couldn't see a bloody thing - it was hilarious. I'm not sure where he got rid of the mind-boggling head wear but I know it didn't get down to the start!

As I've mentioned, another person we trained for was Ray Quincey. Ray would be about my age and loved his racing; I'd often spoken to him but we had our first real conversation at Wetherby one day. He told me he owned a couple of horses called Some Hazard and Galah Bird and suggested I take them over, with a view to organising something to punt on over hurdles. I was naturally very much in favour and they duly arrived at our place. Some Hazard was quite a character, the old horse being built like a prop forward and I'm sure he thought he was playing rugby when he was barging his way past other horses, he certainly would not have got away with it nowadays, with all the cameras about. First time out for us he finished second, though was rather burly for that run but it was three wins on the trot after that. A seller at Wetherby, then a couple of good class handicap hurdles at Catterick and Kelso. Unfortunately, his reign was of short duration for there was a recurrence of former tendon trouble. You might be thinking Colin seems to have had a lot of leg trouble with his horses; I'm afraid that's par for the course with jumpers, it's a rough old game. Nigel was brilliant on Some Hazard, particularly at Wetherby, where they came up the straight with Nigel switching first to the right and then left as they overtook the entire field to win by three lengths. The bookmakers generosity amazed me for he started at 13/2, 11/4 and 3/1 respectively for his successes and we bettered those prices to some pretty hefty wagers. Marie liked the horse very much and no doubt he would have gone point to pointing with her had he stayed sound.

As for Galah Bird, she only had a few runs during her first season with us. What with one thing and another we actually had the mare a couple of years before she was absolutely right; we put her in a two mile selling handicap hurdle at Teeside Park. Both boys had already ridden her and, for no reason in particular, Col had the ride. On the day the mare looked 'par excellence' and ran likewise winning by six lengths but not before having been backed down from 4/1 to 6/4. That sort of drop in price speaks volumes and it was the late John Joyce, the leading course bookmaker in the north at that time, who handled my pretty substantial punt. Ray Quincey was delighted in spite of not having the size of wager he originally intended. But the added bonus for him was that he never expected such a good price and there was no bid for her at the auction.

As a matter of interest, Nigel rode a horse called Gala Lad (no connection) in the previous race for Jack Hardy, they weren't successful that afternoon but the combination won their next six consecutive races.

There was a sequel to the wager we had at Stockton. As Marie, Nigel and I arrived back home at Boltby (Col was in a separate car) we heard the phone ringing from the house. What with the amount I had taken with me, plus what I'd won, I had cash in every pocket; in trying to find the back door key, I put four cellophane packets, each containing £2,500, on top of the car boot. Clutching further money in my hands and stuffing more back into my pockets, I dashed to the phone, forgetting about the money on the car - that's until I saw the vehicle being driven out of the yard. I remembered it then! I ran out of the house as Marie was coming in and she told me "As we didn't require the car, Nigel has borrowed it for the evening". Panic, bloody panic and we had no car phone at that time; what is more it was getting dark. Marie and I ran down the road for fifty yards - nothing, absolutely nothing. They must be in the grass verge for surely they could not have stayed on the car for long; we looked in the grass for what seemed ages but eventually found them, all four cellophanes. A cage full of 'monkeys' had nearly escaped, yes, twenty of them. The manner in which Galah Bird had won meant it had nearly been a question of 'easy come - easy go'!

Three weeks later we took Galah Bird to Wetherby, where she drifted in the market and was well beaten. It was then to Haydock Park with a similar performance. It was however a different story three days later, again with Nigel in the saddle, when we went back to Teeside Park. We knew the track would suit and poured the money on, again backing her down from 4/1 to 6/4. She won by seven lengths and again there was no bid at the auction. We gave her a couple more runs but then she developed a cough, so was given a well earned holiday. It was nice that both boys played their part in the two gambles by sharing the rides but, as always, it had been a Tinkler team effort.

Shortly after that Ray was unfortunately diagnosed as having cancer of the throat; he didn't smoke but was always sucking at sweets. I knew the surgeon who treated him and he remarked that the habit would not have helped matters. Ray wasn't ill that long and soon died. He was married - in fact his wife would often come to the stables but didn't much care for racing. I felt I should go to the cremation so went along and sat at the back of the chapel at the appointed time. The service commenced and the address was all about Harry this and Harry that, then Goodbye Harry - I was obviously at the wrong funeral. I mentioned this to the vicar as he shook my hand as I left the chapel. He was most apologetic and told me Raymond was running late and was next in - I suppose each to his own vocabulary or probably he knew Ray used to play cricket!

I sauntered round the building and in through the main door again, along with others, then sat in the same seat as before. When it came to the chat Raymond was praised for having been a pillar of the community, a great worker for charities (I thought he's laying it on a bit thick). The chat continued "And an inspiration to his sons" - what! the Raymond I knew hadn't got any sons, well not that I knew of. I quickly realised I'd got the wrong funeral again and this must be another Raymond! Mind you I thought it odd that I hadn't recognised any of the congregation either time, though I didn't really know his circle of friends. I heard someone say "I know we are all pleased we came" I thought, does she want to bet on it! Another shake of hands from the Reverend, plus a rather enquiring look and the remark "Wrong one again? well keep fingers crossed; you know what they say - third time lucky." I thought, not for me, I'm going home - 'The dog collar' will be wanting to sell me a season ticket if I hang around much longer!

Another successful gamble that comes to mind was when Nigel rode Torcross at Fakenham, in the summer of '78. The betting that day certainly had a rather fascinating and intriguing look about it but I will start the story from the beginning. Nigel had not long turned professional when he took the mount on the horse at Catterick and finished a well beaten fourth in a novice hurdle. Torcross was trained by Mick Naughton at the time for Bill and Mary Price, who owned a nightclub in Middlesbrough and, on dismounting, Nigel told them that their horse would definitely win a seller. It was not his intention to infer that they should change stables but that's what happened and we got the horse to train.

After four months Marie reckoned she had the horse ready and had managed to keep him sound despite his bad legs. A selling handicap hurdle at Fakenham was chosen for the punt and as always secrecy was the order of the day. With Bill and Mary knowing so many people, I decided they would not be told to have a bet until half an hour before the race. Marie had stressed to me all along that, because of the condition of the off fore, we would have to have him ready for a 'crack' first time out. When Bill discovered we intended running at Fakenham he wanted to hire a helicopter to make the journey less tiring but I soon put a stop to that; we would want to arrive at the course a little more conventionally and be a little less conspicuous!

Marie took Torcross down to Fakenham the day before the race and walked the course a couple of times to make sure the ground was suitable. She was terribly concerned about the going for the rain was belting down and kept phoning me with hourly bulletins. The following morning Marie gave the thumbs up sign; the ground was all right, so the Price's, Nigel and I headed south. I wasn't personally going to use the small band of bookmakers on the course as there would be no more than a dozen in total. I knew Bill wasn't going to have a fantastic punt so I left them to accommodate him. Neither was it going to be difficult to place my bets at starting price but whether any large money would filter back and drastically shorten the price was another matter. We stopped for a coffee on the way down and it was from there that I phoned off my bets. I placed £2,000 with Colin

Webster, the Leeds bookmaker, who assured me he was going to off-load rather discreetly in Scotland and none would get back to the course. I had a similar amount on with John Joyce, who was just as emphatic about no money getting back to Fakenham. Apart from those two wagers I had a further thousand in bits and bobs with other layers. I assumed each thought theirs was the only bet I was having and didn't enlighten them otherwise. I thought as Torcross was not going to be a large price, 'Blower' would not be contacted. For those who don't know what 'Blower' was (I use the past tense for the service no longer exists) I will explain. Basically when a starting price bookmaker wished to hedge some money for one reason or another he could contact the 'Blower' firm at their main office. They, in turn, would phone through on their private lines to their representative at the racecourse and instruct him to back the horse in question. 'Blower' made a charge for the service and the advantage to those wanting to off load is obvious, particularly if they were getting rid of inspired money in a weak market. 'Blower' would endeavour to back it for them at higher odds than the starting price; it wasn't guaranteed to work in their favour but usually did. Most office bookmakers used 'Blower' from time to time but I suppose its usefulness ran out when such as Hills and Ladbrokes offered the trade less complicated facilities.

How wrong I was in thinking that 'Blower' was unlikely to become involved. On arriving at Fakenham we first met Marie who was very enthusiastic about Torcross's chances and she just couldn't see him getting beaten. I then bumped into Bernie who worked for 'Blower'; I'd met him once or twice when racing down south. Apparently he had a load of money from the north to put on Torcross and wasn't long before breaking confidence and telling me it was from John Joyce. What had happened was, the person in Scotland who had received my money from Colin Webster had coincidentally passed it on to John Joyce, who already had my wager of his own to contend with. All this was too much for the Hartlepool layer, hence he contacted 'Blower'. Bernie was obviously looking for a little 'appreciation' as we got into conversation "Colin, there is no need to ask whether you have backed your horse, I know you must have done and, if I put Joyce's cash on, Torcross will go odds on and you don't want that". I remember his next remark "Sod them, we go back a long way". Actually we didn't go back that far but the rest of what he had said was correct! However, I felt there was more to matters than he was letting on. He most likely had a couple of punters he was feeding information to and didn't wish to spoil the price for them either.

With tongue in cheek, Bernie reported back to his bosses after the race, that the course bookmakers wouldn't take his money and the official tag was "No business done". Bill, however, got his cash on at 7/4 using half a dozen of the bookmakers present; mysteriously Torcross then drifted to 2/1 second favourite! There were only eight runners, our horse was the senior of the party and was giving weight away to all bar one. The 6/4 favourite fell at the first but after a circuit Torcross started to go short in his stride and was in trouble; all seemed lost though Nigel had other ideas and didn't push him until they came into the short home straight, with one hurdle to jump. Torcross broke down and jumped across the horse that was alongside, the pair being well clear of the others. Even then Nigel somehow got home, four lengths to the good. There was obviously a stewards' enquiry and no way could we keep the race - but we did. One of the stewards came up to me afterwards and said "We didn't take the race off you because your horse did pass the post first". I appreciated his philosophy and wondered had he also had a punt!

There was, of course, no bid for Torcross with him being lame and sadly he never raced again.

There was an aftermath of inquisitions. Bernie very nearly lost his job and John Joyce pointed a finger at my integrity, until I reminded him of his assurance that he was not going to send any money back to Fakenham. No way did John Joyce, who was a perfect gentleman, and I fall out over the matter; in fact we conducted a lot of business over the following years. He was never afraid to lay a decent bet and was one of the stalwarts of the ring right up to him dying in the mid eighties. Reverting to the hullabaloo, The Sporting Life were anything but complimentary about the whole affair. As for myself, I was just jolly pleased to have won the money and be thankful for a clever trainer (Marie), good jockey, understanding owners, a curious stewards decision, a hell of a game horse - Oh, yes, and the 'Blower' man who didn't Blow It!

Fakenham is the only time a stewards' enquiry has gone in my favour. I have lost a few, one being when Nigel was riding at Bangor in a novice chase. I was watching the race from the hill directly in front of the last fence and looking straight at it. In my opinion and that of many others the result should not have been changed. Nigel had jumped the last alongside the horse that came second to him, admittedly the two horses came close together, but neither obstructed the other. A couple of days after the Bangor farce it was brought to my notice that the vendor at the sales when we bought our horse, had been one of the stewards at the enquiry! I think it prudent to say nothing further. Exactly!

There were a couple of other times when I was involved with enquiries when Nigel was in the saddle or, to be more precise, in one when he wasn't in the saddle but should have been. The absurd situation occurred at Market Rasen at one of their summer evening meetings. Nigel had been riding at Newton Abbot in the afternoon and had hired a plane to get him to the Lincolnshire course as he had a ride for Jack Hardy. Time was going to be tight but he could manage it as long as there were no hitches; unfortunately several developed. The first was when the race prior to the one Nigel wanted to ride in was late starting; this left Nigel circling the course at two thousand feet. I let the Clerk of the Scales know the position, then took a Land Rover to where the aircraft would land; this was in order to speed Nigel to weigh out. Eventually the three mile chase got on its way and as soon as the race was over the plane landed. It was then one big dash to the weighing room and arrived one minute late. Cyril Greenland was Clerk of the Scales though usually he was the number cloth man but, because of the many meetings that day, he had been temporarily promoted. By the time Nigel arrived at the scales Mr. 'G' had already ordered Jack Hardy to find another jockey as he said Nigel was not going to make the time limit for weighing out.

Col took the ride and was beaten a neck. I am not saying Nigel was a better rider than his brother but he had previously ridden the horse and surely that would have been more than a neck advantage. It was a ridiculous situation because Cyril Greenland was well aware of what was happening and should have asked for guidance from the stewards secretary. Yes, Nigel was a minute late to the scales but that often happens when a rider has a fall in a previous race. In my opinion Greenland was being bombastic and I told him so; I did moderate my language, though I was rather angry. The racecourse judge who, incidentally, had got nothing to do with it, reported me to the stewards for causing a disturbance. The stewards were perfectly affable but wished me to apologise and, when I refused, referred the matter to Portman Square. At the London Enquiry I didn't change my stance and was fined £200. Ironically, on my train journey home

I met Bill Smith, a motor trader I knew from Newcastle. We discussed cars and I mentioned I was taking delivery of a new 'Merc' the following week. He knew the car I had, having seen it at the races, and offered me £1,000 more than I was going to receive in the part exchange deal. It was only because new 'Mercs' and, consequently, clean used ones were in short supply at the time; no matter, we shook hands and that was that. It had been a fairly expensive morning but a very profitable day!

There was another stewards enquiry involving Nigel and myself; it was when we ran a horse called Nickadventure at Newcastle in October 1980. I'm going to refrain from saying too much about it, though I have very definite views, but I don't wish to use these pages as a platform for controversy. I will explain briefly what happened: We ran the four year old in a novice hurdle there, Nigel having only recently taken over my trainer's licence and therefore was the trainer as well as the rider. The horse was owned by Norman Heslop, a Newcastle bookmaker, and ran an absolute blinder, starting at 20/1 and was only beaten eight lengths by a couple of potentially useful hurdlers. Unfortunately Nickadventure finished lame; this was confirmed by the racecourse vet and he didn't run again until the following September. I'm sure Nigel would have pulled him up as soon as he felt his stride shortening, had he not been lying third at the time with only one hurdle to jump. The farcical situation was, had he done so, nothing would have been said. We hadn't discussed tactics before the race because we never did but obviously Nigel was going to be fairly sympathetic, with our horse having fallen heavily in his only previous run at Wetherby a couple of weeks earlier. The fact that the Stewards knew that I'd had an even £1,000 on Pay Related, the horse that won the race, didn't help Nigel's cause. I don't believe it was appreciated that I would often back against the stable when not fancying our runner. The subject of Nigel not fully trying was referred to the Jockey Club, where there was a dogmatic lack of understanding. Twenty years on I'm still smarting over the run being misinterpreted, though I suppose it doesn't really matter now and Nigel was philosophical about his holiday.

There was, however, a nice sequel to the story. When Nickadventure did eventually return to the racecourse at Perth eleven months later, Nigel rode a superb race on him to win by half a dozen lengths, with me having backed him down to even money with a major punt. Nickadventure won his next race as well but the injured leg he had sustained at Newcastle, and dismissed by the Stewards, became a problem, further highlighting the injustice that occurred there.

Nigel had his fair share of falls whilst he was riding though, in the main, escaped really serious injury. However, one in particular was rather nasty. It occurred at Wetherby and when I went to see him at the course hospital the doctor told me he was unconscious and, as there was blood coming from one of his ears, they suspected a fractured skull. Actually, it transpired it was the ear drum that had been damaged; I'm not making light of the injury but, whilst not as severe as first thought, it had given Marie and I a hell of a fright.

Apart from the falls, Nigel enjoyed his time as a jockey and never more so than when riding for me on the favourite in a two horse race. His forte was to win by a short head or a head at the most. It is usual, in such races, for some bookmakers to bet on the distance a horse will win by and that was the reason Nigel put his 'finesse' into practice. Mind you, one could never get a lot of money on but I suppose sufficient to make his efforts worth while and it was a lot of fun. Nigel reckoned a head was a long way if one was in front and going the better; besides, it was no use choosing to win by a neck for the judge might make it half a length! I remember at Catterick one afternoon we got Kim's brother Lee to put a couple of hundred on at 5/1 and by the time I stepped in the odds had become what appeared to be a ludicrous evens but even that price turned out to be very generous. At one of Hexham's holiday meetings we'd had a good bet and Nigel cut it really fine - I thought he'd got beaten but he was full of confidence and rode into the winners enclosure. The photo finish print showed he had beaten Ron Barry by the whiskers that had been left on Nigel's mount when the horse was clipped - in fact Ron Barry had literally been beaten by a whisker!

There was another time when Nigel was over confident, though it had nothing to do with a winning distance. Marie and I had gone to Doncaster to back a couple we rather fancied, the first of which went in at 5/2. The bookmakers were under cover in the grandstand that day and as I went to collect my winnings I bumped into a punter I knew and respected. Tapping his pockets he told me he'd been given a couple of thousand to put on Nigel's mount in the novice hurdle, and inquired where I knew anything about the horse. I told him "Absolutely nothing, I never ask either of my boys about their mounts when they are riding for other trainers". The horse in question was Helping Hand and had only ever had one previous run, in which he unseated Nigel at Teeside Park. On the face of it, not the greatest of credentials to warrant a sizeable punt.

There were eight runners and, apart from Nigel, the other jockeys were Col, Ron Barry, Bob Champion, three lesser knowns and an amateur called Heath, who was riding the 50/1 outsider. I expected Helping Hand to open up at 33/1, but sixes was the best price on offer. There was no mad rush but quietly the horse was being systematically backed. I was rather intrigued and, because I had already won a fair amount that day, I decided to go along with the flow of money. I went in with six monkeys (£500 at 6/1) and I could see Marie darting about, with tenners here and twenties there. I had a further bet at 5/1 but the price was tumbling and generally closed at 7/2 - all rather amazing when one considers the form of the horse's only outing.

Raceform's description of the race read - HELPING HAND (N Tinkler) - made headway, led two out, well clear on flat, eased down, won cleverly by threequarters of a length. That does not tell the whole story; jumping the last Nigel was so far in front and hearing over the loud speakers that Helping Hand was well clear he commenced pulling up. It's a long run in at Doncaster and the amateur on Sergeant Boots, seeing what was happening, gave chase. Nigel was not aware of this and was very nearly caught - in fact a stride past the post he was overtaken. I watched, completely aghast; I was stunned and in a state of shock. The money was important, but the fact that Nigel had won a race he'd nearly thrown away is what really mattered. Incidentally, I never did get to know why Helping Hand had been so strongly fancied and had won with such comparative ease.

By the time Marie had collected from a host of bookmakers and I'd picked up my winnings I thought I'd recovered, but the shock had caused the loss of my voice. After several minutes I was able to stammer a few words but nothing too audible. It was amazing the drama should have had such an effect; it was not until well into the evening before I'd fully recovered.

One of the biggest gambles we brought off was when Nigel rode a horse called Helexian at Ayr in the early part of '83. My part in the coup was comparatively small; I'm not saying I was just the 'bottle washer' but with Nigel both training and riding Helexian, he was very much the man. The horse was owned by Barry Stamper whose business at that time was double glazing. He lived in a country mansion near Pontefract and characteristically owned a couple of 'Rollers' - a his and a hers - though he personally didn't drive. I can't recall how we first met but the rest of our association I remember in minute detail. We never had a dispute of any description but I found Barry difficult to understand and was in the mould of a successful Yorkshire businessman.

Helexian had two or three runs over hurdles in the South before Nigel took charge of him for the '82-'83 campaign. His first outing for him was at Wetherby in the November when 20/1; there were twenty four runners and he finished in the middle of the pack. Raceform's quote was 'a bit backward'. He went to Wetherby again for his next outing the following month; was still rather on the plump side yet managed to finish fourth and was only beaten five lengths. To convince the bookmakers that I'd fancied Helexian, I threw £1,000 away by backing him with that amount of money. Nigel considered one more run would put him absolutely 'right' so he took him to Nottingham, where he again finished fourth.

We had learnt that he required soft ground and a flat course to show his best and, as conditions came right at Ayr, Nigel decided to go for the gamble. He had always liked the course and had the distinction of having ridden a winner on the flat, over hurdles and over fences there, whilst only sixteen. It was the last race on the Friday of their two day weekend meeting and, when we discovered the opposition consisted of only Jamastino (trained by Peter Easterby) and half a dozen real mediocrities, I wondered what sort of price the bookmakers were going to offer about our fellow and how the hell were we going to get the money on. Peter Easterby had trained the winner of Helexian's Nottingham race and obviously believed he had the measure of Helexian.

Jamasino had won his last race in a canter at Catterick with Peter's son Tim in the saddle and he was to ride the horse again at Ayr. The Easterby entourage thought they had the race in the bag and went up to Ayr to lump fortunes on their stable runner. We had dotted the I's and crossed the T's and Helexian was bouncing but unfortunately, because of the rain, there were only a few hundred race goers present, and, of course, one of those was Barry Stamper. He was walking about with a small briefcase carrying £30,000 in readies with which to punt. He also had with him a couple of friends who, coincidentally, and I say that without reservation, were his bank manager and his accountant!

As the final race of the day approached the wet weather had not dampened the Scottish bookmakers' vocal chords or their spirits - the last three favourites had been turned over and they were in full cry. As the odds were called pandemonium broke loose; it was equal 5/4 the field about the two main rivals - the layers couldn't possibly win. The more money they took the more they were going to lose - they were committing financial suicide. A further avalanche of money came for Jamastino and it was at this point that Barry Stamper went quietly down the rails, sharing the contents of his briefcase between the bookmakers standing there - £5,000 - £5,000 - £10,000 - soon the entire £30,000 was on at something like 7/4. In fact he even got £5,000 of my money invested, which certainly made life easier for me, though I got £20,000 to £10,000 about the rest of my wager. The ring was so volatile that at one time both horse were odds on - yet at the off it was 8/11 Jamastino and an incredible 5/2 Helexian but I doubt if the bookmakers would have taken any more bets.

I had never known Nigel more confident as I 'legged him up'. He said "I've only got to get alongside Jamastino and he will chuck the towel in - I know the horse, it isn't going to be a race" and it wasn't

- Helexian won by eight lengths. In the whole of my time in racing I've never known such a betting pattern. The volume of money that went on Helexian, in what was virtually a two horse affair and with him still managing to start at 5/2, gives light to the amount that must have gone astray on the Easterby horse. Of course, one must take into account that Helexian had most likely been 'pushed out' in order that he could be backed back, away from the course, at S.P. by some of the bookmakers at Ayr.

John McCririck was writing for the Sporting Life at the time and wrote a rather snide article, about the gigantic gamble, Barry Stamper's briefcase and his two 'minders'. Mr. 'S' took exception to some of the words used and there was talk about suing the paper. Personally I thought it good reading and the perfect 'Italian Job' had been executed. Helexian went on to win again though next time it was at long odds on. Nigel brought off other coups for Barry Stamper who, after a very successful gamble at Redcar - I'm talking megga bucks again - suddenly announced he was calling it a day as an owner and going out on a winner; I haven't seen him since.

During the mid eighties Nigel rode in an invitation trainers race on the flat down at one of Kempton's evening meetings and for his ride he chose a horse called Ahona, owned by the late Pat Phoenix (the actress). In his two previous runs the horse had been to Ascot and York and was just touched off by a short head, carrying a big weight, at the latter. Nigel felt that by taking him to Kempton and winning in a canter it would do the horse's confidence a power of good. We went down the day before and Nigel was decidedly unhappy at something that occurred at the stables on our arrival. It certainly caused us both to be suspicious that not all was as it should have been. The following morning Ahona seemed to be perfectly all right so we assumed we had over reacted to what had happened the evening before.

The race was over a mile and the best of the opposition was no better than a selling plater and as for the riders, Nigel was in a league of his own. The eighteen runners were only competing for a trophy and the Kudos as there was no prize money. It was all very Mickey Mouse but Nigel was anticipating the excursion would fulfil a purpose. I'd gone down to Kempton not only to keep Nigel company but also to have a punt. The morning papers were quoting that Ahona would be around 1/8 and I reckoned that £8,000 to win a £1,000 would be a nice little earner. Just before I legged Nigel into the saddle I did say Ahona didn't seem too lively and, watching him canter down to the start, I was rather apprehensive. As I approached the rails bookmakers I knew something was wrong, the suspicions we had the day before and in the parade ring were suddenly confirmed. Ahona was not 1/8, in fact not even half those odds but something like 2/5, with a rumour flying round the ring that the Tinkler horse wasn't busy. Even so, money was being shovelled on by some of the professionals. I couldn't understand them as surely they knew bookmakers are not charitable institutions; some can be generous at times but they never lay 4/6 (that was the eventual starting price) about a horse where 'no betting' would have been more realistic! I'm not pointing a finger at any particular layer - most saw what was afoot and took advantage of the situation.

Ahona ran a listless race and did well in the circumstances to finish third beaten only two and a half lengths (quote from Raceform - hard ridden final furlong, no impression). Nigel was relieved that I hadn't had a punt but terribly worried about the horse. There was no stewards enquiry - surely the activities that had taken place in the ring demanded investigation - and there was also no dope test ordered, absolutely nothing. I suggested to Nigel that he ask for a dope test but he was fearful that the stewards might think he was really the one responsible if anything were found and was just trying to divert suspicion. I have always said that one of the main things wrong with racing is that the stewards are not on the same side as trainers and jockeys. Here was a case that a horse had been doped and, because of certain attitudes, nothing could be done about it. Unfortunately I must close the episode on a sad note; Ahona never won another race in this country nor, I believe, did he do so after being sold to go abroad.

In the late seventies Col and Carol married, her parents farmed at Rillington, a few miles east of Malton and her father, Roland Stephenson, who has since died, was a former international cross-country runner and Master of the Middleton Fox Hounds for a number of years. He was also very successful with showing sheep. I asked him one day at the Great Yorkshire, how had he fared and was told "Only middleun - I won best pen and best pair of lambs, best ewe, best tup and got Reserve Champion - oh, aye, and Champion, but he looked a bit woolly". Well sheep do, don't they!

Col and Carol's first home was adequate, in fact saying that is not doing it justice, it was a nice place but had no land. They then bought and moved to Musley Bank Stud, on the outskirts of Malton; put down their own all weather gallop, had an indoor arena and fifty boxes. They were preparing to commence training on Col's retirement from the saddle but it came all too prematurely. He had been a brilliant jockey, always gave one hundred per cent and throughout never lost his sense of humour. He tells how one afternoon at Carlisle the stipendiary steward excitedly said to him, with a fair amount of condemnation "You overtook me as we were driving in to the car park". Col coolly replied - "Well - at least it shows I was trying!"

The appalling fall which Col suffered at Newcastle completely shattered the Tinkler family, ended his riding career and very nearly his life. He was on a horse called O'er The Border in a four runner chase, on November 13th 1982. The horse ducked out just before the ninth fence, throwing Col against a concrete post. I was watching the race on television - it was terrible. I contacted a friend of mine, Norman Heslop, who was at the course and he told me Col was in a bad way; naturally Marie and I dashed up there and discovered he had multiple fractures in one of his legs and in the other the ligaments were badly torn. He also had massive bruising and his right eye was badly damaged. Even though he had been race riding for thirteen years he was only twenty eight and had suffered his fair share of falls, fracturing more than a dozen bones in separate crashes. Had it all been worth it? The memories of some unbelievable successes will surely dim a little over the years but the results of his injuries will always be with him. I recently asked him the same question and he told me that for his part it had, as it is very easy to do nothing in life - those, of course, are my sentiments. After a couple of weeks he was moved nearer home to York and stayed in hospital there for two months. He has negative vision in the eye that was damaged and unfortunately his legs, with all the nuts and bolts, will never be right. The number of visitors he had whilst in hospital was a sign of his popularity and it was John Francome, because of what had happened, who was instrumental in having the concrete posts removed from courses and replaced by plastic ones. Incredible as it is some hazards still exist but, hopefully, they will soon be rectified.

I will close the chapter by saying how much I appreciate Col, for all the pleasure his riding gave me over the years; also for his courage, perseverance and attitude against adversities. It can't have been easy at times; I also acknowledge his contribution to many of our personal successes.

Chapter thirteen

Marie dons the silks on the flat

Now for the period when Marie wore the red and yellow silks on the flat. Her initial impact was to cause a change in fashion. She was the first to wear a cotton polo neck jumper under the colours, as against the traditional cravat, which jockeys had been using for more than a couple of centuries. It wasn't long before their modern counterparts followed suit, once they saw the advantage of Marie's innovation.

Girls initially commenced riding on the flat (other than the Newmarket Town Plate) in '72, and then only as amateurs, with the first race being at Kempton Park. Marie didn't take part because I hadn't at that time been granted a licence to train on the flat and we didn't want a horse for her to ride which was trained by other than ourselves. In fact I had to wait until '76 before I received the necessary go-ahead. It wasn't that I was ever actually refused a flat licence but had to wait until the required number of horses were in the yard and had the right facilities. Marie was fifty one, an age when most jockeys have long hung up their boots, before she had her first ride on the already documented Milesian Star at Thirsk; they finished third at 50/1! To be perfectly frank, it was not such a shock because nothing Marie achieved or did was ever a total surprise.

We were continually on the 'look out' for another horse for the girls races; it was not easy for, in those days more than now, the races were restricted to horses of a certain standard that was not too high, yet we wanted a horse that would do justice. We temporarily missed out when not going down to Sandown, when Guy Harwood's Il Magnifico won a mile seller there. He only won by a head but was the sort of horse we were looking for and I'm sure we would have bought him at the subsequent auction. The horse next ran in a non seller at Salisbury where he was unplaced so I contacted connections. A figure in the region of two thousand pounds was discussed so we bought him unseen there and then which, one would say, was rather a risky thing to have done. He was not a robust sort of horse, in fact not dissimilar to Milesian Star and apparently (but unknown to us at the time) had a reputation of not being that genuine. That was soon in the past for Il Magnifico had only been with us a few weeks when we noticed a change in his attitude, as well as his physique. He seemed very happy cantering through the woods on his own and away from a large string. His first run for us was when we took him up to Newcastle, where he finished fourth and not beaten that far. Marie had very quickly altered her style of riding and looked even stronger than before. Chester was next on the agenda and they were only a head and half a length off winning; they went round the bends as if on rails and there was certainly no sign of any roguishness. A couple of weeks later we went down to Newbury for a race over one and a quarter miles, there were sixteen runners and Il Magnifico was drawn right on the outside - a daunting prospect from such a position at that course and distance. The race was on a Saturday in September and on the way down on the Friday somehow one of the wheels of the horse trailer sheared off, flew over a hedge and away across a corn field. Fortunately we were quite close to a Rice trailer distributor and limped there on three wheels. There was only one solution - half an hour later we were cruising along with the Merc towing a brand new trailer with Il Magnifico nicely installed!

On our overnight excursions I always saw to it that Marie stayed in a nice hotel. We would have a meal together then I would go back to the racecourse stables and sleep in the trailer. It sounds rather uncomfortable but it wasn't and besides it was my choice; I could keep an eye on things and be on hand early next morning. By the time I went to the hotel for breakfast our runner would have been out for a nice leg stretch, brush over, fed and set fair for the morning. I would choose a stable well away from the main activities in the yard, away from the entrance gate; rest was important. Usually I would have shod the day before with racing plates; the selection was as important as the correct choice of tyres on a Formula One racing car though I know the majority of trainers wouldn't give a thought to such a detail.

Even though it appeared we had no possible chance at Newbury, for the opposition was not exactly Mickey Mouse and there was the appalling draw to overcome, Marie was not deterred. When walking the course she noticed that the grass over on the other side of the track, where the mile and a quarter start was situated and that on the rails, were two distinct colours. The watering system hadn't reached onto the outside of the far straight, making the ground faster from an outside draw. That was so long as one kept in a straight line and not go over to the rails until the first bend was reached. In the race itself Marie's plans worked to perfection; she was never really headed and won unchallenged by three lengths. Just one tap with the whip at the furlong pole and it was all over. We had a monkey on at 12/1 but, just as it was with our boys when they rode their first winners, the punt was secondary. As I ran from the stand to lead in, I gave out a gigantic holler, a whoopee - all the packs of hounds in Berkshire must have heard me. It came over on the video tape of the race - the whole recording is magical - the clanking of the stalls as the gates opened - then the commentator's voice - "It's Il Magnifico from El Muchacho - the favourite's going nowhere - they won't catch this one - Il Magnifico is streaking away - it's Il Magnifico". It certainly was, Marie and the little chestnut were both MAGNIFICO.

Our boys were racing somewhere, I believe it was Warwick, and saw the race on television. Most of the jockeys watching, quite understandably, thought Marie was their sister, for no way did Marie look or ride like someone who was over fifty - utterly incredible really. By the time Il Magnifico had rested there were no other races for him that season and unhappily he met with an injury when in training the following spring and was retired. He only ran four times for us but, yet again, another horse that gave the Tinklers so much pleasure.

Disappointing as it was not to have Il Magnifico for the '77 season, Marie had however managed to get another horse to ride, a three year old filly by Be Friendly called La Bambola. We bought her at Tattersalls; Horses in Training Autumn Sale for a little over eight thousand pounds which, at the time, was the most expensive horse we had ever purchased. Though I suppose expensive is the wrong word to use for she turned out to be an absolute bargain.

La Bambola had so much charisma; she was a robust explosive power house on legs and another that had a reputation before we bought her of not being all that genuine. However Marie found her attitude to be one hundred per cent genuine and their runs together proved the point. Her breeding suggested she should be a sprinter but that was not so for one and a quarter miles seemed to suit her best. Marie's first six rides on La Bambola, commencing in April, were at Beverley, Thirsk, Hamilton Park, Redcar, Wolverhampton's old turf course and Yarmouth; the trips varied between five furlongs and a mile and a half. We learnt that La Bambola became unbalanced when galloping downhill, no matter how slight the gradient; she was all right on the level but much preferred to go against the collar. Taking everything into consideration we chose a race over a mile and a quarter at Newcastle, towards the end of August, as ideal for a gamble.

Yarmouth is slightly downhill in the home straight and the distance of her race there had been only a mile and the opposition most formidable, with a couple of them topping £30,000 at Tattersalls later in the year. To finish fourth as she did was a most satisfactory effort. It was Beverley Races on the same afternoon and I was told the 'guessers' lumped on and one or two bookmakers at the Yorkshire track took a lot of money for our horse. We were happy with the way things had gone at the seaside course; in fact throughout her preparation for Newcastle, which was in five days from then, there hadn't been a single hiccup. La Bambola was given a complete rest for the remaining few days and spent a couple of hours out in the paddock during the afternoons. She was bouncing and absolutely 'on song' and Marie was full of confidence that the task in front of them was not going to be much of a problem.

Apart from the Yarmouth race where La Bambola surprisingly started second favourite, she had, in all her other runs up to then, been friendless in the market and on two occasions was a 20/1 outsider. John Joyce again handled our wager at Newcastle and we backed La Bambola down from 6/1 to 100/30, with Cabin Boy the market leader of the dozen runners. The start for the mile and a quarter there is at the furthest point from the stands but it was plain to see that Marie had got away well and held a good position early on. By the time she turned into the straight she had La Bambola well clear of the field and going further away with every stride. They seemed to literally saunter past the post ten lengths clear.

The race was televised and as Marie pulled up Lord Oaksey, the T.V. presenter, remarked in his own individualistic way "I don't know where the Tinkler brothers are riding today but I hope they are near a television set and have seen their mother ride that winner"; he went on to pay Marie a host of compliments. Everything had gone to plan, another gamble had materialised; it couldn't have been more successful.

Marie gave La Bambola two further runs that season, the first of which was at Chester but unfortunately Marie was suffering from a ghastly attack of shingles. The rash was extensive and how she rode, or even wanted to with such irritation and pain, I fail to comprehend. In spite of everything they managed to finish third, beaten less than a length. Knowing what I did, I didn't have a bet, though on the strength of her Newcastle run, La Bambola started the 5/4 favourite. By the time October arrived and La Bambola's final outing of the campaign she was over the top; it had been a long season but a most enjoyable one.

It was then full steam ahead with the jumpers and a couple of nice touches were landed during the winter months. But our main priority was to prepare for our next campaign on the flat by getting an additional horse. Were Marie to have any chance at all of landing the Lady Jockey's Title she would have to have further ammunition to fire. The majority of the girls that won the Championship in those days, and I suppose it hasn't really altered, had the backing of powerful stables. However, I felt if we could find another good horse and keep them both sound the task would not be impossible.

As well as scanning through the sales catalogues, we also put an advert in the Sporting Life. The advertisement read - Wanted for Ladies Races sound young horse with form over a mile to a mile and a quarter (but not too high a rating) £10,000 available - contact - etc., etc. We received several replies and the most interesting was from a Mrs. Hammond, an American who spent much of her time in this country at her small stud in Cambridgeshire. She thought we might like to look at a three year old she had bred called Atoka, the filly had won a race at Yarmouth the previous year from only four starts and was perfectly sound.

The reason Atoka was for sale was to help balance the books but it was clear her owner really wanted much more than £10,000 for her. Nevertheless, Marie still went down to have a look, anticipating she would be able to do some negotiating. On seeing Atoka Marie immediately fell in love with her; she was an absolute giant and dark brown in colour. Marie found Mrs. Hammond a charming person and they did a deal at our figure. What swayed the transaction was Marie's assurance that Atoka would never be sold and at the conclusion of her racing would form the nucleus of a small band of mares Marie was eventually hoping to breed from. There was no contingency plan drawn up to that effect; besides Marie's word was worth as much as any written agreement.

The filly was not entirely without fault; we could have done without some of her antics and her highly strung attitude. She possessed a fetish about stable doors - she would make a dash through them as if they were on fire. All rather dangerous for her as well as for whoever was doing the leading. On one occasion when Marie got badly trapped and suffered severe bruising, that was even after we had widened and made higher the doorway into her stable. With her being so tall she had obviously at one time knocked her head and hadn't forgotten the painful incident. One of Atoka's pranks was to rush about the yard before going on exercise and before Marie could get mounted; she would fly around the place in playful jubilation, bucking and lashing out. There was no badness in her - she was gorgeous and, apart from her fear of doorways, it was just one big game to her. To prevent Atoka getting injured on the stone walling I would cover it all with dozens of horse rugs and several mattresses. This was a daily procedure - all very time consuming. There was one further minus in her makeup - she was rather a choosy eater and would only pick about if given hay. As for oats or nuts, I found her interest even more negligible but she did like grass and this was the solution to her eating problem. I would cut her sack after sack full and always looked for the best quality - she was literally trained on the stuff.

I never rode either La Bambola or Atoka at exercise because I didn't feel I was efficient enough to do so. The boys helped when they could but more often than not Marie rode both out every day. It was the same procedure as with all our horses, mainly cantering in the woods on the undulating grass tracks with the occasional piece of fast work and, of course, the excursions to the coast to splash about in the sea and canter on the sand. The art was on how much work to give them.

By the time the flat commenced in March Marie had the two horses fairly straight and it was certainly an exciting time with all the expectations we were harbouring. Marie's first ride of the season was at Doncaster on La Bambola, at the beginning of April. She drifted in the market from 6/1 to 20/1 and was unplaced. We then took her to Ayr where she surprisingly finished second, again unbacked but notching some vital Championship points for Marie. Atoka was next on the agenda, in the mile and a half Haywards Military Pickle Stakes at Thirsk where there were nineteen runners with Marie drawn three off the rails. It was a scorching hot Saturday in May as we planned a rather unusual course of action. The racecourse was only half a dozen miles from our place at Boltby and, as we assumed Atoka would be rather a handful at the races, we decided to saddle her at home. Marie first walked the course, after which she weighed out, then brought the saddle, weight cloth and number cloth back to Boltby. We saddled Atoka in the quietness of her own stable, loaded her and set off for Thirsk. There was very little time to spare, certainly none if delayed by a traffic jam, but that's just what we encountered about a mile from the course. It really was panic stations and, as soon as we arrived at the races, we immediately unloaded in the owners and trainers car park. Once in the parade ring and after helping Marie into the saddle, I went across to the stewards and apologised for being late. One of them asked "What has the problem been?" I told him "We got into a queue of traffic", which was entirely true, though refrained from mentioning the full circumstances!

Our filly looked magnificent and was certainly on her toes; as Marie left the paddock she called out to me "Put plenty on". To be perfectly honest I didn't have that large a punt as I wasn't sure whether she would stay the mile and a half. It was also her initial run for us and the opposition looked anything but easy. You can see I am trying to justify my negative approach but really I shouldn't have lacked confidence. Atoka broke well from the stalls and was never headed, other than for a few strides when Marie gave her a breather turning into the straight. After that it was ding-dong all the way to the line, with Marie and Atoka beating the two market leaders by three quarters of a length and a short head. I watched the race from the open stand opposite the winning post and I can't remember going down the steps after the race - I probably just floated down! The race had been on television, so not only had the big crowd at Thirsk seen the incredible run, the whole country had. That was one hell of a fit filly Marie had produced and what a fine ride she had given her. It was absolutely Marvellous - with a capital M.

The race was worth over a thousand pounds to the winner, which was quite a sum in those days and with regards to the punting I placed a couple of bets on the rails, one of £200 at 14/1, the other of £350 with Ladbrokes at 12/1. Admittedly we won a few thousand pounds, but only because of the odds being what they were. It was a rare occurrence for the bookmakers to be so generous about a Tinkler winner. After what Marie had said, the punt should have been considerably more - but no hassle, it was still a Jewel of a day.

Atoka's next couple of runs were at Beverley (the unique character of the course didn't suit her) and Redcar (the mile was too short a trip). I'm not dismissing the two outings as non events and there was logical reasoning as to why she didn't perform better but we learnt a great deal. During that period La Bambola put a further three notches on her stable door, the first of those being at Warwick. It was an evening meeting and we went the day before to allow La Bambola plenty of time to recover from the journey. On arrival we discovered the gates to the stable complex locked and bolted and not a security guard in sight. It was early evening yet none of the racecourse staff were about either. In the circumstances there was only one thing I could do and that was break the locks; it was an absurd situation. While this was going on Marie was walking the course and, by the time I'd fed La Bambola, made her comfortable and completed all the other routine chores, Marie was back with some interesting observations. She said "There is a lot of grass on the track, it is thick and very long and horses drawn close to the inside (which La Bambola was) will be at a severe disadvantage". This was because the grass there had been rolled against the direction the horses would run. I realised it was going to be extremely hard work for La Bambola and those drawn close to her, so the following morning I persuaded one of the ground staff to re-roll the grass in the opposite direction. I was not seeking an advantage for La Bambola but neither did I wish her to be at a disadvantage.

Nothing was said about the break in, the security people seemed rather embarrassed about the whole thing, and so they should have been. The amateur race which was not due off until seven o'clock was one of a series being sponsored by Brooke Bond. Points were given to the riders of the first three home in each of their races, concluding with one at Haydock in October. The rider with the most points would receive a car which (as the series was not just restricted to girls) he or she would be presented with at that final meeting.

There were twenty two runners for the Warwick race and La Bambola was made favourite at 5/2 with the Tinklers having a substantial punt. When the stalls opened the field went a hell of a clip. This was because all the weights were reasonably low for such a race and some of the runners literally bolted. This left Marie with a lot to do as they came into the short straight, but she weaved her way through the field and went on to win by a couple of lengths. That was some ride and only those who have been connected with winners, in some form or other, know the pleasure and excitement such a performance can bring. After La Bambola cooled off I went over to the bookmakers to collect and one rather cynically said "Mr. T, are you sure that wasn't Greville Starkey riding your horse". He must have been thinking about L'Arc de Triomphe of a couple of years back for, I must agree, Marie's manoeuvres were very reminiscent of Starkey when he won the race on Star Appeal.

Next for the versatile La Bambola was a race at Redcar over one and three quarter miles, where she carried a staggering twelve stone plus. Marie literally toyed with the opposition, leading throughout and winning by just over a length. The race was not just confined to girls and I gathered Wilson, the rider of the well backed Bailador, became rather stroppy after the race and said something about "It's that F*****g Mrs. Tinkler again". They had obviously crossed swords before! Redcar were having a concession day for miners from the local collieries, with the Andy Capp Handicap being the feature event. Apart from the language from the rider of the favourite, there were some choice words from Marie in the paddock before the race as she reprimanded La Bambola for her spontaneous rodeo display. I don't think some of the coal face men could believe what they were hearing! I didn't 'lump on' at Redcar, in fact the only bet I had was one of £1,500 to £600; naturally, I'd been a trifle apprehensive about La Bambola's ability to carry the weight over such a distance of ground. The tag of ungenuineness which she possessed when first coming to us was a complete fallacy, for there could not have been a more sincere and honest racehorse. La Bambola's third win in succession was at Carlisle over one and a half miles; now I certainly lumped on that day, backing her down from 11/10 to 8/11. The opposition wasn't great but it was a handicap and La Bambola was giving everything else practically a couple of stone. She did jolly well considering and got up close home to win by a neck.

A couple of weeks after the Carlisle success we took La Bambola down to Ascot to run in the prestigious Diamond Stakes. With Ascot being so far away it required another overnight stay but, unfortunately, she somehow got cast in her box during the night, kicked out and badly bruised a tendon. We were obviously very concerned about how serious it might be and to run her would definitely have been courting disaster. When we both walked the course the previous evening, just before the light started to fade, I looked up the long home straight and thought I heard the cheering crowd - but it was not to be.

During the summer we'd had a three year old sent to us called Rarely Equalled. He wasn't a great horse, though had been placed but had never won, so I put him in a seven furlong maiden for amateurs at Leicester. The race was a couple of days after our disappointing Ascot journey; there were a host of runners and Marie managed to finish third on him, beaten less than two lengths. It was a good effort and another example of Marie conjuring a little extra from her mount; I thought at the time the run could make a difference at the end of the season were the Championship to be decided on place positions. As a matter of interest, the horse had a further outing for us at Thirsk, in a professional race with Col on board (he occasionally rode on the flat) but unfortunately went wrong so Marie never got another chance with him.

All along we'd had the Brooke Bond race, over Kempton's mile and three furlongs, as Atoka's prime target but the filly was not the best of travellers and we assumed it would be a nightmare of a journey getting there. Actually, it wasn't as bad as expected, though once in London with all the stopping and starting Atoka became restless, despite my giving her confidence by travelling in the trailer with her. There were not as many motorways then and, as we weren't completely sure of the way, we took a direct route and hired a London taxi cab to guide us through the city. It was early evening by the time we arrived at the course but I soon had the filly 'set fair' for the night. I'd brought a good supply of grass and it amazed people the amount I gave her, particularly the following morning just a few hours before the race.

For security reasons as well as keeping a watchful eye on what Atoka was doing, I parked the trailer beside some large iron gates and just a few yards away from the stable I'd chosen for her. The security at Kempton was, as at many courses, extremely poor - in fact a farce. The iron gates I've referred to led into the stable complex and were used for maintenance purposes; admittedly they were locked but easily climbable.

Marie walked the entire course a couple of times and said there would be no problems - an expression she used often. The weather was glorious with brilliant sunshine as I led Atoka round the parade ring for the first race of the afternoon; as usual with a Tinkler runner she was looking exceptionally fit - absolutely buzzing. There were a dozen runners and Atoka opened in the betting at 11/2 but soon became 4/1 third favourite. I'd enrolled John Pegley, the southern bookmaker, to put some of our money on. I also had a couple of people from the north, one whom we trained for, to help place our money. By the time Marie was cantering down to the start and I was able to do some punting myself the ring had become very jittery. The three firms I had accounts with had Atoka at a lesser price than was being quoted on the boards but the ludicrous situation was, the board bookmakers wouldn't lay me a bet of any significance and it wasn't as if I was wishing to bet each way. It was a Saturday afternoon, there were thousands of people at Kempton, yet nearly impossible to get on. I did however eventually do so though it had been difficult.

Kempton is a right handed course, with the one mile three furlong start being quite close to a sharp turn. It is imperative to get away well; this Atoka did from a good draw, got to the front and stayed there. Marie sat motionless as the combination went further and further ahead, winning by eight lengths, but it could have been double that distance. I was on clouds nine, ten, eleven and twelve; Marie was getting ever nearer to winning the Championship and another gamble had been landed. Yet again, everything had gone according to plan - just brilliant - and the journey back to Yorkshire didn't seem to take that long!

Marie's next ride was on La Bambola a couple of weeks later at Newcastle, where she was trying to capture the race they had won the previous year. La Bambola's leg seemed to be perfectly alright from the Ascot accident, though obviously it wasn't, by the way she ran. She started at 4/7 to beat her four opponents but unfortunately finished second, going down by a couple of lengths though was never really striding out; we didn't run her again that season.

Atoka, on the other hand, was going great guns and had three more races before the end of the season. The first was around the soup plate course at Chester, where her long stride proved unsuitable and she was beaten into third place. It was, however, entirely different at Ayr the following month over a distance just short of two miles. There were a dozen runners and, because of the trip and some heavy backing of Ian Balding's horse (ridden by Jenny Pitman's sister), Atoka was on offer at the unbelievably long price of 7/1. I didn't have an excessive punt yet it still shortened her price to 11/2. I watched the race with Joe Mercer who could not believe what he saw when the favourite turned into the straight a hundred yards in front of the field. Marie had ridden Atoka to get the trip and gradually bore down on the well backed leader, going on to win by half a dozen lengths. Another cracking performance.

By that time there were a further four amateur races the girls could compete in but it was most unlikely that any of the chasing pack would snatch Marie's lead at that juncture. One of the remaining races was the final of the Brooke Bond Championship, with a brand new Austin Mini up for grabs. Both Marie and Tim Easterby were so far ahead on points that, no matter what the result of the race, no one else could possibly win the car. It was rather an intriguing situation for the Tinklers because, if our runner Atoka were to win, the amount of prize money gained would prevent her being eligible for the majority of the amateur races the following season. To win the 'Mini' Marie had to finish in front of Tim Easterby. It didn't matter what the positions were - if Marie beat Tim the car was hers and vice versa.

I was so confident of the outcome that, before leaving for Haydock on that damp misty morning in October, I took out insurance so that Marie could drive the vehicle home. On arriving at the course the first thing we saw as we walked to the weighing room was the glorious little red motor parked near the winners enclosure; admittedly, it wasn't an Italian flying horse, nevertheless it still looked a very nice car and it was, coincidentally, in Marie's racing colours. As the twenty runners cantered down to the start the bookmakers were calling the Easterby horse, Ruabon, the 4/1 favourite with Atoka second best at 7/1. It was a pretty open affair and when the stalls opened Marie took Atoka to the front, and remained in that position until turning into the straight. Lord Oaksey was commentating on television that afternoon and I will quote his comments of the closing stages "Martial Game is well clear of Hay Ride and Silken Swift but the real battle is between Marie Tinkler on Atoka and Tim Easterby on Ruaban. All she has to do is stay where she is in fourth place and beat Tim - this she is doing; actually she doesn't seem to be doing very much, she doesn't need to, she is still in front of Tim and now she's passed the post; Marie's won the Brooke Bond Championship and the car and it certainly couldn't have happened to a nicer person".

That was Marie's last ride of the season; she had won six races from 14 rides and had only been unplaced a couple of times. None of the girls came with a late run, so she also won the Lady Riders Championship and, as an added bonus, the overall Amateur Championship (gentlemen riders included). It meant keeping an appointment with the scales in the weighing room, at Doncaster's final meeting, where she was presented with her weight in flagons of Champagne. 1977 was drawing to a close - it had been an utterly fantastic year and there aren't enough superlatives to describe my emotions. Practically everything we set out to achieve had been accomplished. La Bambola had suffered a mishap but we were hopeful that the trouble was only minor and she could resume training in the spring. Both she and Atoka had been superb and no one could have ridden them better.

Marie and I had won a fair amount of money during the season and the punting remained successful over the following months. We did however have a quietish time with our own jumpers, just winning that one race at Fakenham. Over the years Marie had become a very astute punter and disciplined herself to record every bet she made. I was talking to her quite recently when she told me she'd won £19,000 over a period of time and I wasn't surprised.

Two very delightful stories come to mind. The last race on the card had been run at one of the Thirsk meetings and I was waiting for her in the car park. When she did eventually appear, she was clutching a considerable amount of money; I'm talking about several large wads. Marie apologised for keeping me waiting and mentioned the obvious "I've been collecting from the bookmakers". I said "Jolly good, I can see you've had a winning day". Marie's reply was "No, about level, but I got out on the last!" Thank goodness she did!

The other story occurred when Col was riding at a meeting down south and uncharacteristically rang to say that a horse called Tempting Times would most likely win at Catterick that afternoon. He was adamant that we shouldn't back it on the course or with any of the office bookmakers I normally used; it had to be very hush-hush as the horse had never run before and he believed it was to be the subject of a stable gamble. He hadn't given us a lot of options but, as it was the last race on the card, there was time to do the betting shops in the Stockton and Middlesbrough area. I knew exactly where the majority were as I'd made a previous reconnaissance for such an occasion. Marie thought up an ingenious idea to guard against those at the betting shops from recognising her or thinking she possessed some inspired information. Firstly there was the visual disguise - a pair of glasses, an old coat and a head scarf; then the vocal one, an Irish accent. I stayed in the car as Marie went into the first shop on our list. She strolled over to the counter and, pushing a casually written out betting slip (well we had all afternoon) and a dirty old twenty pound note through the grill, she said, in her so called Irish brogue "I'm backing this horse because he was bred in the village where I used to live over there in Ireland, he was, I want the punt to be on the nose, I do, even though I don't think he's a serious horse at all". Marie was absolutely scuttled when the cashier replied in all sincerity "I didn't know you were Irish, Mrs. Tinkler!!" After that Marie returned to normality as we went from one bookmaker to the next. The horse won but his price was shortened dramatically on the course, to start at 11/10. The scanty price was due to Joe Lyle, the one time heavy gambler cum night club owner and charismatic Johnny Heenan, both had noticed the trainer's daughter place a small bet on the horse at a Tote window - they realised that was significant enough and acted accordingly!

Throughout the years Marie and I did a tremendous amount of motoring and, as Marie much preferred to drive than being a passenger, it was she who was usually behind the wheel. There were very few dull journeys and the following stories may not be classics but I believe they are worth telling.

On the way back from Perth Races the trailer had a puncture. It was holiday time and the roads were absolutely choc a bloc, so we pulled into a lay-by to change the wheel but unfortunately had to unload the horse to do so. With the wheel changed we were just about to re-load when a car coming in the opposite direction, and from a slight bend in the road, suddenly steadied. The driver seemed rather interested in what we were doing and his speed dropped from fifty to twenty miles per hour. The cars immediately following didn't stop in time and bumped into one another causing a concertina crash. It was bang, bang, bang, bang, bang, a six car pile up - an utter shambles. No one was seriously hurt but there were a lot of very angry people running about. We soon left the scene and, not wanting to be called as a witness at half a dozen court cases up there in Scotland, I told each of the drivers I considered it was partly their fault; no one seemed to want to take my name and address after that!

One day we were going through Collingham Bridge, near Wetherby, with the Land Rover and empty trailer. The village is on a busy main road and has some traffic lights; as we approached them I remarked to Marie "There is some bloody fool with a van overtaking us." As the lights turned to red we stopped but this 'van' shot past and on into a pub yard, up a bit of a bank and stopped. I said "Crikey, there are some idiots about." All this happened while the lights were still red. I must mention it was raining and visibility on the passenger side of the Land Rover was not good because that side was without a windscreen wiper. Marie, totally unruffled, coolly answered "Stop taking the piss - you know it's our trailer"! Apparently I had not secured the coupling correctly or put the safety chain on. End of story and it was very nearly the end of the trailer!

Marie and I stopped for some petrol with the car and, yet again, an empty horse trailer which had a small gap at the top of the back ramp for ventilation. One of the girl petrol attendants came over and asked had we got a horse with us. Jokingly I said "Yes, it's a jumper." She replied "It's a warm day, I'll get him a drink" and returned with a saucer of milk; I continued the farce by telling her to open the little side door and let him lap it up! Wait for it - she ran back looking shocked and said "It's a jumper all right - bugger's jumped out, it's not bloody there!"

To finalise - we were on our way through Malton with the car and trailer plus a horse, the Mercedes was practically new and the trailer not more than a couple of months old. Marie ignored the red lights and tried to beat the gates at the railway crossing. As we approached, the barrier came slowly down and somehow ended behind the car and in front of the trailer. Marie stopped quickly and we both got out. Fortunately the signal box man had noticed the 'pantomime' and raised the barrier to allow us to move from the track. In doing so, the traffic in the opposite direction started to cross, assuming it was in order to do so but, of course, it wasn't. I could hear the sound of the train's whistle and could see the monster approaching in the distance. I felt a little decorum was necessary at this juncture - so we bloody scarpered and, what's more, didn't look back!

The spring of '79 arrived with things not going well with the jumpers. A couple had gone wrong causing a shortage of runners but worse was to follow. Marie was busy getting her two flat horses, Atoka and La Bambola, fit for the season ahead, when a major disaster struck. We had taken Atoka for a gallop on the tan, in the park at Wetherby, but she somehow got cast in the trailer and severely damaged one of her shoulders. We were devastated and I felt guilty that I'd not travelled with her on that occasion. I'm not necessarily saying the accident could have been prevented as that is something we will never know, though inwardly I believe it would have, had I been in the trailer. It was such a terrible tragedy.

We waited until August before running La Bambola, at Redcar over a mile. She had appeared perfectly sound in training but ran another very much under par race; just as she had done at Newcastle in her previous outing, the season before, only this time it was far worse for she finished lame. Obviously the Ascot mishap she had suffered the previous year had been more severe than we had dared imagine and if she was to race again it was going to take some considerable time for the injury to heal satisfactorily, just as it was with Atoka.

How things had changed over the months, from a near Utopia to an unbelievable catastrophic shambles - an utter nightmare. It is bad enough when horses break down in races or on the gallops but the bizarre circumstances we had encountered had robbed Marie of so much - in fact had robbed us both of so much. Marie had been left with literally nothing of consequence to ride. It was not just a question of buying replacements; if they could be found they would also have been very expensive. That apart, Marie felt she wanted to be patient and wait to see if either recovered sufficiently enough to race again. Deep down we both realised it was going to require a near miracle for that to happen. That miracle didn't materialise, with the result that neither ever raced again. With them both being mares Marie was able to retain them for breeding, but that was something that had come far sooner than had been envisaged.

Marie did have a further couple of mounts before eventually saying "That's it" and putting her riding boots away. It was not done by choice - I know that, had she had a decent horse to ride, Marie would undoubtedly have continued. It was very sad the way the cookie crumbled; at the close of the previous season some television people came to our yard to do a programme on the Tinklers, though mainly focusing on Marie because of her achievements. There was some rather nice filming and the interview Marie gave was typical of her and very much to the point. She said "I'm like an apprentice really, I haven't had that many rides - I'm still learning as far as I'm concerned". When asked how long she intended to keep race riding, she replied "I don't know, I'm like an old horse, one day I'll be galloping about and the next I'll just pack it all in. The bruises have always been there after a fall but they take a little longer to heal as one gets older".

Marie had carried on riding at a high level longer than anyone had done before. In all the spheres she'd tackled she had never been satisfied with second best; the words 'also ran' were not in her vocabulary. Marie would always help young riders. I remember a girl who'd just had her first ride telling me what an enormous help Marie had been, even down to fitting the silks on to her crash helmet properly. Marie had ridden some very nice horses though it was never a question of having a sledgehammer to crack a nut (the bookmakers' odds substantiated that) but she often made it look that way. Marie was always so exciting to watch, which was the reason for her popularity with race goers and she certainly deserved the further success she had when her attentions turned to breeding.

It's unfair to single out specific instances in Marie's long list of successes for they all, without exception, gave me so much pleasure. Nevertheless, I'm going to mention some occasions that are more prominent in my memory than others.

Seeing Marie jumping the final fence on Fanny Rosa to capture the Queen Elizabeth Cup, at the old White City stadium, back in 1953, is unforgettable. Then there was the time she jumped a straight up five bar gate on Nigel's small pony, to win an open competition at a minor Sunday show; one would have thought it impossible - it was pure magic. Turning to the point to point scene - Too Dear's win at the Sinnington, when he never jumped a twig; I swear he never saw a jump; he was flat out the whole way round and it was electrifying stuff. Some of gorgeous little Flexodus's terrific leaps are also firmly imprinted on my mind. As are Marie's two memorable Newmarket Town Plate successes on Blake and Ocean Sailor, both winning by twenty lengths; that was before the demise of the historic event. Now on to flat racing proper and please excuse the terminology. The video tape of El Magnifico winning at Newbury, giving Marie her first success, says it all, the clanking of the starting stalls as the gates opened and the holler I gave as the gutsy chestnut passed the post is something I never tire of hearing and the race itself, never tire of seeing. La Bambola's zigzag through the field at Warwick and Atoka's brilliant triumphs at Thirsk and Kempton are such marvellous memories. Yes - so many unforgettable days filled with emotions. But sadly nothing lasts for ever and when the cookie crumbles, it certainly crumbles, sometimes in devastating fashion.

MARIE'S CAREER - FLAT RACE WINNERS

	Won By	
1970	Blake	Newmarket Town Plate - 20 lengths at 20/1
1971	Ocean Sailor	Newmarket Town Plate - 20 lengths at 5/2
1976.	Il Magnifico	Newbury - 3 lengths at 10/1
1977	La Bambola	Newcastle - 10 lengths at 10/3
1978	Atoka	Thirsk - 3/4 length at 11/1
	La Bambola	Warwick - 1.5 lengths at 5/2
1978	La Bambola	Redcar - 1.5 lengths at 5/2
	La Bambola	Carlisle - a neck at 8/11

Atoka	Kempton - 8 lengths at 4/1
Atoka	Ayr - 6 lengths at 11/2

The odds quoted are the starting prices.
Usually more advantageous odds had been obtained.

Chapter fourteen

Marie and I part company

Apart from the major things that happened over the following three or four years, and they were certainly of great importance, I remember very little of the ordinary day to day happenings. For relaxation Marie played a fair amount of golf but, also, she had the usual mundane things to see to. Both our boys were doing really well and riding plenty of winners and Nigel married Sandra early in '79. Actually the wedding nearly didn't take place as scheduled because there were ten foot drifts of snow blocking the church entrance, obviously somebody was trying to say something! The reception was held over at Helmsley some ten miles away and to get there meant a rather precarious journey through a blinding blizzard and on treacherous roads. There were abandoned cars all along the route but miraculously everyone made it, including Dave Goulding, who was Nigel's best man and a contemporary of his in the weighing room. The champagne drunk was extra special as it was that won by Marie the previous year and presented to her at the final meeting of the flat season. Nigel and Sandra had bought a delightful little cottage at Ampleforth a few miles away and moved in there when they returned from their honeymoon.

We did very little during the 79-80 jumping season; our enthusiasm had disappeared and both Marie and I were finding life difficult. There was not enough anticipation or excitement, without question we were needlessly drifting apart. The boys say we argued, yet I don't recall doing so, though Marie always laid claim to being jolly good at bollocking. She reckoned she could have made a living from it, advertising bollockings given for a small fee - distance no object; but enough of the frivolity because it was a serious matter. Marie told a reporter and it was printed in the press that I had dumped her for a younger girl. The statement was absolute rubbish and obviously very upsetting for me. You may say, there is no smoke without fire, but I categorically say there wasn't a fire, not even two sticks being rubbed together. The whole time I was with Marie I certainly never had an affair or even a one night stand; neither did I go socialising without her. It's no big deal but that's the way it was. Of course, I had been propositioned many times; I was younger and decidedly better looking in those days but still, I always managed to keep my feet on the ground, in more ways than one! A girl who was married and who I knew reasonably well once said to me "What's it matter Colin, so long as our partners don't find out". To me it mattered. I owed Marie so much and I wouldn't have cheated her, for half an hours fun with a pretty face; enough said. The whole thing was crazy and a ridiculous situation; I suppose it was just one of those things that shouldn't have been happening but it was.

We used to go to the races together until Marie bought herself a separate car. We'd reluctantly sold the red mini, nice as it was, because I feared with it being so small it wouldn't stand up to much of a crash. Since I first met Marie I've never failed to send her a Valentine; yes, I still do. On the particular occasion in mind I left a carrier bag in the back porch where it would be seen; it contained a card, some flowers, a nice box of Swiss chocolates and a most expensive sweater. It was completely ignored so, after a couple of days, I dumped the card and the flowers in the trash bin, ritually burnt the sweater in the stable yard and ate the chocolates. One of Nigel's staff called out to me "What a f*****g waste". I'm not sure which she was referring to, the burning of the garment or me eating the chocs! I used to get so frustrated with the whole stupid business that I would get into the Merc, lower all the windows for some fresh air and drive as fast as I could up Sneck Yat (a steep hill leading out of Boltby). I'd then do over a hundred miles an hour along the top of the Hambleton Hills and return home by way of Sutton Bank with its one in four gradient. I would arrive back utterly exhausted but with some of the tension gone. The old sensation of being on a roller coaster became more and more prevalent again. It was rather disturbing for the problem had become less troublesome over the years and I had hoped it was completely disappearing.

I ceased training in 1980 and got the approval of the Jockey Club for Nigel to take over. He was then, at twenty two, the youngest trainer in the country and his licence covered both the flat and over jumps. A few years back Marie and I had the stables full but recently it had been different. However Nigel soon filled the fourteen boxes again and, as I'd appointed myself as yard man cum farrier, I was kept very busy cleaning out all the stables every day and doing all the shoeing. Matters between Marie and myself didn't improve with the influx of horses owned by people she didn't know and the staff to look after them. The kitchen became a canteen, consequently the place was never as tidy as she liked to keep it, and that must be the understatement of the year, but her indignation spread to more crucial issues than that. Nigel, who had also kept his Jockeys Licence, was riding lots of winners and his training was progressing satisfactorily. So for him, apart from the odd hiccup, things were going jolly well.

Nigel, however, hadn't taken over the entire yard. There were two large boxes in the barn permanently reserved for Atoka and La Bambola. By that time the two mares had embarked on their breeding careers with Atoka proving to be by far the more prolific of the two at stud. She had her first couple of foals whilst we were still living at Boltby (both later won races). The first of those was 'Rainbow Vision', a brown filly by Prince Tenderfoot who, when sold as a yearling at Newmarket's Tattersalls Sales, realised 11,000 gns. Atoka's second foal was a brown colt by Young Generation, which arrived three or four weeks prematurely. Because of this he was rather weak and his first forty eight hours were crucial, with Marie or myself staying by his side the whole time. Actually he grew into a very nice horse and made 20,000 gns when sold at Tattersalls Yearling Sales. There is no question about it 'Oh Boya', as he was called, was very fast and would have had a brilliant career had he not developed joint trouble. I actually bought him back when he was re-sold after incurring his injury; in fact I owned several of Atoka's offspring at various times, after Marie and I had parted and she had moved down to Buckingham to develop her new venture - Whitegates Stud.

Despite all the discord between us Marie and I never completely lost our sense of humour. On one occasion I was doing my midnight round of the stables, straightening rugs, feeding, filling water buckets and that sort of thing. It was mid winter, yet I hadn't noticed how frosty it was nor that the fountain in the pond, from where I got the water, had blown spray onto the surrounding path. It had built up quite a sheet of ice and suddenly - swoosh - I was in four feet of water. I tried to climb out but couldn't get a grip with all the ice about. I called out for Marie, who was asleep, but eventually she opened her bedroom window which faced on to the yard. As the moon was shining and some of the stable lights were on, she could see I was in the pond and casually said "What is all the noise about? Stop showing off, there's nobody watching". Before I could answer she shut the window again, switched off the light and went back to sleep! I got out of the pond eventually by taking my shirt off and letting it stick to the frozen path, enabling me to get some sort of grip; I can tell you I was bloody cold. You might ask what did I find so funny about the episode - why, Marie's nonchalant attitude; the manner in which she shut the window and drew the curtains said it all!

The following story has the roles reversed. We must have been having some disagreement for, as Marie got into her car, she put her tongue out at me, maybe not as adult as sticking two fingers up but decidedly less offensive! In retaliation I chucked the bucket of water I was carrying all over the vehicle but without realising the sunroof was open! Not giving me time to apologise, Marie sped off down the road to Thirsk. Twenty minutes later a police car pulled into the yard and two six footers emerged, one asking "Are you Mr. Tinkler, Sir?" I answered "Yes, you know I am". There was then further dialogue "Mr. Tinkler, you are in very serious trouble; your wife has reported that you have tried to drown her". I bounced back with two words "That's Rubbish" - on reflection it was three words! More dialogue "Watch your language, Sir", and "This is no time for frivolity; besides there is strong incriminating evidence to substantiate her accusation". I wanted to know what that was and the officer replied - "She is Very Wet!" Marie recently told me, and it's over twenty years since it happened - she sat in her car in Thirsk's market square waiting for the police car to return and was so disappointed when it did and I was not sitting on the back seat wearing handcuffs!

I seem to have a thing about buckets of water, for I once threw one over one of the Doncaster Baldings when at a Nottingham meeting.

I'd just had a runner break down, yes - another one, and there was a dispute over a saddling box. I wanted to use it for sponging the filly and leave her there until I fetched the horse box to take her home. Balding had other ideas as he required the box for saddling a runner; technically I was in the wrong but I thought that he should have been more considerate so I threw the bucket of water over him. He didn't say a word, but just plonked me one on the nose and that concluded the issue. No way was I going to retaliate and fortunately the incident was hushed up; thank goodness it was, because it could have had serious consequences for both of us.

As time went on Marie and I decided we would utilise the space above the coach house by converting it into a flat for me to live in, as we both considered it best if we lived separately. One day, during the time of the alterations, I found myself walking about the yard having lost my memory. I had a theory about what had happened - I'd been putting a bandage on a horse's leg and somehow got kicked. I knew who I was but not where I was and unfortunately Nigel didn't believe my predicament; he thought I was pulling his leg. I did have an inkling he was my son and that he had a brother. I also knew of Marie and that she was away playing golf but couldn't recall much else. I went up to talk to the builders and couldn't understand what they were doing there; they just laughed at me so I chucked their radio and all their tools out of the window and pushed them down the stairs - not surprisingly they never came back. When Marie did return home we had a sensible chat then she drove me to see the doctor who, in turn, sent me to the hospital at Northallerton. Those there remembered a previous visit I'd had and curiously didn't invite me to stay! It was a good job they hadn't because on the way home my memory started to return and by the time we got back to Boltby I was fine - it had been just another day!

Nigel was being offered further horses to train but, because of the lack of space, he was having to turn them away. It was a question of building more boxes at Boltby or moving on and, because of the general climate of things at our place, he sensibly chose the latter. It wasn't long before he found a property on the outskirts of a charming little village called Langton and only a couple of miles from the Malton gallops. When Nigel made the purchase there was absolutely nothing there apart from a few acres of neglected land, some rotting greenhouses and a dilapidated bungalow. Over the years Woodland Stables has been developed into one of the most imposing training establishments in the area. It now has a delightful house, seventy boxes, a magnificent horse walker, a tan canter and lawns all surrounded by a twenty foot high conifer hedge; incidentally, it was I who planted the Leylandii nearly twenty years ago, time certainly flies. Nigel has invested a large amount of money into the place but the transformation has been incredible.

Within a month of buying the property Nigel had built a dozen boxes, transferred the horses over there, said "Goodbye" to Boltby and sold his cottage at Ampleforth. He was soon churning out the winners and has been doing so ever since. Obtaining planning permission for the initial alterations caused some unintentional amusement. There was an on-site meeting of councillors (who were to do with planning) and I went along to give Nigel support. At one stage a lady member of the party asked "Mr. Tinker" (not a spelling mistake) "It's all very well, but if your son demolishes the hedge along the road side, what on earth will happen to my little blue tits in the winter?" I thought, steady on you little Tinker, don't answer that one, that's if you want the planning application to be approved!

I'm mentioning the following because it is part of what happened during the latter part of our time at Boltby. The subject is a delicate one because some might prefer me not to discuss what is, after all, a private matter. I will therefore skim over things lightly. I have said earlier that Marie's father had been immensely successful and built up a fairly large screw manufacturing business. He also had some property in central London and, before he died, he set up a trust where his daughters became the beneficiaries and, because of Marie's generosity, each of the Tinklers also benefitted. Initially the Inland Revenue valued the assets at a figure far higher than their true value, consequently the Capital Gains and Inheritance Tax demanded was excessive. There was only one solution and that was to put everything on the market, which would give a correct valuation and also raise the money to pay what was owing. In practice each individual was responsible to the Inland Revenue and that's why I considered it correct to take an active interest. The property boom had been missed as far as the buildings were concerned and it was imperative the same mistake was not made with the sale of the business. I'd heard that Armstrongs, the Yorkshire Engineering Company, were interested but, as no headway was being made, I decided to intervene, had several meetings with those at Armstrongs and was instrumental in setting up the negotiations. They did eventually buy 'Ormond' and many years later I was at Beverley Races when I happened to meet once again Armstrong's agent. He told me he hoped the Delfosse family had appreciated my participation in selling the Company because, without my intervention, the transaction would not have materialised. He went on to say how his company had regretted the purchase; enough said.

Once Nigel had left Boltby the place seemed empty, though Atoka, La Bambola and a couple of their offspring were in residence. On the occasion I'm going to mention, they were out at grass, about half a mile from our home when, in the early hours of the morning, an almighty storm erupted. The rain came down in sheets, it thundered and lightened and the ground was unable to absorb all the water. I'd never seen anything like it and we were very concerned about the horses; no way could we have left them out in such conditions. We got dressed and made our way down to the field as quickly as we could and, it goes without saying, got drenched to the skin in the process. It was pitch black and, with the driving rain, finding the horses was not easy. However, we eventually located them trying to get some shelter under a large tree. All four were shivering and looked very distressed and I was extremely relieved when we'd got them back home, dried off, and bedded down into warm dry boxes. Marie and I had done a good job together and if the marriage could have been kept intact that was the time, as mutual appreciation for each other was at a high but it was not to be. In any event we would not have stayed at Boltby; the one time quiet unspoilt hamlet had changed so much since our arrival twelve years before.

I don't recall precisely how the decision was reached but Marie and I eventually agreed to divorce, the grounds being my unreasonable behaviour. I do however believe Marie was very much influenced in the matter. I didn't go near a solicitor. This rather angered Marie's legal man who, I could tell, was wanting a fight but didn't get one. I know there must have been a better solution to the whole sad affair, if only we had looked, but the bottom line is, we didn't. The annulment was finalised towards the latter part of '83. It was all so ridiculously stupid. Most marriages endure and survive considerably more hassle than ours ever encountered. There was no animosity on either side, nor were there any financial arrangements, however I will add that financially Marie put a great deal into the partnership. Emotionally we were both drained; thirty years had been a long time and surely the fact that neither has remarried tells its own story, or does it; most probably we both said never again! There was one thing I learnt throughout, it was the saying "It takes two to make an argument" is a complete fallacy. Exactly!

When Whitegates was put up for sale at £100,000 plus it was very quickly snapped up; in fact a couple of prospective buyers did a spot of private gazumping, with a comparatively young person making the higher bid. He never actually moved in for, soon after taking possession, he had a nasty car crash just outside the village and re-sold the place. The new buyer practically demolished the house and stables and tore up all the landscaped gardens. It's funny how people buy somewhere because they like it and then proceed to knock it down!

After we sold Whitegates and prior to going our separate ways, Marie down south and I, initially, to the Green Man Hotel at Malton, we stayed for a while in the same hotel near Thirsk. The reason we didn't move on immediately was because we had various things to see to, such as the auction of some surplus furniture, lawn mowers and that sort of thing. It was at the sale that Marie's wit again came into play when a double bed was offered up; she called out "Very little used and I can assure you the springs in the mattress are like new!" Another funny story was when Marie later asked "What would you like for Christmas?" I told her "To do a parachute jump and it will only cost £60". Marie's reply was "Cheap at the price, particularly if the chute doesn't open!" Actually she started to doubt my courage and said "OK, I'll pay for it but I bet you £100 when it comes to the crunch you won't jump"; I believe using the word crunch was a tactical manoeuvre on her part. Marie continued, saying "What's more, I will go to the middle of the airfield to check if you do". I replied "But I might land on top of you". Marie had the final word "I'll take the chance because it's a long time since you have done that!" I've just remembered, I never did pay Marie that £100! I asked Marie the same question that she'd asked me, about a Christmas present, and she jokingly said "A tractor for the Stud" so, much to her surprise, I bought one and had it delivered.

I can't remember the last few days that we spent at Boltby, nor seeing the furniture van leaving and heading south. Neither do I recall loading any of the horses into a horse box for a similar journey. I can't even remember Marie driving off from the hotel. I have somehow managed subconsciously to erase it all from my mind - thank goodness I have because I wouldn't want to relive any part of it again.

Marie and I had some marvellous times during the years we were together; so much happened and I would like to think so much was achieved. When the break up occurred anger outweighed the sadness but those sentiments were soon reversed. The anger disappeared altogether but the sadness remained.

Chapter fifteen

The Flockton Grey affair

While Nigel was training at Boltby the Tinklers unwittingly became involved in the notorious Flockton Grey affair, when a three year old was substituted for a two year old. The skullduggery that took place in an attempt to bring off one of the most cunning and fascinating racing coups in the last half century is mind boggling. The reason for the failure of the whole crooked business was that far too many people became involved and the entire operation was too complicated. There is no doubt similar schemes have been successfully carried out, but I would wager that in such cases the number of persons involved were few and a degree of simplicity used. When all is said and done the perfect crime is when it does not appear that one has been committed, which was certainly not the case in the Flockton Grey intrigue. The much publicised race in question was The Knighton Auction Stakes at Leicester on the fourth day of the 1982 flat season. It was won by a staggering 20 lengths at 10/1, by the three year old Good Hand when masquerading as the year younger Flockton Grey.

A great deal has been written, much of it speculation, on what exactly took place. I've spoken with many people who were either directly or indirectly involved in the amazing charade. It's surprising how much people have been prepared to reveal, once a fair length of time has lapsed, though most was said in confidence which I must respect. Before giving my version of the incredible story with all its complexity, I will introduce the key players, though there were others who were closely linked.

Ken Richardson - Was in his middle forties at the time and lived with his wife and family at their stud farm in the village of Hutton Cranswick, near Driffield. He had various successful business interests, including the manufacturing of paper bags. He was also known to be a very heavy gambler and raced horses in this country as well as in Belgium, where he also owned another stud farm. At his trial at York, in the summer of '84, which was two years after the dubious race, Richardson was found guilty of plotting the swindle and given a 12 month suspended jail sentence. He was also fined £20,000 and faced costs of a staggering amount. The Jockey Club subsequently warned him off all racecourses and from running horses for 25 years. He has always maintained his innocence which, in my opinion, has not necessarily been the sensible thing to do, but, of course, it's been his prerogative. I have only ever met him the once, it was at Doncaster Sales, he didn't say much but the court case was pending, so very little could be said.

Colin Mathison - Was very much involved in the conspiracy. A close friend of Richardson and had joint business interests. He was fined £3,000 and warned off by the Jockey Club for 15 years.

Peter Boddy - Richardson's chauffeur and horse box driver cum confederate. Was given a 12 month conditional discharge and warned off by the Jockey Club for three years.

Freddy Wiles - In the racecard he was credited as being the owner of Flockton Grey but it was established this was incorrect and it was only his name that had been used, as a guise. In my opinion he was most fortunate to escape with little more than a reprimand; or had he turned Queen's evidence?

Steve Wiles - Son of Freddy Wiles. Trained in a small way from stables near Barnsley and had connections in Belgium. Was warned off for five years for, among other things, knowingly allowing a horse to run in a race, purporting to having been trained by himself when, in fact, that had not been so. He, too, seemed to be punished lightly and I ask the same question, as I did of Wiles Senior.

Kevin Darley - Was the jockey who rode Flockton Grey (Good Hand) in the notorious race. He was rightly completely exonerated.

Steve Perks - Rode Good Hand in all his three races as a two year old, including the one when he was claimed. I'm sure I'm correct in saying he was never questioned by the police nor any investigating officers of the Jockey Club; if my assumptions are correct, I find it extraordinary, for surely he might have been able to throw some light on to the events.

Flockton Grey - The supposed runner in the notorious race at Leicester. Foaled in 1980, grey colt (later gelded) by Dragonara Palace out of Misippus. Was originally sold as an unnamed foal in November 1980 at the Doncaster Bloodstock Sales for 700 gns. He was then re-sold the following October for 1,700 gns at Tattersalls Yearling Sales, Newmarket; to either Ken Richardson or his associated stud. It must be remembered that by this time Ken Richardson already had the year older lookalike called Good Hand in his possession. At the trial Freddy Wiles stated Richardson had subsequently sold him the Dragonara Palace colt for £2,250 in cash so that it could be entered in his name, thereby making it appear that Ken Richardson no longer had any connection with the horse. The grey was eventually gelded and sent to Steve Wiles' stables and named Flockton Grey, a fact that later caused much controversy owing to a discrepancy of markings.

Good Hand - Foaled 1979, grey colt (later gelded) by Some Hand out of Aberside. He was the three year old used in the switch. As you read on you will discover how the energetic little fellow firstly became involved, then trapped, in what could easily be mistaken for a fictional racing thriller when, in fact, it was very much reality.

I will commence right at the beginning. It all started in the summer of 1979 when George Patching, who had a small stud near Stratford upon Avon, invited my son Col to go and have a look at a couple of foals he had for sale. Col was still riding at the time but he and his wife Carol had already commenced a business of buying foals then selling them on as yearlings. Col rather liked the youngsters and bought them at quite a reasonable figure. One was a grey colt by Some Hand out of Aberside, a real sharp little fellow who was later named Good Hand, and that is how I will refer to him from now on. The following autumn Good Hand unfortunately met with a slight accident to his off fore, nothing serious and mainly superficial, but it prevented him being sent to the yearling sales, so Nigel bought him privately from his brother. The injury which never caused any problems did however leave a scar on the shin of about three inches in length. The disfigurement played a crucial part in proceedings, when identification became such an important issue later in the Flockton Grey trial.

It didn't take Nigel long to find an owner for Good Hand, nor did it take him long to break the colt in and he soon had him in full training once spring arrived. Most of his fast work was done on Jack Calvert's gallops, which were at the top of Sutton Bank and about four miles from Boltby. He was an exceptionally tough character and the work he was doing was bringing him on 'leaps and bounds'. Jack was more than mildly interested in the youngster and considered we had a real flying machine in the yard. Nigel was just as enthusiastic and was confident he could get him ready for a gamble first time out;

the target was a two year old seller over five furlongs at Catterick towards the end of July. Four days prior to the race Nigel rode him in a spin against older horses and he went brilliantly. There was no doubt about it, Good Hand over five furlongs on a comparatively easy track was going to be very difficult to beat in a low grade event.

The omens certainly looked good when Nigel discovered there were only going to be nine runners and Good Hand was drawn perfectly, three off the inside. It happened to be the first race of the afternoon and, as I didn't want people asking me about the horse's chances, I thought it best if I kept out of the way. In the circumstances and with the five furlong gate being adjacent to the road I decided to take the car down to the start. I'd already given John Joyce £4,000 for Good Hand; he laid me a little at 5/1 and the rest at 4/1, but the starting price was half that figure. As for the race, it was a calamity, Steve Perks, who had been engaged to ride, appeared to lose his balance as the gates opened, which caused the horse to rear. Perks could have argued it was the other way about but he didn't - in fact when asked for an explanation none was forthcoming. The following is a quote from Raceform - Good Hand reared, was slow away losing several lengths, headway after three furlongs, finished well to be third, beaten just over two lengths. I was neither the owner nor trainer of Good Hand, but he was in my yard and I had an awful lot to do with him, including his shoeing. To say I was upset is putting it mildly - I am known to be normally an exceptionally good loser, but I wasn't so on that occasion.

The horse's next engagement was the following week at Thirsk, this time over six furlongs. It was another seller but a decidedly better contest than the one at Catterick. As far as I was concerned, because of the extra furlong and the fact he was not well drawn, I was not going to be on a retrieving mission. Nigel had his reasons for keeping with the same jockey and they again finished third, beaten a similar distance as before. I will again quote from Raceform - Good Hand was 5/1 third favourite, looked well, led until headed and weakened inside the final furlong, beaten a neck and two lengths. Considering the pros and cons it was a good run and Nigel had learned a lot from the outing. Good Hand had proved he was genuine, that he was capable of breaking fast and had the ability to make the running for five furlongs. Nigel had always thought six furlongs would be a trifle too far for him and so it proved. His next run was at Ripon a couple of weeks later, again it was a seller, but back to five furlongs. The ground and the draw were not a problem and the horse was really buzzing. He was not that big in stature but very, very, sharp and athletic and I just couldn't visualise him getting beaten. Nigel's logic for again having Steve Perks to ride was that Perks knew the horse's capabilities and would realise he could win if ridden correctly.

Right up to Good Hand being led into the parade ring everything had gone according to plan. I intended to split my bet between several bookmakers and put the first £2,000 on with John Joyce at 13/8. Before I could even say "Thank you" one of his floor men sprinted across to a bookmaker on the rails and laid the bet off. John had said nothing to him, it must have been telepathy! I quickly placed another £3,000 in a couple of places before I realised that the bookmaker who had taken my John Joyce wager kept extending Good Hand's price and taking a fair amount of money for him - Why? Exactly. For one reason or another, he obviously didn't fancy the horse; he knew I was backing him and usually he would respect my judgement - it had cost him enough in the past. The long and short of it was I 'shut the shop' and didn't bet any further; as it was I'd had £5,000 on. I'm not suggesting in the least what the bookmaker on the rails did was in any way wrong, the worst scenario being he had heard Good Hand wasn't busy and which bookmaker wouldn't take advantage of such information!

By the time the horse got down to the start I'd made my way over to the owners and trainers stand, where I met Nigel, who was not at all happy. Perks had been late into the paddock, seemed agitated and got straight on to the horse, without any sort of conversation. The following are quotes from the Sporting Life and Raceform and they certainly tell their own story - Good Hand opened in the betting at 6/4 and, despite heavy support, drifted out to 3/1 at the off. There was also money for Blue Rain (finished second) from 14/1 to 9/2 with very little for the others. The race - Good Hand made headway two furlongs out, not quicken, finished fourth beaten four and a half lengths. It goes without saying I wasn't at all surprised he'd failed to win, what with all the shenanigans that had taken place. The questions I would like answering are - Why was Perks late into the paddock? Why was he on edge? Why did he keep Good Hand covered up for a late run that didn't materialise, when he knew that was not the way to ride him? His blatant excuse of "I forgot about the way he went at Thirsk" certainly didn't hold water with me.

As Perks was dismounting from Good Hand, Nigel told him he would phone the following day (Sunday) to discuss what had happened. Perks however failed to disclose to Nigel that he would not be at home, as he had arranged to go over to Belgium for a couple of rides and wouldn't be back until the Monday. I have mentioned this because it later has some significance. After a selling race has been run the winner is automatically put up for auction, but of course connections can always buy the horse back if they so wish. As for any other runner in such races, the rules state it can be claimed and that's exactly what happened to Good Hand. As soon as I learnt the bad news my priority was to discover who had made the claim, offer some profit and try and secure Good Hand back for the stable; this was permitted in those days. I was told by several people in the weighing room it was either Ken Richardson or an associate of his called Colin Mathison who had put up the £3,100 it had cost to claim the horse, and was most likely the former. I saw Colin Mathison, who said he had bought Good Hand for himself and it had got nothing whatsoever to do with Richardson. Because he had offered the information regarding Richardson, before it was asked for, I doubted him. He wasn't interested in taking profit and I remember remarking "I'm not really surprised because you know he is better than he showed". Incidentally, I gathered Good Hand was to race in Belgium - Yes! Belgium. And who do you think I discovered Perks was going to ride for in Belgium, Exactly. As it transpired, all the talk about Good Hand going to race there was to mislead - just another piece of unnecessary intrigue.

After talking to various people, I walked over to the racing stables for one final look at the young horse and to mention to Nigel's staff what had occurred. I was surprised to find that Good Hand had already been removed; it was within the claimants rights to do so but I wondered why so quickly. I asked those on security if they knew who had taken him and to where? They informed me they had been told that he was going over to Ken Richardson's place near Driffield; yet Mathison had said the claiming had got nothing to do with Richardson. I later learnt that the little grey left Ripon Races in a horse box owned by a Newmarket trainer but, of course, it could have done a detour via Driffield on its way back to base.

I believe that after leaving the racecourse stables he went straight to Richardson's stud near Driffield and remained there for several months. During that time he was gelded and given a complete rest.

As the race chosen for the intended coup was not until the end of the following March, Good Hand would not have needed to start work before sometime in December. Whether that was done at Ken Richardson's place or not is immaterial, the interesting question has always been who eventually did the final training? I know of a couple of people with yards in the north who were wrongly suspected; it must also be assumed Ken Richardson himself didn't and we know from what was said in court that Steve Wiles was not entrusted with the job. It is my opinion it was Newmarket Heath that saw the little grey's dancing hooves. I don't wish to elaborate further - it's sometimes prudent to dodge an issue. I'm not even saying it was a licensed trainer who took charge of Good Hand. Newmarket has always had individuals who will rent a couple of boxes in the corner of a yard and work independently

It seemed everything connected with the whole business was other than straightforward. Even so, I am still prepared to be "generous" and not to say categorically that there had been anything untowards about any of the three races Good Hand had been in, or that he'd been specifically targeted to be claimed. All I am doing is cataloguing the events; coincidences do occur, consequently things aren't always as they seem, no matter how ominous the signs.

As we left Ripon racecourse we counted the cost which had been high and thought we'd probably never hear of the horse again. Little did we realise he was to become a major player in a gigantic deception. After Ripon the next time we heard Good Hand's name mentioned was the following June. It was when George Edmondson called in at our stables at Boltby, to ask us to identify a photograph of the horse. Edmondson was a former detective with the West Yorkshire Police who had become an investigation officer for the Jockey Club. I remember his visit well. There were some rumours circulating in the north that not all had been correct with the Leicester race; they were very 'low key' and we had no reason to connect Good Hand with the matter as Richardson's name had not openly been connected at that time; well not until Edmondson descended upon us. First he showed Nigel a photograph, saying it was of the Leicester winner and asked was it Good Hand? Nigel was obviously surprised, yet straight away confirmed that it definitely was the horse. George Edmondson then walked across the yard to where I was standing and produced a photograph for me to see. I told him in my opinion it was not Good Hand. This caused a mild argument between Nigel and myself, as Nigel was adamant that it was and I was just as adamant that it wasn't. Edmondson eventually interrupted, saying "Hold it boys, I've shown you different photographs I wanted to test your judgements". He then proceeded to show me the photograph Nigel had seen. Yes - this one was without a doubt of Good Hand. It was then Marie's turn to scrutinize. The horse happened to have his mouth wide open as if laughing his head off, which in all probably he was! When Marie saw this she immediately said "That's Good Hand and no way could it be a two year old because it has three year old teeth!" Armed with Marie's exciting observation the man from the Jockey Club proudly drove off with his findings; subsequently others tried to take credit for what Marie had first detected. Incidentally, some time later the police asked Nigel and I to do a further identification of Good Hand at some stables near Beverley. They took us over at different times, making some lame excuses for doing so and what's more, pathetically tried a similar scam to the one used by Edmondson, but this time with live horses. The one they showed me looked more like a Suffolk Punch and couldn't have run fast enough to win an egg and spoon race!

I asked for and received some newspaper cuttings from the

Jockey Club, relating to the trial and matters arising from it. It seems there never was such a horse as Flockton Grey legitimately registered. From that one must assume, rightly or wrongly, Good Hand's markings were used. If that is so, it meant there were two horses with identical markings lodged at Weatherbys. The people there are always extremely affable, but I fear I got lost in bureaucracy in my endeavour to obtain some concrete answers from them.

My idea of what transpired on the day of the race is pretty well what was said in court. It was Monday, 27th of March, 1982. There were two meetings that day, one at Ayr and the other at Leicester. The going at the latter course was officially good to soft and a strip of turf just off the far rails and about 3 yards wide had mysteriously been rolled the entire 5 furlongs - this made for better and faster ground. Flockton Grey was in the first race on the card, a 2 year old Auction Stakes (not a seller) and top apprentice Kevin Darley booked to ride. None of the other 8 runners had previously raced, they had all been cheaply bought as yearlings and it didn't appear much of a contest. However, and it is only incidental, as it turned out three of the runners did go on and win races during the season.

I contend that in the early hours of that Monday morning Ken Richardson sent Peter Boddy and his horse box to Steve Wiles' yard near Barnsley, to collect Flockton Grey as if he was going to run. He had even been fitted with racing plates, which was all a gigantic smoke screen. The horse box didn't go straight to Leicester but, instead, did a wide detour by way of Newmarket to pick up the super fit Good Hand. The box then headed back north to Leicester, and was seen at a service station on the way. There was no real urgency because Peter Boddy didn't want to get to the course too early - in fact the later the better. To say that the two greys were in the same horse box when they swapped over is only academic as was the pre-race identification check. The important factor is, they did exchange places and it was Good Hand that ran in the race.

Now to the contest itself! The stalls were on the far side of the track and 'Flockton Grey' was drawn in the middle, bang in line with the strip that had been rolled. He bounced out of the gate, led all the way and won pulling up by 20 lengths. There were more than just a few raised eyebrows around the winners enclosure after the race and God knows how much the grey would have made had it been a seller!

No money was put on 'Flockton Grey' on the course. It was purely a starting price operation, though I doubt the correctness of the word 'purely'! I would have found it utterly impossible to have backed an unraced 2 year old in a mediocre race at Leicester, to win £200,000 but that was the figure Ken Richardson was purported to have won. With the number of people involved there was bound to have been additional money punted, yet none seemed to get back to the course, which would have been rather amazing were the figures correct. Nevertheless, a great deal of money was involved.

It certainly appeared at first that the gamble had been landed but it was only temporary; no way were the majority of bookmakers going to pay out without an Enquiry and those that did soon demanded and got their money back. They had been caught and bookmakers don't like being caught - Who does? I know several people, including a couple of well known trainers in the north, who would have been exposed had they not returned the thousands of pounds they assumed they had won. Yes, they were the two who were on many people's short list as having trained Good Hand. I also know of a bookmaker who was standing at Ayr on that fateful day who was heavily involved.

The biggest gamble that took place at Leicester was not on Flockton Grey but the one that Ken Richardson took, in fielding against a Tinkler not being at the meeting. Because, if any of us had been there, surely we would have recognised Good Hand. The fact that I wasn't has saved me the embarrassment of asking myself a hypothetical question - Exactly!

As soon as the dope test on the supposed Flockton Grey had been satisfactorily concluded he was loaded into the horse box where Flockton Grey was patiently waiting and both were driven up to Yorkshire. On arriving back at the Wiles' stables Flockton Grey was unloaded and Good Hand proceeded on to Driffield. Steve Wiles returned separately with his wife who, incidentally, had been helping at Leicester; in fact she went down to the start to make sure all was well with their runner.

As soon as George Edmondson heard the shouts, for they were more than whispers, that matters had not been kosher, he commenced making enquiries and starting with Steve Wiles. He was told that Flockton Grey, alias Good Hand, had been sent over to Ken Richardson's stud farm for a rest. George Edmondson's next move was to travel the seventy miles to Driffield, where he was informed by the stud manager that the horse was not there and he knew nothing about him. Back went the Jockey Club's security man, this time to take a statement from Wiles which also turned out to be a pack of lies. A second statement was taken a few days later, which also contained a litter of 'porkies'. On that second visit George Edmondson was shown Flockton Grey who was, of course, minus the scar on the off fore and Steve Wiles admitted he was not the horse that had raced. I understand it was not until the third visit before the whole truth was eventually told in yet another statement. Freddy Wiles, Steve's father, also put pen to paper and the picture became clearer. By this time both greys had not surprisingly gone missing and were incriminatingly discovered sometime later in a field on the

Yorkshire Moors near Whitby. After being found they were taken into police custody and sent to a small farm near Beverley, owned by a police officer. Good Hand was retired and never raced again - Flockton Grey never raced at all!

Of course, George Edmondson didn't realise at the beginning of his enquiries that a horse called Good Hand was involved. It was only later that he suspected it might have been a horse older than a two year old which had actually won the race. Edmondson's colleagues had been through the archives at Wellingborough, where the details of all racehorses' passports are kept. They show a horse's markings and, in Good Hand's case, the scar on his off fore, which was obviously a good identification mark. This had been noticed at the dope test after the race, when the horse's bandages were removed; it could only have been that Good Hand's markings were used when Flockton Grey's naming form was being compiled. When George Edmondson discovered Good Hand's passport, showing he was a three year old grey gelding with a scar on the off fore, he thought he'd struck gold and, after visiting the Tinklers and noting Marie's observations, he knew he had; the Fraud Squad were then called in. It was more than two years before the trial was held at the Crown Court, York, and the defendants found guilty by a jury's majority decision. The judge was Harry Bennett, QC, and he told Ken Richardson "You were clearly the mainspring of the enterprise and, but for you, the others would not have become involved". Richardson's Defence Counsel, George Carman, QC, said in court "K.R. lost his private kingdom for a horse", a remark I find difficult to understand coming, as it did, from one representing the defence that had pleaded 'not guilty'!

Ken Richardson had several attempts to have the case re-opened, always stating there is fresh evidence with grey areas. As I see it there were only two grey areas, Flockton Grey and Good Hand, Exactly!

There is a sequel to the Flockton Grey affair that has not been told before. Leading up to and during the trial, the press were very inquisitive. They were continually on the phone or calling in to interview us. I had one particular phone call, asking if there had been any further developments I would like to talk about and had Ken Richardson been in contact. He seemed surprised when I replied in the negative. Actually something had transpired and I am convinced it was that reporter or his paper who had initiated it. Two extremely rough characters came to Malton, stayed overnight at one of the pubs, had a meal at Florios Restaurant, and asked where did Tinkler the trainer live. They were wanting Nigel's stables but were directed to his brother's place, as Col also was training at the time; those at Florios had mixed up the two Tinklers. The couple of scruffs waited until the following morning before going to Musley Bank, having most likely changed the number plates on their car. They saw Col and on realising they had gone to the wrong Tinkler, told him to pass a message on to Nigel. It was that he would be in serious trouble if he didn't change the statement he had given to the police and they indicated with their fists they meant business. Actually the only statement Nigel had ever made was the same as given by others - that in their opinion the photograph of the horse in the winners enclosure at Leicester was that of Good Hand. It was obvious the caller on the phone knew of the supposed threat, wanted me to mention it and implicate Ken Richardson, thereby creating another story to report on. Pitiful, wasn't it?

One last word on the Flockton Grey affair - I don't think Ken Richardson's sole motive was money; I honestly believe he primarily wanted the thrill of 'Robbing a bank'.

Postscript - Nearly fifteen years after the Flockton Grey trial Ken Richardson was again in trouble when tried at Sheffield Crown Court for conspiring to burn down the stand at Doncaster Rovers, at which he was Chairman. Even though extensive damage was done, the torching was another botched up job; nevertheless he was sentenced to four years imprisonment.

Chapter sixteen

The Full Circle story

During the last few months of my time at Boltby I had been working on an idea I had for group ownership. It was an entirely new concept, which I actually put into operation the following June (1984), when I launched Full Circle. By the end of that year there were quite a number of other copycat groups formed and, since those early days, there have been numerous others. I opened the door to people who otherwise would never have thought it possible to have a share in a racehorse. The pleasure shareholders get from being so involved is monumental and the phrase I used when advertising - 'Make dreams come true' - has been widely used by others because that's exactly what racing companies are all about. The racing industry has also benefited in many ways, notably by the millions of pounds subscribed by the shareholders. Without a doubt Full Circle was one of the most successful groups, with over 170 winners to its credit. Unfortunately, as is often the case where money is involved, there were at the beginning some unscrupulous minds managing groups but they have been very much in the minority; generally, racing clubs, as they are usually called, are totally honest.

The work involved in 'setting up' Full Circle was intricate and very time consuming. I concluded that if I could enrol a couple of hundred people at between £400 and £500 each I would have enough capital to pay all the initial expenses and to buy and have in training three horses. But, of course, as there had been nothing previously with which to compare, it was pure speculation whether the figure of two hundred shareholders would be achieved. The Jockey Club had very strict rules about ownership and I don't believe they have varied much over the years. Not more than four people could be in partnership in an individual horse and not more than twelve could belong to a syndicate, though a club, such as a golf or cricket club, could be registered as an owner, so long as it had been in existence for a number of years. Another way a group of people could have had an interest, would have been if they were shareholders in a Public Company, for example a manufacturing business, though, if one of the shareholders happened to be a disqualified person with the Jockey Club, the company in question could not have become a registered owner.

After numerous discussions, with many people who specialised in Company Law, I came up with a formula to work on. After depositing the required £25,000 in a bank I would form a limited company with the sole purpose of owning racehorses. I would endeavour to make a profit though, at the same time, stress that I didn't expect to do so. The shares would be put on the market at roughly the figure I had in mind. The company would be dissolved each year with whatever assets there were being distributed equally among the shareholders. The reason for dissolving each year would be to enable a repeat of the exercise, thus generating the flow of further capital. To all intents and purposes it would basically be an administration matter, for the name of the company would remain the same. However, as that on its own would not technically be in order, I would add a different suffix each year, in the form of a single letter of the alphabet, A, B, C, and so on.

I went down to the Jockey Club to discuss the matter but

understandably I was rather apprehensive; I need not have been, for I was told at our meeting that so long as the concept didn't violate Jockey Club rules they were happy and wished the enterprise every success. I returned home elated and spent literally hundreds of hours designing a brochure and compiling a prospectus to go with it. The former was difficult and required much research. In fact the first I submitted to Company House was turned down but, after certain alterations, was accepted. The law did not permit the advertising of shares for sale in a Limited Company but that's exactly what I wanted to do. I did however find a legal way round the obstruction, though I was walking very close to the cliff edge.

For the public to buy a share in the newly formed, therefore unknown, Full Circle the brochure would have to convey sincerity and sell a dream that could come true. The following are extracts - People become racehorse owners for various reasons. They may wish for privileged information or are primarily fascinated by the power and splendour of gorgeous horses. Then there are others who just want to be part of the prestigious sport of racing and enjoy all the fun and excitement it generates. But, whatever the reasons, Full Circle affords the perfect opportunity for ambitions to be fulfilled and a new fascinating interest in life acquired....... Being an owner and having a string of racehorses is a totally different world and you don't have to go racing to experience all the emotion and fantastic excitement. Just to talk about your horses or see them on television is a tremendous thrill and brings so much happiness. Imagine the sensation of having a runner in the Grand National or the electric atmosphere of being part of a successful gamble. All enchanting magic. As for the prospectus, I achieved the near impossible; it was set out in a way which was easy to understand yet kept scrupulously to the intricate language of Company Law.

Initially the company was called Full Circle Thoroughbreds Limited. But later the Jockey Club required all such racing groups to be a PLC. The move was, basically, to give people greater protection. I had to make alterations at Company House and the title then became Full Circle Thoroughbreds (followed by the appropriate letter indicating the year) PLC.

It was January '84 before I moved to the Green Man Hotel in Malton and had an office in a large mobile home at the back of Nigel's stables. I'd planned to launch Full Circle at the beginning of June, which I did with adverts in the Sporting Life, the leading racing paper at that time. I thought that by waiting until the flat season was in full swing, the timing would be correct. For the initial launching it was but I soon realised it would be more convenient if the company's year end coincided with the end of the flat season. This policy was eventually adopted, though it took a number of years of extending each Full Circle term to longer than a bare twelve months. My brother Peter, who then lived in a village close to Skegness, had maintained his interest in racing over the years so I appointed him as company secretary. Even though the registered office was at the stables, for convenience I used Peter's address and telephone number in the adverts. I decided to offer the shares at £450 each but I hadn't the foggiest notion what the response would be. The advert went into The Sporting Life on a Saturday and I stayed with Peter and his wife Lorna on the Friday evening, to be ready for the phone calls the following day. The first came just before seven o'clock and they continued throughout the day; it was literally non stop. We had over 300 calls and took it in turn to answer the phone. Peter and his wife were marvellous; to talk to so many people and write down their names and addresses, all from one phone, took some doing. With further calls throughout the following week, plus all the postal requests for brochures, we'd soon sent off practically all the thousand I'd had printed. Obviously the following Saturday's advertisement didn't bring about the same response, with most people having already seen it the previous week. Nevertheless, the calls were still considerable and required more brochures to be printed.

It was only a matter of time before the avalanche of cash, postal orders and cheques came pouring through the letter box at Peter's place - roughly £160,000 worth. I was absolutely delighted with the response. Coincidentally, the final number of shareholders in the first year was 360. I say coincidentally because, as you know, there are 360 degrees in a full circle! A couple of weeks after the company was launched the applications to buy shares suddenly ceased - there wasn't even a trickle. I was totally mystified, that is until I had a phone call to my office. The caller pleaded with me to let him become a shareholder. Apparently he'd sent his cheque along with the necessary forms to Skegness but Peter had returned them, together with a curt note saying just two words - 'Full Up' I wondered how many more Peter had sent back at nearly a monkey a throw! His explanation to me was that he considered there were too many joining. I didn't understand his reasoning because the date of the closure for the sale of shares (which was required by company law to be stated in the prospectus) had not yet been reached. I honestly felt he was under enormous pressure and that it would be better if Nigel were company secretary and this was amicably agreed. I greatly appreciated what Peter and Lorna had done during those first couple of weeks; it had been exceptionally hard work and they wouldn't accept any remuneration.

To put the record straight, Full Circle was the first company of its kind to be registered, but another such organisation, 'British

Thoroughbreds' came into being at about the same time. I never made a secret of what I was contemplating, so it might or might not have been that my idea was imitated. They were initially tremendously successful, spent massive amounts on advertising and enrolled far more shareholders than Full Circle. Nothing seems to last forever for, as with Full Circle, the company ceased operating several years ago.

It was soon pretty obvious Full Circle had enough capital to have three or four horses in training. I had kept down to a minimum the cost of setting up the operation but there had still been numerous items to contend with, such as legal fees, advertising, printing, to mention just a few. With Full Circle being a limited company, even registering at Company House and the Jockey Club cost close to £1,000. I realised the administration expenses I'd yet to encounter would be considerable and that was the reason I decided not to take any directors fees for at least the first couple of years. Budgeting was going to be the all important factor and, of course, I was going to be dealing mainly with people (shareholders) who knew little about the cost of keeping racehorses in training. What I feared most and had to make provision for, was horses not staying sound. It is a fact of life that a great percentage of horses in training go wrong in one way or another; some just require rest to heal their troubles but, with others, it is often far more serious. Whichever, a reserve of money would have to be kept available for replacements.

It was decided that Nigel would train all the Full Circle horses even though Col had also taken out a licence. It wasn't a question of favouritism on my part; it was Col who was not over keen to take charge of any of the new venture's horses, believing there could be too much hassle with so many shareholders being involved. It was nothing other than that.

The occupations of the shareholders varied considerably. Over the years there was a brain surgeon, a member of parliament, a tax inspector, even a VAT inspector, there was also an Irish priest. There were young secretaries who goggled at the two year olds and members who goggled at the secretaries! Also an airline pilot, several publicans, one or two from the building trade and a well known racing commentator stayed in the Group practically throughout. A big game hunter from South Africa, a professional gambler from Brighton and a bookmaker from Birmingham swelled the numbers. Then there was the taxi driver from near Fontwell; we used his services when flying down to the races there, getting picked up from a local landing strip and taken back after racing. A couple of bank managers, several postmen, a policeman and a prison warder had shares. Plus a great many who had retired and, at the other end of the scale, a schoolboy spent his savings to buy into the Group, the list was endless.

From a mere handful at the beginning, Full Circle would have at its height as many as a couple of hundred visiting the stables on a Sunday morning and the number would double that on an Open Day. They would come from far and wide armed with polo mints and carrots for the horses to nibble at and cameras by the dozen for themselves to click at. Nigel and I would always be at hand to make them welcome but, I know some went away convinced they had been snubbed because we'd not had a one to one conversation. It was inevitable that would happen with there being so many milling around but I can assure those who felt slighted, it was never intentional. A shareholder who resided in Ireland used to come over regularly; I'd book him into a local pub and he would stay for a week. He would go to the gallops every morning and thoroughly enjoy himself. That's what Full Circle was supposed to be all about, fun and enjoyment.

Many who came to visit the stable would say "It's nice seeing the horses but it's worth coming just for the crack"; there was certainly a great deal of laughter on those Sunday mornings. I recall a couple from Halifax, they would be in their mid sixties, he a small thin chap and his wife decidedly the opposite; once I hid the husband in the office and then threw his cap into one of the stables. Of course, 'someone' saw the cap amongst the straw and suddenly it was panic stations because, with a little help from me, everyone assumed the horse had eaten him. The wife however didn't get at all distressed, all she said was "Serves silly bugger reet, I told him not to get too near doors and it's a good thing I've learnt to drive!" I can assure you when he did eventually come out of hiding there was a jolly good bollocking waiting, though somehow I escaped any kind of reprimand.

There was another time when a mother, whose baby was crying incessantly, said to me "Colin, do you mind if I change the baby?" I answered "No, I don't mind, but, whatever happens, get one that's not bloody howling!"

Of all the shareholders in Full Circle Don White stood out. I renamed him 'Clint Eastwood' because he was never far away from a camera lens and must have led in over fifty per cent of our winners. On one occasion we had three winners at two separate meetings, all on the same day, and the times of the races were such that Clint was able to lead them all in; mind you, the two courses were only a hundred miles apart! I don't know exactly how many racing groups there are at the present time but I'm sure Clint will belong to most. The photo finishes sometimes catch him out when two different clubs own the horses concerned, he doesn't know which to lead in until the result is announced!

The ink was hardly dry on the share certificates when I bought Full Circle their first horse. It was towards the end of June and it had just won the two year old seller at Warwick. He was a brown colt called Octolan and at the auction after the race I had to go to 5,250 guineas to secure him. He had been trained at Newmarket by Hinchliffe, was ridden by Ray Cochrane and had started favourite to win first time out. It wasn't long before Octolan was carrying the newly registered Full Circle colours of blue with red seams and cap; in fact it was at York's July meeting, again in a seller, though a better quality contest than the one at Warwick. A fairy tale start would have been ideal but it was not to be; nevertheless, he ran a most respectable race, finishing sixth with Eddie Hide in the saddle. A third at Thirsk the following month was another pleasing effort but the climax came a couple of weeks later, on August the sixteenth at Catterick. It was there that Octolan won the opening race on the card, The Radio Times Selling Stakes, over seven furlongs. He was ridden by Tony Ives on that occasion and, of course, trained by Nigel. It was an exciting contest with Full Circle's first winner going to the front close home and scoring by a head; incidentally, he was retained at the subsequent auction without a bid. I had been reasonably confident about the outcome and had a bet of £3,500 to £2,000, which for me was the icing on the cake.

There was jubilation all around with about a dozen shareholders crowding the winners enclosure. People at Catterick that afternoon had witnessed the beginning of a new era; soon there would be group owned horses winning every day of the week and on every racecourse in the country. I had changed the face of racing. Whether for better or worse is not for me to judge.

Octolan had one further run for us after that; it was at Yarmouth when Lester Piggott rode him, he was unplaced and we subsequently sold him on. There is a delightful story about the race and Lester Piggott which I tell often but unfortunately can't put into print! - Sorry.

By that time I'd already bought Rainbow Vision, a brown two year old filly, by Prince Tenderfoot out of Marie's exceptionally talented Atoka. 'Rainbow' was the first horse Marie had bred and originally realised 10,000 guineas when sold at Tattersalls Newmarket Yearling Sale. However, eight months later I was able to buy her for half that figure from Charles Booth the Malton trainer; this came about because of the financial collapse of his patron. She was a beautiful filly and what a thrill it was for me when she notched up Full Circle's second success at Ayr and I was able to lead her into the winners enclosure, just as I had her dam six years before. Tears literally rolled down my cheeks; mind you they might still have done so had she got beaten, for I had a hell of a bet! 'Rainbow' had already had a couple of races for us at Redcar and Chester and, even though her coat had been a little on the dull side, had managed to finish third on both occasions. At Ayr she was entirely different, absolutely oozing well being. It was that sparkle that persuaded me to have the £7,000 to £2,000 about her. Tyrone Williams rode a peach of a race and, without resorting to too much pressure, got home by the narrowest of margins. Unfortunately she only managed one further run before developing a leg problem and was retired to Stud, with Marie giving Full Circle a nominal sum to get her back. I'm not dismissing the leg injury lightly but it's a lovely story with a happy ending.

Meningi was Full Circle's next acquisition, a chestnut colt (though Nigel had him gelded). Being a strong, good looking horse I was surprised to get him for only 3,000 guineas when Michael Jarvis sent him to Tattersalls Newmarket September Sale. He was a cast off, having made no show in any of the three races he'd been in. There was, however, a transformation as soon as Meningi arrived in Yorkshire. The horse's attitude completely changed; he won three hurdle races in as many months at Ayr, Kelso and Catterick. Then ran a blinder when finishing fifth in the Waterford Crystal Supreme Novice's Hurdle at Cheltenham, each time ridden by Nigel. The following year Meningi also won a couple of flat races. He was a gorgeous horse and I managed to win a great deal of money backing him at odds even more generous than the starting prices of 3/1, 7/1, 6/1, 11/2 and 5/1.

By the time Full Circle had reached the conclusion of its first year I was all geared up to launch the second. A newly designed brochure had been printed and sent to the existing shareholders and an advertising campaign was in full swing. Because the stock had been valued and other assets known, the company was able to finalise the first twelve months accounts earlier than had been anticipated. It had been my intention, at the end of each term, to return to the shareholders in the region of ten percent of their original outlay. This could only be achieved by retaining a considerable amount of cash to add to the other assets. I found this to be unrealistic, if I were going to utilise the funds I had to their true potential, so the target figure was dispensed with.

I was delighted with the way things had materialised; five winners and a fifth at the Cheltenham Festival was more than I could have wished for in the first year. Throughout the whole time of Full Circle I alone made all the administrative decisions and, because of my indifference to what I personally paid for, I lost out financially on numerous occasions. In spite of my 'generosity' to Full Circle a large section of the press, though I must emphasise not all, were continually after my scalp and gave me bad coverage. Such headlines as 'Tinkler's racing company loses thousands' wasn't particularly good publicity and, when the actual figures were given, it read even worse. Anyone with a grain of intelligence knew that Full Circle was not expected to be a profit making organisation. It was in existence to own horses to race and give pleasure to all those connected. People don't join golf clubs or go sailing in order to enlarge their bank accounts. One venomous press attack stated that Full Circle had paid a £450 fine I'd incurred for drink driving when, in fact, I've been teetotal all my life. I was continually reading damaging inaccuracies and the space the papers gave to the lame apologies, when forced to retract their untruths, was pathetic. I never understood the aggression, for what I had introduced was so beneficial to racing.

Full Circle had just commenced its second year when I decided to move their account away from Malton and, as Lloyds in York had touted for the business, I went there. Twice a week, I would gather up the cheques and cash I'd received from the shares that had been sold, put them in an envelope, take it through to York in the evening and put it through the bank's letter box.

I was soon to encounter my second fracas with a bank, in the space of a few years; on looking through a statement one morning I noticed a bunch of cheques and some cash, totalling in the region of £5,000, had been omitted. I phoned the bank's manager and, after he'd made some enquiries, I was told the envelope had not been seen by anyone there. Now, I didn't wish to contact any of the shareholders whose cheques were involved, for that would have caused too much of a disturbance and for me to ask "Has your cheque been presented?" would not have shown a great deal of competence on my part. Fortunately there was no need to because I had taken some cash out and replaced it with one of my own personal cheques, and, if that cheque had been cashed, it meant whoever had done so could be traced. I didn't hold out much hope, I assumed the cash had been stolen, by a bank employee, and the cheques destroyed. Thankfully, this was not the case, for I discovered my cheque had gone through another account at Lloyds. Armed with that information I went over to York to see the manager, but he was not at all affable - in fact most aggressive. For some obscure reason he still denied the bank had ever received the envelope and took exception to me saying there had either been some fraudulent goings on or some utter slackness. Whichever it had been, I was not leaving the bank until the matter was resolved. The bank manager saw the situation differently, I was informed it was closing time and, if I didn't go, the police would be called in to escort me out! That was 'a red rag to a bull' situation. I went to the counter where there was a queue of customers and 'gave tongue', I let rip, shouting that the bank had lost £5,000 of my money and I wasn't leaving until it was found. Surprisingly there was not a 'bloody' in the outburst, I had used them all up in the manager's office with a few f*****gs thrown in for good measure and that was besides what I called him!

The chief cashier eventually decided to bring some sanity to the situation; he told me the money had been located in another Mr. Tinkler's account, and had now been transferred over to that of Full Circle and gave me a receipt. Actually, I'm sure they were trying to save face, because if they did have another Tinkler with an account, surely they would have looked there earlier. Besides, the paying in slip which had accompanied the cash and cheques, was made out to 'Full Circle'! He was most apologetic and whether or not they had traced the £5,000 at that time I don't know; I didn't make an issue of it for I hadn't come for an argument, but just to locate the money. I had been at the bank five hours and was back again a couple of days later, this time to close the account. I was told the manager was on sick leave as he'd had a nervous breakdown - I wasn't at all surprised!

After the Lloyds fiasco I transferred Full Circle's business back to the NatWest in Malton, where I had my personal account. Several years later I was in there when invited to look at a new computer that had been installed. It meant passing the safe which had its door wide open and I could see the stacks of money on the shelves. I jokingly said to the manager "You are taking a bit of a chance leaving the safe door open - I could rob it". He nonchalantly replied "Mr. Tinkler, you wouldn't benefit if you did - because it all belongs to YOU!

In spite of the adverse publicity, Full Circle continued to flourish. It mustered more than twice the number of shareholders and triple the number of winners in the second year (Full Circle B). A quote from The Sporting Life, 'Fearless punter Colin Tinkler Snr, hit the jackpot at Hamilton Park on Saturday. He'd had an even £5,000 bet with a Tyneside bookmaker, last August, that his Full Circle Company would have ten winners within the year. It was when Wessex, a former unreliable character, won the Airdrie Handicap that the required number of winners was reached. It was the same again for Full Circle C with further increases in both shareholders and winners, there being 25 of the latter, with the most notable being The Ellier, ridden by Gee Armytage to a superb victory in the Kim Muir at the Cheltenham Festival.

It was in June of that year, 1987, that I introduced my premium rate racing information service; it was a great innovation and has only lasted so long because of my sincerity and the information I give. For a time, I also continued to operate the ordinary answering machine from the office; this was for news regarding the Full Circle horses only. I signed a contract with Telecom to rent the premium line numbers for £500 a week and didn't initially advertise, but I have since done so, very occasionally, in some premier racecourses and William Hill Action Line magazines. Of course, all those in Full Circle were given the number and, fortunately for me, freely gave it to others. As the service was the first of its kind people were curious and the press reports about all the money I was winning, by punting, worked in my favour. The first two years generated over a million calls but that was before most firms and Government Departments put a barrier on employees phoning premium lines. Even so, the total number of calls I've received over the years is more than five million. I've never sent out less than three messages a day, with usually one being from the races. It has been continual without a single break and the percentage of winners I have given has been staggering, with not a losing year. I get the papers delivered by taxi each morning at six o'clock and work on from there. I back ninety per cent of the horses I select and there is always a logical reason if I don't; also my policy of advising on all aspects of betting has been very profitable for punters, or pirates as I call them. I never read form, it's what is going to happen and not what has happened that counts!

I once said to Nigel "My eyesight is not as good as it was but as long as I can spot pretty girls and non triers I will be all right". His quick reply was "Don't count on it - they can both get you into trouble - I know!" From the outset I've never tried to con callers by keeping them on the line longer than necessary, in order to bring in greater revenue. Admittedly, until comparatively recently, I would not only give betting advice, my conversation would digress to amusing happenings. The whole idea was to try to be entertaining as well as informative but, with Telecom continually increasing the charges for calls, I have felt it necessary to curtail the length of time I'm talking and concentrate entirely on punting matters. My major coups have been when I gave Norton Coin when 200/1 before he went on to win the Cheltenham Gold Cup and my correct forecasting at 50/1 and 40/1 respectively when the Nigel Benn/Chris Eubank and Holyfield/Lennox Lewis fights ended in draws. I recently went public with my Company and thought by so doing the volume of calls would increase, but they haven't, which is rather disappointing though not calamitous. Incidentally, at the time of writing, calls cost £1 a minute and the main information line number is 09068 200 700.

Full Circle D mustered approximately 2,000 shareholders and more than a couple of dozen horses in training; ending the campaign with 38 winners. Another magnificent achievement, but even that figure was surpassed the following year. Full Circle E had close on 40 individual horses in training at various times during its twelve months and trotted out an impressive half century of winners. They also had a further hundred placed and became the leading British based owner for races won. There was an enormous amount of work involved, Nigel in particular doing a marvellous job; I trebled the office staff to three and bought an additional brand new horse box to transport all the runners. I had been living in a room next to the office since practically the commencement of Full Circle. It was convenient as I could then work until the early hours of the morning - never having more than four hours sleep a day. I was receiving applications for shares from all over the world, with the final number issued being in excess of two and a half thousand. There were dozens at the races every time there was a runner and never less than a hundred for a Saturday meeting. All wore the Full Circle owner's badge, though only a handful were allowed a free entry. It was a question of the first few who presented themselves at the owners entrance receiving the official racecourse owners badge for the day; it was they who were also invited into the parade ring. It was not entirely a fair procedure but it sufficed and I couldn't think of a better system.

As to the winners' enclosure, I didn't restrict the numbers, though I did try to keep everyone to the front of the horse, often to no avail. At times it became more than a little congested and my enthusiastic cheering didn't exactly offer a calming influence. It's rather amazing that no-one was ever kicked. My antics when buying in our seller winners were not exactly the norm and would attract a large crowd around the ring. To do the bidding I used hand puppets, of which I possessed quite a collection, with Mr. Frog being the favourite. The razzmatazz was always greeted with lots of laughter and clapping, so obviously most people enjoyed the banter. On one occasion John Botterill, the Auctioneer, called out to me "Mr. T., can that frog pay for the horse he's bidding for?" With that the puppet dived into one of my pockets and brought out a wad of £50 notes. It was all rather hilarious and made light of the usually boring five minutes that follows a selling race. I would, or rather the puppets would with my assistance, invariably advance the bidding at £1,000 a call. It brought further entertainment and the final figure reached would not necessarily have been lower, had the bids been of a more conventional nature.

We actually had over 600 at the Full Circle Annual Dinner Dance that year, which was held at the York Racecourse and I'm sure I spoke to everyone present. The dances, and the A.G.M's, were great fun and I introduced giant television screens showing videos of all the Full Circle winners. I always invited the press, which caused surprise amongst some of them considering what they had written, Exactly!

No one person was allowed two shares in Full Circle, the idea being to keep everyone equal. Of course a husband and wife could have a share each, but a member from Ireland who was single was determined to have two shares. He 'slipped through the net' as it were, by having one issued to a Mr. G. Fish from the same address as his; yes, he paid £450 for his goldfish to become a shareholder. His Irish logic was he would receive twice the amount when the assets were distributed at the end of the year! Opposite to that was the man who didn't wish to keep the share he had. It was at Haydock Park on a wet Saturday afternoon when Dale Park, one of the Full Circle two year olds, romped home rather unexpectedly at 11/1. I hadn't backed the youngster though several shareholders did have a few quid on; but not the irate member who stormed into the winners' enclosure shouting "The whole thing's a bloody twist, I want out". He was still blasting off when he threw his Full Circle Owners Badge to the ground; he was fortunate not to be arrested for causing a disturbance.

The whole time Full Circle was in being, that oafish prat was the only shareholder with whom I had a real disagreement; obviously there were others with grievances that never came to my notice but all in all they appeared a nice crowd of people. Of course, there was the odd bore that seemed to demand my attention more than others and they were always the ones that thought they knew absolutely everything there was to know about racing, including who could train and who could ride, or rather, who couldn't train and who couldn't ride.

Next it was Full Circle 'F' but where had all the shareholders gone? Only half had decided to stay involved and there were only a handful of new faces; though the vibes had not indicated this would be the case. Nevertheless, Full Circle notched up a further 26 winners but it was obvious the wheels were coming off, indeed, had come off by the following year when there were even less shareholders. Obviously I had less money to spend resulting in less winners. In fact the blue and red colours passed the post first on only nine occasions with one horse being responsible for six of them. Money doesn't necessarily guarantee success in racing but it's not possible to have a continual stream of winners without it.

The next two years netted only half a dozen winners, then in '94 none at all and finally, in '95, it was left to the enchanting Rawaan to virtually wind up proceedings with a couple of successes, firstly at Perth and finally with number 176 at Market Rasen on 17th June. Of the hundred faithful shareholders that remained only a dozen of them saw the race which marked the end of an era. In the space of eleven years I'd climbed to the top of the mountain, admired the view, then crashed down to the bottom; it was one almighty fall. There must have been many contributory factors as to why the 'cookie crumbled' so dramatically and with such devastation. Some shareholders had become owners in their own right and still have horses in training with Nigel; though the numbers were only marginal. Then there were those who left Full Circle because they found being involved was unaffordable, of course, I appreciated their position. Also a large number joined other racing groups for one reason or another, many probably imagining the grass was greener on the other side of the fence. Those shareholders didn't deserve Full Circle, nor all the hard work and personal finance I had put into the Company. No, I don't harbour any resentment but quite naturally it was very disappointing. Taking everything into consideration, it was extremely difficult to understand how something so incredibly successful should suddenly and catastrophically collapse, though at no time had I been conceited enough to believe it couldn't happen.

My integrity was flawless but not all the decisions I made were the right ones. I came to the conclusion that the main bone of contention, existing amongst the majority of the shareholders, was that they considered, though wrongly, the whole enterprise to be a

Tinkler benefit; that the horses were solely for me to punt on, Nigel to train and his wife, Kim, to ride. They seemed to forget about the pleasure they should have derived from owning them. I'm sure that most shareholders had become spoilt, with too many runners and too many winners. It was just like a child having too many toys to play with, it becomes quickly bored with them all. Apart from the first couple of years, I should definitely have had fewer horses in training and put through a resolution to alter the Company's Articles of Association; enabling me to retain some money for the future. I don't believe that some of the adverse press coverage I received, over the years, played any significant role in Full Circle's demise - though it would have been better without it. With regard to my premium rate information line, I believe some held the view that Full Circle should have derived the income from it. I don't know why, for 'Racing Communications' was my personal company. It might also have been more sensible had I repressed my cavalier manner and curtailed my sense of humour. For instance, one of the shareholders asked, in an exaggerated Lancashire accent "Mr. Tinkler, have I said goodbye to my £450 - will I ever see any of it again?" My reply was "Yes, if you go into the trainers' car park". I don't think he appreciated my humour and what I'd said couldn't have been further from the truth. In fact, I took very little from Full Circle and what I did take I gave back in numerous ways. Nigel, likewise, didn't charge for anything other than training fees. He received no remuneration for being Company Secretary, nor any expenses incurred while on Full Circle business and likewise no commission for buying or selling the horses. Company Law demanded that Full Circle should have two Directors and that's why my other son Col was on the Board, but he received absolutely nothing for being so. I now realise that the stringent monetary policy I adopted, which was solely to show my genuineness, was neither necessary, sensible nor appreciated and my stupidity in the matter certainly didn't enhance the Tinkler coffers.

Full Circle's brilliant success had been a team effort and I thank everyone for the hard work they put in, in whatever capacity, whether it was training, riding or administration; my appreciation was enormous. As for the horses, the majority were superb and it is impossible to praise them too highly. For my part, I know I derived an enormous amount of pleasure being involved but, 'Nothing can be relied upon to last forever'.

Much happened within the Tinkler clan during the Full Circle years, though, before I venture in that direction, I'll conclude the Full Circle story. There were 54 individual horses who won 176 races, 69 being on the flat and 107 over jumps. A similar number of horses also ran without winning, though most of those managed to be placed. Nigel trained all the winners with the sole exception of Monanore, when he won for us at Fairyhouse; Bill Harney, the horse's original Irish trainer, was in charge of him on that occasion.

A total of 23 jockeys rode the Full Circle winners, at 38 different courses. In the majority of cases I left the riding arrangements to Nigel, though at times we did discuss the matter. On one such occasion after rejecting numerous jockeys suggested by him he said "How about Fred Archer, at least he will be able to do the weight!" When I asked who was his agent Nigel answered "The devil and I'm sure you will have his phone number"!

Another interesting point is that less than a third of the winners started odds on. Surely this fact puts paid to the notion, held by many, that the Full Circle runners were always at too short a price for the majority of punters. The following are some race position figures which show outstanding sequences and the marvellous consistency that prevailed:-

3332WW3 - 224W22W - WOW332WW3 - 22W3320W2 -
WO224WW3W3W - 2WWW3W - 3WW2W - WWWW2W -
32W4W2434W - 3W22242 - 23WWW204 - WO2WO2WW -
WOW22WW - WW34WW

In my general review of Full Circle I've already referred to the
winners the Group had in its first year. I will now reflect upon some
of the other successes Full Circle had throughout the years. Tony
Ives was again in the saddle on the Group's first success in its second
year. The horse was a gorgeous two year old filly called Wow Wow
Wow and the race was at Thirsk; she won by just under a length from
a large field having made all. The filly had been working
exceptionally well at home so I had a bet of £5,000 to £2,000 about
her. She won a further twice during the summer, both in Scotland, but
with them being rather competitive events my punting was only
negligible. It was a similar story the following spring, for she again
won first time out at Thirsk, though this time Kim was on board; I
got 4/1 to my money which netted me £8,000. The person leading
her round the parade ring before the race was wearing a smart
lightweight blue windcheater; with a blazer type badge of under
three inches diameter, bearing the Full Circle logo. A very agitated
official rushed across to where I was standing and excitedly informed
me that the garment would have to be removed. The badge
apparently was braking the rules regarding advertising. What a load
of absolute diabolical rubbish and how things have now changed.

Wow Wow Wow had a further two outings before we took her to
Edinburgh for a Mickey Mouse seller. Kim had become the filly's
regular pilot so was again entrusted with the job of, what appeared to
be, just a question of guiding her home. Obviously the odds were

322

going to be cramped so you can imagine my surprise when 6/4 was on offer; because of this I was more than a little apprehensive but still went in with six thousand to four. More so in those days than later, there would always be a dozen punters or so who would religiously pursue me around the betting ring and as soon as I made a move they would follow suit. It was no different on this occasion: the money poured on the Full Circle runner, yet her price eased to 7/4 at the off. The filly finished third and wasn't beaten that far though it was the manner of her performance that disturbed me, for she ran a listless race. It could have been a combination of things but, because of the market, I was more than a little suspicious. After the race the first person of authority I saw was McHaig Senior, the Clerk of the Course at that time. I asked him if he would arrange for a dope test on our filly as I was not satisfied all was in order. His response was negative and his attitude most unhelpful, so I approached one of the stewards with a similar request but again met a 'brick wall' with a remark something about "We don't want to ruffle feathers do we?" I returned home completely baffled by the system; horses had been tested for dope at Edinburgh that afternoon which, by their very performances, one could see had not been 'got at', yet in my opinion Wow Wow Wow had been. My fears, my suspicions, call it what you like, were confirmed when we ran her again four days later at Ayr in a very mediocre apprentice handicap. She started favourite, was virtually tailed off throughout and beaten a distance. Again, there was no inquiry and no dope test; sadly Wow Wow Wow never recovered sufficiently to race again. Official mismanagement had been the cause of the whole sorry mess.

Controversy seemed to follow the filly; there was an occasion when Full Circle were fined £70 (fixed penalty) when I withdrew her from a race at Hamilton. There had been a change of going, to heavy, and had I offered that as the reason nothing would have been said. However I preferred to be truthful about not wishing to run, this being, because of the ground conditions, starting stalls could not be used. The state of the going would not have inconvenienced her but without stalls she would have been very slow away and I didn't wish to put her to that disadvantage. As the race was a sprint and Wow Wow Wow would have been favourite, I was disappointed the Stewards had not shown some understanding and to hell with the directive.

There was a sequel to the Wow Wow Wow story, because of her name. I noticed a bra manufactured by Playtex being advertised, called the Wow bra. I contacted Playtex down at Woking with the view to their sponsoring a race for lady riders and this they did at Thirsk the following August. I planned a real coup for the event which we won with Domino Rose, a filly we bought specifically for the race and sold back later to the original owner. I had a small fortune on and along with many of the Full Circle shareholders, of which there were hundreds there that day, backed her down to 11/8. Domino Rose was ridden by Gee Armytage and won by a neck. There was a Stewards Inquiry because of some bumping which occurred in the last furlong and in different circumstances I wouldn't have been surprised to lose the race.

It was a very warm summer's day and on the way to the meeting I shot past Mark Birch and then, as I was about to overtake Lord Grimthorpe, I noticed there had been some tarring and stoning of the road. I suppose I should have dropped in behind but that would have meant getting peppered and, as I was sort of committed, I went on, inadvertently kicking up stones. Whilst at the races Lord Grimthorpe, a hell of a nice person who was a steward at Thirsk, came up to me and jokingly said "Colin, you showered me with bloody stones when you went past, I only hope you are not involved in a Stewards Inquiry today." I'd wager he regretted making the humourous remark. We kept the race - we had to after all the joviality!

There was rather a delightful little piece in the following Monday's Sporting Life - I quote: "The racing at Thirsk last Saturday was dominated by the sheer theatre of the activity around the selling race. It featured Colin Tinkler Senior, the moving force behind the successful Full Circle Syndicate Group. Several hundred of the members were at Thirsk and clearly most had supported their runner Domino Rose. To their delight it won and they crowded the winner's circle to such an extent the horses could not get in! A broadcast appeal for them to follow Mr. Tinkler's example and leave the scene was only spoilt by the fact Mr. Tinkler wasn't playing a penny whistle as he led them away like the Pied Piper!"

During the Autumn of '85, when Full Circle had been on the go for a little over a year, Nigel and I paid a further visit to the Newmarket Sales and returned to Yorkshire with a couple of really nice young horses. They were Caro's Gift, a 4 year old colt from Pritchard-Gordon's yard who had won at Brighton during the summer and Romiosini, a 3 year old colt who had recently been successful for Clive Brittain. We paid in the region of £35,000 for the two and both had been placed second the last time they ran just over a couple of weeks previously; so obviously were straight enough in condition. I believe Nigel schooled them over hurdles no more than half a dozen times; there was no need to do more for they jumped brilliantly. We put them in a couple of novice hurdle races at Catterick towards the end of November, the first and last races on the card. I went in rather heavily on Caro's Gift in the opener, backing him down to even money, but the race was not without incident with our runner nearly being brought down. Somehow Nigel, with his usual calmness, survived and went on to win by half a length. In those days, when having a bet, I would always 'pay on' before the race and on this occasion as I approached John Joyce to collect he got off his stool and came towards me, putting several bundles of notes into my hands, he asked, was I going to have another substantial punt in the last. On learning that I was, he told me if I were to keep well away from the betting ring he would guarantee me a decent price. Nigel was again on board the Full Circle horse; this time it was a trouble free run with Romiosini winning by 6 lengths and bringing off a fantastic double. J J kept his word, paying me out at the generous odds of 6/1 - so ended a perfect day's racing.

I lost money the next time they ran; it was at Wetherby when they finished second and fourth in their respective races, and running a trifle jaded. Even though we'd only recently purchased them they had been without a break for some considerable time. After looking at all the pros and cons, Nigel sensibly decided to go easy with their training for a while and aim at a Spring campaign on the flat.

The policy paid dividends, when some pretty substantial bets were landed when Caro's Gift won at Haydock at 9/1 and Romiosini was successful at Ripon and York at 2/1 and 8/1. Racing is all about winning, though I thought at the time, just as important for the prestige of Full Circle was Romiosini's brilliant run at Royal Ascot in the 'Bessboroug' that year. A quote from Raceform: 'Romiosini made up a lot of ground on the inner until severely hampered a furlong out. Finished sixth beaten three lengths.' Kim was in the saddle and was becoming well established as Full Circle's regular pilot on the flat. Caro's Gift and Romiosini were so genuine but sadly they developed leg troubles; one could very easily despair but I'm afraid it's 'par for the course' with racehorses, as it is with athletes

326

FULL CIRCLE

BE A
RACEHORSE OWNER
HAVE A SHARE IN A STRING OF RACEHORSES

Right: (p301)

Above:
Full Circle's first winner Octolan (Tony Ives) at
Catterick *(p309)*

Above:
Romiosini with Kim winning at York *(p326)*

Above:
Meningi (Nigel) winning cleverly at Catterick
(p311)

Above:
Wow Wow Wow with Kim winning at Edinburgh. *(p322)*

Above:
Kim brings home Lake Omega at Hamilton (in the year C)

Above:
Wessex the winner of seven races for Full Circle
(p327)

Above:
Authentic (Kim up) getting up on the line at Ayr
(p327)

Above:
The Ellier and Gee Armytage winning the 'Kim Muir' at the Festival *(p329)*

Above:
'Nice one Ellier' *(p329)*

Above:
The presentation *(p329)*

Above:
'Another dream comes true'. *(p329)*

Left:
Monanore going on to finish third at Aintree in the
'88 Grand National *(p344)*

Below:
Monanore and Tom Taaffe taking a fence in the
'88 Grand National *(p344)*

Above:
Nigel and Foot Patrol notch up Full Circle's fiftieth winner
(p333)

Above:
'Bought In' *(p333)*

Left:
Tiklas foils a Barney Curley gamble at Ayr
(p335)

Above:
Judi (my chauffeur) leads in Foot Patrol, winner of six races for Full Circle, after one of his successes.

Above:
'The Saint', Colonel Dave (Dan) Grieg and 'The Sinner' chatting at a Saint and Sinners Meeting at Hamilton

Lotus Island

Flyway

Arum Lily.
Completes a Full Circle treble at Nottingham.
(p350)

Above:
Something to shout about: Lotus Island after
landing Full Circle's hundreth winner *(p352)*

Above:
Oh, to be a fly on the wall! *(p361)*

Right:
Nigel and Gold Sceptre land an almighty
gamble at Catterick *(p346)*

Above:
Ghadbbaan (Kim) winning 'The Very Much Alive Marie Tinkler Stakes' at Redcar *(p354)*

Below:
My brother Peter (left) and Don Wright lead in another Full Circle winner

Above:
Corn Lily *(Kim)* winner of seven races for Full Circle

Left:
The loveable Rawaan winning one of his nine races for Full Circle (Including their last at Market Rasen) *(p362)*

from every sphere. It goes without saying, the more game a horse is and the harder it works the more likely it is to succumb to injuries.

The day Romiosini won at York I forgot to put on a tie and as I tried to enter the club enclosure was politely told by a gate official "Sorry sir, but you can't come in here without wearing a tie". I immediately whipped off one of my socks, tied a knot in one of the ends and tucked it into my shirt top, and asked "Will that do?" Back came the reply "Certainly Mr. Tinkler" and in I went!

Wessex was another horse we had early on. In spite of him being a wind sucker he won seven races for us under both codes. His stupid habit often caused colic, consequently he didn't run two races alike; this annoyed the stewards, foxed the layers and sometimes cost me dearly, though I did have one or two nice punts with him, for he kept popping up at such good odds. On one occasion, when looking rather miserable and running atrociously at Thirsk when favourite, we sent him up to Ayr four days later. He was as happy as a sandboy in the paddock, literally sparkling, came from last to first and won by a couple of lengths at 14/1. That was the day I doubled up on a Full Circle 2 year old called Authentic, backing him from 5/1 to 5/2; in the race Kim beat Pat Eddery on the short priced favourite in a photo finish.

There was rather an amusing incident when the horses arrived back home the following day. Not so much nowadays, but Ayr was always renowned in racing circles for the high jinks that took place when staff stayed overnight; it didn't affect the well being of the horses, it's just that there was often a lapse of memory as to the numbers on their bedroom doors! At that time Nigel had a girl working for him, nice she might have been, but she was certainly not beautiful, in fact decidedly very plain. The horses had been unloaded and, as she carried a couple of hay nets to the barn, she called out to me "I scored twice last night". My reply was instantaneous "Well they must have been own goals!" Think about it - on second thoughts, don't! Soon after, we sent Authentic back to Ayr for a repeat performance; Kim was again in the saddle and again they beat the favourite in a photo finish; the race must have been of a higher grade for I got 12/1 to my money. It was winner number twenty six for the Full Circle Group.

The following spring, and still incorporating Full Circle 'C', came The Ellier. I was determined to find a horse to run in the Grand National and decided to go over to Ireland to have a look at a strongly contested three mile chase at Leopardstown. It was early in February and as Aintree was only eight weeks away time was at a premium. The race was won by Last of the Brownies ridden by Peter Scudamore but only after cutting the corner at the bend into the straight and failing to go round a marker doll. After a Steward's Inquiry the race was automatically awarded to The Ellier. He was an eleven year old gelding, a lovely stamp of a chaser, was owned by a Mr. Jones and trained by Arthur Moore who, incidentally, had also bred him. Pat Taaffe's son Tom, The Ellier's usual pilot, was again in the saddle. The horse had carried eleven stone and I was immensely impressed by his performance. I had a chat with the connections and discovered I could buy the horse; the exact figure escapes me but I believe it was £30,000. I'm sure the only reason I was able to buy him was because of his age and my promise that he would be returned to Ireland when retired. It was not a condition of sale, though had The Ellier won the National I would have given a further £5,000 each to Arthur Moore and Tom Taaffe.

Following a veterinary examination the horse duly arrived at Woodland Stables. After a few days Nigel suggested we should take in the prestigious and steeped in history amateur riders 'Kim Muir', at the Cheltenham Festival, before going on to Aintree. I booked the pretty and extremely talented Gee Armytage to ride; I'd known her mother and grandmother, both international show jumping riders. Gee's only fault was that she was too brave, if one can say that's a fault; she had no fear whatsoever. The run at Cheltenham was supposed to be a tune up for Aintree but, because of a sparkling piece of work the horse had done in his pre race gallop, Nigel was confident he would run a corker and was adamant that I should not let him run unbacked. The Ellier was spot on and Gee gave him a marvellous ride - winning by half a length at 16/1. I'd had a punt, though hadn't really shared Nigel's confidence; nevertheless, because of the price, I still won £8,000. Once again The Ellier was involved in a Steward's Inquiry; I couldn't see what he was supposed to have done wrong and, of course, he kept the race. But it certainly spoilt the immediate post race celebrations in the winners enclosure, and I was on edge until the loud speakers announced "Result stands". As I was presented with the trophy, attired more for Cowes than Cheltenham in my trainers, track suit and windcheater, I made some sort of crack about having "left my yacht in the car park!" The only memento I got to keep, or should I say Full Circle got to keep, was a bronze medal, but no matter, I treasure it a great deal. It must have been a tremendous occasion for all those in Full Circle. Many owners spend a lifetime and fortunes trying to have a winner at 'Cheltenham' and the group had achieved it in less than three years and with only its second runner there.

Next on the agenda was the Grand National just a couple of weeks away; Nigel knew what was required to have the horse 'on song' for the gigantic task ahead. He took him to the coast to canter on the sands and splash about in the sea once or twice and tried to give The Ellier a complete rest to help recover from Cheltenham's exertions; but it was impossible with all the hype going on. Dozens of reporters and only a small percentage were racing journalists, with their camera men colleagues, descended on Woodland Stables; then there were the television crews all wanting a piece of the action. The bait, for want of a better word, had been that here was a live chance that a horse ridden by a girl could win the Grand National which had over 800 owners. Not quite National Velvet stuff but definitely different to the norm. The headlines read - Full Circle's visions of Aintree Glory; then there was - "The Ellier will win says Tinkler" (a complete misquote but what the hell) but the zaniest of them all was "Brain surgeon heads for Aintree". Now that was my fault entirely, I should not have told one of the reporters that a shareholder in Full Circle must be a brain surgeon because he wrote offering to have my head examined for buying The Ellier; I must add I received the letter prior to the running of the 'Kim Muir'!

I had assumed and hoped that Gee would keep the ride at Aintree but Nigel wanted Mark Dwyer. Mark was, over the years, always a leading contender for the jockeys title, knew the Aintree fences and had ridden The Ellier a couple of times back in Ireland. Needless to say I was disappointed but there was no confrontation whatsoever between Nigel and I. I didn't like what the press said when making the comment that Nigel had beaten me to the draw in booking Mark Dwyer: it most certainly wasn't like that at all. The same paper also quoted Mark as having said "If Colin makes it worth my while I'll stand down and watch from the stands". Well, I sincerely hope he didn't say that, in fact I'm sure he didn't do so.

As it turned out neither were able to ride the horse following a bizarre string of events; the race was due to be run on the Saturday and on the Thursday Gee was unseated when the horse she was riding refused in a novice hurdle. She severely damaged a knee and spent the rest of the meeting in and out of hospital having treatment. Next it was the turn of Mark Dwyer who fell in the novice chase on the Friday breaking a wrist. Of course, this left The Ellier without a jockey. Gee realized the ride was hers if only she could get the OK from Dr. Allen, the Jockey Club Medical Officer. I confirmed this with her but naturally we would have to have a replacement standing by. I've never understood why Nigel didn't fill the gap and take the ride. Admittedly since he'd commenced training he had ridden less but was still very fit and hadn't stopped conjuring up the winners; though it must be said he never liked Aintree, it was nothing to do with courage, but more that he'd not had any success there. As for the replacement, Tom Taaffe who rode The Ellier at Leopardstown was ruled out as it would have meant carrying too much overweight. I suppose we were stuck for choice with so many jockeys already booked. One that wasn't was Frank Berry, the crack Irish rider, and he could do the weight. By Friday evening all was arranged. Frank Berry had been told to catch a flight into Liverpool, all his expenses would be met plus £1,000 whether he rode or not and, if he did ride and won, there would be a very substantial present. However, at that juncture there was still a slight possibility that Gee would be fit to ride, though this was ruled out when she hobbled into the weighing room a couple of hours or so before the race. By the time The Ellier was saddled I must have spoken to over a hundred shareholders who were at Aintree; the anticipation was tremendous and there had been such a build up all morning, what with television interviews and everything else that was occurring and the jockey situation certainly hadn't helped. The race itself was an utter anticlimax and the ride Frank Berry gave The Ellier or rather didn't give The Ellier has been well documented. The thousands of people who had backed the horse and were watching the race on television must have been completely mystified, as were those at Aintree, and I'm sure The Ellier was. Berry was a hundred yards behind the leaders jumping Bechers Brook first time round, yet made up so much ground on the second circuit that they managed to finish seventh. We deserved better from someone who was entrusted with the ride; incidentally, though it's of little importance really, he was 18/1 at the off but I'd got 50/1 about him before Cheltenham. By the time I arrived at where the horses were being unsaddled Frank Berry had gone, disappeared, without any explanation at all. I went over to the weighing room and asked the official at the door of the jockeys changing room to call Berry, the normal practice when one wants to talk to a rider, but he was not there, he had flown, or more likely had burrowed his way out as I certainly never saw him come through the door. I did however meet him again, some years later when I was racing in Ireland; actually he approached me but I don't believe we discussed the race; it was long gone. He did however say he'd retired from riding and I thought, you're not a bad judge!

The Ellier ran just the once more, at Wetherby a couple of weeks after the National. Normally one would not dream of running a horse so soon after such a gruelling race but, of course, our fellow hadn't been exerted over much. The race was a three mile chase worth over £10,000 and was won by Mr. Frisk, a future Grand National winner. Nigel rode The Ellier and disaster struck at the fifth fence when the horse broke a leg. There was absolutely nothing that could be done to save him. A very game horse did not get the retirement he deserved over there in Ireland; all so very, very sad.

In a letter to the press I wrote:

"I wish to pay great tribute to The Ellier, a truly marvellous horse, a perfect gentleman, who died at Wetherby on Monday. His manners were impeccable and he loved his racing. I didn't know him long yet together we experienced joy, frustration and sadness, the three ingredients of life. He was a lovely, lovely, horse. Colin T."

The administration of Full Circle was going very smoothly, with no hitches whatsoever. The fact that we were having to suffix the Group's title, at the beginning of each financial year, with a different letter of the alphabet was causing no problems. To all intents and purposes Full Circle was continuous. The winners kept coming in a steady stream as if on a conveyor belt. There were a further 19 during '87 of which only 6 started favourite; the last of those was at Newcastle, late in December, when Nigel took the ride on Foot Patrol. They notched up the Group's fiftieth overall winner and the horse's third of his 6 successes for us. I had an exceptionally large punt to celebrate the occasion; it might have been a little premature of me but as it happened it was not so. I backed most of the Full Circle winners and, of course, some of their losers, though not that many of the latter. I do, however, vaguely remember at Kelso one day having £7,000 to win £4,000 with Macbet on a loser. Apparently the horse, whose name I don't recollect, had a phobia about snow and just as the race began a few flakes fluttered from the sky; the horse lost his cool and I lost my money!

In addition to Foot Patrol during '87, those prolific scorers Lady La Paz and Tiklas also came on the scene, along with Mayor, who was brilliant when winning at Hamilton, Doncaster and Nottingham, each time ridden by Kim. Tiklas was always in the news, even before we bought her, which was after her second run. In her first racecourse appearance at Kempton she was literally tailed off but in her second at Ripon, in a 3 year old seller, it was an entirely different story. She absolutely pulverised the field, winning by 8 lengths. At the subsequent auction the filly was knocked down to Nigel on behalf of Full Circle for 9,000 guineas. Over the following months she had a further 8 races, winning 4 of them, each with a certain amount of authority. The last of those successes was on the second Monday in October; Full Circle had sponsored the race, including giving the trophy, a delightful glass tortoise weighing several pounds. I believe the technique used in France to create such pieces is a closely guarded secret, as is the amount I paid for it, though I can reveal there was very little change out of a couple of monkeys! The combination of a tortoise and a horse race appealed to my sense of humour but that was only secondary, the main reason I originally bought it being, I thought it would look rather nice on my desk!

There were only 4 runners in the race, Tiklas ridden by Kim, River Blues owned and trained by Barney Curley and ridden by his young apprentice, plus a couple of nondescripts. The race was the third on the card and just before the meeting began Barney and I had a chat and discussed the glass tortoise; I'd become obsessed with the damned thing and said if he were to win it I would like to buy it from him. He assured me he wouldn't be winning the race because his horse was no way near straight and wouldn't be carrying any of his money; mind you I've never taken any notice what the opposition tell me.

The following day's Sporting Life said - There were fireworks before and after The Full Circle sponsored selling race at Ayr yesterday. Of the 4 runners only 2 were seriously backed. Tiklas, owned by the sponsors and managed by Colin Tinkler and River Blues trained by Barney Curley; both are well known as fearless punters. As Tinkler went down the line of bookmakers supporting his filly with some very big bets at 8/13, 4/6 and 4/5 money suddenly appeared for Barney Curley's runner; several bets of £7,000 to

£4,000 were noted and he was still being backed when evens was the best price on offer. At the off both horses started at 4/5 joint favourites. The Sporting Life's reporter, John Broadway, had rarely seen the like of it. He said "This sort of thing happens once in a blue moon. The market could not cope with the flood of money for both horses, consequently both started odds on. From the turn into the straight there was never any doubt that Tiklas wouldn't beat her rivals, the winning distance being a length and a half. When auctioneer Michael White asked for an opening bid of 1,250 guineas for Tiklas after the race, Tinkler, who had got wind that there would be keen competition for the filly, immediately offered 5,000 guineas. From there the bidding leapt in stages of 800 guineas a nod from Tinkler, until he got the better of the tussle at 13,000 guineas. This figure shattered the previous highest price a seller had made at Ayr. Yes, I got the tortoise and, yes, it's on my desk.

It had not only been Tiklas's last race of the season but, as things turned out, it had also been the last for Full Circle. All the Group's horses were sent to auction at the year end, whether we wished to keep them or not and Tiklas was no exception. Actually we would have liked to have bought her back but when the bidding reached 26,000 guineas at Tattersalls Newmarket Sales we were forced to call it a day as it would not have been sensible to retain her; incidentally she was bought by a stud in America and I understand had some very nice foals. We certainly had a lot of fun with her, bringing off 4 very successful gambles and making a nice overall profit on the buying and selling transactions.

Earlier in the summer of that year, June the 26th to be precise, a riot nearly broke out at Newcastle's evening meeting, it was because of a controversial incident involving one of our horses, I will start at the beginning.

It so happened that June 26th is my birthday but that is incidental really, though it did play a minor part in the proceedings in the afternoon. Nigel had got a couple of the Full Circle horses ready for the Newcastle evening meeting. George Duffield was to ride Fiesta Moon and Julie Bowker, a girl apprentice of Nigel's (who was later to marry Kieren Fallon), was to be on Love to Dance. Not often everything is perfect when one goes for a 'touch'. It is usually the state of the ground which is the missing piece in the jigsaw but in this case it was getting the money on which was going to be the problem. Johnny Ridley would be there, along with one or two others who would normally oblige, but one could not expect them to be too generous, if there was little other money about. I suddenly thought of an idea - it was Doncaster on the Friday afternoon and I'd had a whisper for one of Alan Bailey's newcomers. So off I went down to Doncaster and disguised my £1,000 treble on Baileys two year old and our couple at Newcastle by saying it was my birthday present to myself - yes, the treble was the idea! No one seemed to take any notice. I had a strong feeling the bet would very soon be forgotten and that no money would be 'sent back' to Newcastle if the first leg went in. It would now, for today is a different kettle of fish. The amazing thing was I just could not comprehend the two year old getting beaten and it didn't; it strolled in at 9/4. I naturally was having to take S.P. on all three legs and the result at Doncaster meant I had £3,250 going on Fiesta Moon, the first of the two at Newcastle. I left the course immediately after the race as I didn't want to start answering any questions; besides, it was a fair haul up to Newcastle. The roads were rather busy with it being a Friday evening, nevertheless I got there with plenty of time to spare. As expected, there were not all that many people about and not more than a handful of bookmakers. Full Circle members were also scarce on the ground. I met Nigel, we went for a coffee and he seemed full of confidence.

Fiesta Moon opened at 3/1, drifted, before reverting to start at 5/2; George rode a perfect race and 'Fiesta' did her part, winning quite comfortably in the end. Absolutely marvellous - just one to go. It meant I now had over £11,000 going on Love to Dance. I decided not to back anything else in the race for 'insurance', as I didn't really fancy any of the others; besides, the layers would have been alerted that something was afoot. I just had to stick it out and as the evening dragged I must admit to a little tension; enough not to assist in the saddling, for I know one can transmit nerves on to a horse just by being there. Ten minutes to the off the bookmakers opened up the betting at 7/1 Love to Dance. I remember thinking what a fantastic price. Then they went 13/2 as the horses arrived at the start - I suddenly feared an avalanche of money would descend, but none came. By this time it was becoming rather dark and lights were on all over the place. A quick glance at the boards on the Off, 13/2 was still on offer, and that was the official starting price.

As the light was deteriorating very quickly the visibility was getting worse. The commentator was having difficulty but as the horses came to the furlong mark he called Love to Dance and Passion King. It was ding dong all the way to the line. Oh, so close, it wasn't a question of on the nod as both horses were striding in unison. There was an immediate announcement 'Photo' and as the horses were being led into the winners' enclosure Mark Birch, the rider of 'the other horse', called out to me "You have won it." There was a crackling of the amplifier - now for the announcement - first, Number 10, Love to Dance - We had done it, I had won over £80,000.

The Full Circle people were overjoyed, the thrill was

unbelievable. More crackling of the amplifier, then another announcement "Correction, Love to Dance, second, the winner Passion King." WHAT? I was, of course, utterly stunned, as was everyone else. There was no apology, no explanation and a lot of people were demanding to see the photo finish; was there one? It was getting darker and darker. A near riot was developing, the police were called in to prevent what looked like a very ugly situation outside the weighing room and some in authority had left by the back door. One of the remaining stewards asked me if I could please possibly convince the mob to accept the result and that all was in order. I told him that I could not even convince myself of that. Eventually after half an hour, in fact just after ten o'clock, a photo print was produced and pinned to the board. Because of the conditions the print was of very poor quality and no way could one define a winner; a dead heat would have been appropriate and accepted by all concerned. It was not long before the photo disappeared - some said a press man had taken it. In fact this was so, for it was reproduced in the Racing Post on the following Monday. It is not generally known that on photo finish prints in those times the horses had not necessarily raced up to the white line, the reverse was often the case - the white line being moved to the horses. It might have seemed that I was taking the whole utter shambles in a philosophical manner. It was just that I was in shock more than anything else.

The following questions were never answered:-

Why was the result changed before the print of the finish was developed?

Why did the photo print take over half an hour to develop?

Why were some of those in authority so evasive to my questions?

Why was there no Steward's Enquiry about the whole incident?

Of course, I protested strongly but got nowhere at all. As I walked over to my car I noticed one of the tyres had a puncture. I thought, now I am pissed off - well, wouldn't you have been? After all it was my birthday - Exactly!

Fiesta Moon went on to win a further two races that season and brought off a 'right touch' at the old Wolverhampton track when winning a claimer by four lengths at 4/1. I remember the club car park filled to capacity that day and, to prevent any more cars entering, they locked the gates. Once Fiesta's race had been run I wanted to be away but the gates were still locked and the car park attendant with the key was nowhere to be found. I suppose it was the only way they had of keeping people at Wolverhampton - lock em-in!

Love to Dance, on the other hand, went to pieces after the Newcastle race - I'm surprised we all didn't! He always had been a bit quirky but became even more so; basically he was over the top. He filled out, and developed into a nice looking three year old though didn't matured mentally. Nigel gave him a couple of runs over a mile and a half and a mile and a quarter with the second run bringing the horse on a 'ton'. He was then found a nice little race at Carlisle that would just suit - 'a mile seller'. As he suffered from claustrophobia, for the journey up to Carlisle, we took a partition out of the horse box to give him plenty of room. We also sent along a pony as a companion in a further compartment and one of Nigel's staff travelled in the back of the box with them. Wait for it - to be doubly sure we also sent along a cattle truck knee deep in straw; this was for insurance in case the horse panicked in the other. A convoy of three vehicles left the yard, the horse box, the cattle truck and my car, all heading for Carlisle to bring off a nice little punt, nothing too big but hopefully some consolation for that Newcastle run twelve months previously. Actually things went pretty smoothly with no stops on the way. We didn't take Love to Dance down to the racecourse stables as that would have upset him, so we just popped him into the cattle truck and, of course, someone always stayed close by. But there could have been a major hiccup. I had used my hand phone from the car park to phone Marie, who naturally was interested in Love to Dance, having bred him. I was phoning to tell her I was going to have a punt and fully expected he would win. Somehow my conversation was picked up by bookmaker Brian Dunn; it was not a question of a crossed line because there were no lines as such but more a case of crossed air space. It didn't make any difference to the price, which was something I was most surprised about, or had Brian thought it was some kind of a ploy and I didn't really fancy Love to Dance!

I got 6/4 about Love to Dance, in three places, to several thousand pounds. One of those bookmakers was John Joyce and on placing the bet he said "Good luck Colin, but I think you will need it." Obviously he didn't reckon the horse and he disliked him less ten minutes later when I went to collect! Love to Dance won by seven lengths in an absolute canter, with Julie Bowker having kept the ride. I retained him at the auction and returned home rather pleased. We had paid attention to detail and done the job right. Love to Dance next ran at Chepstow, this time in a mile and a quarter seller. That run won me a further £5,000 in bets. Actually I got 5/4 about him and he was backed down to 8/11 and won by an eased down couple of lengths but it could and should have been twenty. Julie Bowker was again in the saddle; well she was until she got dumped just past the winning post. Julie was warned that if she relaxed he could stop and so he did but what a fiasco if it had been a couple of strides sooner. As it was a seller Love to Dance was put up for auction after the race and I again managed to buy him back. We gave him a break after Chepstow and because of his nervy attitude he was becoming very difficult to train. Nevertheless, we gave him a further run at Windsor; it was an evening meeting, he got terribly stewed up and didn't want to go in the parade ring. In the circumstances I was surprised he finished second and even more surprised I wasted a couple of thousand on him. He was claimed that evening and for me it was the end of the Love to Dance saga. He never did a tap for the new connections but that was something that didn't surprise me.

There is one rather amusing story to tell. Some years later Marie and I were talking and she said "Do you know Colin, I once got 25,000 gns for a yearling at the sales". I replied "Yes, I do know, I bought the f******g thing". By the way, there are no prizes for guessing which it was!

Full Circle's fourth year, which took in the majority of '88, was certainly an eventful period with hardly a dull moment. The Grand National had always held an enormous attraction for me. I have never considered the race to be a handicap for slow old crocks as do some cynics; to me it is pure magic and I was again in a buying mood to replace the ill-fated 'Ellier'. Firstly I bought Darkorjon after having inserted an advert in The Sporting Life's 'Horses Wanted' column. He was a seven year old chestnut gelding and trained over in Ireland by Pat Mullins. The horse had run some good races, including quite recently when beaten a short head in a £20,000 3 mile chase at Leopardstown. The owner wanted over £100,000 for him, which seemed rather excessive, nevertheless, Nigel and I went over to Ireland to have a look at the horse and try to buy him for a lower figure. We must have liked Darkorjon because we bought him but failed to negotiate a more realistic price. The taxi journey from Dublin Airport to the stables should have taken an hour and a half but our driver had other ideas and drove at incredible speeds. His logic for cutting the corners off right handed bends was "It saves petrol, it does, if you go a shorter distance". I suppose, as we were usually on two wheels, it must have been to save the tyres as well; that was one hell of a scarey ride!

Darkorjon's first run for Full Circle was at Ascot with Gee Armytage in the saddle; they were lying second, having made most of the running, when the stupid fellow put his feet in the open ditch four from home. He came one almighty cropper, breaking Gee's collar bone. We later learnt he had often done the same thing in Ireland but had not fallen, the reason being the open ditches over there are different from those in this country, they have the usual substantial 'take off' bar but the actual ditches are filled in. We gave the horse a couple more runs over fences, at Kempton where he made no show and at Cheltenham where he fell again at an open ditch. It was obvious he was not going to be suitable for Aintree and I'd made one hell of a boob buying him so he had to be replaced. Incidentally, Darkorjon did win a race for us, which was over a mile and a half on the flat, for amateurs at Thirsk. Anthea Farrell, now married to Sam Morshead, was on board and he started at 20/1. The irony of it was I can't remember backing him so in all probability I didn't and the final straw was when he broke down after the Thirsk race.

Next on my shopping list was the 11 year old chestnut gelding Monanore. Admittedly, he had just run a poor sort of a race at Punchestown but had won a £10,000 chase at Leopardstown before that. He was a real Aintree type and I'd noticed him the year before when finishing just behind The Ellier in the National. I had also spoken about him to Bill Harney, the horse's trainer, on one of my excursions over to Ireland. He was naturally not keen to part with his charge but said he would convey my interest to the joint owners, John

Meagher who had bred him, Richard Fogarty and Noel O'Meary. They decided I could buy Monanore if I promised to return him to John at the end of his racing, so he could retire on the farm where he was foaled. Coincidentally, there had been a similar understanding when The Ellier had come to me. The transaction regarding Monanore was soon completed and as I'd made such an error of judgement with Darkorjon I felt I owed Full Circle some sort of compensation. In the circumstances I paid the majority of the £30,000 that Monanore cost; it came from the Director's Fee I'd commenced receiving. It was agreed that the horse should stay with Bill Harney, at least, and probably beyond, the National for which he was already entered and as Tom Taaffe, son of the legendary Pat, had been booked for the ride I felt he should keep it.

I was invited down to London for the Aintree lunch when the weights were announced (Monanore 10 stone 3 lbs) and from then on it was a question of waiting for the big day. Just as with The Ellier there was the media interest though, thank goodness, not to the same extent. I had £250 each way on him at 40/1 and though I expected the horse to run a good race, I couldn't visualize him actually winning, I just couldn't imagine the dream coming true. With Nigel not training Monanore the contingent of Full Circle shareholders seemed reluctant to view the saddling, which I was rather pleased about, for I'm not sure Bill would have coped, but it was nice to see the horse's ex-owners on hand. By the time I'd 'led' Monanore on to the course for the parade it was too late to get any sort of position on the stands so I watched the race from one of the television sets the Tote were operating.

The going was good and the weather perfect as the 40 runners lined up for the near £70,000 first prize but, what was more important, they were racing for the prestige of becoming part of racing's history. Our blue and red colours were easily seen as the silent stands erupted as the horses left the gate and charged towards the first fence. Monanore was in mid-division as the field jumped the water with a full circuit to go. It was then down to the notorious Bechers Brook for the second time and left again after jumping the Canal Turn. As those that were still standing approached Valentines for the final time, Monanore started a forward move and by the time he'd cleared the next, just five from home, the big chestnut was among the leaders. With three left to jump he was lying third behind Rhyme 'n' Reason, the eventual winner and Durham Edition who finished second. Monanore battled on all the way to the line to keep his position, beaten 4 lengths and 15 with the fourth some way off. It was a courageous run from the Full Circle runner, and he had been splendidly ridden; we collected £10,000 prize money and I personally picked up a little over a couple of thousand pounds from my wager. Yes, the dream very nearly came true.

I will continue with the Monanore story through to its conclusion. After the National he returned to Ireland for his summer rest. The following season Bill Harney put him back into training for another crack at Aintree; his age had slowed him somewhat but had not dampened his enthusiasm and he most unexpectedly won a 3 mile chase at Fairyhouse, a preparatory race for the National; Graham McCourt, who was then Nigel's stable jockey, had gone over there specially for the ride.

As in the year before, there were 40 runners for the 1989 race and with the going heavy the four and a half miles was going to take some getting. Monanore looked magnificent in the paddock even though it was a dull afternoon. He was 20/1 at the off and, as in the previous year, I split a monkey each way on him. Graham gave Monanore a great ride and vice versa; they were always in the chasing pack and were running on through tired horses at the close, finishing sixth. It was another first rate performance and on reflection we should have retired him then, but we didn't - we went to the well one more time.

For the 1990 Grand National Monanore was a 13 year old and even though he loved the big jumps and went better there than anywhere else, we decided it would be his last visit to Aintree. It was amicably agreed that Nigel should train him this time around, sort of give the horse a change of environment for he'd been with Bill Harney all his racing life, but it didn't work the oracle.

We brought over Tom Taaffe to ride, he having done so well with 'the old boy' two years previously. In the race Monanore was well behind when he was baulked and pushed out at the jump before the chair; we'd had no illusions and were not at all disappointed, just pleased he finished sound. Mr. Frisk won the race; I'd known him since his point to point days and had always liked the horse. In fact I offered Kim Bailey, his trainer, £100,000 for him some months prior to his National success, but unfortunately for me the bid was not accepted. Monanore didn't race again and went back to Ireland to spend his days on the farm where he was foaled. I spoke to the Harleys recently, they are a lovely family; apparently Monanore is thoroughly enjoying life, gallops about like a two year old and hasn't lost his appetite for living; what a jolly nice horse and so ends the Monanore story.

To revert to the early part of '88, I had an almighty 24 carat punt on a horse called Gold Sceptre, ridden by Nigel, in a four year old selling hurdle at Catterick. I'd bought the ex-American colt out of Paul Cole's yard six months previously, he having been placed on the flat during the '87 season. The horse had grown and matured since arriving in Yorkshire, during which time we'd given him two or three runs over hurdles and finished second at Nottingham in the race previous to Catterick. At Catterick none of the other fifteen runners had even been placed third in any of their last outings, showing what a 'Mickey Mouse' contest it was. The bookmakers went 5/4 Gold Sceptre and virtually any price the others. I had no argument with the skinny odds, at least I wouldn't be knocked back (refused a bet). The bookmakers will always lay the thin ones and they certainly did that Wednesday afternoon. In the race Gold Sceptre made a real howler three from home but Nigel gave him time to recover and got up close home to win by a neck. Though the distance he won by was only marginal, in reality Nigel had the race won a long way out. Being a seller the colt had to be auctioned; everyone knew I wanted to retain him so there was very little interest and I bought him back with just a couple of bids. The planned coup had materialised - the money was important, of course it was, but as was always the case, the fact that the gamble had been successful was the real kick!

Gold Sceptre next ran the following month in another four year old seller, this time at Southwell where he was unexpectedly beaten into second place. I had been alerted that something might be amiss when I discovered his box (stable) at the races had been broken into. I'm not totally naive but that didn't necessarily mean the horse had been got at. The intruder could have been hoping to steal some tack. Gold Sceptre seemed alright so we let him take his chance and run; I did however become uneasy when the market was formed and our horse went out from a particularly generous first show of 6/4 to 2/1. I had intended placing money away from the course but in the circumstances of events I didn't go ahead with my original plans. In fact my punting was very much restricted and on reflection the horse should not have run. Graham McCourt rode him that day and reported him being a little lackadaisical, yet was only beaten a length. I didn't report anything to the Stewards as I'd found in the past it being an utter waste of time. But what a farcial situation to be in - utterly frustrating; taking every aspect into consideration, our horse had obviously been 'got at'. Graham McCourt was again in the saddle for Gold Sceptre's remaining two hurdle races, which he won at Market Rasen and Stratford. In between his hurdling exploits 'Sceptre' was successful in a claimer on the flat at Hamilton, when Kim got him home at 3/1, beating Dandy Nichols on one of Mick Easterby's. Each time I'd had the confidence to have a really big punt; all in all 'Sceptre' had been a real money spinner but unfortunately forced into early retirement.

Mubdi was another horse in the same mould which ran during '88 for Full Circle. As a three year old in '87 he had half a dozen runs without success for Sheik Hamdan Al Maktoum and, when sent up to the Autumn Sales at Newmarket, didn't exactly set the place alight; I was able to buy him for a reasonable figure. From the moment the hammer fell I had in mind a gamble in a selling hurdle; I didn't care how 'Mickey Mouse' the race was going to be, so long as he won it. Actually, during the twelve months he was with us Mubdi ran in 24 races, winning four over hurdles and three times on the flat; I only ever backed him six times and each time he won; quite a little gold mine though his first success was a complete bollocks. We had already given Mubdi one or two runs on the flat as well as over hurdles where he finished third, both at Edinburgh and Towcester; unfortunately at the latter meeting he sustained an over-reach. It would soon heal and we'd learnt enough to know once 'spot on' he would be really something to bet on. Nigel entered him for a novice selling hurdle at Worcester, it was in May and my only concern when I got to the course was the ground. It was very much on the firm side and I would not have been happy 'shovelling on'.

I never interfered with the training and only rarely when and where a horse should run but I felt this occasion was one of those exceptions. I naturally didn't want Mubdi to win unbacked and I didn't wish to back him with the conditions as they were. Basically we should have withdrawn him and I said to Nigel "If you think there is any chance of winning don't run as I would rather wait for another day." The outcome was a nightmare, an absolute nightmare, Mubdi ran with Graham McCourt in the saddle and won in a canter at 3/1 and, of course, I didn't have a penny on! I'd mentioned on my information line that Mubdi would prefer better ground and may not run. Not exactly the right recipe to keep callers happy and many believed I'd 'put them away'. With it being a seller there was an auction after the race and I bought Mubdi back for 5,000 gns which, in reality, meant Full Circle had to write out a cheque for roughly £1,000 to retain him. Sometimes racecourses would bid against me, after winning a seller although not on this occasion. For those that don't know, a racecourse receives half the money that a horse makes above the 'to be sold for' figure. It is immaterial whether a horse is bought in or sold so obviously the more a horse makes at the auction the more lucrative it is for the racecourse.

Actually, the buying back of one's horse and the distribution of the monies is not too complicated a procedure and can be far less expensive than many people believe. I am often asked, why run horses in such races, if I wish to retain them. The answer is simply that sellers are usually easier to win and when the money is down it's a question of the easier the better!

Mubdi had a further couple of runs over hurdles, at Southwell and Market Rasen, both being poorish affairs which he won very easily. I poured the money on, but the odds were extremely short; one must say we had, up to that point, collectively made rather a bollocks of things. His flat campaign was entirely different, winning at Ripon 6/1, Ayr 4/1 and Edinburgh 9/2. I never had less than a couple of thousand on and, incredibly, never backed the horse when he lost. Kim had terrific confidence in him and rode an absolute blinder at Edinburgh getting up in the last stride to win by a short head. That race was at the beginning of November '88 and from then to the end of the year Full Circle went through a golden patch with 13 winners. These included Leon at Wetherby on Boxing Day; in spite of him having to concede lumps of weight to 17 others in a novice hurdle, I still had a fairish punt. Nigel gave him a brilliant ride and to quote The Sporting Life - "Nigel Tinkler rarely dons silks these days - but when he does a nod is as good as a wink. The Langton handler had his first ride of the season on Leon in the Bramham Novices' Handicap Hurdle and gave the grey a classic ride. Leon is not the easiest of mounts, as he showed when throwing away a winning chance at Doncaster this month, but he hardly knew he had a race. Tinkler kept the Full Circle-owned gelding on the rails all the way round and, after taking closer order entering the straight, waited until going to the last before delivering his challenge and strolled home by eight lengths at 10/1." Leon went on to win two novice chases the following season.

To revert to Mubdi; he was the epitome of genuineness, but as soon as the flat season came to a close he had a short rest, it was then back to hurdling. He chalked up a further win, again at Edinburgh, by a couple of lengths. It was a none seller so I only had a small interest at 9/2; in his next outing at Huntingdon he was made favourite even though it was a good class event and not really a betting proposition. Unfortunately he had to be pulled up before the last hurdle and never ran again. With Full Circle having so many runners such things were bound to happen and it was always sad when they did. Mubdi had been like a fruit machine, wedged in maximum payout! He'd won seven races in just seven months and was going to be a most difficult act to follow!

I must mention Lotus Island, who was one of the few greys that Full Circle owned and ran at the same time as Mubdi and Co. It so happened he was involved in three races of some significance to me. The first of those was at Worcester when he finished second in a race he should have won. Then he was the first leg of a brilliant 75/1 treble at Nottingham, the others being Flyway and Arum Lily. And, finally, he was the horse that notched Full Circle's hundredth winner early in '89.

Lotus Island was first successful for us at Nottingham then a year later at Southwell when he scraped home, with Graham McCourt, at 8/13. I didn't punt that day because the ground was very firm and he had exceptionally shallow soles. On returning home I suggested to Nigel that I should make a set of surgical shoes to minimize any jar, he agreed, so they were fitted for the horse's next outing at Worcester; Nigel was at another meeting so I was in charge and had a chat with McCourt before the day's activities got on their way. I explained about the shoes and how much better he would run than he did at Southwell; Graham was not impressed and told me, in his opinion, we wouldn't beat the Pipe horse. I was adamant that we could and reminded him that Lotus Island had to be covered up and must not go to the front until after the last. I have never been one to give specific instructions to a jockey, though I'll quite often discuss the best way to ride a horse, particularly if they have some sort of quirk.

What I heard in the betting ring was most emphatic to say the least and did not please me; the vibes were definitely not good for our horse and experience had taught me to be wary on such occasions so I didn't have a punt. Graham McCourt has ridden some cracking races for me but this race at Worcester was not one of them. He made the pace early on, going well clear of the field of more than a dozen runners. Eventually he was caught by Pipe's horse, Celcius, ridden by Peter Scudamore, and they finished in that order; had Lotus Island not made the running he would most likely have won. I was naturally extremely upset, in fact bloody seething; I'd stated on my information line that our horse would come with a late run and literally romp home. The fact that he'd not won wasn't the issue, the tactics used were the criteria. McCourt's explanation was that as his mount was travelling so well he felt he didn't want to restrain him. I was not a happy bunny and that wasn't quite the end of our conversation! I was so incensed that I decided to make straight for home and as soon as I got into the car the windows immediately steamed over. I was like a volcano about to erupt. It was similar to what happened once before at Kelso; I can't recall the horse's name on that occasion but I do remember the reason for my anger!

Lotus Island's third visit to Nottingham, in the early part of '89, put the eighth notch on his belt for Full Circle and gave the group its century of winners. It was a great achievement and we'd had some bonny little touches along the way, some of them not that little! It had been four months since the Worcester race when Celcius beat our horse; both had been very busy in the interim winning races for their stables, and here they were meeting again. Both were five year olds and carrying similar weights to before but that's where the similarity ended. Graham used an entirely different strategy, the one he should have used at Worcester, I quote Chaseform - Lotus Island looked well: held up: headway 6th hurdle: led flat and won by one and a half lengths from Celcius the 5/4 favourite. The starting price of Lotus Island was 11/2, he was never a larger price than that and I had

£11,000 to £2,000 about him. I've refrained from mentioning anything about the presents I gave when having winners but I will make an exception here. I'd promised Graham four monkeys were he to win which, of course, was a generous sum for a glorified seller and I gave him the £2,000 as soon as he'd weighed in. All in all it was a jolly good day and I'd proved a point, Exactly!

Lotus Island had two or three further races that season though he was decidedly over the top; nevertheless he still managed a couple of seconds. After a short break at grass he was put back into training and won at Stratford being well punted down to 5/4. He had one further run at Southwell, after which he was subsequently retired. As you will have gathered, it wasn't all roses, it never is, but what a cracking little horse he'd been; one always imagined he was having a joke and what's more he probably was!

Incidentally, there was a piece in The Racing Post following the Nottingham Treble, quote: 'All three Full Circle winners were trained by Nigel Tinkler and ridden by Graham McCourt. Colin Tinkler snr, who took more than £12,000 out of the ring, called out in the winner's enclosure when being presented with a pair of grape scissors "I'm going to need these to cut open the cellophane packets holding the money I've won!"'

It was amazing how many multiple winners Full Circle had over the years but even horses with a lesser number of successes were important; they all contributed. The marvellous touches kept on materializing, such as Al Mulhalhal at Edinburgh and Spate when ridden by Dunwoody at Worcester, then the following day Peter Scudamore rode Hanseatic to win at Huntingdon at 2/1. I also had several highly profitable punts with Hanseatic and only once was he ever odds-on. Fisherman's Croft was a big price winner for the Group when Kim rode him at Doncaster in a claimer, I backed him from 20/1 to half those odds and he won rather cosily by just over a length. Many of the gambles were well planned but not all. It was quite often a case of just recognising a horse's ability to win as the races unfolded.

Another memorable day was Full Circle's four timer at Ripon, Bangor and two at Market Rasen, with Kim and McCourt sharing the honours along with Corn Lily, Koo, Rokala and Leon. Incidentally, Graham rode at the Welsh course in the afternoon and drove across country for Market Rasen's evening meeting. I backed Corn Lily at 5/2 but the others weren't really value.

A horse Full Circle owned that absolutely oozed class was Ghadbbaan, he was a winner and placed on the flat for Hamdan Al-Maktoun when trained by Stewart. The horse was then switched to Major Hern's at West Ilsley, from where he contested a Group three as a pacemaker and led the field for seven furlongs. He didn't race again that season but apparently had been used as a lead horse on the gallops and must have been pretty useful to have done that. We had a suspicion he was not entirely sound, nevertheless, when sent up for the autumn sales at Tattersalls, we took a chance and bought him for somewhere in the region of 15,000 gns. He was a giant of a horse and immensely strong; the talk was he had become difficult on the gallops so Nigel immediately had him gelded; it changed his aggressive attitude and he eventually became a real 'pussy cat'.

Ghadbbaan's first run for us was at Haydock in a rather competitive novice hurdle where he opened up at 4/1 but, with no money for him, soon went out to double those odds; though well beaten he jumped superbly and we were very well satisfied. His next race was at Warwick the following week, another novice hurdle, though a poor sort of contest in comparison to 'Haydock'. Ghadbbaan was put in at evens and quickly went to 4/6 after I had three individual bets totalling an even £5,000. Graham McCourt who was Nigel's stable jockey, rode a perfect race winning hard held. The horse then had a further two outings over jumps in quick succession, being competitive affairs and giving weight away to the others, he ran as well as could be expected. It did transpire that our misgivings about Ghadbbaan were correct, every morning he would potter about for five minutes then suddenly stride out perfectly and as it didn't affect his work we had no option but to ignore the matter.

A flat campaign was put into motion, with the initial outing being at Ripon. It was 1990 and the number of shareholders, consequently the number of horses Full Circle owned, had dropped considerably but, with Ghadbbaan, it was similar to having three horses in one. He ran 17 times during the season, winning six and being placed on eight other occasions. Admittedly most were either sellers or claimers though not all. One of his successes was in a seller at Redcar over nine furlongs. I sponsored the race and determined the conditions, which naturally were to suit our horse. I had arranged with Marie to call the race 'The Marie Tinkler Stakes', believing it would please her, but a couple of weeks before the meeting she had a change of mind. She rang the Clerk of the Course to say that having a race named after her might make people presume she was dead, when in reality she was very much alive! Matters were soon rectified, hence 'The Very Much Alive Marie Tinkler Stakes' took place! There was a piece in The Sporting Life about the race which read - "Redcar stages 'The Very Much Alive Marie Tinkler Selling Stakes'. Colin Tinkler Snr, explaining the reason for his first personal race sponsorship, said 'I have done this in appreciation of my former wife Marie, for all the fine races she rode and all the marvellous times we had'."

There were eleven runners, with Ghadbbaan drawn right out in the wilderness in stall ten, but it made not the slightest difference as he still won by seven lengths with Kim having all on to pull him up; surprisingly there was no bid at the subsequent auction. Something happened at Redcar which was to occur every time he ran from then on. He hesitated leaving the parade ring and, once on the course, dug his toes in refusing to go down to the start. There was the odd skip and a buck but in the main he appeared downright mulish. It worked in our favour as bookmakers were always quick to notice the antics and never failed to extend his price, consequently he was always at a far more generous price than he was entitled to be. At Redcar Ghadbbaan opened at evens and at one stage went out to 7/4, with me taking £7,000 to £4,000 about him. It was the same scenario wherever we went and we certainly travelled; he won at Redcar (twice), Carlisle, Lingfield (bought in 10,000 guineas), Windsor and Chepstow. I won stacks with him, though lost heavily on a couple of occasions when unexpectedly beaten. As a matter of interest, his overall starting prices averaged 7/2 and when he won they averaged more than evens, though realistically he should always have been odds on.

At the end of the Company's financial year Ghadbbaan, along with the other stock, was offered for sale at Newmarket but, because of the lack of shareholders, it was not possible to retain them all. I suppose I could have bought some of them back to own personally but I would not have been happy with that, besides it would have caused too many complications. Ghadbbaan was bought by an agent to race in one of the Scandinavian countries; what a fantastic twelve months we'd had with him and what a character he had been!

Dale Park is another horse that Full Circle owned which quickly comes to mind. Nigel bought him at the '87 Doncaster Yearling Sales for 7,000 guineas; he was a leggy colt yet came to hand early the following spring and showed a fair turn of speed on the gallops. We decided to have a crack at the 'Brocklesby' with him which is the first two year old race of the season, held at Doncaster. I had a pretty substantial punt but the youngster ran disappointingly, never really getting into the race, and finished well down the field. Kim, who rode him that day as she did in all his races on the flat, put his mediocre performance down to sheer greenness. Dale Park next ran at Haydock the following month where he absolutely skated in at 11/1. His success was not a total surprise, even though I didn't have a bet, for I knew he had ability and I should not have been so negative about the progress made since his first run. That was the day there was the fracas involving a shareholder in the winners enclosure; he was angry I hadn't advised him to have a punt, though had done so at Doncaster. Dale Park had a further seven races as a two year old and notched up another success at Ayr in a competitive nursery at 8/1 but, unfortunately, went unbacked; once again I'd under-estimated his chances.

I resolved there would be no such mistake with Dale Park in '89. He ran some decent enough races early on, getting placed once or twice, but then came a spate of 'duck eggs', all in decent handicaps. He was then dropped into a claimer at Ayr and it certainly would have been a major shock for the 'Tinklers' had he been beaten; he wasn't and won with a lot in hand by a couple of lengths at the incredible price of 20/1. No way should he have been anything like those odds, in fact 2/1 would have been more in keeping. I had a real touch with my money being placed away from the course. It didn't stop there either, we went back to Ayr for three hurdle races, in quick succession and won them all. The first was at 9/2, though the layers were never that generous again. Over the next couple of years Dale Park was rarely seen on the racecourse either jumping or flat as Nigel was finding it difficult keeping him right. We had to wait until April '92 for his next and final success, in a claimer over hurdles at Kelso. McCourt rode him again and they won by ten lengths in a canter, though I didn't win as much money as I should have done, as I was very apprehensive about his legs. He had three further outings after Kelso, the last of which was in a novice chase at Hexham where he finished fourth. We then retired him whilst he was comparatively sound; at least he was able to enjoy his life.

The last time Dale Park won at Ayr was in fact the last time I visited the seaside course. I had some marvellous times there and possess many fond memories, going back long before Full Circle. A catalogue of successful gambles and emotional runs are imprinted firmly in my mind; incidentally Full Circle won more races there than anywhere else, 19 in number. But something occurred to end my happy association with the place, it was at the time there had been a change of gate personnel. I was about to enter the Club area when I was roughly manhandled, grabbed by the arm and told I would be thrown off the course if I didn't attach my owner's badge to the windcheater I was wearing. This was not possible as there was no place to fasten it. I actually had the badge tied to my binoculars which I had shown and it was only my determination that got me into the enclosure where I wanted to be. The gateman, who was wearing a new styled 'Gestapo' type peaked cap, had been most aggressive both verbally and physically so I reported the incident to the Racecourse Manager. I did receive a written apology but I was not happy, the correspondence also stated that their employee was only doing his job. I felt if that was the attitude I would not go racing there again and haven't done so. I wish to add - I'm sure, in general, there is a mutual respect and a courteous attitude between racecourse employees and myself; that's how it should be with neither superior to the other.

Memories keep flooding back and for me each win I was involved with was entirely different from the next. However I appreciate stories about them could seem rather repetitive to readers, it being a question of the same scenarios with different names. That's the reason why I've restricted the summary of events surrounding the Full Circle winners; though readers should still get the gist of how things were. Whether I have mentioned an individual horse or not doesn't affect the admiration I had for it and all are included towards the end of this chapter, in the list of winners and general statistics.

Of the Full Circle horses that didn't win a race, very few failed at least to get placed. One that didn't win but did collect minor honours was my namesake Geega, a bay colt by Runnett and named Geega for no reason in particular. He was another inexpensive youngster purchased at the Doncaster Yearling Sales and I'm mentioning him as another example of how things didn't always work out as I'd have wished them to. He ran four times as a two year old, without showing much and it was a similar story for the first few races at three. We then prepared him for a seller at Redcar over a mile and a quarter; I backed him down to 13/8 but he was beaten a couple of lengths. There were no tangible excuses; he was just not good enough on the day. Two weeks later we took him to York, again for a seller, where I had a hell of a gamble and got 3/1 about my money. Kim sent Geega to the front at the furlong pole and hung on to pass the post a short head in front. Hung was the operative word for there was a Stewards Inquiry, the outcome of which was diabolical with our horse being placed second. There had been no interference whatsoever and his deflection off a straight line certainly didn't impede any of the other runners; even Ray Cochrane whose mount was awarded the race was surprised at the outcome. It was then down to Leicester for one more crack in a similar race but the result was the same, Geega again finishing second; I'd done my money three times on the trot and I'm not talking about 'Mickey Mouse' amounts. After that I waved the white flag and sold him; I believe he went flapping in Scotland. I've given special mention to Geega to illustrate that it wasn't 'honey on toast' all the time, though I think you will have already gathered that.

Another horse I'm going to refer to is Rawaan; he played a significant part in the latter years of the Group. Rawaan was a bay gelding and bred by the Aga Khan. He was a three year old when Nigel went over to France to buy him for somewhere in the region of £12,000; he was an exceptionally nice horse, not that big but very strong and his general attitude could not have been better.

We brought him back to this country, gave him a couple of runs on the flat and by the time he'd had his first outing over hurdles at Nottingham he was about spot on. His next run was in a three year old claimer at Ludlow where he was sent off 2/1 favourite but could do no better than finish second beaten just over a length. Though no blame was attached to anyone I attributed his defeat to him being in the lead over the last. The 'run in' at Ludlow is notorious; a horse in front sometimes momentarily hesitates at which shoot to take.

It wasn't long before I recouped my losses when we ran him a couple of weeks later in a selling hurdle at Doncaster, ridden by Nigel's second jump jockey, Martin Hill. Again the money made him favourite but this time the little horse won very comfortably by a couple of lengths. There was an added bonus as it didn't cost Full Circle all that much to hear the magic words "bought in" called out, by the auctioneer, after the race. Full Circle was very much on a downward slope by this time and the Company only had a handful of horses in training, yet mustered nine winners for the year carrying the 'G' suffix. Rawaan was the mainstay with a further five after his initial success; one of those was at Stratford when ridden by the delightful Lorna Vincent who some time later went to be a work rider in America. Another charming girl, who I haven't yet mentioned and rode for me over jumps, was 'Pip' Jones, an exceptional rider who also rode a number of winners for Nigel and later became Champion Lady Point to Point Rider. The other Full Circle horses who won that year were Norquay at Stratford and Srivijaya whose successes were on the flat at Redcar and Edinburgh.

Unfortunately, the following year (1992), there was some unpleasantness surrounding Rawaan's 'stroll in the park' at Kelso. Although it was October the ground was very firm and there were only a few runners at the meeting, twenty in total for the six races. Graham McCourt had flown up specially to ride our horse in the last, a handicap hurdle, with only one other runner. When I arrived at the course the talking point was how many winners would Peter Niven ride? It was not inconceivable that all his mounts would oblige; they were in the first five events. Even though the racing was not competitive, there was a good crowd and Niven won the first four races without incident. Race number five was a novice hurdle and as Niven weighed out for it the bookmakers were calling long odds on the Reveley horse. Now this is when things started to happen; Niven was confident it would be five out of five and asked McCourt to help him make it six out of six by giving him the ride on Rawaan. Graham was not happy but told Niven he was prepared to do so if it meant him, Niven, going through the card with all six winners, something no jump jockey had ever before achieved.

There were however two important issues, firstly, I had not been asked and nothing could be done without my sanction and secondly, permission would also be required from the Stewards to change riders, as McCourt had already been declared for Rawaan. I couldn't see an obstacle to that; surely the authorities would not be so short sighted if there was a chance of history being made. However, before I went any further there was the money situation to be resolved; it was more than likely that Rawaan would win so, what with the riding fee, the win percentage, travelling expenses and other monies due, I would be giving McCourt over £500 if he rode and were to win the race. Yes, Niven did ride the fifth winner on the card and as he was dismounting I said to him "I understand you have spoken to Graham and want the ride on Rawaan. OK, but you will have to reimburse him with the money you will be collecting from me, plus his travelling expenses - £500 altogether. You can't expect me to pay for a jockey I'm not having; or Graham to miss out financially as well as handing you a winner on a plate." What transpired was astonishing, I was flabbergasted; Niven angrily replied "All you Tinklers think about is f*****g money." I was stunned by the attitude of a person seeking a favour. I immediately went back to the jockey room and told McCourt to weigh out as he was still riding Rawaan. I had £2,000 to £7,000 about him and he won by twenty lengths. I later heard from the Stewards Secretary that in any event it would have been status quo because the Stewards wouldn't have allowed for a change of jockey. Incidentally, I read in the following day's Sporting Life a different account of events; obviously 'someone' had spoken to the press but I can assure you my version of what transpired is the correct one. I certainly wasn't asking for any money for myself.

Rawaan never ran a bad race unless there was something amiss. There was the occasion we took him on the long journey down to Wincanton only to finish third at 4/7. Dunwoody rode him that day and there just had to be an explanation for the mediocre run, though none was visible. The next time he ran was at Southwell a couple of weeks later; he won but struggled to do so, finishing lame. We then realised what the trouble had been at Wincanton; he must have felt some pain. We were forced to give Rawaan a couple of years rest to allow the leg time to mend and when he came back he won those two final races for Full Circle, in the summer of '95. Rawaan was then retired sound and is now very happy with a devoted family up here in Yorkshire and doing a spot of showjumping. Without question Rawaan was one of the nicest horses the Group owned throughout their entire time. Half a dozen or so really stood out and he was amongst that number; all had quality, a lovely disposition, plus a desire to win.

I was recently browsing through a scrapbook, which contained much regarding the activities surrounding Full Circle and came across an article about myself. It was by Paul Haigh in The Racing Post; I can well remember the interview, it was lighthearted as is the copy and the following few lines contain some quotes from it.

'Colin Tinkler is an unusual and somewhat contradictory character even by racing's fairly generous standards. A four-figure gambler who favours dark glasses, possesses a rather dashing line in hats and more often than not will be seen wearing trainers. He's a former jump jockey (well, I did say it was lighthearted) and trainer who dislikes fox hunting though doesn't believe it should be banned. He is also a non-smoking, vegetarian and teetotaller who firmly believes that "We're only here for about 75 years on average, though I'll live longer, so we might as well enjoy ourselves." One of his office staff is quite a religious lady who chides him about his gambling. "We're both gamblers" is his retort. You gamble every day when you say your prayers and I gamble when I have a bet. The only difference is I know when I've backed a winner!" His "racing manager", who occupies an armchair in Full Circle's office, is a large cuddly bear wearing a genuine Rolex watch, has an expensive cigar in his mouth and a bottle of gin under his arm. Talking to him (to Tinkler, not the racing manager) is an interesting experience. Most conversations have the same pattern as a tennis match. (You serve up a remark; the other player hits one back and the rally continues until one of you runs out of shots). When you're with Tinkler however the effect of that first remark is to set in motion a sort of three-dimensional pinball machine. He's all energy and helpfulness but his mind darts about so fast and his words follow so closely behind that sometimes you have trouble keeping your eye on the silver ball. Every thought he has seems to trigger another one. For example: "I've been a vegetarian since I was about ten mainly because I hate cruelty of any sort. Which is why I can't stand hunting. Still the fox hunts doesn't he? So I suppose he should expect to be hunted himself. And I employ cats to keep down mice. So I suppose that makes me a hypocrite doesn't it? I had my first ride in a race at Stratford when I'd only been on a horse for six hours and I couldn't even bounce at the trot. I got round and had four or five more rides, then I had this most almighty crash at Southwell. My brother looked after the horses then. You didn't need a licence or anything in those days and I remember him saying to me about this one 'Just give it a smack as it comes into the hurdle'. Well, I did and the little bugger looked round to see what the hell I was playing at, fell, then most of the field galloped over me, what an almighty crash. I fractured my skull, broke bones in my back and was poorly for a long time. Very dizzy. How long was I dizzy? Well. I still am, aren't I?" (Lots of laughter).'

Also taken from the scrapbook were the following letters. They had been printed in The Racing Post or The Sporting Life and are representative of what was generally written.

Sir, I would like to say that I, together with a friend, have been a member of 'Full Circle' for several years and hope to continue to be so for many more. I am sure I speak for other members when I say I could not care less how much is paid out to buy in one of our winners after a seller. Many of the horses who have won sellers and gained confidence have gone on to win decent races. It is hardly Full Circle's fault if bookmakers are so nervous of our runners that they make them a false price. In the morning telephone messages, shareholders are always advised whether to bet or otherwise, and consequently, unlike other members of the betting public, seldom get their fingers burnt when a hot favourite is beaten. I joined the syndicate for a bit of fun and entertainment and personally feel that I have had far more than my money's worth. If Colin Tinkler, Senior has £7,000 on to win £2,000, good luck to him. Perhaps it is not known that most of the purchase price for Monanore (third in the Grand National) was paid out of Colin Tinkler's pocket as a gift to Full Circle. Or that, in a free competition to members, he donated a £10,000 yearling together with free training for a year. Colin Tinkler has always had time to stop for a chat whenever I have been at the races. He did so at Worcester on 8 October, even though he was rushing towards the bookmakers with his £2,000 bet on Desert Emperor (won at 5-2) and the horses were on their way to the post. Besides, Colin is always in a jovial mood and he makes me laugh. I could write reams more extolling the advantages and sheer fun of Full Circle, but hardly think it necessary as the results are in the formbook for all to see.' D.P.

'Sir, as a satisfied Full Circle member, disgusted at the recent criticisms levelled at Colin Tinkler, I feel impelled to write in his defence. I believe that the following points need to be made. Firstly, the use of the term "loss", in relation to the accounts, is misleading, albeit there is no other way to portray the company's financial situation in a formal set of accounts. The true position, however, is that I, and 2,000 like-minded enthusiasts, put up a total of some £900,000 as a fund for the purchase, training and racing of 30 horses for a full year. Of that sum, just over £800,000 was spent, leaving in effect, a surplus of £100,000 plus, this surplus was repaid to us. Secondly, I put up my £450 stake voluntarily, having studied the prospectus, which made it absolutely clear that I should not expect any return in financial terms at the end of the year. The prospectus stressed that the principal aim of the enterprise was fun. Full Circle has, to me, and to many other members with whom I am acquainted, delivered more than £450 worth of fun and pleasure. Thirdly, in my case, the cost of membership has been repaid several times over by betting profits which I have made in the last 18 months as a direct result of Colin's advice, which, if followed with intelligence, and some discrimination, is excellent. I can see no valid reason why any member should feel that he has been misled or cheated, and no valid reason why certain racing correspondents should seek to contort facts in order to portray Colin and the Full Circle concept in a bad light.' T.H.

'Sir, in reply to a reader's letter, that most Full Circle horses run in sellers and at such a price that members can't afford to be on, may I point out that three recent Full Circle winners scored at odds of 10-1 (Leon), 7-2 (Wessex), and 3-1 (Lotus Island) - not a seller in sight and Colin Tinkler had advised that all should be backed.' G.F.

Full Circle had some marvellous times and owned a string of cracking horses. I feel guilty that I've not referred to more of them individually for they gave such pleasure; however all the winners are mentioned in the final statistics, (which are at the back of the book)..

Of course, there had been some sad times, which was inevitable with so much happening, though, when we finally balanced the books, added all the pluses and subtracted the minuses, we were well in credit and Full Circle had certainly been something special. But for some reason

'The Cookie Crumbled'

and for me

THE END OF AN ERA.

Chapter seventeen
The foal business

During the mid eighties I marketed a further thoroughbred company. It was entirely separate from Full Circle, though the structure was similar with it being financed by people purchasing shares. The concept of the venture was to make profit by buying foals, then selling them on at the yearling sales the following autumn. I'd hoped the investors would become involved and apart from a monetary gain they would derive pleasure from the enterprise. However matters didn't go according to plan but, before I progress, I will introduce you to the indefinable Clare Bancroft, a girl I first met at the Doncaster Bloodstock Sales during the early seventies; it was just a casual meeting and I can't remember how we got into conversation. She had a small stud in Southern Ireland and would use the sales in this country to sell some of the young horses she bred. Clare, who was in her twenties, looked typically Irish with her diminutive figure, flowing blonde hair and mischievous good looks; but surprisingly wasn't Irish at all, in fact very much English and came from a military family. I didn't see her more than half a dozen times over the next decade and then only at either the Doncaster or Newmarket Sales. During that time Clare had a two year old in training with Bruce Hobbs at Newmarket. She told me that in a conversation she had with him, my name somehow cropped up and he indicated I was a sharp character and not one to be trusted. I don't know how he was qualified to judge, having neither met nor had dealings with me. It was not because of what had been said but Clare and I lost touch when she moved from Ireland to live in this country, I'm not precisely sure when it was but I believe it to be at about the same time that I left Boltby. It was no big deal because we were at that time no more than acquaintances and it was simply that we had not been to the same sales.

The next time we met was a matter of pure chance - I'd been to Bath Races down in Somerset and was on my way home. After passing through Cirencester I took the Fosse Way, heading North to Stow on the Wold. After travelling a few miles I noticed a sign outside a pub called The Hare and Hounds, saying 'Coffee and sandwiches being served', so I pulled in; I was chatting away with the landlord who was asking where had I come from and that sort of thing. I told him I had been racing; then out of the blue he mentioned he had a new neighbour, a girl who had got something to do with racing and kept horses. She had apparently only recently bought the farm which was a couple of hundred yards down the lane which was close to the pub. He asked if I knew of her. She'd come from Ireland and was called Bancroft! Yes, it was Clare Bancroft. Naturally I called in to see her, but not before first phoning; it was a lovely old farmhouse built of Cotswold stone, but the whole place required extensive renovations which were in the process of being done. Clare was obviously surprised to see me and eagerly showed me round the place; she hadn't a partner at that time so just the two of us went out for a meal. Full Circle was in its infancy and I was extremely busy with the project, nevertheless I did find time, over the following months, to go down to 'Long Furlong' quite frequently. On one such visit, we were just about to commence breakfast in the kitchen when Clare asked me to get some butter from the fridge. It was hilarious;

as frequent as they had been.

In spite of all our endeavours the business was a total disaster. By the end of the second year and having had a dozen yearlings through our hands, practically all the capital had been lost. It had been a question of one misfortune after another; though many astute people, with years of experience in foal rearing, lose money from time to time. We unfortunately had two bad years in succession. As I wasn't prepared to approach the shareholders for further funds, I 'shut the shop' and personally honoured all the outstanding debts; in doing so I lost an awful lot of money but it was something I considered I had to do. Clare had naturally been paid for keeping the stock but apart from that neither of us received any remuneration. I genuinely felt for the shareholders but, as with most things in life that are disappointing, there is often a lighter side.

There was the police chase through the streets of Dublin, after we'd been to the foal sales at Goffs. To save time, as we were late for the ferry home, Clare had driven over the centre of a concrete island. The manouvre left a hole in the sump and a trail of oil all the way to the harbour. It also left a very big hole in my pocket, though we counted ourselves extremely fortunate we weren't locked up for the night. I believe it was Clare's short skirt rather than my apologies to the police, after they finally caught up with us, that left the cells empty.

On another occasion, we had been to Deauville for a few days attending their foal sales and our only way home was via Paris; but because of the flight times and our late arrival into the capital it meant an overnight stay. By the time we'd had a meal it was two in the morning and Clare considered it was not worth the expense to stay in one of the better hotels. Now that was one big mistake, for we eventually found ourselves booking into this scruffy, dimly lit place.

on opening the door I was confronted by this big fat mouse perched on its hind legs, twitching its little black nose and licking its buttery paws! Pointing to the fridge I called out "Clare, there's a f*****g mouse in there and its been at the butter!; without looking up from what she was doing she replied, in a matter of fact sort of way "Don't worry Col the fridge isn't wired up yet; I suppose he must have sneaked in when I've had the door open". Actually I wasn't that interested how he got in but very much concerned that he was there. Clare continued "Is there any butter left or has the little bastard eaten it all?" As I had suddenly gone off breakfast, in particular buttered toast, I didn't really care if there was any butter left or not but I did mention there was just enough for one!

Clare's farm consisted of several paddocks, 35 acres in all; because of this and her 'know how' I suggested we start the foal to yearling business which I've already referred to. Clare was most enthusiastic but wondered if I would still go ahead, after telling me she had recently met someone who was going to move in with her. He was considerably younger than Clare and I'm not exactly sure about his occupation but, no matter. Clare and I weren't romantically involved so I couldn't envisage a problem, as long as he didn't interfere with the project. I went ahead with forming the company and put the shares on the market at £100 each, with no restriction on the number an individual could hold. I sold the issues mainly to those in Full Circle and Clare sold some to people who had read an article she'd put in her local newspaper. I don't recall the exact amount raised, though it was in the tens of thousands of pounds; a tremendous amount of work was put into the enterprise throughout and by all concerned, with Clare employing a succession of girls to help. I still kept going down there to keep and eye on the stock but, because of my work load with Full Circle, journeys south were not

The receptionist, who most definitely required a good wash and a clean shirt, asked in broken English "How long do you want the room for?" When I replied "Just the night", he said, gesturing with arms in the air "What, all night?" Then, looking at Clare and still addressing me, continued "Surely it won't take that long". Apparently the room was so much an hour, not so much a night! Needless to say I slept in a chair as no way was I going to get into a bed; I don't know how, on our arrival, the red light had escaped our notice! In the morning Clare washed her hair and, as she had no hair dryer, she stuck her head out of the taxi window all the way through Paris to the airport. Her hair was certainly dry on arrival, it was just a pity she didn't have a comb with her!

During the first year we held an open day at 'Long Furlong' for the shareholders; about a hundred came from all over the country. After my talk the parade of the yearlings took place in a field where there had been some cattle grazing, after which everyone trooped off to the house for the refreshments. Unfortunately, several didn't notice where they were walking and tread in some cow dung. Clare called out "Col, you have been talking a lot of f*****g bullshit to them all afternoon and now they are treading in it!" Exactly!

Soon after that was the most bizarre of events; it all started when Clare's clapped out old Volvo estate went on strike, she needed a vehicle so I bought a comparatively new BMW for her to borrow. There was a proviso - that it was only for Clare to drive. I didn't go down the week the Badminton Horse Trials were taking place, for I expected she would be having guests; I did however phone on the Sunday morning but she was not at home. In fact, according to the girl who was working for her, Clare had not been seen for several days. I was living at Nigel's stables at the time and after the phone call I popped down to Malton for some lunch. On my return I noticed police cars all over the place, then suddenly, I was pounced on and escorted back to the stables. Then the questioning commenced, Where had I been? Where is my BMW? - and so on and so on. They were not local police and not all in uniform. I wondered if my car had been stolen and used for some crime or other. After a while the attitude of the police changed towards me, for they realised I was around Malton all morning. It transpired that a twelve year old blonde girl who lived at Coldstream, on the Scottish border, had not been seen for a couple of days. Apparently my car was noticed in the area that morning, in a layby which was situated near a bend in the road. The description of the driver fitted me and he was seen putting a girl with blonde hair into the boot of a BMW or taking it out of the vehicle. Some people, driving past at the time, saw this, contacted the police and were able to give the vehicle's registration number, which you will have gathered was that of my car.

I was convinced and told the police that what the people had seen was not the missing girl but Clare and the man was her boyfriend. To me it was obvious or why else had she not, during the past few days, contacted her home. I feared she had been either accidentally killed or even murdered and her body taken to Scotland to be got rid of, and I imagined her companion would have been surprised when the other car came from around the corner. The police came to the conclusion there was the possibility they now had two murders on their hands. They got in touch with their Scottish colleagues and the priority was to find the BMW. The car was eventually spotted and stopped at about 11.30 that night just outside Cheltenham. It was a mystery how it had travelled all the way down the M6 without being noticed by any of the police who were watching out for it; both Clare and her boyfriend were in the car and were immediately taken to the police station for questioning. As Clare was alive the police now assumed that the girl in the boot must have been the missing girl as was first thought and, if so, where was her body? After a lot of interrogation and many phone calls to me the police became satisfied with their explanation of events and released them but were far from amused.

It takes some grasping but Clare and her partner had gone up to Edinburgh for a few days, on a business matter, and were on their way back when they had either taken the wrong turning or chosen the scenic route! An argument developed about the loudness of the radio so Clare decided to travel and have a sleep in the boot of the car. She was actually being helped to get in when that other car passed and could quite easily have suffocated, then what! Exactly!

As Clare knew there was no insurance cover on the BMW for anyone other than herself to drive I had no alternative but to send someone down to collect the car. I then sold it to James Lambie, the racing journalist, who named it 'The Bullet'. I can assure you the name was purely coincidental! The whole episode had caused me so much anguish; I certainly hadn't deserved all the hassle.

The missing girl's body was eventually found, tragically she had been murdered and years later a man was charged with the murder of another girl in Scotland. It was thought the two crimes had a similarity.

I only went down to 'Long Furlong' once after that. It was to take a look at the yearlings before they went to the sales at Newmarket, where they made desperate prices. At the end of the sales, Clare commenced packing everything up to go home. Amongst the paraphernalia were a couple of quite sizeable conifers in plastic tubs, they had been used to enhance the look of the row of stables where the yearlings had been housed. Clare had taken them to the car park on a trolley and, instead of putting them straight into the boot of her vehicle, she placed them on the roof of a Mercedes estate car which was parked alongside. I don't know how the hell she got them up there, for they were very heavy, or for that matter, why! She then went back to the stables to collect the rest of the gear and returned just in time to see the Mercedes, with the plants still on the roof, being driven through the sales entrance and away. Clare's only comment was "The thieving bastard!"

By the end of the year I waved a white flag and closed down the company. Clare parted from her boyfriend, sold the farm and moved to London. She took up photography and is now a most highly regarded member of the profession, mainly photographing racehorses at the principal meetings both in this country and abroad. She did, however, once accept an invitation to be one of the photographers at a prestige boxing evening in London; Nigel and I were guests of Terry Marsh. I wasn't aware of Clare's assignment and was more than a little surprised to see her climbing through the ropes and into the ring whilst the two boxers were slogging it out. Apparently she wanted to get a close up of the action! I don't see so much of her nowadays but when Clare first moved to London and was less busy she would frequently come up to Yorkshire to stay for a couple of days and still does for the York May and Ebor Meetings. When I lived at Wombleton in the early nineties Clare always brought Harly, a giant of a dog, a ridgeback. The first time they came Harly chased my black and white 'puddy cat' round the garden and up on to the roof of the house, with puddy refusing to come down until he'd gone back to London. It was uncanny, completely mysterious, but 'puddy' would sense when Clare was coming to stay; every now and again I would discover him sitting on the roof and lo and behold within half an hour Clare and 'The Hound' would arrive! If I put Harly in a stable he would bark, if I let him lose in the garden he would scratch at the front door and when in the house he'd chew at the sheepskin rugs. I mentioned his idiosyncrasies to Clare, who said "Come off it Col, you were young once". I thought, Yes, but I didn't go around barking, chasing cats, scratching at doors and chewing up other people's

sheepskin rugs! Exactly!

A couple of years ago Clare went to Cuba for the winter and returned having married a citizen of that country, but nothing Clare does surprises me. The whole time I've known her there has been a succession of incredible situations and very humorous incidents. If only I could relate them all, but I don't possess the writing talent to make the majority of her actions seem in the least plausible; little she does seems to conform. I recently saw on television Marianne Faithful, the pop star, she was discussing her turbulent younger life. Apart from Clare being more slightly built the likeness was extraordinary. Her looks, her personality, her mannerisms, were all so similar, as was the voice and the vocabulary used; truly amazing!

Because of Clare's charisma I have always managed to forgive her somewhat, at times, nonchalant attitude; that apart, I realise some of my descriptions of events have been a little flippant but it would have been difficult to write about the happenings differently.

Mentioning the Newmarket Sales reminds me of a most amusing incident that occurred while I was once down there. I still go occasionally, though when Full Circle was at its height it would be more often. In those days I usually stayed at The Angel in Bury St. Edmunds, it is a lovely country hotel with a nice atmosphere and the food was always first class fare. On this particular occasion, during the sales on the first day, I bumped into a girl I knew called Katie (please allow me some decorum), she mentioned that all the hotels in Newmarket were chock-a-block, she hadn't booked in anywhere and asked where was I staying. I told her The Angel over at 'Bury' but said they were also full. Now, to be perfectly truthful, I didn't want to think of her sleeping in the car, I'd much rather think of her sleeping with me! As my room had a double bed, I was diplomatically about to make that suggestion when pretty Miss Katie beat me to it. So everyone was happy - the hotel had another guest - Katie had somewhere to stay and, of course, I was extremely happy! Exactly. We took our separate cars to the hotel, arriving there at about seven in the evening, signed in at the reception and were given room number 31, it being one of the nicest at The Angel. While I was bathing Katie somehow smuggled her puppy past the staff and up the stairs and into the bedroom. We had dinner and, for some reason, I can't think what it was, we decided to have an early night!

Now for a hilarious couple of hours. As we settled comfortably between the sheets, I turned the lights out then suddenly Katie jumped out of bed, ran across the large room to the window, knocking her toe in the process. "Ow, f*****g Hell - Col, those people in the bedrooms at the other side of the courtyard can see right into here." At that she gave the curtains a good yank - I did say the curtains, to try to close them and down the lot came, pole and all. "Bloody Hell, Col, give me a hand." I was hoping to do that later on but, for now, I most definitely wasn't getting out of bed in my birthday suit and start galloping around the room. For Katie it was different, at least for the time being, she had a nightie on, be it very scanty. "Col, I can put this curtain pole halfway up the window, have you got something to wedge it with?" Now, that was a stupid question, of course I had something to wedge it with but I didn't fancy 'standing up' there all night. The curtain idea was soon abandoned and moving the dresser across the room was next on the agenda for Katie. Another call for help but I wasn't budging; I thought it better if I reserved my energy! Katie eventually got the piece of furniture in front of the window. "Col, that will stop those nosy bastards peering in." Actually she had a point, two in fact! Katie got back into bed saying "Col, I'm exhausted." I thought, crikey, please don't be. Lights out again, then immediately the phone rang. "This is reception here, Sir, would you tell your guest there is an outside call for her." - it was her boyfriend, it was also panic stations, she had apparently rang him earlier to say where she was staying. "Sorry about this Col, tell them I'll take it downstairs at the desk but where are my Bloody clothes?" Well, she hadn't got them on, that was a certainty! Ten minutes later Katie was back "Col, I told him I'd been for a walk - I couldn't sleep because there was too much banging going on." I thought, chance would be a fine thing! Katie undressed, back into bed, lights out - then the phone rang again - I don't bloody well believe this. "Yes, what is it?" "This is the hall porter Sir, I'm sorry to disturb you" not as sorry as I was "Would you like a Sporting Life in the morning?" To that I replied "I'm trying to get one tonight but I'm not having much f*****g luck." With that I put the phone down and turned the lights out for the umpteenth time. Five minutes elapsed and then a knock, knock on the door - this was getting ridiculous. "Your champagne, Sir." "Go away, I've got nothing to celebrate yet, besides you have the wrong room." Katie then chipped in "No, Col, I ordered it, I didn't think there would be all these hold ups." I thought 'hold ups' not a good choice of words, anyhow he 'came in', put the tray on the table and 'out' again, which was a hell of a lot more than I'd been able to do. Then.... another disturbance, what the hell, the fire alarm was ringing. I could hear people running along the landing and down the stairs when the phone rang. "Management here, Mr. Tinkler, it's a false alarm but I'm just inquiring, Sir, are you smoking?" I couldn't resist replying "I haven't looked but I don't imagine so, not yet!" Everything quietened down in the hotel - well not quite everything! .... It must have been a couple of hours later when I felt Katie nibbling and licking my ear; well I thought it was Katie nibbling and licking my ear until I discovered it was her blasted Bow wow! I switched on the lights. Katie asked "What's the matter Col?" I replied "Nothing - by the way, I'll try and not disturb you but I want to be up at six o'clock." More dialogue from Katie "It won't disturb me, far from it - Col, you certainly like it don't you." Of course, I hadn't meant that! And to think we were booked in for a further two nights!

Chapter eighteen

Wheels and wings

The following chapter is an assortment of additional short stories with wheels or wings as their theme, mostly of an amusing nature and all occurred after I left Boltby. I've been in quite a number of accidents over the years, but only rarely have they involved other vehicles and miraculously, when they did, no one has been genuinely injured.

I was on my way to Newcastle; it was pouring with rain and I was certainly shifting. The windscreen wipers were going bingerty bong, bingerty bong and the visibility was atrocious. Suddenly I came to some road works and not having seen any signs was late applying the brakes. I hit the road barriers sending them scattering and then crashed into a stationary steam roller. In fact we both ended up stationary! with my car being a complete 'write-off'. You might ask "Where is the humour?" Well, the driver of the steam roller apparently hasn't worked since, supposedly suffering from whiplash! Yes, he was in the steam roller and supposed to have suffered whiplash!

Another time I had taken delivery of a new Mercedes in the morning and went to Thirsk Races in the afternoon. When returning home after the last race it started absolutely pouring down; consequently there was a lot of water on the road. I came to a bend at the bottom of Sutton Bank where I somehow got into a terrible skid, lost control and bounced off an oak tree straight into the path of one of those little French cars that look rather like a dustbin. The driver somehow got out of the crumpled wreck, ran over to me shouting very excitedly "I'm OK but the car must be a write-off, I'm fully insured, I've been trying to sell it for ages." I was pleased to know someone was happy! Actually, both cars were write-offs. I phoned the Merc garage in Pickering, luckily they were still open and asked them to collect the two crashed motors but not to bring the breakdown wagon, just a skip.

Neither was the replacement car that lucky. A couple of months on I was down for the sales at Newmarket. There was a bit of a lull so I decided to take the Merc for a 'face lick' at the automatic car wash. Now, I didn't realise it was that frosty. In fact the car wash was like a skating rink - crash, bang, bang, wallop, crash, bang. The car limped back to the sales and then on to a garage in Cambridgeshire, where the bill for the repairs came to a staggering £4,000! Some face lick and only I could cause such mayhem in a car wash.

I have dozed off more than once when coming back from Scotland. There was the time I had been to Kelso Races alone and the last thing I can remember it was daylight. But when I awoke it was practically dark and I was sitting in the car in the middle of a field oblivious to what had happened. Apparently, I'd gone to sleep as I came to a bend in the road which was steeply banked at that point. Then in true James Bond fashion had driven straight on and over the fence, without touching a twig; I must have kept on going across the field until my foot came off the accelerator. The amazing thing, there was not even a scratch on the car and I'd slept through it all! A very lucky day for me, even Logamimo had won and there was over £15,000 in the car when it took the leap!

My first permanent chauffeur was Judi, a gorgeous girl, always so bubbly and enthusiastic, great company and a jolly good driver. It was a marvellous job for anyone, particularly taking into consideration the generous perks. The position was full time but Judi only worked three or maybe four days a week, though on occasions, the days would be lengthy. Actually she kept the job for about eighteen months until there was a disagreement on a certain matter, though we have kept in touch over the years. Judi was a regular guest at my place at Wombleton and at Helmsley's Black Swan Hotel, when I lived there for a while. However, though there has been no fall out, her visits to my present home have been rather spasmodic, I believe that is the appropriate phraseology to use! I've never understood her fully - in fact I've never understood her at all! She has frequently 'gone missing' for months on end; then suddenly re-appears with no explanation, not that I've ever asked for one (I believe I should have phrased that differently!) Once when Judi was staying I had been working in the study then, on going through to the kitchen, I found a note saying "Colin - I have gone for some milk - Judi". Six months later I was gardening when she drove into the yard, full of the joys of spring, and called out "I'm back". I answered "I can see that, was there a long queue at the dairy?!"

We were down in London for a Bruno fight at the Tottenham Ground and had booked in at the Hilton; the only rooms they said they had available were a couple of luxury suites with fantastic views across the city. I said to the porter "Do you get many guests jumping over the balconies?" "Not until they have seen their bill, sir!" was his reply. When we were at the fight people recognised me and thought Judi was Kim, my daughter-in-law and, as she had ridden Mayor to win at Doncaster that afternoon, they wanted her to take a bow in the ring but we gave that idea the body swerve. Next morning Clare Bancroft, who was then living in London, called round for breakfast.

She also practically emptied the drinks fridge in my suite into a bag, saying "They'll never notice." Oh yes they did - the computer lights flashed in the accounts office as if a disco was taking place. I'm sure my excursion to London cost me more than Bruno got for fighting.

Judi once drove me down to Buckingham to see Marie and we all went our for a meal. During conversation, Marie's advice to Judi was "Don't let Colin sack you, but if he does just stay put - don't go". I thought, strange words coming as they did from someone who had left me of their 'own accord'!

There was another time when I wished to do a couple of meetings on the same day. They were at Thirsk in the afternoon and Stratford in the evening; with only having three hours to spare it was going to be pretty tight for time, even without having to contend with the unexpected ten mile queue of traffic north of Doncaster. To escape the hold-up Judi took a route on roads so minor and narrow that they weren't even on the map. I looked at the speedometer at one stage and we were doing over ninety. I said "What if we meet a car?" Judi replied "We will have to just hope it's got a sloping bonnet!" The hedges were so high on either side of the road it was like being in a crazy maze but it saved us many valuable minutes. There were more queues near Stratford but we had made up good time by then, doing well over the hundred most of the way. After sprinting through the car park we arrived in the paddock just in time to give Graham McCourt a 'leg up' on Gold Sceptre and then go to the betting ring where I poured the money on our horse, backing him down to 4/9. It had certainly been some drive to Stratford but the journey home was more relaxing as I put my winnings into £1,000 bundles!

Once when we were at the Newmarket Sales I asked Judi to bid for a horse. When it reached 25,000 gns Nigel went over to her and said "No more" but she thought he said "One more" and went again.

"Thank you" said the Auctioneer to Judi, then continued "27,000, thank you, sir", turning to Judi again he asked "Any more, Madam?" she didn't say anything but just shook her head, and we were off the hook; it's the only time I've ever been pleased to see Judi shake her head!

Following the Judi era as my chauffeur, I went on to short term 'chauffeurs' for a while and Dave Magson's 'Term of Office' was very short indeed. 'Fat Jack', as Dave was known because of his slimness, had just left Ladbrokes and, being at a loose end, approached me about doing some driving. I agreed and our first excursion was to go over to Wombleton to take a look at a place I'd just bought. The car I had at the time was a special white Mercedes '190', wide wheels, the whole works, fast but safe - a lovely car - a real humdinger. On the outskirts of Malton we came to a junction. Being on the main road Dave didn't take much notice when out came this old codger who hit us broadside - Bang! - Dave swerved and straight into an eight foot stone wall. We actually bounced back a couple of yards.

The following is a piece that was in the 'Sporting Life'. "Yesterday's car crash involving Colin Tinkler senior was quite hairy by all accounts but, as you might expect when Full Circle's boss is involved, it did contain a lighter moment. Former Ladbroke's racecourse employee Dave Magson, who was driving Tinkler's Mercedes when the accident occurred, said "If there is one thing that Colin absolutely forbids it is smoking in his car. After the crash it was pandemonium. Colin had banged his head on the mirror and there was blood everywhere. The car was a complete write-off. I was shaken up, as you would imagine. We were still in our seats and there was no smell of petrol, so I asked Colin whether it would be OK if I lit up a cigarette. He said 'Oh, all right, Fat Jack, just this once but don't let any ash drop on the floor!"

Dave didn't drive for me again; his nerves were utterly shattered and he left Malton the following year to live in Barbados and is still there.

At one time there was a rumour going around that I bought my chauffeurs Rolex watches as a sort of symbol and even a cuddly bear, which was in the Full Circle office, wore one. Let's put it this way, I'm not denying the "speculation"; a girl also became aware that it might be correct and wished to become my driver. So as not to embarrass her I will call her Miss B. She worked in stables and apparently was well-known around the Yorkshire circuit, particularly in the jockeys' saunas! There was one occasion when she led a horse round the paddock at Thirsk wearing a white, rather tight fitting, T-shirt with 'I'm a nymphomaniac' written on the back in big red letters. These might not be the exact words but they had the same implication! The stewards can't have failed to notice. They miss an awful lot but must have seen that. I suppose they were too embarrassed to say anything. Miss B. came over for an interview and squatted in one of the armchairs. Derek and Isabel Wright were in the office at the time, having just popped in to see me. I'd known them for a long time, in fact since the early days of Full Circle; I write in the past tense because, sadly, after a long illness, Derek recently died. He had several good horses with Nigel, but he will best be remembered in racing circles for his association with the superb Group winner Sugarfoot. Whenever I had a conversation with Derek it was enjoyable because we shared the same sense of humour. He had a dog called Gruff; I remember that for a short while he had a sore spot on his shoulder and Derek, in his inimitable style said "His car seat belt must have been too tight!" As they were leaving the office Isabel beckoned me out and with genuine concern for my safety said "Colin, you can't employ that girl. I don't know if you noticed but I know Derek certainly did, she wasn't wearing any panties." I nearly quipped back "Well, it will save me time taking them off", but I thought I'd better not. I found Miss B. pleasant but the driving job was a non-starter. Nevertheless, I mentioned I was going down to Malton for a meal and would she like to join me, which she did. I stayed on for a while after she left but that is not quite the end of the story. On the following Wednesday, at Ripon Races, I was standing outside the weighing room when Miss B. came into view. She was wearing the same T-shirt and called out as loud as she could across the crowded paddock "Coo-ee Colin, thanks for the other night, it was great!" If only I could have bolted down the nearest rabbit hole I would have done so - now that is the end of the story.

The most airy-scary journey I have ever had was when Tony Charlton drove my car back from Ayr Races. He literally threw it round the bends, on with the brakes, off with the brakes, into the dip, over the brow, and never seemingly doing less than a hundred for the whole of the 200 miles back to Malton. The car wheels were black with disc dust. I said to a fellow passenger "Tony will kill himself, that was suicidal driving." Tony was a nice fellow and had ridden for me several times in the past and had just set up training outside Malton. Ironically it was on the way back from Ayr's next meeting when he crashed and was killed, all so sad - such a waste.

How absolutely crazy can the law be? I received a load of parking fines relating to a car which was in the Pontefract district and one that I had sold in a part- exchange deal two years previously. Naturally I told the police that the 'Merc' was no longer mine and it was not I who should be involved. My solicitor advised me to pay four of the fines, a £100 worth to save me going to court and he would sort the job out; I did and he didn't! The summonses still kept rolling in. Apparently what was happening or rather not happening, the computer at Swansea was not accepting the change of ownership. I completely ignored a further bundle of demands for money as I was getting bored with the whole business. Then one afternoon I was in the office at Nigel's stables when this big fat overweight policeman arrived to arrest me for non payment of fines, "sub section" this "sub section" that. I told him to "piss off". At that he got his handcuffs out. Now that manoeuvre made me a little bit cross. I got my gun from the drawer and I shouted "You know that it's not my bloody car." I fired one shot through the open window and in two seconds flat the policeman was out of the office and across the yard. As he ran bouncing up and down to his 'panda' car he put one hand on his backside as if for protection! Strange but nobody ever contacted me again about those unpaid fines - I wonder why?

We now have shades of Hellsapoppin! I was driving to Hamilton Park in Scotland and Nigel and James Lambie, a racing journalist, were in the car with me. It had been a slow run over from Scotch Corner but once on the M6 I thought things should be OK. We were cruising along nicely until we got behind a little red Ford, that wouldn't budge from the outside lane. There were a couple of fellows inside and as they were wearing blue shirts Nigel thought they could be police. I opted for ambulance men and overtook them on the inside. They weren't ambulance men! The police caps went on and the lights started to flash. I thought as we were in a new high powered Merc it would be no contest so I put my foot on the accelerator, but the trouble was the traffic. The road was so busy they kept catching us up. At one point, for no reason, the boot lid of our car flew open scattering racing colours, paddock sheets and God knows what all over the M6. Of course, we had to stop to gather them, I don't know how the hell I wasn't knocked down. I had just got back into my car when Jamie announced "I can see them coming, you are just in time." That's exactly what I thought I would be doing - 'time' - at the end of this crazy chase. By now we were over the border and in to Scotland. Another 30 miles on there was a police road block and we were beckoned down. I jumped out of the car and excitedly announced that I'd learnt I was going to be robbed on the way up to Hamilton Races that day and that the muggers, masquerading as police, were chasing us in a red car. While we were talking the 'said' car had pulled up and I was told in fact they were police, not crooks, which, of course, I really knew. There was further dialogue between all the police - in fact they were arguing fiercely - then one of the Scottish group said to me "On your way Sir, the incident is closed, but drive more carefully." The two from Cumbria objected but were told "You have no authority in Scotland, and had better buck off back to England" - but I might have misheard! James wrote in the Sporting Life the next day "Amazingly Colin got off with a light caution and, playing up on his luck at Hamilton, was still counting his winnings - "Five thousand - six thousand - seven thousand" - as we re-crossed the border, with Nigel driving, at a more leisurely pace on the return journey."

Reading the following Victor Meldrew would have said "I don't believe it!" It takes some believing but it is perfectly true. We were coming through Malton on our way back from Redcar Races. There were four in the car and I was driving. The other three, who also had horses with Nigel, had left their vehicles at his stables and were returning to collect them. In those days I used to carry a lot of money on me; in fact I was known as the travelling Bank of England and nearly always had in excess of ten thousand in my pockets (though that is no longer the practice!). I felt safe when at the races but a little uneasy when in the car, until I started carrying a gun; it was kept loaded in the pouch behind the driver's seat. As I never took children in the car I naturally assumed it was a safe enough practice but obviously it was not. One of my passengers spotted the gun and decided to play gangsters. Lowering the window and not knowing the gun was loaded, he took a pot shot at a man mowing his lawn. There was an almighty BANG. I suppose the fellow with the lawn mower imagined it was the car that had back-fired, the game would certainly have 'back-fired' if the shot had hit its target! and just think of the repercussions.

Nigel had ridden a winner at Market Rasen in the afternoon at one of their August meetings and was doing a dash across country to Wolverhampton, as he had a two year old running in a Seller there in the evening. Bill, a friend of ours, was also in the car and as we approached a roundabout in the middle of Lincoln there was a traffic jam and utter chaos but this hold up was not going to deter Nigel. He drove down the outside of the stationary vehicles and straight across the grassed island, bump, bump, over the kerb and away, well not quite away, there was a sound of bur-bur, bur-bur. I said "Pull in Nigel, get out and tell the police I have had a heart attack and you are rushing me to hospital. I have just seen a sign pointing it's this way." I then slumped into the passenger seat trying to look poorly. Bill, who was in the back of the car, looked poorly without even trying! The police and Nigel had a few words then the bobbies got into their car and Nigel ran back to us and announced "It's OK, we are going to be escorted to the hospital." "What!" We followed the police and when they drove through the hospital gates we went straight past and on to Wolverhampton! Just like an old Key Stone Cop film. Our car number must have been noted but we heard nothing further. I suppose there would have been too much ridicule, from colleagues, had the matter been reported. We arrived at Wolverhampton just as the stalls opened, consequently not in time to place a bet, saw the race and Nigel's colt was beaten a short head but brought off rather a nice gamble at Nottingham two weeks later.

I've had a number of car break-ins, a couple of which were at Ayr Racecourse. On one occasion, we left the car in the centre, about twenty yards from the winning post, and in full view of the stands. Nevertheless, the car boot was forced open and two cases removed. They contained clothing, some business papers and an address book. Through adverts and press reports I offered £1,000 reward if they were found but there was no joy. Ironically the louse of a person missed £5,000 that Nigel had put in the boot wrapped in a bit of sacking.

I had been to Beverley Races and called in to see Nigel at the stables. I don't recall why I left the car near the yard entrance - and unlocked - but I did. Anyhow £3,500 was taken from the floor in front of the passenger seat. Admittedly the bundle was covered by an 'evening paper' but that was no great protection, especially if someone wanted to know tomorrow's runners! The police were called and made some rather nasty insinuations! I informed them that the loss of the money did not carry insurance; in fact I told them who I suspected. Actually I don't just suspect him anymore - I know it was he and I also know he will read this Autobiography and will know I know it was he.

On a more pleasant note; I was travelling to York from my home at Wombleton and, because of road resurfacing, I took a different route to normal and by doing so I had to go over a narrow wooden bridge. On getting there I saw this perfectly attired little girl in smart jodphurs, hacking jacket and a rather large riding hat. She'd be only about eight or nine years old and was riding a very mischievous but cracking grey pony. The little girl was having difficulties persuading her mount to cross the bridge, so I got out of the car and asked could I be of any help. In beautiful English back came the reply "Yes please, Sir, would you lead the pony across the bridge, I'm afraid he is being a teeny fractious." Wow! All the way across she was scolding the pony telling him how naughty he was. On reaching the other side she thanked me for helping and assured me she would be alright, as she would take another road home but asked me for "Just one more favour, Sir." And handing me her riding whip said, still in the same beautiful voice "Now smack its f*****g arse!" I declined by telling her it might bolt, though I didn't use the word bolt. She sort of agreed and, thanking me again, rode off down the road, turning her head as she went and called out "Hope to see you again, Sir." It wasn't only a cracking little pony I saw that afternoon!

Rose Carter was the last of my drivers and only ceased being so because I'd had a clean driving licence for some considerable time. She had been with me since the early days of the racing club, first working entirely in the office, then driving occasionally and eventually most days. She and her husband used to train in Malton back in the eighties and had a lot of success until an accumulation of misfortunes. They now run a horse transport business; actually Rose sometimes drives the box but naturally she would prefer to be behind the wheel of a SL500 - who wouldn't. I say with respect, she is one elegant chick, has immaculate taste, a great sense of humour and whatever Rose wears she looks good in, whether it's jeans and a jumper or an Ebor Meeting outfit. If I seem full of compliments, so be it, they are deserved.

Rose recalls the time, with a certain amount of sarcasm, when I asked would she drive me over to Redcar Races because I had a touch of flu and I didn't wish Judi, my chauffeuse at the time, to catch it. If I can remember correctly, I believe her answer, with justification, was "SOD OFF!"

When I was doing the renovations both at Wombleton and my present house Rose helped me with the decor. She thought the bedspread on the single bed in the guest room could be improved upon and suggested a certain very nice material - something special. I agreed and had it made up into a gorgeous cover. The bill was £1,600. I enquired from Rose as to when could I expect the twenty four carat gold tassels arriving!

Rose had driven me to Worcester Races for one of their summer meetings and it was a boiling hot day. I had won a few thousand pounds on a horse of ours called Rokala, which I'd backed down to 5/4 favourite; I collected the money and before heading for the car park and then home, I bought a couple of ice cream cornets. We were sitting in the car enjoying the delicious ice creams when I said to Rose "Eating ice cream beats sex." Rose's reply was "I would rather have sex." I quipped back, jokingly "Well throw your ice cream away, get in the back of the car and wait until I have finished mine." Rose is adamant she did not say that. What she says her answer was "If you think ice cream is better than sex you must be doing something wrong!"

The following occurred when my driving licence was intact so I wasn't in need of a chauffeuse. However a friend of mine gave me a call and mentioned a girl who wanted a job; She could drive, help about the house, answer the phone and be generally helpful. I was living at Wombleton at the time and as she lived a distance away it would mean her living in. I didn't wish to squash anyone so I said I would "Give it a whirl", words that were to become very appropriate! Sue duly arrived, young petite and pretty but had this appalling voice. When she spoke you had to listen to a cacophonous sound. On her first evening I had been working in the study until very late; in fact it was after midnight when I decided to make some coffee. I thought Sue was fast asleep in bed but I was wrong for into the kitchen came this very short nightie with legs; she stood there for a moment, then screeched "Don't you like sex then?" I was caught off guard but managed to answer "Yes, if the girl is discreet and doesn't talk about it." To that she replied "Don't worry, I never say owt when I'm shagging, I'm too busy riding a f*****g finish." Well I knew there was no ice cream in the fridge!!!!!

The next morning Sue was on the phone to her boy friend, I just heard the end of the conversation, it went something like "Well, he don't knock me about." I thought, but someone is going to if I don't quickly say "Bye, bye Sue". Exactly!

I have practically gone through the whole range of Mercedes from the 190 E upwards and must have had a dozen altogether. The previous car to the one I now have, was a 500 SL sports - that was one seriously fast car. The road holding was brilliant, a great pleasure to drive; I called it my vacuum cleaner because it picked up bits of fluff! I sold it because, yet again, I was banned from driving for a while and it wasn't a car to own and then sit in the passenger seat! I had to attend court near Doncaster regarding the speeding offence and, whilst it was not my usual practice to have a solicitor on such occasions, this time I did. He was John Cardon and when we met up in the morning he said "It's odds on I will be driving your car back so I might as well drive it there." He did, and went off the clock at 175 mph along the motorway. It was ironic that he was going to represent me for speeding! Tragically he was seriously injured in a hurdle race at Southwell shortly after and will not walk again. He is such a very nice person - a terrible, terrible shame it happened. My present 500 SEC Coupe, in black, is without a doubt the best car I have ever had, that is why I have kept it so long. It will cruise all day at a 130 plus. Oh, what have I said!

Another amusing incident occurred in Malton when I had parked my car outside the Nat West and, as it was only going to be for a couple of minutes, I didn't bother to lock the doors. When I came out of the bank the car had gone. At first I thought it had been stolen, then I noticed quite a commotion and a traffic jam near the traffic lights a couple of hundred yards away and my car was in the middle of it all. I had apparently left the car out of gear, the hand brake not fully on and, as there was a slight incline, the car rolled away playing tiggy with the oncoming vehicles. At that moment a fellow was coming out of 'The Gate Inn', saw the 'dilemma', ran across the road, opened the door and somehow managed to jump in and stop the car at the traffic lights, though on the wrong side of the road! Just as the 'candidate for a bravery award' was getting out of the Merc along came a policeman. "Now, what have we here Sir, looks as if you are quite the centre of attraction." Still in sarcastic mood the policeman went on "Are you a foreign gentleman, Sir? because I have noticed you are driving on the wrong side of the road." Recognising the car and knowing it to be mine he continued "Have you Mr. Tinkler's permission to be driving his car, Sir?" The poor fellow could not say anything, could not get his thoughts together because he was pissed, as he must have been to do what he did. On again went the man in uniform "I am just going to use my mobile phone and call for a back up while you blow in this bag, Sir. I am sure you will be well aware of the procedure." I arrived on the scene just in time to explain all and by this time there was rather a large crowd looking on. Large enough for the policeman to start waving his arms about and declare "On your way, everyone, the fun is over, on your way please" but now in more subdued tone. The Merc escaped without a scratch but one car required a face lift costing me over £500, including the cost of the hire car which I immediately got for the owner. I didn't claim from my insurers for what could I have put on the claim form? Exactly. I was prosecuted but as I had personally paid the £500 out of my own monies the bench thought that was enough punishment.

A couple of weeks after the above happening, I was at the stables waiting for my car to come back from being serviced, when I realised I had some shopping to do in town. Kim said I could borrow her runabout, a little white three door Fiesta. I scooted down to Malton and was lucky enough to find parking space in the busy main street. I left the key in the ignition switch and didn't bother to lock the doors - I seem to make a stupid habit of doing that; I did my shopping and then drove back to the stables. Half an hour later Kim came into the office, where I was having a chat with Nigel, and said "Nice one Colin, it appears you have swapped my three door for a five door model." "Bloody Hell", I then realised I'd taken the wrong car in Malton, but what a coincidence. The two cars must have been parked near each other, both white Fords with the doors unlocked and the ignition keys left in. I phoned the police to explain the embarrassing situation and that I would be returning the car immediately. Back in Malton I pulled up beside an excited crowd who gave me a big cheer. The police apparently had been to tell the owner I was on my way back with the reported stolen car and with all the cheering I felt as if I had just won the 'Le Mans'. I apologised to the lady owner, who said "It's alright Mr. Tinkler, if I'd known it was you who had taken my car I wouldn't have worried, I'd have known my car was in safe hands." WHAT!

One of the funniest sights I've ever seen was when Marie and I got caught up in the evening rush hour in Warwick. As we waited at some traffic lights we were passed by an open sports car being driven by a bare chested young fellow. He was towing a little A30 with an expressionless blonde 'Barbie Doll' at the wheel. Obviously her car had broken down and our knight had come to her rescue. Guess what was being used as a towrope? It was a shirt and a pair of jeans! Now we know who the shirt belonged to, but whose were the jeans? Marie and I were reminiscing recently, when she asked "Do you still have a bit of a snooze when you come to roadworks and the traffic lights are at red? I often had to waken you when they turned to go". I told her "Yes, I do, but instead of getting a prod in the ribs, as of old, I now just wait for the driver behind me to blow his horn!"

A few years back I decided to buy a motorbike; apart from the fun aspect, I thought it might even be useful at times. I didn't want anything too powerful like those lively Italian jobs with a name that sounds more like an expensive pair of shoes; just a simple, dare I say it, 125cc outfit. I called into a showroom in Leeds and bought a spanking new Honda, paid for it, arranged the insurance and placed a 'licence applied for' note in the disc. Once shown where the controls were, I was ready for off - OFF being the operative word. I started the engine, did something with the throttle, the bike suddenly rose in the air like a bucking bronco and I baled out backwards with the Honda shooting straight through the showroom window! That was the end of my motorbiking.

I first commenced flying to meetings in the middle of the eighties; it was when Nigel took a share in a five seater light aircraft; Mark Birch, Kevin Darley and Peter Savill, among others, were also in the syndicate at various times. Peter Johnson, who ran the project, had a landing strip on his farm on the edge of the Yorkshire Moors, near Kirkbymoorside. He had then, and still has, a couple of planes and usually pilots one himself. Apart from Haydock, where aircraft can land in the centre of the course, and the occasional run down south,

I've used planes mainly to go to meetings north of the border, though I don't now fly as much as I used to. On our excursions we will phone, from the plane, for a taxi to pick us up when we land. The technology is amazing, I feel we take so much for granted.

On returning from Perth's summer meetings, Peter, who is a first class pilot, will invariably give a guided tour of all the castles along the east coast. It's surprising how many there are, some lived in and others derelict. As the plane circles the castles, which are steeped in history, one's imagination goes back over the centuries.

There have been occasions when I've used other than Peter's aircraft; in fact the first time I flew to Ayr was when one of Nigel's owners borrowed a plane and flew us up there. As we approached the now little used Prestwick Airport, just a couple of miles from the racecourse, a sea mist suddenly engulfed the entire area so we flew around for a while. I'd noticed that our pilot always whistled when losing money at the races - no tune in particular, just a whistle - and he started to whistle then which meant one thing - 'yes' he was lost! I could also hear some crackling from the radio link, then a voice saying "Come in to land - use the runway with the control tower on your left", or words to that effect. As we swooped in I realised that what we'd heard was intended for another plane because it was not the control tower we'd passed on our left but the lighthouse adjoining Turnberry Golf Course. We were actually some 15 miles south of Prestwick and about to touch down in the Irish Sea. The plane just caught the top of a couple of waves before climbing out of trouble, fortunately, the mist cleared as we headed north for Prestwick and I was more than pleased the whistling had ceased!

There was another time when, as we were about to land at Yarmouth, the battery operating the aircraft's flaps suddenly went dead; the landing strip there is very short, with the drome being recently converted for the North Sea gas helicopters. Because of our predicament we had to fly a couple of miles out to sea; the tail piece must have worked independently from the flaps as our pilot was able to turn the plane round, he then switched the engine off and glided in. He contacted those on the ground, telling them of our difficulties, and asking for the hanger doors to be opened, thereby giving a few extra yards in which to stop! It was not a question of luck that we landed safely but the undoubted skill of our pilot. Once again, not the nicest way to spend a Saturday afternoon, or any other afternoon for that matter.

Matters became rather critical one evening when we were returning from a meeting in Scotland and flying over Thirsk; it was dark and we could see little on the ground except lights. Gymcracks Gordon Holmes, who has a pilot's licence, was sitting alongside Peter with me in a seat behind them. I realised Peter was trying to contact the small airfield at Bagby. Though I didn't know at the time it was because our plane was practically out of fuel. The call was to ask for the landing lights to be switched on so we could touch down. Peter couldn't make contact yet all the lights were suddenly aglow, my companions gave out a big cheer which was the first I knew of the severity of the trouble we'd been in. Apparently the groundsman had run out of cigarettes and gone down to the clubhouse for some. He only put the lights on when he heard our aircraft giving out a splutter and thought we may be in trouble. We landed safely but couldn't refuel as all the tanks were locked up for the night so we took a taxi back to base, where our cars had been parked in the morning. We had used the two engine plane and I later said to Peter "I suppose we could have limped home the remaining few miles had you turned off one of the engines." Peter replied "I already had done that several miles back"!

They used to build light aircraft at Kirkbymoorside, and maybe still do. One of the directors, Alan Clark, was a leading aerobatic pilot in the early nineties and it always fascinated me seeing him practising high in the sky above my home at Wombleton in his tiny red plane. I was telling him this one day when he invited me to join him and experience the thrills for myself. I declined the invitation for two reasons, one being, my head would not appreciate doing loop the loops and the other, utter fear! A couple of weeks after our conversation Alan was killed when the plane fell from the clouds and crashed. There were several theories as to what had happened.

When Full Circle was in full swing I sometimes popped over to Ireland to look over a horse which had been recommended to me. I didn't always take a large amount of cash, but did so on the occasion to which I'm going to refer. I intended it being only a fleeting visit so I travelled light; everything, which included £50,000, went into an ordinary inexpensive black briefcase, which bore my initials. Obviously I locked the case and it was not going to leave my side. On arriving at Dublin Airport I went over to the newsagents to buy something or other and momentarily put the case down between my feet; suddenly it was gone having been replaced by one similar. It was a Sunday and the reception area was not over crowded, yet I couldn't see anybody carrying a briefcase. I did however see a security man who told me that none of the known rustlers were about and he was sure it must have been a traveller that just might have accidentally picked up the wrong case and would hand it in when realising the mistake. The officer's optimism was certainly stronger than mine and that's putting it mildly; as far as I was concerned I'd said bye bye to the £50,000. I can't remember where I was going but I found myself on an escalator and in front of me was a tall well dressed man carrying my briefcase; I'd noticed the initials. Of course, I confronted him, he was full of apologies and was adamant it had been a genuine mistake. The lock had not been forced and the £50,000 was intact; the flabbergasted look on the fellow's face when shown the money didn't really reveal much for he was bound to have been surprised whatever. It was very noticeable he didn't bother to examine his briefcase! I left matters as they were, it being little use doing otherwise, but without question it had been a switch and I'd been incredibly fortunate. Had I not recovered the money I'm afraid I would have been obliged to stand the loss. As a matter of interest, for some reason I didn't buy the horse I'd gone over to Ireland to look at.

There was the occasion when I was flying back from Chepstow; in the plane was Raymond Gomersall for whom Nigel has brought off some real gambles. We detoured slightly in order to fly over Raymond's home and what he saw didn't please him, or rather what he didn't see didn't please him. His new Jaguar was not where it should have been - in the driveway, in fact it was nowhere to be seen. Raymond's immediate reaction was to phone the person who was supposed to be looking after the place; he was not exactly a bodyguard, that would have been difficult with him being well under five feet. There was no answer from the house but there was when phoning the mobile; Raymond asked 'Mighty Mouse' "Where are you?" Back came the reply "I'm in the driveway, polishing your car boss - where are you?" I can't reveal exactly what Raymond's words were but the gist was "I'm looking down from the clouds, just as you will be doing when I get back home, you little liar!"

I will close the chapter with a most amusing incident, which occurred at Heathrow, on a journey over to Ireland. Our plane was parked on the other side of the airfield from the terminus and required a bus to take the passengers to it. As the vehicle sped around the perimeter a little Irishman, who looked like a leprechaun and was hanging on to a roof strap, suddenly called out "Bejasus - you'd never tink dis ting would take off, you wouldn't!" - it was incredibly funny.

Chapter nineteen

Some bookmakers I've known. Some punting stories and a little auctioneering.

Bookmakers, whether they stand at the races, have offices or own betting shops, are continually being attacked; most people label them as greedy parasites who make a great deal from racing yet put little back. Such criticism is grossly unfair as nothing could be further from the truth. Many bookmakers are extremely generous and put much into racing in one form or another. I'm entirely opposed to a tote monopoly and I'm sure it will never come about in this country. Admittedly there are more opportunities for skullduggery as things are and I'm sure there's no need for me to elaborate on that, but where money is involved, no matter in what sphere, there will always be dealings of a dubious nature.

So many changes have taken place in the betting ring in recent years that I find it not such a friendly place as it used to be and I certainly don't get the same pleasure out of punting as I did of old. The humour has disappeared and many of the characters along with it. Tradition and all it stands for is gradually being drowned in technology but that is also the case in all aspects of horse racing.

Now for a few names, I would like to mention more but space dictates that is not possible. I will start with George Yates, who was my neighbour for a while when I first came back to Yorkshire to live and years later we joined in several successful gambles. However, the bookmaker I did the majority of my punting with at that time was

John Joyce. He was extremely shrewd and I got the feeling he resented losing! John had a habit of pretending he was deaf; I would say something like two thousand to one so and so and by the time he'd cocked an ear and said "Pardon", one of his workers would be away in a flash backing the horse back at 9/4. I always went to J.J. when the horse I wanted to back was at a slightly shorter price with him than elsewhere. That way I could get on without any hassle and no fear of being refused the bet. John was highly respected amongst his colleagues and they would often lay him a bet which they wouldn't have done for others.

Peter Rawson was another I did business with about that time; unfortunately he died from a heart attack when comparatively young. I once asked him if he would handle the entire punt of a gamble I was engineering for Market Rasen but he declined saying "I would rather not because it would entail me laying the bet off amongst my fellow bookmakers and I wouldn't want to catch them out." I appreciated his attitude and eventually did the job myself a couple of months later. I used thirty betting shops in and around Leeds; the punt was a success but the way I put the money on was too much of a hassle.

The present Victor Chandler's father, also called Victor, was a hell of a nice fellow; I had my first ever £1,000 punt with him down at Fontwell Park many years ago. The horse was Ocean Sailor ridden by Col when he was only 16. I backed them at odds against but they soon went long odds on, for a £1,000 punt in those days was quite a sizeable bet. As I was paid out Victor Chandler added a fiver to the amount, to buy a bottle of champagne! Well, it was some time ago. Because most of my racing was done in the north I didn't have that many bets with him, though amazingly never backed a loser, the last wager I had being an even £5,000 one day at Windsor.

There is rather a nice story involving the present Victor

Chandler's name, which I must tell. Peter Savill, for whom Nigel has trained and ridden many winners, was giving an after dinner speech at the Hilton Hotel on Park Lane. There were four or five hundred guests listening and they were there in connection with some association or other to do with racing. Peter went on to thank his trainers and jockeys for the marvellous year he'd had. To conclude, he said he had been talking to Michael Stoute recently and asked him if Nigel had ever ridden for his stable when a jockey. Stoute's reply was "Yes, several times; he never rode a winner for me but always rode strictly to instructions; the trouble was they weren't my instructions but those of Victor Chandler!!" Even the chandeliers shook with laughter.

Another name that comes to mind is Pat Whelan; I can't imagine him ever refusing a bet no matter how lopsided his book. Then there is Colin Webster, Leslie Steele and Francis Habbershaw, though recently Champagne Francis, a charming person whose grandfather founded the firm back in 1905, decided to retire from the rails. Regrettably another family firm, that of Morry Peters, has taken a similar course of action; it was a sad day for Tattersalls when they decided to sell up, all of them such characters what with their 9/10 and 11/12 odds. I first knew Morry nearly half a century ago when I was connected with the motor trade.

I will take this opportunity to recall another amusing story. During my visits to the nursing home in Leeds, when Col was born, I met a bookmaker (who will remain anonymous) whose wife had also had a baby boy there. Years later - I'm talking about thirty years later - I mentioned the fact to the son in question. He gave one whacking big smile and with his arms outstretched said, in a pronounced Yiddish accent and a touch of the Marx Brothers "Just to think, if they had got the babies mixed I would have ridden in the

Grand National". Somehow I don't think so!

Scotland have some fearless bookmakers; just to mention a couple, they have Alex Farquhar (Macbet) and Ricky Nelson, both 22 carat. I've done a tremendous amount of business with Alex over the years; he has opinions and if he doesn't fancy a horse he will really lay it to a substantial amount. Johnny Ridley, who operates from the north is also 22 carat, a perfect gentleman whom I've never seen ruffled. Johnny once asked me "Are you related to Don Enrico Incisa?" I told him I wasn't, though we were both often referred to similarly, he a Count and me a .... Exactly!

I never want to see boards on the rails in this country as they have them in Ireland; they are on a swivel over there, one moment the prices are shown to those in the Club area and then to people in 'Tatts'. I much prefer things as they are here with the boards only facing into the club, though I'd rather not have them at all. It used to be so easy to approach, say, John Smurthwaite or one of his colleagues at William Hills, place one's bet and leave matters in their hands. They are first and foremost company men yet scrupulously fair with their clients. Whilst on the subject of rails bookmakers, we have two complete opposites in John Pegley and Micky Fletcher. John usually works entirely on his own; when he wants to lay one off, which he usually does, he shuts his bag and darts up and down the line. I'm sure he once stayed with Marie and I for Thirsk Races and he is always welcome. On the other hand, I can't imagine Micky Fletcher ever playing safe and hedging his bets. He is undoubtedly one of racing's characters par excellence and there is no one in racing with more integrity. When Micky reads that he will laughingly say "That's not saying much for the others!" I'm not sure whether he is a Cockney or a Brummie - who cares. It might be a myth but I believe he first came into racing by selling freshly picked asparagus at the Cheltenham Festivals. I expect it to be true for anything would be possible where Micky's concerned. He spends most of his winters abroad in the sun and comes back in time for Cheltenham, as brown as a conker. He shouts the loudest and pays the quickest. If you have backed a winner with him and haven't collected immediately he'll come looking for you.

He is a very amusing fellow; some time ago I had a runner at one of the Midland courses which I strongly fancied. The horses had gone down to the start when I wandered over to the rails and asked him "What price is my horse?" He answered "Col, they tell me you're not off a bloody yard and it comes from a reliable quarter; so I won't take your bet". I assured him we were very busy indeed. He just stood for a moment then said "Col, you may own the horse, you may train the horse, but you're not riding the f*****g horse, are you?" You can guess what happened; I didn't have a bet, the horse got beat and Micky saved me losing four monkeys!

He was on the rails for a recent Royal Ascot Meeting where it is correct, though not essential, for bookmakers to wear top hat and tails. But not Micky, who went along in jeans and a T-shirt; "Well, it was a bloody hot day". For one of the races he was shouting "I'll take 11/8" (translated - 11 on to win 8) as Lord and Lady Toffee Nose approached from across the lawn with champagne glasses in hands. Lady Toffee Nose asked "Tell me my man, what price is the favourite?" Micky replied that he'd been bawling his f*****g head off for the last quarter of an hour with 11/8 on. The two with the wine glasses then had a board meeting between themselves and announced they would invest £5 each way. One can imagine the adjectives Micky used in his reply!

I have mainly mentioned bookmakers who are from the north, largely because of where I live and where I usually go racing, though

I don't go as often as I used to. In fact I don't do anything as often as I used to! There was a time when I very rarely missed a day and would also frequently attend an evening meeting in the summer months. I'm not saying all bookmakers would appraise me favourably but I would be disappointed if those that know me well failed to do so. That even includes Brian Dunn, whose jaw he insists I broke at a Zetland Point to Point many years ago. I suppose, in truth, it was all about nothing and I have mentioned the incident in more detail in a previous chapter. I've known Brian ever since he rode ponies as a small boy at the local horse shows. I remember one Saturday afternoon him riding in two events, one for children eleven years and under and the other for those over twelve years! It figures!

I can truthfully say there's only one bookmaker I've really resented and that was the late 'Chummy' Gaventa, who had offices in London. My dislike for him had got nothing to do with punting but stemmed from a transaction with a horse he owned, one of many he had in training over the years and most bearing the prefix 'Chummy's'.

It was back in '77 and no way does it seem all that long ago. Marie and I had placed an advert in The Sporting Life stating "Flat horse required for amateur up to £10,000 available", the result being we acquired Atoka. We also received a call from Gaventa, who offered one of his string trained by John Sutcliffe for £10,000 but we told him we had already purchased. Later an amateur rider contacted us, asking if there were any 'left overs' from the advertisement so I introduced him to Gaventa, though only after the bookmaker had agreed to pay me £500 commission if a sale materialized from the introduction. Incidentally, I asked the amateur £2,000 above the figure Gaventa would have been satisfied with. The transaction went through but I wasn't paid any commission. All Gaventa said to me on the phone was "F**k off, you have nothing in writing" then hung up. Obviously it was no earthly good phoning him back at that stage; one thing I knew, it would cost him more than £500. Gaventa would often run horses in claimers and sellers; my idea was to 'nick' a suitable sort when he did so. All perfectly legitimate, though not quite the done thing among friends but who the hell said anything about friends.

It must have been about a year later when I noticed Gaventa had a nice horse in a £8,000 minimum claimer at Doncaster. Firstly I must explain that the rules governing such races keep changing but, at that time, if one put in a claim for a horse which was higher than the minimum required it would most likely be successful. Nigel and I had a chat in the weighing room and agreed a figure of £9,000. Nigel then obtained the necessary form, filled it in and was just about to deposit it in the appropriate tray when I called out "Just a second Nigel, could I have a quick look at the form". I haven't the foggiest notion why I said what I did but, on opening the envelope, I discovered not £9,000 had been written but £90,000. Wow and wow again. That was a near one. We tore the form to shreds and decided to give that particular horse a miss!

Shortly after the Doncaster 'near calamity' a horse of Gaventa's won a seller at Windsor trained by Geoff Lewis and I happened to be there. I told Geoff the whole story and he wasn't all that chuffed but it made no difference; I knew they didn't want to sell so I was hell bent in bidding for the horse, thereby making it as expensive as I could for Gaventa to retain; at least the racecourse would benefit by the surplus. I don't remember the exact figure I went to but I know it cost Gaventa several thousand pounds to retain the horse. I phoned him the following morning; he was fuming once he realised it was I that had done the damage. Well, what did he expect!

I've had two accounts closed by leading firms, the reason given on both occasions being that my business was not profitable to them. They were not disputes for I agreed my business was not profitable for them! However, I do recall three occasions and only three when there have been disagreements where punting was concerned:-

I was at Carlisle and had backed a horse in a photo finish as insurance, for I'd backed the other horse in the photo prior to the race. I paid on as was the norm at that time and gave the money to one of the floor men. Somehow, whether intentional or not, the Clerk recorded the wager as owing. It so happened it was a losing bet and quite naturally the layer was of the opinion he wanted some money from me. I had no intention of paying twice and there were some sharp encounters and that was that. I'd not previously had a bet with that particular bookmaker and now very much regret not 'forking out' twice, for it is obvious he himself didn't get paid; but it is too late now.

The other two incidents became very much a matter of principle, the disputes being with bookmakers I had punted with regularly before the differences occurred. The first I'm going to mention was, in my opinion, a genuine misunderstanding but was handled badly due to an untruth being told. It all started at Beverley Races one afternoon some years ago. It has often been my policy to split my bets and this was one of those occasions. I had an even thousand with Hills on a horse trained by Mary Reveley, then had another even monkey with one of the board layers, indicating that wager by saying "Monkey" and nodding towards the bottom right hand corner of the board. The horse won, as did another I backed that afternoon with the bookmaker in question (not Hills). At the end of racing I was owed £1,750 which I went to collect. I hadn't paid on so it was just the winnings I wanted. I stood around for a while and was eventually told he would settle with me at Market Rasen the following day. He said something about he was concentrating on an away meeting which was still taking place.

At Market Rasen I was handed £750. When I asked him to explain I was told he considered I had lost £500, and not won that amount on the race in which Mary Reveley's horse won. I was also led to believe the bookmaker had a tape where I could be heard making the losing bet. This turned out not to be so. Yes, there was a tape but it was not audible. There was absolutely nothing I could do other than go to arbitration, which neither of us wanted. I took the £750 but have not punted with the firm since. Actually, I would have been satisfied to have treated the matter as a no bet situation but cold water was poured on that suggestion. However, some months later the senior partner of the firm offered me £500 to do exactly that but I declined the offer as the gesture should have come sooner.

The other disagreement I've referred to occurred about ten years ago when I did Redcar and Leicester on the same day. While at Redcar in the afternoon I received some pretty lively information about an unraced two year old running in the seller at Leicester in the evening. It was for a colt called Poppy Charm trained by Mark Tompkins, to be ridden by Ray Cochrane and The Racing Post's probable starting price had the youngster at 6/1. I was going to the midland meeting in any case with Nigel and Kim, for they had a runner in the fourth. But with the seller being the second contest on the card it meant I was going to find it rather tight for time to do any punting.

I had been told that connections were in action elsewhere in the afternoon and would be helicoptering to Leicester; it was emphasized there would be a lot of money for the horse, so it was suggested I get on early. There were a number of bookmaking firms doing both Redcar and Leicester but, of course, using different staff. I said to one who was representing at the Yorkshire track, the following being my precise words, "Phone the boss down at Leicester and tell him Colin wants £1,000 on Poppy Charm at first show, not to keep the money because the horse will win, no question about it".

Nigel drove down and we arrived just in time to hear the course commentary; I'd already phoned Hills to discover Poppy Charm had been 2/1 but was being backed down. Rather a disappointing price, nevertheless he won by a couple of lengths. I went straight over to the bookmaker in question and asked "What price did you get for me?" He sheepishly replied "Evens". Nothing was going to be gained by a lot of conversation. I just said "Give me the thousand but that is the end, I'll never have another bet with you" and I haven't done so. I'd won a lot of money from him over the years but, of course, he had gained from me in many ways. Incidentally, Poppy Charm had officially opened at 7/4, though there had been a lot of 5/2 about early on and, because of the weight of money, he eventually started at 4/5.

Later in the afternoon, just as with the other incident, I was offered an olive branch of £500, which I didn't accept; principles have usually cost me money, but still, I wouldn't wish to be without them.

You may be wondering what happened to Kim's mount in the fourth event. Well, it was backed down from 6/1 to half that figure, started favourite and got beat, though I didn't have a bet.

I have never considered myself a heavy punter and certainly not a gambler of any significance, though I have lost £10,000 on a couple of occasions on horses that were rather unfortunate in running. The largest amount I've ever lost was on a football match; I'd just received a cheque from Ladbrokes for £11,000 and had the lot on Liverpool at 4/11 to beat Wimbledon at Wembley, which needless to say they didn't! As a matter of interest, the maximum amount I've parted with at a casino in an evening is £200; surely that confirms something.

I'm flip flopping about but I must tell you an amusing story about myself when visiting a casino. I was in London on business, just for the day, when Nigel rang me from Newbury to say he was coming to town and suggested I stay over and meet him later at the 'Alexander' for a meal. I was wearing trainers and took the chance they would be allowed but they weren't. I got a polite "Sorry, Sir, not that footwear". As we were discussing the matter Nigel arrived with one of his Irish owners and told me he could solve the situation. Apparently he had a swish pair of blue coloured Wellington boots in his car. On hearing this 'Paddy' became very enthusiastic and suggested I turned the tops of the wellies down to give them a bit of class! Obviously I put them inside my trousers; we all congratulated ourselves for our ingenuity and had a pleasant evening. It was all very amusing and would have been even more so had there been dancing at the club!

The largest amount I have ever won is, to be precise, £61,250; it was when Norton's Coin captured the 1990 Cheltenham Gold Cup. I will explain how the bet materialized. Nigel was down at The Festival for the whole meeting but, for some reason I can't recall, I had not been for the first two days. On the Wednesday evening Nigel phoned suggesting that, instead of driving down on the Thursday, I should fly from Bradford Airport with one of his owners. Peter Robinson had bought the plane only recently and had told Nigel I could go along. We landed about six miles from Cheltenham, just the other side of the M5 and Nigel was there to take me to the racecourse; Peter and the rest of the party took a taxi. While in the car we discussed the Gold Cup; apparently Nigel had breakfast with Graham McCourt that morning and learnt that Norton's Coin had done a jolly good gallop on the Monday and that Dunwoody thought Graham's horse would make a race of it with his mount, Desert Orchid. I took note of what Nigel told me because I was looking for a value bet each way, as I didn't really fancy the favourite; also I had made note of the horse myself, with it having previously won at Cheltenham and the going would suit.

The first thing I did on arriving at the course was to make my way to the rails where the bookmakers stand. On doing so I bumped in to a friend of mine, Jim Beaumont, who is a stalwart at Musselburgh Racecourse; he also has a restaurant in Edinburgh and is married to Wendy, a lovely girl and a brilliant artist who I am sure must be a descendant of Peter Pan. I told Jim of my plans about the outsider in the Gold Cup and also said I was going to put the information on my 'Hotline from the course'. We both had a chat with the Ladbrokes team. Jimmy got 200/1 to his tenner each way but I had to make do with 100/1 about my £250 each way and I could only have 66/1 if I wanted any more on. I tried Hills but they didn't really want to lay me and laughingly said "Colin, you must know something." I did however repeat my Ladbrokes bet with another rails bookmaker but only got a fifth the odds a place from him. The rest is history, Norton's Coin winning with Graham McCourt in the saddle and I'd netted a fabulous £60,000 plus; Nigel hadn't backed the horse so I gave him £5,000 for himself and £2,000 to give to 'someone else'.

By the way, I heard a person say if Desert Orchid had won there wouldn't have been a dry eye on the course; well I certainly would have shed a few tears!

I had another marvellous day's punting at Aintree the following month, on Grand National Day. Just before the first I met the late Frank Scotto who owned and had transformed Sedgefield Racecourse. He told me Peter Easterby fancied their horse in the first; actually I was going to back it in any case but his remarks gave me further confidence and I took £5,000 to £500 about him. I then followed it by having £40,000 to £2,000 Mr. Frisk for the National. Both horses won and I collected £45,000, amazingly I hadn't backed either each way which was completely out of character.

Beverley has always been my favourite course though I've only ever had a couple of winners there as an owner. It's a real country meeting with a lovely atmosphere and only 25 minutes from Malton. I only hope they don't do any more building for the recent work has most decidedly robbed the course of some of its intimate charm. As for the punting, it has been an absolute gold mine for me. The course has distinct characteristics, the home straight (which isn't straight at all) is very much on the collar. The bends are especially sharp with the final turn being slightly on the wrong camber. The draw is also all important, no matter what the distance of the race and, when assessing this point, the going must be taken into account. It is one thing knowing what is required to give a horse an advantage over the others at Beverley but it is also crucial to recognise the right sort of horse that is required.

Incredibly, I've hardly ever had a losing day there and one of the most memorable winning ones was at a July evening meeting. On that particular day it was certain that Cecil's two runners would be long odds on and I didn't fancy either. There was Proud Crest in the mile and a half three year old maiden and Dragons Wrath in a seven furlong two year old event. Both were to be ridden by Willy Ryan and I had seen each of their latest outings; Proud Crest had been second at Windsor and I just didn't reckon his action would suit the

Yorkshire course. As for Cecil's other runner, he had scraped home at Ripon only recently at the prohibitive odds of 1/3. Many so called shrewd judges considered the colt had won cleverly but my opinion did not coincide; I didn't like his attitude. I refrained from having a punt in the first three races though I had fancied the winner of the seller at 11/4 and by the time Proud Wrath's race came along the meeting was in full swing. It was an exceptionally warm evening with a clear blue sky. Proud Crest opened up at 2/7 and quickly dropped half a point to 1/4, a crazy price. The second favourite at 9/2 was a horse trained by Hindley at Newmarket, which had run only once, finishing second in a good class maiden there; it was then 16/1 and more, any of the other half dozen runners. I approached a bookmaker I did a lot of business with and mentioned I didn't like Cecil's horse and asked for four and a half monkeys the Hindley runner. My bet was accepted and I noted a touch of sarcasm as I was asked "Would you like the bet again and make it £4,500 to £1,000." You can imagine what my answer was; I felt my judgement was being questioned. Proud Crest was never at the races and beaten most convincingly by the horse I'd backed. Incidentally Cecil's horse went on to win five consecutive races after that, all on courses totally different from the East Yorkshire track, two in fact being at Lingfield and Catterick.

The next race on the card was that of Dragons Wrath; the layers asked for 1/3, then 7/2 young Col's runner which had won his previous race at Carlisle, a course not dissimilar to Beverley. As with the previous contest it was 16/1 bar the two. I didn't even ask Col about his horse; there was no need as I knew the score and had £7,000 to £2,000 about him. Dragons Wrath was rather reluctant to go to post, which didn't surprise me, and was sweating profusely. In the race the two market leaders were held up until a couple of furlongs out, it was then ding dong to the line with the Tinkler horse Kafu Warrior getting up to win by a head. Cecil's Dragons Wrath had a further two races, started favourite each time but won neither. I'd won £11,500 that evening; the money was important, of course, but so was being correct with my judgement.

What a difference a couple of hours can make. I was driving over the moors to Redcar and contemplating a difficult day ahead with 120 runners at the meeting. Then the car phone rang, just as I came out of a poor reception area; it was Nigel with some rather inspiring information for the 2 year old seller. It was for a horse named Call Me I'm Blue, the only youngster in the field without a previous outing, the others being a fairly mediocre bunch. Call Me I'm Blue was trained by Ben Beasley from stables at the top of Sutton Bank and was to be ridden by a 5lbs claimer. I'd no sooner put the phone down when it rang again, this time the caller being from Ireland advising me to have a crack at Mark Tompkins runner in the other two year old race at Redcar. Well, at least I now had something to work on.

Call Me I'm Blue looked a picture in the paddock and went down to the start fly jumping and taking a hell of a hold. The bogey was going to be the draw, right over on the far side. I once heard it referred to as like a girl wearing cami knickers, one had no chance! Nevertheless, I intended having a real punt. I got 8/1 to a sizeable bet yet, to quote Raceform, "Opened 4/1, backed down to 5/2". There was also another quote "Made all, soon clear, won unchallenged by five lengths". With it being a seller there was obviously going to be a fair amount of interest at the auction and I intended to be in the thick of it. You will have noticed I've discreetly refrained from saying how much I won; well, I wouldn't want anyone thinking it was I that was the cause of his price shortening so dramatically.

Actually I learnt Nigel wanted the horse for one of his owners so I quickly dropped out of the bidding. He eventually bought the colt very cheaply at 9,200 gns. Call Me I'm Blue won five good class races the following season, including a couple at Ascot and Goodwood. It certainly showed what a good thing he must have been in that seller at Redcar. Oh yes, I nearly forgot, Mark Tompkins two year old also won and 'someone' backed it down from 9/4 to 6/4 and that 'someone' is again being rather discreet!

I'm sometimes asked by people if I would place a bet for them but I always decline; I don't need the hassle, small amounts would be a nuisance, large amounts a headache. The most bizarre request I've ever encountered was in the late eighties and was regarding placing a wager on a snooker match. At the time, Nigel was training a horse for an Irish bookmaker, a dapper sort of fellow in his early thirties but unfortunately his name escapes me. It was he who asked had I an account with Ladbrokes and could I get £20,000 on Terry Griffiths to beat Silvino Francisco in the Benson and Hedges. What's more, he wanted the wager to be on the exact number of frames Griffiths would win by. At first I thought surely anything so outrageous had to be a wind up, but no it wasn't. Before I had time to answer he tried to assure me the whole thing was perfectly straight but admitted to being a little bit useful forecasting snooker events! I told him "Sorry no can do, I never punt on snooker, consequently if I asked Ladbrokes for £20 on such an outcome, never mind £20,000, it would certainly start alarm bells ringing." Incidentally Griffiths did beat his opponent and the winning margin was, as I was told it would be, five frames to one! A couple of years ago I asked Nigel had he seen the 'snooker' punter recently but apparently he had died, I thought, that sounds rather ominous, though Nigel didn't know from what cause.

Some layers refused to pay out on the event; such a practice is a real bone of contention with me. When bookmakers accept a wager they should honour it even if they believe, after the event, all was not Kosher. They certainly don't allow me the privilege of not paying them when I back a non trier!

Finally - some years ago, in fact it was the last time I was down at Portman Square for a Stewards Enquiry; it concerned a filly which had won at Warwick for Nigel and a Chinese owner of his. I was asked by one of those officiating "Mr. Tinkler, is it correct you had £1,000 on the horse?" I replied "I sincerely hope it was more than that Sir!" Exactly.

AUCTIONEERING

I've done a little auctioneering at times, mainly after selling races, when for one reason or another the regular auctioneer was not available. But the most amusing bit of auctioneering that I've been involved with occurred at Pontefract races. The management asked me to help with their charity evening which was in aid of the local apprentice school. Various items were up for grabs such as bottles of rare wine, signed footballs and all that sort of thing. The auction took place in the winners enclosure between the first and second races. 'Business' was not brisk and that is putting it mildly. At one stage I had £50 bid for a number cloth from a classic winner and it was my bid! I went up to a middle aged couple leaning on the rails and tried to persuade them to get involved. I chatted away to them and got no response as far as bidding was concerned but a conversation emerged:-

He "A number cloth would be no good to the likes of us lass."

She "Ask him is he a Lord like that Oaksey."

Me "No, I'm not a Lord."

She "Ask him does he shag"

He "Who, that television chap."

She "No, not Oaksey, this here that's laughing."

He (looking at her) "Don't you think of owt else lass."

She "Well, it's shape of microphone he's holding!"

While I was bantering away I was also taking bids for the number cloth and magically got £200 - who bought it? I did!

There was more to come, the next 'item' on the agenda had been given by Guy Harwood when he was training. It was for a morning at his stables for two, coffee, then to the gallops to see the horses work, back for a lavish breakfast, followed by a tour of the stables. I laid it all out in detail. Before continuing I must go back a few years to Newmarket Sales. There was a horse in the catalogue entered from Guy Harwood's stables that interested me; so I approached him, asking about it and, in a very condescending manner, was told "It will be far too much money for you", then made no further conversation. Actually it made roughly what I would have been prepared to give but because of his attitude I didn't pursue the matter.

Now for the auction. I called out "Who will start me at £5 for the morning with Guy Harwood, thank you, I have £5 bid!" - bang - sold. So that the charity would not lose out, the next lot was a morning for two with me. I pointed out the breakfast would not be of the same standard as the previous lot, particularly if the guests to be weren't partial to cornflakes! Again, the bidding commenced at £5 but quickly rose without any help from me to £85 - bang and sold. I understand Guy Harwood was not amused - but then neither was I, some years before, at Newmarket Sales. Incidentally, I've never been invited back to Pontefract for any further auctioneering; I wonder why!

Chapter twenty

The Tinkler Clan

I have already mentioned most of the following dates and why they were significant but by putting them in the list, along with some more recent happenings, it will make events easier to follow.

1979 - Nigel and Sandra married - their daughter Maria was born.

1980 - Nigel commenced training at Boltby.

1981 - Marie and I split.

1982 - Nigel moved to Langton to train and built Woodland Stables.

1982 - Col's terrible fall at Newcastle finished his riding career.

1983 - Marie and I divorced and left Boltby.

1983 - Col and Carol's son Nicky was born.

1983 - Nigel and Sandra parted.

1984 - Marie bought a small farm near Buckingham.

1984 - Nigel and Kim joined forces - Amy was born.

1984 - I launched Full Circle.

1984 - Col started to train at Musley Bank near Malton.

1985 - Col and Carol's second son Andrew arrived.

1987 - My telephone information business went into service.

1989 - I bought the place at Wombleton.

1989 - Mumso died aged 91.

1989 - Nigel retired from riding.

1992 - Nigel and Kim's son Lewis was born.

1994 - Col handed in his training licence.

1994 - I sold my place at Wombleton.

1994 - I moved into the Black Swan at Helmsley.

1995 - Full Circle had its final runner.

1995 - I bought my present home at Huttons Ambo.

1999 - Nicky rode his first winner.

2000 - Andrew rode his first winner.

2000 - Marie returns to Yorkshire to live.

Over the years Marie has occasionally had a horse in training with Nigel; in fact has a couple at the moment, one of those being the home bred Wishful Thinker. The Tinklers had a bit of a touch on him when he was backed down from 7/2 to 9/4 to land a seller at Redcar. Marie came up for the race and stayed with me for a couple of days. She mentioned she'd become discontented with life at her stud farm near Buckingham and was finding the work hard and not sufficiently rewarding. She hinted that she'd like to come back to Yorkshire to live and be closer to the rest of the Tinkler clan and their activities. Since then Marie has sold her stud farm and is now staying in a cottage locally until she finds a place of her own - the possibility of us ever getting back together again is not an equation, but it's nice to be friendly. We talk on the phone daily and meet up frequently. Her sense of humour has always been paramount; she was telling me recently about someone she was not particularly endured with and thought a generous spray of insecticide was the answer! It was not necessarily what was said but how it was said, delivered with an impish grin, that was so amusing.

Looking out from the stand at a local meeting we attended recently, Marie said to Kim "When I was training we used to come here on a Sunday morning for a gallop". Kim answered "We are not allowed to do that now". Back came Marie with "Neither were we allowed to do it then!"

The fact that I've not until now introduced my grandchildren is no true reflection of their importance to me, nor does it minimise my affection for them; it's just the way the composition has been compiled.

Col and Carol have two boys, Nicky aged 18 and Andrew 16. Whereas Nigel has two girls and one boy, Maria aged 21, whose mother is Sandra, Nigel's first wife and, from his second marriage to Kim, there is Amy aged 16 and little Lewis, very much the youngster of the pack at 8. They give me enormous pleasure and I'm greatly interested in whatever they do. They are all so different in many ways but their attitude to life is similar. All are ambitious and possess the right attributes to succeed. These qualities plus his striking personality even shines through in Lewis, young as he is. I could not be more pleased with each of them.

I see them quite often though not as much as I would like, but I don't wish to become an overbearing old buzzard. No matter how close our relationships, I am of a different generation which I'm sure, even with the best will in the world, can be boring for young people. I might be wrong but that is my philosophy. I've never interferred with their upbringing nor passed judgement on anything they might have done which has displeased me, though I can't think of anything offhand. They know I'm here if needed, that's what counts and I'm sure our respect is mutual. As for the future; they are my future.

When it became certain, because of his appalling injuries, that Col would not be able to race ride again he commenced training and was granted a licence early in '84. He made a dream start winning with his first runner; it was Trickshot at Hexham on Cheltenham

Gold Cup Day and brought off quite a gamble having been backed down to 7/4. Col was quick to improve the facilities he had by putting down a further all weather gallop and building new boxes. Having started with a dozen horses the string soon grew to over forty. Carol and he were a great team and numerous successful gambles materialized over the years; I particularly remember Ernie Bilko at Nottingham and Swingit Gunner in the '87 November Handicap at Doncaster. I'm not saying Col was exactly secretive about the coups that were planned but neither was he especially informative! Of course, I was always delighted when he had a winner, whether I'd backed it or not - usually not!

After ten years and close on 250 winners Col became rather disillusioned; one or two of his owners didn't play it straight, the majority did but the odd bad apple in the tub caused him to throw in the towel. The whole time they were training Col and Carol had not ceased buying foals and selling them as yearlings. All they did from then on was to increase the turnover and venture into other aspects of the bloodstock business. Col didn't regret the transition in the least though I believe Carol would have been happy to have continued with the training. However, they are now established and highly respected amongst those in the profession. Nicky and Andrew had grown up with the training which had become a way of life; still, they had no problems coping with the 'switch over'. At least it meant they didn't become sour with too much racing, something they might otherwise have done.

Even though there is a two year difference in ages the boys have always been the best of friends. They went through the usual tribulations which all children encounter, though probably less than most endure; they have had a very happy upbringing playing the same games that all children play but ponies were their lives from a

Above:
Clare Bancroft *(p367)*

Above:
Clare leading a yearling *(p367)*

Above:
Johnny Ridley *(p404)*

Above:
Leslie Steele *(p403)*

Above:
I won over £60.000 when Norton Coin (nearest
camera) won the 1990 Gold Cup at Cheltenham
with Graham McCourt in the saddle *(p411)*

Below:
The controversial photo finish print *(p336)*

A quote from the Racing Post.
There were ructions at Newcastle on Friday night when police had to be called to help disperse
angry punters after the announcement that Passion King had beaten Love To Dance in the last, the
Angerton Graduation Stakes. Earlier there had been an announcement that Love To Dance was the
winner.

Andrew aged seven waiting for his imaginary
ride at Pontefract *(p 423)*

Andrew and Nicky when very young.

Andrew and Nicky at a Hunter Trail

Nicky and Andrew looking forward to the future

Below:
Nicky's first winner: St. Lawrence at Southwell
(p425)

Above:
Andrew's first winner: Nafith at Musselburg
(p428)

Left:
Nicky's winning on Brevity at Hamilton *(p429)*

Below:
Andrew going to Post at Haydock

Left:
Marie and little Maria at Thirsk Races

Below:
My Granddaughter Maria and Paul marry.
The car is unmistakable with the distinctive
number plate! *(p432)*

Above & Right:
Amy *(p433)*

Below:
Lewis *(p434)*

Above:
Lewis and Nigel at Epsom
for the Derby

My home at Wombleton *(p439)*

The study at my present home at Huttons Ambo and from
where my autobiography was written *(p464)*

very early age. Both were keen on hunting and taking part in Hunter Trials, though never had ponies good enough to take them to the top at show jumping. Just as Col and Nigel had done when they were at a similar age, Nicky and Andrew built miniature steeplechase courses and raced round them flat out in racing colours and giving running commentaries as they went. Watching them was like being in a time warp machine. Apart from such games being a lot of fun they were also teaching them to ride. From a very early age it was evident they were a cut above the average child rider and would most likely become jockeys.

Remarkably they steered clear of serious injuries though I would occasionally see a plaster cast hobble by. When Andrew was no more than six or seven he would often pack a holdall with racing boots, silks, white breeches, the whole regalia, plus a whip protruding from the top of the bag. He would mention to Col and Carol that he was riding at wherever they had a runner that day and would they take him there. Once at the races he would make his way to the jockeys changing room, change into the kit, pop on the scales and then come out with the riders as they made their way to the parade ring, signing autographs as he went.

The jockeys loved him, he was their mascot. I've no idea where he went while the race was being run but afterwards people would ask "Did you have a good ride?" All marvellous make believe.

Nicky's imagination came to the fore one day when at a similar age, or maybe he was a couple of years older. He arranged a two a side football match at my place when I lived at Wombleton and decided that he and I should be on one side with Andrew and my Secretary on the other. I put up the goalposts, Rose sliced the oranges ready for half-time and the boys changed into their strip. Nicky then marched on to the marked out pitch and announced that not only was he to captain our side but he was also the referee and that he would stand no nonsense! He blew a whistle and the game 'was on'. I don't recall the score at the time but, after about ten minutes and much whistle blowing, Nicky ran over to where I was standing and pointing a finger towards the touchline screamed "Off". He was also waving a red piece of cardboard, obviously prepared for the occasion! It was hard for me to keep a straight face as I asked him "Why, what have I done wrong?" He informed me "It was for handling the ball". But when I reminded him that it was he who had made me goalkeeper he accused me of arguing and said "I will now have to report you for bloody insolence". As he ran quickly backwards, which is something he'd obviously seen referees do, he shouted "And don't try and sneak back as a f*****g substitute!" At half time Nicky took the opportunity to also become manager and gave me a bollocking for being sent off. He inferred that because of it we might lose the game. Now that was something I thought most unlucky for, despite not having a goalkeeper, we were leading by 12 goals to nil. The lop-sided scoreline was by courtesy of some of the referee's rather curious decisions. Every time Andrew popped one into the back of the net it was deemed to be offside! The game fizzled out when Andrew was also given a red card for going on a cross-country run before the game was supposed to have ended. It had all been brilliant, humorous make believe, though Nicky had taken it all so seriously.

Actually Andrew became an above average runner and represented Ryedale Schools, but both boys only real interest has always been riding. Neither of them went away to school yet academically they are bright enough and certainly not lazy in any shape or form, in fact very much the reverse, with Nicky being a workaholic. There is very little he can't do about the place and sees to all the maintenance. He's also made a mechanical horse which I thought worked most efficiently though, according to the boys, was not a good enough mover so has been replaced by something better.

Both Nicky and Andrew have grown too heavy for the flat but will be the ideal build for 'over the sticks'. They ride regularly for trainers around Malton and at a very young age rode in the Newmarket Town Plate. Andrew, even though he is the younger, has up to now been the more adventurous. Some time ago, when still only fourteen, he decided he should broaden his 'education' and had spells with Jack Berry, David Nicholson, Oliver Sheerwood, Lenny Lungo, Martin Pipe, Philip Hobbs and Ferdy Murphy. He also spent a month with Michael Dickinson over in America. It reads like a Who's Who and what a marvellous experience for him to be able to ride work and school over fences for such notable trainers. I know Andrew is very appreciative of them for he learnt a great deal from the visits. Only recently he spent a couple of days at Nicky Henderson's and it was agreed that after leaving school in the summer he should commence there as an amateur. Andrew is delighted, as I am, that he is to join such a prestigious yard, but he has no illusions and fully realises to be successful will not be easy.

On reaching sixteen Nicky was granted an amateur licence and had his first ride on the flat at Musselburgh. It was actually on his birthday and, though it was not expected to be a dream start to his career, the horse ran respectably and got a most efficient ride from Nicky. Carol and Col then bought a five year old maiden, St. Lawrence, out of Clive Brittain's yard for him to ride on the all weather tracks. After several outings, which included a second and a third, they won a race at Southwell. Riding his first winner was marvellous but the style in which it was achieved also gave me a terrific thrill. To mark the event I gave him a mounted sovereign with a gold chain and had another made ready for Andrew.

The second winner Nicky rode will not be in the official records as such, for it was at an Arabian meeting held at Market Rasen. The occasion was made special because the colours he wore were those of Hamdan Al Maktoum, who is a great supporter of Arabian racing in this country and has his horses trained by Jill Duffield at Newmarket. Since that initial winner Nicky has gone down to Newmarket on a regular basis, to ride work, and has had further successes in the famous blue and white silks, including a double at Wolverhampton and a treble at Fontwell. I particularly liked the report in the 'Horse and Hound' on the latter meeting; it was headlined "Tinkler works his magic". He is, as I write, currently leading rider in the 'Arabian Racing Jockeys' Championship'. One can't say other than the experience is teaching him so much. Nicky has also ridden a winner at Mijas in southern Spain, a new racecourse which holds its meetings under floodlights; they incredibly commence proceedings very late in the evening and run through to the early hours of the morning. Apparently thousands attend though I don't imagine such unusual hours would be appreciated in this country. Nicky's mount was backed down from 5/1 to 1/3, won comfortably and obviously brought off quite a gamble for Mick Lambert and connections. Incidentally, Mick used to train at Malton a few years ago and is now one of the track's resident handlers. What impressed Nicky most about the meeting was the number of gleaming Bentley convertibles in the car park; well he was in southern Spain!

After the excursion to Spain he had his first ride over jumps, in a handicap chase, at Carlisle and finished second on a horse trained by Malcolm Jefferson. It was then back to the flat at Wolverhampton for Nicky's next winner, Colonel Custer, in a mile and a half handicap.

The horse was trained by Brotherton and because of the appalling draw they seemingly had no chance whatsoever, but Nicky rode a blinder and won by several lengths. There are some good young amateurs about at the moment and Nicky is certainly amongst them.

There was an amusing sequel to Nicky's first ride over hurdles; it was at Fakenham, the horse was Needwood Spirit and trained by Hamish Alexander it won by three and a half lengths at 33/1. 'Needwood' had previously been competing in similar company so the starting price indicates there must have been a significant improvement in the way the horse had performed. There was no official Stewards Inquiry though the Stewards Secretary wanted to know why there had been such an amazing discrepancy of form. Neither Hamish or the owner were at the meeting, in fact nobody from the stable, other than the boy attending the horse, was present. Realising there was a minor problem Andrew, who had accompanied Nicky to Fakenham, put himself forward as the stable representative. His answer to the stipendiaries query was "My brother had not ridden the horse before today and I just think he gave him a peach of a ride". The explanation was duly noted!

On one of his excursions to Lambourn Andrew rode some work for John Hills who paid him a great compliment when saying "He is years ahead of his time". It's clear that he would have applied for his amateur licence at fifteen had the rules governing age limits not changed. However, the rules of racing did allow him to ride at that age in a charity race at Newcastle. It took place on one of their jumping cards, was on the flat and over a mile and a half. The horse Andrew rode was Clarinch Claymore, trained by Malcolm Jefferson, started favourite at evens and won by four lengths. Even though it was only a minor contest, the Tinklers were thrilled to bits and Andrew had ridden with such confidence. I've since reflected on all the highs and lows the Tinkler clan have experienced at the Northumberland track and there's certainly no need for me to mention which category Andrew's win was placed.

Six months after the Newcastle race came Andrew's sixteenth birthday, it was on May the third and with it his amateur licence. He had already been to a seminar held in Newmarket; these must now be attended before the Jockey Club will issue a licence to ride. As fortune had it, the day following his birthday, there was a two mile flat race at Musselburgh for amateurs. One of the horses entered was Nafith, a five year old gelding with a string of duck eggs and a bit of a reputation to his name. The horse was trained by Lee Lloyd-James here at Malton and, after Andrew had ridden him a gallop, there was a half promise from Lee that he could have the ride. However it was not until the last minute, before the declaration of riders were made, that it was finally confirmed. Andrew had to lose several pounds, which he did, and with the aid of a six ounce saddle was able to do the weight.

It was a lovely day, the sun was shining and what a dream start Andrew had to his riding career. He settled Nafith off the pace for a mile then gradually made steady headway; sticking to the rails he took up the running a furlong out and went on to win by a couple of lengths at a staggering 100/1. It had been a copy book ride and what gave me further pleasure was, as they were pulling up, Nicky, who also rode in the race, gave his brother a tap on the back with his whip as a gesture of congratulations. The fact that the win was so unexpected put the icing on the cake and did I have a punt? No, but it was irrelevant. I'm not going to fill the page with a string of superlatives, besides, I can't spell half the words I would want to use; I will simply say it was a fantastic and wonderful day. Tom O'Ryan, the racing journalist, wrote - 'Fairytales do not only happen in fiction, as Andrew Tinkler has discovered to his delight. Dreams turned to reality for the Ryedale schoolboy at Musselburgh, when just a day after his sixteenth birthday he made his debut as an amateur jockey - and recorded a 100/1 triumph on the totally unconsidered Nafith'.

The following week the Tinkler brothers were again in action; it was in a sprint at Hamilton, only this time it was Nicky's turn for the winners enclosure. He rode the consistent Brevity for Milton Bradley, led for the whole six furlongs and won by three lengths with Andrew finishing in sixth place. A couple of weeks later the friendly rivalry continued when they rode the two market leaders in a twenty six runner, six furlong, Maiden Handicap at Redcar. Nicky could have ridden either horse but, as he was riding out for Tim Easterby on a regular basis, he felt committed to the stable's 'Day Lily'. This left Milton Bradley's 'Currency' free for Andrew, who took full advantage of the opportunity and won by a length at 7/1; Nicky was a further two lengths back in fourth place. Excluding the charity race at Newcastle, it was Andrew's second winner from only three rides, though he has since had a couple of unplaced mounts, one being Marie's 'East Cape' at Haydock. I'm delighted they commenced their careers whilst I'm still writing my memoirs, it has enabled me to record their initial successes. Both boys seem to have the right attitude, not only with matters relating to their riding but in all other aspects of life; something which is so very important.

Before I venture on to Nigel's side of the Tinkler clan I must refer to one further matter, though I'm rather reluctant to do so. Unfortunately there has recently been a breakdown of relations between Col and Carol; it is personal to them so I will say very little. They are still affably in business together, which is prospering, but that is not the issue. Naturally I'm sad about what has happened but it's not for me to intervene.

I've already written about some of Nigel's training escapades but, before going on to discuss his family, I'd like to mention that he has so far had over 500 winners. The figure being helped along the way by some fantastic horses, including The Ellier and Sacre D'Or, both winners at the Cheltenham Festival. Rodeo Star was another prestige winner when romping away with the Chester Cup, the Tote Gold Trophy at Newbury and the Queen's Prize at Kempton. As 'Rodeo' didn't possess the soundest of legs, the fact that he won on the flat, over hurdles and over fences, made his triumphs even more remarkable and certainly the more rewarding. He was brilliant and the same can be said of Nigel's handling of him. Sugarfoot, a superb stamp of a horse, is the most outstanding individual Nigel has trained so far. The chestnut colt, foaled in '94, has won nine races to date which include successes in group and listed events. He's also won the Bradford and Bingley at York twice; carrying top weight he absolutely trounced the opposition on the latter occasion. Sugarfoot was so unlucky when badly hampered in the Lockinge at Newbury; he also ran a couple of cracking races when just touched off in Group 2 events at Longchamp on L'Arc de Triomphe days. He's becoming worldly travelled, having also raced in Hong Kong and Dubai and wouldn't it be nice for connections were he to win one more high class race. He is still entire and is destined for stud, but what a cracking hurdler he would make; though Nigel doesn't believe he would stay two miles.

Nigel and his first wife, Sandra, decided to part early on in their marriage and finally divorced in '84, with Maria, the oldest of my grandchildren, being their only child. She was and still is a lovely, lovely girl but, like me, over sensitive which can be rather a drawback at times; it puts others at an advantage. When relationships collapse it's not necessarily a calamity though it certainly is when young ones are involved. Sandra and little Maria moved to a house not more than three miles from their former home but it was in town which was something I was not overjoyed about. Nigel had wanted them to take a more pleasant place which was closer to Woodland Stables but for some reason Sandra used her prerogative and declined to move there.

It's a fact of life that a large percentage of marriages and relationships don't last. The percentage would be even higher were more couples in a better financial position and able to afford to go their separate ways. I'm stating the obvious but people only become partners with those they meet and nobody meets that many people. What I'm trying to say is - it's odds on that there will be someone 'out there' more compatible than one's existing partner, no matter how affable that partner might be. I'm not a cynic nor am I endeavouring to excuse the number of marital breakdowns within the Tinkler family; I'm just philosophising.

Obviously the lifestyle of little Maria changed when Nigel and Sandra parted but with her being so young she probably didn't notice that side of the equation. As for Sandra who has recently remarried, she was naturally terribly upset at what had happened but never showed any real resentment and coped the best she could in the circumstances. I've always remained on good terms with her and the fact that she became a Jehovah's Witness didn't alter that. However, with that religion being the opposite to my beliefs I'd rather Maria had not been channelled in that direction. When I was talking with Sandra recently she said that "In the next world there will be no cars polluting the air, everyone will travel by pony and trap". I thought, if that's going to be the case I won't be having any runners at Wolverhampton on a frosty and foggy night in November; I live a hell of a long way from the potteries!

For me, Maria's childhood seems rather a blur and I've seen her far more often since she left college. Her first job was with a firm of travel agents and during that time was involved in a terrible motor accident. It occurred on a dual carriageway leading into Scarborough; a car came out of a slip road straight into her path, resulting in both cars being complete write offs. Maria suffered injuries though, thankfully, were not too serious. Sandra on the other hand, who was the only passenger in Maria's car, was not so fortunate; she was detained in hospital for a few days and may always feel some discomfort. The others involved in the collision were elderly; the driver of the other vehicle was killed instantly and his wife died later. This bears out the severity of the crash though remarkably Maria handled the tragedy extremely well; what had happened did not affect her confidence in the slightest and she was soon driving again. In the not too distant future all my grandchildren will be driving and it's my worst fear that they will become involved in crashes.

Maria became engaged early in '99 and she and Paul were married in the August. Little Lewis, all three feet of him, who acted as a pageboy, cut a real dash in his topper and tails. Paul was employed at an administrative bank in Newcastle at the time and when he was transferred to Livingston near Edinburgh in the autumn, it meant selling the delightful little house they had just bought and required them to purchase another in Scotland. Maria had been offered a position with British Airways but took a post as a temp, moving from one firm to another; the trouble was, if one can call it trouble, everywhere she went they asked her to stay permanently. The outcome was a complete coincidence; after doing a stint at the same bank as Paul's she stayed on there and secured a very good position. I have been up to see them a couple of times and they come down to Malton at regular intervals. They both seem perfectly happy and ideally suited, though I'm sure Maria would rather be living in Yorkshire.

Nigel is a very amusing person and always has been, whenever he is around there is usually the sound of laughter though, having said that, some subjects are surprisingly very much taboo. He hates confrontation, though that's not saying he would sweep all unpleasant issues under the carpet. Soon after the divorce with Sandra Nigel married Kim, arriving at the Registry Office minus his shoes; no, it was not some religious ritual, he simply forgot to put them on! Nigel had known Kim for some time and gave her the opportunities all jockeys require at the start of their careers; one would have thought that having Amy and Lewis to look after would have curtailed her riding, but that has not been the case. I much admire her for the way she combines her two roles, on one hand a wife and mother, on the other a rider of close on 200 winners, with neither suffering because of the other. Kim has even found the time to take Amy and Lewis to countries as far afield as Australia, New Zealand, America, Africa, Spain and France.

As can be seen by the summary, which appears at the beginning of this chapter, '84 was a most eventful year for the Tinklers and no date was more important than that of July the tenth. It was on that day that Amy was born and the photograph shows what an exceptionally pretty child she was. Amy seems to have grown up so quickly and now has Royal Ascot pencilled into her diary. I haven't been for the last couple of years but I'm told she has caused more than a few heads to turn at the most prestigious of all meetings. She is seemingly quiet to the point of shyness, though that is an illusion; Amy is in fact a most self assured, sophisticated young lady. When she leaves college I don't necessarily expect her to take up a career in racing; though there are always opportunities in administration that can be interesting.

As with Maria, much of Amy's earlier days are a haze in my memory. One cannot expect otherwise. The more eventful a life one leads and the more active the brain the more there is to remember. However the memories I do recall of her are happy ones and mostly amusing. There was the occasion when the Tinklers went down to Florios, the 'Italian' in Malton, for a meal and, for a prank, I parked Amy's peculiar shaped 'Noddy pedal car' outside on the double yellow line. It wasn't long before the police arrived; they then came into the restaurant and spoke to the first person they saw, which happened to be me "Tell me Sir, have you any idea who the vehicle outside belongs to?" There was a great deal of laughter when I answered "Yes, it's Noddy's car and he pissed off through the back when he saw you come in." I continued the leg pull with "Are you going to clamp it or tow it away?" It was hilarious.

The same adjective, hilarious, can be used to describe Lewis, the youngest of my grandchildren. He was born on October 5th, 1992 and possessed the same laughing eyes that Nigel had when I first saw him so very long ago. Lewis is just a bundle of fun, everything he does having a humorous connection. He's as bright as a button and incredibly generous for one so young; it's not surprising that everyone he comes into contact with absolutely loves him. He's on the small side but athletic and so determined, making him very competitive. I see so much of myself in him, even to the food we like, whether it's raspberries with cream or mashed potatoes with lashings of butter. He also likes money - you may say who doesn't - but I think, for his age, he more than most and I'm sure he will make a lot when he grows up. In fact he hasn't waited for that. I'll explain -

when I called in recently he was sitting at the office computer churning out twenties; they were practically indistinguishable from the real thing. On seeing me he called out "Geega, how many do you want - or would you rather I made some fifties for you?" I asked him where did he get the paper and was answered by a tap on his nose by one of his fingers, indicating that I shouldn't have asked! As I left the office with my pockets bulging with his twenties he gave me what he called "Some sound advice". "Don't spend them in Malton Geega because they know you there; you don't want to end up behind bars!" Actually I wasn't intending to, though I did get the notes mixed up with some genuine ones and it took quite a time to sort out. While on the subject of money, he once told me with outstretched arms "I'm in financial trouble and a 'twenty' won't put it right." Apparently his newly acquired puppy had damaged a leg and an operation at the veterinary surgeon's was going to cost £500; Lewis was under the false impression, with it being his dog, he would be footing the bill. He went on, still gesturing with his hands "Geega, how can I afford a 'monkey', I've only got £914 in the whole world!" He was seven at the time and with that amount of money he reckoned he was in financial trouble! There was a happy ending - mister puppy came right without the operation and recently accidentally sired a litter of pups with a terrier Kim has at the stables. Incidentally, I wasn't at all surprised to learn that Lewis had charged his mum a stud fee for the little dog's services! One of the first things I can recall about Lewis was when we were once at Doncaster Sales; he wouldn't be more than two at the time. He had gone to the snack bar and somehow managed to buy a Scotch egg but it had slipped off the cardboard plate onto the floor. When I saw him he was sitting there, not having much success in trying to redeem the situation. I asked him "Can I help?" and was told "No, Geega, it's alright but I'm trying to get the f*****g egg back into the sausage."

One Sunday morning at Woodland Stables, when Lewis was a little older, he was holding court to quite an audience. They had come to see the horses but the rascal's repartee held them spellbound. He was telling them that the scruffy old Tom cat that had just walked by was the only puddy cat left on the place. According to Lewis, "There was Twinkle - she died when she got run over by a tractor - stupid Twinkle. Then there was Harry, a horse trod on him and he died." We were then treated to a demonstration of what had occurred, including the stamp. Lewis went on "Then there was Rusty. He was a ginger cat; he went down a rabbit hole and didn't come out - he died. Blacky got his head stuck in a jam jar and 'suffycated' and he died." The list of unfortunate pussy cats and how they met their end went on and on until Lewis finally came to Fluffy. "Poor Fluffy! I loved Fluffy - he was my favourite." The little fellow's voice lowered and I thought I saw a tear in his sparkling eyes as he continued to talk about Fluffy. "Poor Fluffy - he died when the hoover sucked him up." What! I later learnt from Kim that none of the cats had ever existed, other than in Lewis's mischievous mind. In fact it was the listeners who had been sucked up; he'd so enjoyed stringing us along! At one time Kim kept a mini zoo at the stables; there were birds and small animals of all descriptions. I'm sure Lewis would have crossed a monkey with a parrot if he'd had his way!

From a very early age Lewis knew which horses were in which stables; on one occasion when Nigel was trying to sell a yearling to a prospective buyer, Lewis popped his head round the stable door and said "Dad, is this the one you gave too much money for?" Thankfully the deal went through and even more thankfully the horse won races. Lewis once remarked "When wasps sting me they die." I told him "That's not true." He said "It is, I kill them!"

He recently made up a drink from the drinks cupboard and sold a bottle to one of Nigel's Irish owners, who was staying for a couple of days. John took rather a large gulp of the lethal concoction, dived into his pocket and gave Lewis an extra £20. He reckoned he'd been cured of the drink in five seconds flat. "I'll tell you what Lewis, my boy, if that's what drink tastes like when I'm sober, I'll never touch another drop." Diving into his pocket again he brought out another £20 saying "And give this to your sister." John continued "Lewis, you should sell the recipe to Alcoholics Anonymous; you would make yourself a bloody fortune!"

Lewis phoned me recently and mentioned, during the conversation, that he thought I was putting on weight. I agreed but told him "It's not life threatening". He said "It could be Geega, if it caused you to take too long to cross the road!"

I'm not saying Lewis is spoilt, anything but, though I'm sure even his toys have toys, he's got that many. At the present time he's not over keen on riding but Nigel wasn't at an early age; so long as he's good at something that's all that matters and if he gives me as much pleasure in the future as he has up to now I'll be a very happy bunny, but, of course, the same applies to all my grandchildren. Lewis asked me recently "What do you do for a living Geega and how much do you earn?" I put him right on both accounts. There was then quite a pause before he announced "Geega, that seems like my sort of job when I grow up!" Lewis also said something to me the other day, something which I enjoyed hearing him say; it was "Do you know, I've got the best mum and dad in the whole world." - nice one Lewis.

Chapter twenty one

I move to Wombleton and then to Huttons Ambo

Looking back I find it incredible that, after parting from Marie and selling up at Boltby in '83, it took nearly six years before I bought somewhere else to live. During that time I spent a short spell at The Green Man in Malton, after which I lived in a room next to my office in a mobile home, parked at Nigel's stables. More often than not I worked on until the early hours of the morning so I found the arrangement very convenient. I had things quite de luxe, though having said that, it was not exactly the way a 'top executive' should live! Eventually a property came up for sale in which I was very much interested. It was a charming detached cottage in Langton village and only a few hundred yards from Nigel's place; it required extensive renovations but that would not have been a problem. At the auction I was the underbidder at £75,000, which was a ridiculously low figure considering the location. The fact that I didn't buy the cottage probably had far reaching effects, because the property I eventually purchased the following year soaked up an enormous amount of money. It was a very much neglected 23 acre small holding close to Wombleton, a village on the edge of the North Yorkshire Moors. I bought it at auction for £205,000 and took immediate possession. This allowed me to send in a couple of JCB's which must sound rather ominous - it was! I took up most of the hedges, demolished all the farm buildings other than those directly

439

adjoining the house. All the overhead electric cables and telephone wires were put underground, thus dispensing with dozens of poles. A complete new water and sewage system was installed and the renovations to the house were on a massive scale. Much of the work had to be re-done time and time again until I was satisfied - all escalating costs. It was not that I kept changing my mind but more a question of the work not being the standard I required. However the pond was another scenario, I did keep altering its position and it became a standing joke. One day hundreds of tons of earth would be excavated only to be put back the next. This happened several times until I was sure I'd got the right position for it.

Wombleton would be approximately 15 miles from Malton and I would do the journey each morning to inspect what had been done the previous day; quite often it was very little! I would stay for about an hour and then go on to the races. On one occasion I got half a mile down the road, realised I'd forgotten something or other, so returned only to find a card school taking place. It only involved a few of the 30 working there that day though that was a few too many; I shan't elaborate on what I said but another type of card came into the conversation! I didn't employ just the one builder to oversee but several supposed specialists in their field; mind you they weren't all nincompoops, I also had some real craftsmen there.

On one of my morning excursions I discovered the wrong roof tiles had been delivered and subsequently fitted. I wanted simple pantiles and not the abortions that were stuck on the roof, they all had to be changed. The same thing happened with the guttering; I'd arranged to have wood lined with lead but what did I get delivered and, again, fitted? Plastic! It all had to come down. The house was not large and when the renovations were completed there were only three bedrooms though all had bathrooms. It also had two staircases, a snooker room and a study, apart from the norm which is associated with a house of its size. I brought in a wealth of timber and there were many exciting features; a beautiful home was created.

The stable complex was just as extravagant with the leaded light windows being double glazed and all the boxes had fans and heaters installed. The garden was extensively landscaped with the walling costing over £30,000 and the large pond was stocked with 200 Koi. All the fields were re-seeded and post and railed into suitably sized paddocks. Thousands of Leylandii were planted and I built a three hole golf course. The long sweeping drive was constructed to main road specifications and was curbed with stone from Cornwall. To get the perfect curves I drove the car when there was some snow on the ground and took the lines the tyres had made.

In order to give the grass verge along the roadside a decent width, the open ditch was channelled underground and the existing hedge uprooted. This was replaced roughly five yards further back into the field by double post and rails with leylandii between. With that done I then had a crazy innovation, I decided to have artificial grass some 1,500 square yards of it, between the newly erected fence and the road. I laid down the tarmacadam and was just about to add the strips of 'grass' when I was told by the local Council that they would not allow it. It was a question of having to dig up all the tarmacadam; this was not a problem but getting rid of the stuff certainly was! As a matter of interest and with much appreciation on my part, it was Norma Macauley, the Midland trainer, who supplied the 'grass' and took it back without charge. Reverting to normal turf it soon became an imposing frontage but didn't meet the approval of an utter lout; one night, soon after the turf had been laid and thoroughly watered, he, I presume it was a he, drove his car up and down, braking to make skid marks. He did the same the following night causing further damage. I decided to put an end to his malicious lunacy; I dug a deep hole where the skid marks were then filled it with grass cuttings - when all was said and done it was my land he'd been trespassing on. I had to wait until the following week before he came back, well I assume he did by the condition of the hole! and there was no further trouble.

Eventually I moved in but it had taken over a year for the transformation to take place. As I walked from room to room on the plush green carpet, I thought, if ever it became known exactly how much 'Geegas Place', for that's what I called my new home, stood me at I would be certified insane.

I realised I'd spent too much money and not enough time supervising the renovations but I was managing both Full Circle and my Information Line at the time; this meant there were just not enough hours in a day. I bought quite a lot of antique furniture to fill the rooms along with all the other things a house needs for I had very little in the way of possessions at that time. I did however have a rather exquisite chair; it was feminine against being masculine and I had just the one from an original set of four. I mention this chair because there is a story behind its survival. Many years ago Marie had bought the set from the antique department at Harrods and only acquired them because a sale to an eminent film actress had fallen through, the reason being, the bank wouldn't honour her cheque! When Marie and I decided to go our separate ways we divided the chairs between us and my pair found their way into my office at the stables. Unfortunately they became damaged when I climbed through a window, slipped and crashed on top of them. I wasn't pissed - I'd merely mislaid the keys to the door. The chairs weren't badly damaged but definitely required some restoration. I contacted a restorer and asked him to call and collect them but as I wouldn't be about I would leave the chairs in the tack room. On seeing them Nigel's gardener thought they were just a couple of old discarded chairs so took them home to use as firewood! By the time I realised what had happened pieces from both chairs had already gone up in smoke. However, I rescued enough for the restorer to make up a single chair, which has now becomer rather special.

I hadn't been living at Geegas Place long when my brother Peter came over to see me. He looked terribly dejected and before he even said "Hello" remarked, in an agonising tone "You have got trouble with one of the cannon balls on the top of the gate pillar." Fearing the worst, whatever that might be, I asked "What the hell has happened?" Peter dryly replied, and not meaning to be humourous "A bird has done a dropping on top of it!" I told him "We can soon put that right" and handed him a bucket of water and a scrubbing brush, then pointed him in the direction of a ladder. On any of his subsequent visits Peter never again mentioned the gate pillars or the offending birds!

I once overheard an awfully funny conversation on a crossed line. One of the fellows talking could obviously see 'Geegas Place' from where he lived because he told the person he was chatting to "There are some jolly nice sorts keep visiting that Tinkler chappy, I'd better call round and introduce myself and see if I can meet one of them". The talk then drifted to other things so I 'hung up'. I imagined him sitting for hours at his bedroom window with field glasses at the ready. I wonder if one of those 'nice sorts' happened to be the girl with the bicycle? I must tell you about her. I was in the garden one Sunday evening when this girl came up the drive pushing a bicycle with a punctured tyre, though I'm surprised I noticed the tyre! I soon learnt she was Norwegian, on her own, and mainly over here to visit York and soak up the history. She was a little off course going back for the ferry but I didn't mind! She wanted to know where she could get the tyre repaired; we chatted and I told her with it being a Sunday it would be impossible but she could stay if she wished then we could take the wheel to a garage in the morning. I would not say Joanna was exactly pretty though she had a gorgeous smile and a slender figure and, as she walked, her bottom had a tantalizing mischievous wiggle! It actually took five days to get the puncture repaired plus a further two to get the wheel back on! Enough said.

A girl I knew quite well, who worked for a finance company, would sometimes stay over when in the area. I remember her once saying "Colin, you know what we did together yesterday" - how could I possibly forget - "Well, if I lived here permanently we could do it every day." I thought, Oh no we couldn't, or at least I couldn't, I would not be able to stand the pace; though on second thoughts she possibly wasn't referring to our expensive shopping excursion to York! I heard from her recently, she now has a job in Miami as Personal Assistant to an American; apparently she met him whilst on holiday there. She told me her salary is treble what it was in this country, plus an apartment and the use of a new BMW coupe. I said "It certainly sounds as if you have landed on your feet". To that she replied "Well, not exactly on my feet, more on my back, with my feet in the air". Again, enough said! I had many visitors whilst living at Wombleton though it wasn't always what it seemed. I also employed a 'Jeeves' for a while, that was until I discovered, by the sound of broken china, that he thought the tumbler dryer was a dishwasher!

As soon as I'd settled in I moved the Full Circle administration to Wombleton, it had a comfortable office in the house with photographs of all the winners on the walls. Just to see row after row of them was incredible, so much had been achieved in so short a time. During its closing years I hosted a couple of open days at my new home. The members visited Nigel's stables in the morning and then came over for refreshments in the afternoon. I remember one small boy not only stuffing his face but also stuffing all the pockets of the snooker table with apple cores and sticky sweet wrappers from sweets he devoured by the hundredweight. All smiles he came up to me and said "Do you know, I'll soon be five". I answered "Don't count on it sonny!"

Another guest I had at Wombleton was a crow, yes, a crow; the first time I actually saw him he was taking a swig of gin and tonic. It was the morning after there had been a party and someone had left the half full glass on the bridge wall next to the pond. From then on I would leave a tipple out for him every morning and he would come along as I was making the recording for the Information Line. I'd discuss Mr. Crow and say how he was strutting about the lawn; though quite often he would be staggering about the lawn. He became quite a favourite with callers and, as he was in a way earning me money, he was entitled to his daily drink. I often wonder what became of him after I moved on; he probably flew to a health farm to dry out!

A ridiculous rumour persisted in the area that I was breeding Geegas and that they lived in the enclosed plantation. It was also assumed that that was the reason the hunt didn't go on my land. Incredibly the local Council even sent a couple of their staff round to investigate, but I don't know from what department! They quizzed me about all manner of things, such as "How big is a Geega, what do they look like, how many have you, what do they eat and where do they come from?" Now, the latter question I could answer truthfully. I said "Some of them have 'Made in Korea' stamped on their bums". We all laughed, but only I knew how right that was! I thought, enough is enough and was just about to tell them, there weren't any

Geegas, they didn't exist, other than half a dozen 'Giles like' cuddly toys. At which point one of the Council men stopped me in my tracks by proudly mentioning that his wife had recently seen a programme on television about Geegas. I just hadn't the bottle to destroy his illusion. Eventually the two men left feeling rather cheated that they'd not actually seen any Geegas, but as I said to them "They will be in the undergrowth - bonking away!"

Actually my departure from Wombleton was not as sudden as it must have appeared to outsiders. It had been building up for some time and after five years there I decided definitely to move. There was no specific reason but rather an accumulation of things which collectively caused me far too much hassle. I suppose others in a similar position to myself would have been perfectly happy there, I presume the present owners are but I was not. For me it was too large a place and the work involved keeping everywhere looking immaculate was enormous and at times rather soul destroying. I suppose the soil there was adequate but one could not say it was anything special; it certainly required to be well fertilized and I was continually fighting the elements. We were at that time having a succession of scorching hot summers and a general shortage of water, consequently a hose pipe ban became the norm. Apart from that, with 'Geegas Place' being on high ground it meant the water pressure was usually non existent. To counteract that I hired tankers to bring in water, thousands of gallons at a time. They drove around drenching everywhere - that was alright but the cost of such weekly operations wasn't and I didn't dare ask from where they got their precious cargo.

From the outset I had a fieldman for the paddocks and a couple of gardeners, though none were on a full-time basis. I did quite a lot of the work myself in keeping everywhere neat and tidy, I also designed a most ingenious rake consisting of five spring rakes in a line, it was a great time saver and kept the gravel yards and drive always looking immaculate. One of my many self inflicted chores was to sweep the road, for a couple of hundred yards, either side of the main entrance. This I did every Sunday morning wet or fine; one Sunday I was sweeping away when a car stopped and the driver asked "Who lives here?"

I said "Colin Tinkler."

He replied "Oh, the gambler, they say he's an eccentric millionaire, is that correct?"

I answered "IT'S HALF CORRECT." EXACTLY!

Another reason for wishing to move was the fear of further break-ins. It was becoming a near annual occurrence, but there was never anything taken. The intruders were obviously looking for money, though I don't imagine they hung around for long once the burglar alarm sounded. The alarm was connected to the police station, which I'm sure any intruder would have assumed; it was however more of a deterrent than anything else and of little use if a light aircraft was used for a quick departure. I'm not being dramatic, in fact it would have been the logical thing to do. There was a landing strip no more than a couple of hundred yards from my main entrance, it being part of a disused airfield and frequently used by me to go racing.

Whilst at Wombleton I bought a rather expensive young greyhound from Ireland, I'm talking several thousand pounds; she was a gorgeous bitch who had just commenced racing, was well related and had speed to burn. She won a couple of races at Sheffield for me though I felt something was amiss as she was not showing her true potential. I'd bought her primarily for breeding as I wanted another interest away from what I was doing. However, this never materialised for she died from an internal complaint when I'd only owned her for a short while; it was very sad and I doubt I'll repeat a similar venture again. I had been trying to recapture some of the good times I had when associated with greyhounds all those years ago but seemingly forgot the heartaches.

It would be late into August '94 when I eventually contacted Alan Black, an Estate Agent I knew through racing, and asked him to put 'Geegas Place' on the market. The price we agreed upon was a long way short of what I originally thought I would get for the property. The actual figure was not made public as such; I certainly didn't wish to see it in print - it would have been far too painful! I lost bombs, in fact a frightening amount, but I'm a realist and taking everything into consideration I would not have given, at the time of sale, the figure I received for it. Within a couple of days of Geegas Place being advertised I received a call from the Agents saying a Mr. W. wished to view. He came, liked what he saw, and said he would purchase, there would be no haggling about the price though there was a proviso, it being that he was allowed to buy everything in the place down to the last teaspoon, all at valuation and he would stand the cost of that being done. As for the trophies and photographs, I could retain what I wanted so long as I replaced them with something similar. My first reaction was thinking him a 'nut case' but, after the valuation had been completed and learning that he'd recently sold a commercial property in Otley for over a million, I crossed my fingers. After a couple of weeks of further visits and numerous enthusiastic phone calls a date was made for signing the contract but, instead of that happening, I received a letter from Mr. W. saying unfortunately he was not now in a position to purchase Geegas Place as he was going abroad for a couple of years. I suppose I'd half expected it but what on earth possesses a person to act out such a fantasy, knowing that's all it was. In general there was not a lot of interest shown; admittedly it would require altering to meet most people's needs and the property market at that time was not exactly on fire, nevertheless, I had expected more enquiries. What there were mainly came from people with racing connections; however it was left to a couple from the Isle of Man to sign the contract of sale and their interest in racing was only minimal. I moved out in the December and was I pleased to go? Yes, most definitely! I sold a lot of the things I had and put the rest into storage; I felt a sense of freedom and it was time to take stock.

I'd reached 68, was not committed to anyone, and was in jolly good health apart from the troubles caused by too many accidents. A knee joint and my right hand were in rather a mess and had been so for some time. However the turbulent sensations I'd endured for half a century had become far less frequent and easier to cope with. Financially I was sound though matters had suffered a few hiccups of late. Wombleton had been a ludicrous fiasco and my accountants at that time were not handling my affairs with any efficiency. There was the incident of them losing an invoice, which Full Circle had paid, to an advertising agent who had folded and gone abroad; rather than cause any misgivings I repaid from my own monies the near £50,000 involved. I'm not a person that harbours regrets but no way should I have been so stupid as it was a hell of a lot of money and not necessary. I also had trouble with late and incorrect Company House and VAT Returns, which at the time cost me several thousand pounds; I did however manage to recover these lesser amounts from the accountant's insurers. My accountants had also miscalculated my tax position over a number of years; this I had to rectify plus the fines incurred and we are not talking Mickey Mouse money here.I only fully discovered the extent of the deplorable situation when one of the partners had a nervous breakdown and the other was sent to prison for embezzling clients' money, though none of mine.

There was, however, a brighter side to the coin - I had money in the bank even before picking up the cheque for the sale of 'Geegas Place'. Admittedly Full Circle was no longer a force, though it had never really been an earner for me, but the Information Line was an entirely different scenario. I'd also won a fantastic amount punting whilst living at Wombleton, with over £150,000 in one year alone, the bulk of that amount being on Norton Coin in the Gold Cup and Mr. Frisk in the Grand National. I'd also put a large amount of money into a pension fund which was about to mature. It's relevant really but I certainly wasn't endowed with wealth, though had I been more astute matters would have been different; on the other hand, neither was I exactly on the rocks.

Without a doubt the most amusing thing that occurred whilst living at Wombleton was when I'd just left 'Geegas Place' to go to Thirsk Races. As I shut the iron gates a car went past which was going in the same direction I was to travel. The driver immediately slowed down and drove in the middle of the road, which prevented me from overtaking. The three scruffy urchins on the back seat started pulling faces and sticking their tongues out at me, through the rear window. I blew the horn gently, indicating that I wished to pass. On hearing the sound the 'fright' in the front passenger seat looked round angrily. At the same time the driver, peering through his mirror, put a finger to his stupid little head, and waggled it about, indicating to me that he thought I was crackers. Eventually I did manage to overtake by going on the grass verge. I then pulled up across the road forcing the other car to stop. The driver was a very small man or was sitting very low in the seat, but no matter. I smiled as I walked over and he seemed relieved at my friendliness. He wound down the window and the following conversation took place:-

Me "Tell me is this your car?"

Driver "Yes."

Me "Are these your three children and is this your wife?"

Driver "Yes, why?"

Me "Well you are driving this bloody old heap, you have three screaming brats and a f*****g ugly wife and you think I'm crackers!"

With that I turned and did my impression of a John Wayne walk, back to my new Mercedes SL 500 and away I roared.....with laughter!

After leaving Geegas Place I went to live at the prestigious and very comfortable Black Swan in Helmsley, which was only three or four miles from Wombleton. The Black Swan is a gorgeous hotel and Helmsley a small picturesque market town; both steeped in history. I thoroughly enjoyed my stay, which was not only fascinating but most of the time hilariously funny; unfortunately the majority of the stories cannot be told as it would cause too much embarrassment for those involved. The majority of the guests would only stay a few days and usually at the weekends; I would try to analyse them and imagine what their home lives were like. I met a very amusing couple from Ireland, they were over for the York Races and the Black Swan had been recommended to them; the hotel was always chock-a-block when there was York Races, so I suppose they were fortunate to get a room without booking. On their last evening there I invited them, along with another couple of guests, to my table for dinner. They really were hilarious and uncannily similar to Mrs. Bouquet nee Bucket's sister and brother-in-law; though, I hasten to add, far better attired than their 'cousins' of television fame. During the meal 'Paddy' was saying his advice to a young man wishing to marry was "Choose a wife that can cook but make sure she's ugly then no one will run off with her!" He didn't want a dessert and declined a brandy with his coffee, but his wife, who was wriggling about on her chair, announced, in a little girly voice "I'd like some passion fruit". Paddy took one long look at her then, turning to me, said, in a delightful Irish brogue "On second thoughts I tink I'll have dat brandy after all, in fact you'd better make it a double!". As you can imagine we all had a most enjoyable evening.

However most guests were a complete bore; it's amazing how many, after learning that I was connected with racing, would insist on telling me about the one and only bet they'd ever had. It was nearly always because they had drawn the horse in the Grand National office sweep. None could remember the horse's name but most could recall the jockey being Lester Piggott! Coincidentally, each had invested £5 each way at 90/1 or some such unfamiliar price and in every instance the horse had won, netting, so I was told, the jubilant story teller a cool £100. Who was I to point out that the betting shop cashier had been a little dishonest when settling! There would also be the snobs, usually the wrong side of middle age and dressed in tweed skirts or cavalry twill trousers. They would say to me in a rather haughty manner "We come here every year for a few days, it's so relaxing, is this your first stay?" I'd tell them "It is, but as I rather like the place I've decided to live here!" Actually, I find snobs amusing, with their many forms of idiosyncrasies, however there is nothing funny about racism, it's particularly vile but unfortunately they usually go hand in hand. Having said that, I'm not one of those who consider all are equal, of course, they are not - just as all racehorses are not on a par with each other. To be fair, people should not be judged by their colour or heritage but solely on what they are, what they do and what they think.

From the outset I had my own direct phone line installed, which meant as calls didn't have to go through the hotel switchboard I always had a free line. This was important because at that time Helmsley was in a poor reception area for portable phones. After a short while I changed rooms to a really charming one at the front of the hotel - overlooking the Market Square. As I was a long term guest, in fact the only one they had, I was allowed to do some refurbishing and put down new carpeting. I also brought in some of my furniture and paintings, all very civilised. Talking about furniture; all the tables in the dining room were far too high. Many a little old lady had great difficulty manoeuvering a spoon full of soup from the plate to her mouth, as her face would be lower than the table top! Some joinery was necessary; I only ever used two of the tables and rather discreetly had a few inches cut off the legs of both!

Still on the subject of furniture; when Prince Charles stayed at the Black Swan for a few days, I understand a consignment of antiques were brought in to enhance his rooms. They had been borrowed from some high class dealers in Harrogate but unfortunately were never returned. On the day the furniture was due to go back a bogus van arrived a couple of hours before the legitimate one was due! Need I proceed? I thought not, but what a crafty little earner. On another occasion the elegant grandfather clock which stood in a corner of the dining room went walkies but was found in the nearby churchyard. It had obviously been left there to be picked up later. There was another sort of robbery, whilst I was at the Black Swan, it occurred at a Christmas Eve gathering for those staying at the hotel. Black ties were the order of the evening and after dinner the fun began; well, the game of horse racing began; to tell you the truth most of the guests were so old they must have forgotten what fun was! Back to the game, it consisted of five horses being moved across a table to a winning post all on the throw of a dice. The hotel acted as bookmakers with a maximum bet allowed being £10 a horse. They went 4/1 the field with 7/1 bar one - no wonder they lost £350 on the night. How much did I win? Well let's put it this way, I managed to pinch a few quid! But I did warn them.

I got on very well with most of the staff, in fact all but two, one of those being the Manager; there was definitely a clash of personalities. On our very first meeting he said "They tell me you will liven up the place, I hope not too much." I thought, not a good start; he seemed to be under enormous pressure and matters of little consequence became large issues. However, I believe his main bone of contention was that I was a fixture; I'm sure he preferred guests that came and went and wrote in the visitors book "Had a nice quiet stay, everything perfect." The other member of the staff I chilled against was a waiter. But this was an entirely different scenario to that of the Manager. I found him the most unpleasant and obnoxious of people, every remark he made was abrasive, he had a face I wanted to punch and I'm surprised I never did. I could fill a book with reasons for disliking him and I was not alone by any means. I would not allow him to serve me and cut him out of the £100 monthly draw I had for the staff; the draw was my way of giving a gratuity to them. I could never understand why the Manager was not more aware to what was afoot; he was alert enough to object to most of the girls that worked there calling me Colin and of some of them using the sun bed I'd installed. He spoke to me about this saying "Such familiarity is not good for the image of the hotel." I suppose he had a point, though nothing changed.

Virtually the only people frequenting the bar were those staying at the hotel. Amazingly very few outsiders came in and the fact that one had to pass through the reception area could have been one reason. Another, and the more likely, was the price of the drinks! One thing is certain it wasn't the bar girl. Tracy was outrageously funny and definitely a 'one off'; if I were to liken her to a show biz personality it would be Zoe Ball. I hadn't been there long when she asked "Col, which would you rather have, a really good shag, I mean a really good f*****g shag, or just make gentle love?" I presumed she was talking metaphorically; I'm sure she was talking metaphorically and, if not, well it's too late now! I replied to her fiery question by saying "Tracey, at my age I haven't got an option."

Judi, who was once my chauffeuse, would come over most weeks and stay a couple of days and the two girls became friends. One Saturday the weather was so appalling I didn't go racing but watched it on the television in my room. The two girls came up after doing some shopping so I rang reception for some coffee and sandwiches. Soon there was a knock on my bedroom door; on impulse I told Judi and Tracy to jump into the bed and pull the sheets up so only their beaming faces showed. I slipped out of my slacks and into a dressing gown, all in ten seconds flat. I opened the door and in walked two young porters with our refreshments. On seeing me dressed as I was and then the girls in bed, who, of course, they recognised, was just too much. They put the trays down on the table, stood for a moment or two, then made a bolt for the door; God knows what they told people. Actually it was a hell of a lot funnier than I've been able to describe. You might wonder what has become of Tracy, well, she ran off with Keith, the Restaurant Manager. We still keep in touch, no, not literally!

There was one weekend I remember rather well, the hotel was exceptionally full and in the early hours of the Sunday morning the smoke alarm sounded. Suddenly it was panic stations with guests running up and down the corridors; no, they weren't all evacuating the hotel, most were merely returning to their own rooms, where they should have been in the first place. How do I know all this? Well, I was caught up in the stampede! Some guests did leave the hotel and stand in the car park, but most stood outside their bedroom doors rubbing their eyes innocently, as if they had just been awakened. As the firemen made a room to room inspection they discovered smoke in a bedroom that was supposed not to be occupied. It had got nothing to do with me but earlier on in the evening I happened to see a girl I knew go in there. Next day I asked "Where did you hide when the firemen came into the room, under the bed?" She replied "No, Col, I went in the wardrobe but I put my fag out first."

Still on the same humorous theme - I awoke one night to the sound of bang, bang, bang, the noise was coming from the next bedroom to mine. It was obviously the bed, which was also creaking in rhythmic harmony. The banging and the creaking went on for ages and ages and then sudden silence. When the couple did eventually emerge from their room the following morning I had a quizzical look and soon realised why the bonking had taken so long! Exactly!

One evening I was leaving the hotel, to go to a jockey's dance at York, when a Porche pulled up. The girl in the passenger seat had difficulty getting out of the car; apart from the seat being low to the ground the door kept shutting. I couldn't just walk past so stopped to hold the door open. On seeing this, and dressed as I was in a tuxedo, her companion mistook me for a member of the hotel staff. He asked me "Where shall I put my car?" and also mentioned they had no luggage as they were not staying but just having dinner. Realising what he thought I got straight into the part; I indicated where he should park, then guided him into the spot and threw in a couple of 'Sirs' for good measure; he then handed me a tenner. I don't know whether he was naturally generous or was just trying to impress the girl; he certainly impressed me!

Another time when I pretended to be a member of the staff was even more humorous, in fact bordering on the ridiculous. I will start from the beginning - I'd had a bath and was drying when I noticed a tray with the usual tea things on, so I decided to put them out into the corridor. To do this I only needed to stretch my arms, but somehow the door slammed shut pushing me out. There was I, completely naked and not being able to get back into my room. It was the perfect comedy situation that Mr. Bean would have revelled in. With the tray coming to my rescue I ran down the corridor looking for help and, by chance, a maid was turning back the bed cover in one of the rooms. I dashed in and before I could grab a towel or explain to her what had happened a girl in her early forties came into the room. On seeing me and believing she must have mistaken the number on the door, commenced to apologise. My sense of humour suddenly took control; I interrupted saying "Yes, this is your room and I'm room service". The situation was ludicrous and both girls, the one whose room I was in and the maid, went into hysterics. What would I have thought if I'd returned to my bedroom to discover a naked girl standing there with only a tray as cover. Well, to start with, I'd assume it was either the twenty fifth of December or it was my birthday! The phone then rang so I took the opportunity to borrow a towel and make a quick exit; the maid had the good sense to follow and unlocked my bedroom door; she then asked "Is there anything else I can do for you?" and I stupidly said "No".

Part of the old section of the Black Swan was once a convent and one of the bedrooms overlooking the church yard was reputed to be haunted with the sound of a child crying. Apparently, at the beginning of the last century some builders who were doing repair work discovered the skeleton of a baby. It's only speculation but the story has it that a nun had a child that died and to conceal this she buried the baby in the wall of the bedroom; it was there where the remains were found. I was curious, not about the ghost, to me they are non starters and a lot of Mumbo Jumbo, but I wanted to see inside the room. Actually it was pleasant enough in itself but, of course, the unnatural association and the proximity of the church yard weren't exactly a plus. I didn't get any eerie vibes, though in no circumstances would I have dared sleep in the room. One of the porters told me, when on night duty, it was his job to tour all the corridors, but the narrow one leading to the room in question was one he never went down, the icy atmosphere terrified him. One night shortly after the conversation with the porter I was asleep when a gale blew up; I woke and thought I'd sleep better if I closed the half open window. I was just about to do that when I distinctly heard a baby crying, it was frightening, not a normal cry. I shut the window very quickly; the hairs on the back of my neck stood on end and a shiver went down mu spine. The following morning the wind had dropped and the sun was shining, which seemed to give the happening of the night before an entirely different concept. I was rather late returning to my room after breakfast, racing was at nearby Thirsk so I was in no particular hurry. As I put the key in the door I noticed a couple with a baby were about to go in the next room. Ah, I thought, all is explained, and the weirdness of the crying sound must have been caused by the wind. We introduced ourselves, then the girl said "I hope little Harry doesn't keep you awake tonight, he's teething". I assured her he wouldn't and mentioned that I'd heard him the night before and it hadn't disturbed me; I thought, that's one hell of a lie I've just told, but no matter. The girl answered my remarks with "You couldn't have heard Harry, we have just arrived this morning". At that moment, for some unaccountable reason, the church bell gave three slow chimes - I literally froze.

Shortly after that I had a runner down south and stayed over at an hotel I'd not used before. I was given the only available room in the place, it was drab, the furniture heavy and the four poster bed most uninviting. It might have been the lighting, or rather the lack of it, but the walls seemed to close in on me; I thought opening the window would help, but it didn't, there was such an icy chill in the air. I was tired and hoping for a good night's sleep, but in the early hours I awoke in utter fear. I had not been dreaming and didn't know what the problem was until I heard drip, drip, drip. I quickly put the light on and went to the bathroom but there was nothing wrong there. The sound was not loud yet seemed to engulf the whole room. I rang for the porter but there was no answer; I dressed, then went to look for him with the same negative result. No way was I going back to that room, so went to the car to sleep. The following morning I asked questions and was told, rather reluctantly, that in the early twenties, just after the First World War, a girl who worked at the hotel was murdered. Apparently she was stabbed to death in the room above the one I'd been in! To some, but not me, that would have explained the ghostly trip, trip, trip that had caused so much fear. Mysterious, yes, but as with the previous story, I'm sure there were simple explanations far removed from the supernatural; anyhow it's more rational to think so.

After ten months my stay at The Black Swan came to a close; the manager called me over and tackled me about a joke a guest of mine had told in the almost empty bar the previous evening. My response to the manager's reprimand was a curt "This is not a prep school and you are not my headmaster - I'll be away by the end of the week." I had objected to his attitude and not the fact that he'd complained. He did try to persuade me to stay on and to be perfectly honest I should have done, but I didn't, it's as simple as that.

Whilst I was at The Black Swan everyone there thought I had retired; they would see me come down for a late breakfast, then mooch about the place before going off to the races. I would next be seen in the evening having dinner and was always casually dressed. I suppose life for me did appear to be somewhat leisurely though, in truth, it was nothing of the sort. I would go for the morning papers at six o'clock and never go to bed until the early hours and what I did most of the time between was anything but relaxing; running a successful racing line is a very precise business.

I was once at the Newmarket autumn sales when the talk turned to winter vacations; I happened to mention that I'd not had a break for more than fifteen years. A girl in her early twenties, who was standing close by, heard what I said, came over and suggested I take her on holiday to somewhere nice and sunny. I admired her cheek and said I would if the weather became severe enough to stop racing. We didn't exchange telephone numbers but she did say she knew I was Colin Tinkler.

I gave the matter no further thought, not even a couple of months later, when arctic conditions descended upon us. However, Michelle didn't have the same lapse of memory; she rang Col's number, thinking it was mine and it so happened Carol answered the call. Michelle told her that Col had promised to take her on holiday if bad weather came; I won't elaborate on Carol's immediate reactions but it was soon sorted out. Michelle then gave me a call and by the following evening we were installed in the airport hotel in Newcastle ready for a flight to Tenerife the following morning. I'd gone up to Newcastle by car and she by rail, both arriving simultaneously and in time for dinner; but all Michelle ate was beetroot, yes, beetroot. Apparently she was on a diet of virtually nothing else. I soon realised it was not going to be much of a holiday, in fact more of a nightmare.

Denys Smith and his wife were on the plane and he thought I was being very discreet by sitting four rows apart from 'that smashing blonde', as he called her. The truth was, we both preferred to sit next to a window than to one another. Michelle didn't like the crowds at the airport when we landed, nor the journey to a really nice hotel in the north of the island and volcanoes were definitely not on her shopping list. She was also allergic to the flowers in the hotel foyer and waited until we were in the lift before telling me she suffered from claustrophobia and had a fear of heights. I thought, what the hell am I doing here so pressed the stop button, then the one sending us back to the ground floor. I told Michelle she didn't like a bloody thing so I was going home. Unfortunately I found it impossible to get a flight back to England. I tried, but to no avail. Of course, if I had done so I wouldn't have left Michelle stranded. We were in Tenerife for only a week, though it seemed an eternity and didn't have one single meal together; I didn't want to watch someone devouring plate after plate of that horrible vegetable. We did however have the occasional coffee beside the pool and it was there that I learnt she was having a rather steamy affair with one of the Newmarket trainers, though I'm not divulging which!

I met a couple from Glasgow; he was in the rag trade, but apart from them the others I came into contact with were boring to the extreme. Eventually it was time to return home and the leather holdall Michelle asked me to carry, which I had bought for her, was bulging at the seams, I didn't ask what was in it, I assumed souvenirs. On arriving back at Newcastle I got her a taxi for the two hundred and fifty mile journey to Newmarket; now that was money very well spent! I haven't been on holiday since and don't ever intend to do so again if it has a blind date tag. I've seen Michelle since, again at Newmarket, she was with some friends and called out "Hello Colin,

I've just been saying what a good time we had in Tenerife". For once I was speechless!

My next port of call after The Black Swan was The Fox and Hounds Country Hotel in Sinnington, a quiet village not that far from Helmsley. The style Country Hotel, was given to enhance the place by the owners at the time of my stay. I must stress, there is now an entirely different management and I understand they have made many sweeping changes. With that said I will continue; from the day I arrived to the day I left it was like staying at 'Faulty Towers'. The similarity was unbelievable, right down to the personnel; they not only looked like those in television's comedy classic, they behaved as they did. The more I saw the tall lanky manager and his wife the more they resembled Basil Faulty and Sybil. The foreign waiter was indistinguishable from Manuel, as was the waitress from her counterpart. It didn't stop there and I was convinced the two chefs were one and the same! There was however an additional member of staff at The Fox and Hounds, it was that of the restaurant manager, a position which seemed totally unnecessary, for most of the time, other than at the weekends, I was the only one eating in the dining room.

I'd been there a couple of days when I saw a mouse doing a grand tour of the skirting boards of my room. I dived down to the reception to report the intruder and with a request to change rooms. 'Basil Faulty', in his excitable voice asked "What colour is it?" As if it mattered a damn what the colour was. Basil then grabbed a broom, presumably as a weapon, ran up the stairs, then down again, to enquire as to the little bastard's size. I said "Well let's put it this way, I know it's not big enough to attack you but it didn't stand still long enough to be measured!" I did change rooms only to get one with an even harder mattress!

They didn't serve afternoon tea, lunch finished at two o'clock and dinner began at seven, with nothing in between. On the particular Sunday I'm going to mention, a group of guests were staying the weekend for a walking break. They had been hiking across the moors and arrived back at the hotel in the late afternoon. As often happened, I was mistaken for management and was asked "Will there be any chance of some tea and toast". I explained my position but said I would ask the owner for them as I could see he was just about to come through the glass door. On hearing my suggestion that he should be obliging, the 'Faulty Towers' act really came into play - striding up and down and waving his arms about he ranted "I'm sorry Mr. T., I didn't know it was your hotel, how silly of me, but I thought I was the owner and made the rules but apparently not." He then announced "Afternoon tea will be served in the lounge, for all those wishing to partake, in precisely ten minutes." He then went into the kitchen and disappeared out of the back door; we never did get the tea!

Some time after that incident 'Basil' told me his wife was hopeless at organising. He continued "There are seven days in a week and she takes her day off at the same time as the restaurant manager; can you believe it?" Well, yes, I could actually!

'Manuel' was also extremely amusing and would purposely imitate the television character; there was the time he put a currant into my soup with the pretence that it was a dead fly "Poor little fly, you have drowned, I get a matchbox and bury you in the garden". There was further dialogue - all so funny! But in general, the humour was not strong enough to override the discomfort of the place. I would make a weekly tour of the villages around Malton looking for my next home and eventually found it in Huttons Ambo, a quiet hamlet just three miles west of the market town. I'd been at The Fox and Hounds about three months and it took a similar length of time to renovate the new 'Geegas Place'. Shortly after I left the hotel, early in '96, there was a complete break up there, everyone going their separate ways. This was something I could have forecast; one hadn't to be that bright to realise it couldn't have lasted.

The cottage I bought had marvellous views and directly overlooked fields; that was until I planted well grown Lelandii which I'd obtained from Italy. For me it was more important to have privacy than anything else. The place had already been renovated to a certain extent but I'd never seen anything more hideous or workmanship so atrocious. Actually that was of little concern because I gutted the building to such an extent there was virtually nothing left other than the outside walls. It was 'Wombleton' all over again, though because of its size I was able to be even more extravagant. I spent more time on the site than at Wombleton, consequently fewer mistakes were made. Hundreds of tons of earth were removed in order to landscape the garden and much of the stone walling I did myself. Similar iron gates to those at the former 'Geegas Place' were fitted and as I wanted the garden to be instant, hence the mature Lelandii and similarly everything else that was planted; of course, I had to have a pond and went back to Wombleton for a dozen large Koi. No one could fail to recognise the Geega 'stamp' inside or out. I liken doing a renovation to that of painting a picture and when all was completed I knew I'd be happy here and that's how it's been.

My days commence early with the papers being delivered by taxi; incidentally in the five years I've been living at Huttons Ambo that service has cost me a staggering £11,000! The next caller is either the postman or one of the post girls, all have emerged from racing, and what a nice group of people they are. I recently said to one of the girls "A witch is going to turn me into a frog if I accumulate fifty points and I've already got ten." She asked "What would you have to do Colin to get a further forty points?" I told her "Make love to a post girl." After a lengthy pause she curiously asked "What did you do to get the original ten points?" I said "Thinking about making love to a post girl!" No wonder I have a notice outside the gate saying 'Beware of the Geega'. My neighbour recently bought a metal post box for her gate; I decided to do likewise though I fixed mine to the wall of the balcony. On seeing it one of the girls wanted to know "How am I going to get up there?" I told her "Through my bedroom!" All such delightful humour we cried with laughter.

I recently underwent laser treatment for one of my eyes and booked in at the nursing home in London. After some time a pretty young nurse approached me saying, in a Far Eastern accent "I have been asked to take your blood pressure Mr. Tinkler." I told her "Everyone calls me Colin". She answered "OK, I do that also from now on Mr. Colin"! The count showed a high reading, in fact high enough for a doctor to be called. He asked "Are you at all disturbed about the surgery you are about to have?" I told him "Not in the least". After further questions he suggested I relax on the bed and they would take another count in ten minutes. The pretty little nurse then decided in the meantime she would measure me for surgical stockings. Naturally I didn't enlighten her to the fact that I was only there for laser treatment to an eye and wouldn't be requiring the leg wear; though I did ponder on what the hell it was going to do to my blood pressure! Eventually it was time to again take a count - pump, pump, pump - as I expected the reading hit the ceiling causing little 'Miss Oriental' to again seek help. Were I writing a stage play I would scribble - enter the male nurse. It was pump, pump, pump once more, then gesturing with his hands, and in a somewhat feminine voice, he said "You won't believe this Mr. Tinkler but you are as normal as me. These young girls can't do anything right." I thought, Oh yes they can!

I had a girl staying over recently, she remarked "I wish I was twenty one again". I said "I wish I was seventy one again!" During her stay she came down for breakfast wearing only a skimpy nightie and asked "Does it tease you, me walking about the place in just my nightie?" I told her "It would tease me a hell of a lot more if you took it off." I've known her for quite some time and once when staying at Wombleton she remarked "Col, I really like your company". I asked her "Which one, Full Circle or Racing Communications PLC?" Exactly!

Chapter twenty two

To close

Compared with former years, my present lifestyle here at Huttons Ambo is less hectic by comparison; yet I'm busy enough and writing my autobiography has taken longer than anticipated. This has resulted in being beaten to the punch by Graham Bradley and others in racing, with their life stories. Mentioning 'Brad' reminds me of something very amusing that occurred when the two Grahams, McCourt and he, were riding. I had a runner at Kelso and agreed to pick them up at Scotch Corner. McCourt took over the driving and 'Brad' got into the back but he was soon leaning forward; he kept looking at his watch and urging our 'chauffeur' to get a move on. He was riding in one of the earlier races and feared he would not get to Kelso in time. McCourt told him it was odds on that he would make it, but Brad was not convinced and gave a pretty vigorous "Go on, click click." I then entered into the conversation; with tongue in cheek I said "Brad, it's a long time since you said that to an odds on shot!" Incidentally, he was a brilliant rider, is now a successful bloodstock agent and a very nice person to boot.

As my seventy fifth birthday approaches, my autobiography comes to a close and as you will have gathered by reading through the pages, I've had a marvellous life. It's been exciting and, without a doubt, extremely happy. I've faced some tragedies, but even those have been limited and who hasn't at my age. Luck and good fortune have played their part but I'm sure, no matter which direction I'd taken at the many crossroads I've encountered, it would have been the same outcome. Basically, life is what one makes of it; admittedly, there are exceptions, some people are dealt appalling cards, just too dreadful to comprehend, but that's a different scenario. Ever since I was a child I have been an individualist, never going along with the flow; I've also been very much influenced by my feelings rather than by rational thinking. Being emotional can be a drawback, though I wouldn't have had it any other way. I don't know how people perceive me but I'm certainly not conceited, I've got nothing to be conceited about, but I always have confidence in whatever I tackle. I never relax and have found it easy to make money, but even easier to get rid of it. I still run my very successful racing information service but will come up with a further idea before long; there are always opportunities for a well thought out new project.

I was born with no great attributes, other than I was going to have the right attitude in life; which has been sufficient to carry me through. There are, however, many who aren't even blessed with that credential and go through life with a permanent chip on their shoulders. On the other hand there are some truly brilliant people about, unbelievably so; one feels so insignificant by comparison which, in point of fact, most of us are. You might ask, have I many regrets? Well, not that I harbour but, of course, I've made many mistakes most of which could have been avoided. Having said that, it would have been so easy to have done very little but then life would have been so boring and my life has been anything but that. I would like to have achieved more but I haven't always taken full advantage of some of the opportunities I've created. I suppose I should have taken more risks, though to be perfectly frank I'm not a gambler. As you will have gathered, I've been known to have some pretty hefty bets, though not large enough to cause concern had they lost or should I say "When they lost"! I suppose it's relative really, but I have never considered myself a big punter, not in any stretch of the imagination; though I don't imagine Alec Russell, the racing photographer, would agree. We were talking recently, when he reminded me of the time I came out of a bank, in Malton, as he was going in. He noticed I was clutching several plastic wrappers containing £10,000 when he asked "Are you going to buy a horse?" and I replied "No, this is my amunition, I'm going to back one!" Strangely, I can't remember whether it won or lost.

The late Alex Bird once said to me after his retirement "I ceased punting because I didn't need the money and didn't want to loose what I'd won; besides, there are other things in life than racing". My sentiments entirely, though racing has been my life and how the business, for that's what racing has become, has changed over the years; it no longer possesses the carefree, friendly atmosphere of old. I have my views on the subject but don't wish to enter into controversy. I'm interested in most things, with all manner of sport being high on the list. I do, however, stay well clear of religion because I only believe in what I know to be true. Party Politics is another none starter for me, I find them a complete bore; though they do take on an entirely different dimension when Mary Nightingale, television's delightful news reader, is reporting!

I love beauty and quality, no matter in what capacity; they come in so many forms and without them life would be pointless. I'm so enthusiastic about anything nice, it's not a question of taste or opinion, something is either nice or it's not, it's as simple as that. Unfortunately we don't live in Utopia, there is also much ugliness in the world, with crime, disease, cruelty and squalor being responsible for most of the ugliness.

I believe a person's character can often be judged by the music they favour; for me, some of the tunes of the late fifties to the late seventies had something special about them. I remember Marie and I going to see and hear James Last, during that time, he had the audience dancing in the aisles - fantastic stuff. Stephane Grappelli always intrigued me - he was brilliant on the violin. The same adjective can be used to describe so many jazz pianists I've heard. I must mention Abba, Tina Turner, Barry White and the music of Bacharach, individually so different, yet all are more than just a pleasure to listen to, especially Bacharach with the lovely 'Raindrops are Falling'. The most 'catchy' little number in my book is 'In The Summertime' and the most moving melody - Barbara Streisand and Celine Dion singing 'Tell Him'. But really there is so much fantastic music to appreciate. I once heard a busker in Oxford Street playing a tin whistle, he conjured up a magical sound, it was fabulous, and that's how I would describe my life, it's been fabulous, I've had such a marvellous time.

Sadly, all good things come to an end, nothing lasts forever. One day there will be no more tomorrows for me, no more gorgeous views to see, no more sunshine, cool breezes, anticipations, laughter, no more music, no more happiness, and no more love, absolutely and totally nothing. Then my ashes will be scattered to the winds. I really don't want to think about that, besides I expect to be around for a long time yet. In fact I am very excited about the future, I feel I have much to look forward to, especially within the Tinkler clan - Exactly.

CONCLUSION

I thank you for taking the time and for having the patience to read what I have written, I hope you have found it of interest and amusing.

Appendix I

The Full Circle Winners

Venue	Horse	Jockey	S.P.
'A' - 5 winners			
Catterick	Octolan	T. Ives	6/4
Ayr	Rainbow Vision	T. Williams	7/2
Ayr	Mening	N. Tinkler	3/1
Kelso	Meningi	N. Tinkler	7/1
Catterick	Meningi	N. Tinkler	6/1
'B' - 15 winners			
Thirsk	Wow Wow Wow	T. Ives	15/8 Fav
Ayr	Wow Wow Wow	D. Nicholls	3/1
Edinburgh	Wow Wow Wow	K. Spink	6/1
Catterick	Caro's Gift	N. Tinkler	Ev Fav
Catterick	Romiosini	N. Tinkler	6/1
Haydock	Caro's Gift	K. Tinkler	9/1
Ayr	Wessex	K. Tinkler	6/1
Thirsk	Wow Wow Wow	K. Tinkler	10/3 Fav
Thirsk	Meningi	J. H. Brown	11/2 Jt Fav
Market Rasen	Miss Maina	N. Tinkler	5/2
Beverley	Meningi	K. Tinkler	5/1
2Southwell	Miss Maina	N. Tinkler	5/6 Fav
Hamilton	Wessex	K. Tinkler	7/4 Fav
Ripon	Romiosini	K. Tinkler	2/1 Fav
York	Romiosini	K. Tinkler	8/1

VENUE	HORSE	JOCKEY	S.P.
'C' - 25 WINNERS			
Leicester	Princess Singh	K. Tinkler	Ev Fav
Redcar	Girdle Ness	K. Tinkler	11/10 Fav
Ayr	Wessex	K. Tinkler	14/1
Ayr	Authentic	K. Tinkler	5/2
Catterick	Wessex	N. Tinkler	8/11 Fav
Ayr	Authentic	K. Tinkler	12/1
Nottingham	Doon Venture	M. Dwyer	4/11 Fav
3Ayr	Lady la Paz	P. Tuck	2/1 Jt Fav
Cheltenham	The Ellier	G. Armytage	16/1
Hamilton	Lady la Paz	K. Tinkler	9/2
Hamilton	Lake Omega	K. Tinkler	7/2
Nottingham	Hyokin	K. Tinkler	2/1 Jt Fav
Hamilton	Tiklas	K. Tinkler	5/2
Newcastle	Fiesta Moon	G. Duffield	5/2
Ayr	Lady la Paz	K. Tinkler	8/1
Thirsk	Domino Rose	G. Armytage	11/8
Ripon	Lake Omega	K. Tinkler	14/1
Nottingham	Tiklas	K. Tinkler	5/4 Fav
Hamilton	Tiklas	K. Tinkler	2/5 Fav
Nottingham	Fiesta Moon	M. Birch	10/1
Hamilton	Mayor	K. Tinkler	8/1
Wolverhampton	Fiesta Moon	G. Carter	4/1
Ayr	Tiklas	K. Tinkler	4/5 Fav
Doncaster	Lady la Paz	K. Tinkler	9/1
Doncaster	Mayor	K. Tinkler	14/1
'D' - 38 WINNERS			
Doncaster	Lady la Paz	K. Tinkler	4/1 Jt Fav
Newcastle	Foot Patrol	C. Grant	14/1
Wetherby	Foot Patrol	C. Grant	1/3 Fav
Nottingham	Lotus Island	G. McCourt	7/2
Newcastle	Foot Patrol	N. Tinkler	6/5 Fav
Newcastle	Foot Patrol	G. McCourt	7/2 Fav

Appendix I - Full Circle Winners

VENUE	HORSE	JOCKEY	S.P.
Catterick	Gold Sceptre	N. Tinkler	5/4 Fav
Hamilton	Gold Sceptre	K. Tinkler	3/1
Haydock	Dale Park	K. Tinkler	11/1
Stratford	Arum Lily	G. McCourt	8/11 Fav
Beverley	Foot Patrol	J. Bowker	11/1
Southwell	Arum Lily	G. McCourt	10/11 Fav
Market Rasen	Gold Sceptre	G. McCourt	4/5 Fav
Southwell	Design Wise	G. McCourt	4/5 Fav
Thirsk	Darkorjon	A. Farrell	20/1
Worcester	Design Wise	G. McCourt	2/5 Fav
Worcester	Mubdi	G. McCourt	3/1
Stratford	Gold Sceptre	G. McCourt	4/9 Fav
Southwell	Mubdi	G. McCourt	1/3 Fav
Market Rasen	Mubdi	G. McCourt	30/100 Fav
Carlisle	Love to Dance	J. Bowker	6/5 Fav
Kempton	Foot Patrol	N. Tinkler	9/4 Fav
Newcastle	Street Party	K. Tinkler	7/1
Chepstow	Love to Dance	J. Bowker	8/11 Fav
Nottingham	Mayor	K. Tinkler	5/4
Thirsk	Arum Lily	K. Tinkler	13/2
Catterick	Desert Emperor	N. Tinkler	4/9 Fav
Ripon	Mubdi	K. Tinkler	6/1
Southwell	Good Point	G. McCourt	4/7 Fav
Ayr	Mubdi	K. Tinkler	4/1
Perth	Good Point	G. McCourt	4/7 Fav
Worcester	Arum Lily	G. McCourt	7/4 Fav
Southwell	Lotus Island	G. McCourt	8/13 Fav
Worcester	Desert Emperor	G. McCourt	9/4
Ayr	Dale Park	K. Tinkler	9/1
Edinburgh	Mubdi	K. Tinkler	9/2
Catterick	Good Point	M. Dwye	Ev fav
Uttoxeter	Lotus Island	G. McCourt	6/4 Fav

VENUE	HORSE	JOCKEY	S.P.
'E' - 50 WINNERS			
Market Rasen	Good Point	M. Dwyer	Ev Fav
Hexham	Arum Lily	G. McCourt	1/3 Fav
Sedgefield	Arum Lily	G. McCourt	4/9 Fav
Nottingham	Lotus Island	G. McCourt	4/6 Fav
Nottingham	Lotus Island	G. McCourt	4/7 Fav
Nottingham	Flyaway	G. McCourt	12/1
Nottingham	Arum Lily	G. McCourt	3/1
Edinburgh	Flyaway	G. McCourt	Ev Fav
Wetherby	Leon	N. Tinkler	10/1
Newcastle	Wessex	G. McCourt	7/2
Ayr	Lotus Island	D. Sullivan	3/1 Jt Fav
Catterick	Al Mulhalhal	L. Wyer	8/1
Edinburgh	Mubdi	G. McCourt	9/2
Fairyhouse	Monanore	G. McCourt	8/1
Catterick	Lotus Island	N. Tinkler	8/13 Fav
Edinburgh	Al Mulhalhal	G. McCourt	85/40 Fav
Nottingham	Lotus Island	G. McCourt	11/2
Edinburgh	Al Mulhalhal	G. McCourt	7/4 Fav
Catterick	Spate	G. McCourt	1/4 Fav
Market Rasen	Arum Lily	G. McCourt	1/2 Fav
Southwell	Spate	G. McCourt	4/9 Fav
Hexham	Arum Lily	G. McCourt	1/7 Fav
Worcester	Spate	R. Dunwoody	1/2 Fav
Huntingdon	Hanseatic	P. Scudamore	2/1 Fav
Cartmel	Hanseatic	G. McCourt	11/10 Fav
Cartmel	Hanseatic	G. McCourt	4/6 Fav
Hereford	Spate	R. Dunwoody	30/100 Fav
Stratford	Rokala	G. McCourt	11/10 Fav
Market Rasen	Hanseatic	G. McCourt	5/4
Doncaster	Fisherman's Croft	K. Tinkler	10/1
Ayr	By Choice	K. Tinkler	11/2
Southwell	Koo	G. McCourt	20/1
Worcester	Rokala	G. McCourt	5/4 Fav

Appendix I - Full Circle Winners

Venue	Horse	Jockey	S.P.
Catterick	Corn Lily	K. Tinkler	8/13 Fav
Ripon	Corn Lily	K. Tinkler	5/2
Bangor	Koo	G. McCourt	2/13 Fav
Market Rasen	Rokala	G. McCourt	2/13 Fav
Market Rasen	Leon	G. McCourt	11/8
Perth	Leon	G. McCourt	4/5 Fav
Hamilton	Corn Lily	K. Tinkler	9/4 Fav
Perth	Bold Try	G. McCourt	8/11 Fav
Stratford	Lotus Island	G. McCourt	5/4 Fav
Market Rasen	Fisherman's Croft	G. McCourt	11/10 Fav
Ayr	Dale Park	K. Tinkler	20/1
Uttoxeter	Fisherman's Croft	G. McCourt	1/3 Fav
Catterick	Tenderloin	K. Tinkler	5/1
Edinburgh	Corn Lily	K. Tinkler	11/10 Fav
Stratford	Fisherman's Croft	G. McCourt	5/4 Fav
Market Rasen	Norquay	G. McCourt	8/11 Fav
Hexham	Fisherman's Croft	M. Hill	1/5 Fav

'F' - 26 WINNERS

Venue	Horse	Jockey	S.P.
Ayr	Dale Park	G. McCourt	9/2
Catterick	Corn Lily	M. Hill	11/8 Fav
Nottingham	Fisherman's Croft	G. McCourt	1/4 Fav
Warwick	Ghadbbaan	G. McCourt	4/6 Fav
Worcester	Wessex	G. McCourt	11/2
Uttoxeter	Norquay	G. McCourt	13/8 Fav
Ayr	Fisherman's Croft	G. McCourt	2/1
Ayr	Dale Park	G. McCourt	4/11 Fav
Catterick	Fisherman's Croft	G. McCourt	2/1 Fav
Ayr	Dale Park	C. Grant	4/5 Fav
Edinburgh	Logamimo	G. McCourt	4/9 Fav
Catterick	Estonia	M. Hill	3/1 Jt Fav
Kelso	Logamimo	G. McCourt	9/4 Jt Fav
Edinburgh	Hercle	K. Tinkler	5/1 Jt Fav

VENUE	HORSE	JOCKEY	S.P.
Perth	Fisherman's Croft	G. McCourt	4/5 Fav
Market Rasen	Logamimo	G. McCourt	9/4
Redcar	Ghadbbaan	K. Tinkler	13/8 Fav
Carlisle	Ghadbbaan	K. Tinkler	6/4 Fav
Carlisle	Norquay	K. Tinkler	9/2
Carlisle	Tenderloin	K. Tinkler	7/2
Lingfield	Ghadbbaan	K. Tinkler	11/8 Fav
Thirsk	Corn Lily	K. Tinkler	10/11 Fav
Nottingham	Corn Lily	K. Tinkler	Ev Fav
Windsor	Ghadbbaan	K. Tinkler	8/11 Fav
Redcar	Ghadbbaan	K. Tinkler	8/11 Fav
Chepstow	Ghadbbaan	K. Tinkler	7/4 Fav

'G' - 9 WINNERS

Doncaster	Rawaan	M. Hill	Ev Fav
Nottingham	Rawaan	G. McCourt	5/2 Fav
Stratford	Norquay	G. McCourt	13/2
Redcar	Srivijaya	K. Tinkler	9/2
Edinburgh	Srivijaya	K. Tinkler	4/1
Market Rasen	Rawaan	G. McCourt	1/4 Fav
Market Rasen	Rawaan	G. McCourt	4/9 Fav
Stratford	Rawaan	L. Vincent	5/1
Kelso	Rawaan	G. McCourt	2/7 Fav

'H' - 3 WINNERS

Edinburgh	Wessex	G. McCourt	4/6 Fav
Kelso	Dale Park	G. McCourt	10/11 Fav
Southwell	Rawaan	G. McCourt	3/1

'I' - 3 WINNERS

Fontwell	Society Ball	G. McCourt	6/4 Fav
Worcester	Operation Wolf	G. McCourt	7/2
Perth	Operation Wolf	G. McCourt	1/2 Fav

Appendix I - Full Circle Winners

VENUE	HORSE	JOCKEY	S.P.
'J' - 0 WINNERS			
'K' - 2 WINNERS			
Perth	Rawaan	A. Smith	11/4 Fav
Market Rasen	Rawaan	A. Smith	7/2

54 WINNING HORSES - WON 176 RACES (69 Flat and 107 Jumping)

Arum Lily	9	WowWowWow	4
Scrivijaya	2	Fisherman's Croft	9
Fiesta Moon	3	Tenderloin	2
Rawaan	9	Al Mulhalhal	3
Bold Try	1	Lotus Island	9
Logamimo	3	By Choice	1
Corn Lily	7	Leon	3
Darkorjon	1	Dale Park	7
Mayor	3	Domino Rose	1
Ghadbbaan	7	Rokala	3
Doon Venture	1	Mubdi	7
Romiosini	3	Estonia	1
Wessex	7	Authentic	2
Girdle Ness	1	Foot Patrol	6
Caro's Gift	2	Hercle	1
Lady la Paz	5	Desert Emperor	2
Hyokin	1	Meningi	5
Design Wise	2	Monanore	1
Hanseatic	4	Flyaway	2
Octolan	1	Gold Sceptre	4
Koo	2	Princess Singh	1
Good Point	4	Lake Onega	2
Rainbow Vision	1	Tiklas	4
Love to Dance	2	Society Ball	1
Spate	4	Miss Maina	2
Street Party	1	Norquay	4

Operation Wolf	2	The Ellier	1

WON ON 38 COURSES

Ayr	19	Carlisle	4
Fairyhouse	1	Catterick	16
Kelso	4	Fontwell	1
Market Rasen	14	Redcar	4
Hereford	1	Nottingham	14
Ripon	4	Huntingdon	1
Edinburgh	11	Hexham	3
Kempton	1	Southwell	9
Uttoxeter	3	Leicester	1
Hamilton	8	Beverley	2
Lingfield	1	Worcester	8
Cartmel	2	Sedgefield	1
Thirsk	7	Chepstow	2
Warwick	1	Newcastle	6
Haydock	2	Windsor	1
Perth	6	Wetherby	2
Wolverhampton	1	Stratford	7
Bangor	1	York	1
Doncaster	5	Cheltenham	1

23 JOCKEYS RODE THE WINNERS

G. McCourt	73	R. Dunwoody	2
D. Nicholls	1	K. Tinkler	56
T. Ives	2	P. Scudamore	1
N. Tinkler	14	A. Smith	2
D. Sullivan	1	M. Hill	4
M. Birch	1	P. Tuck	1
J. Bowker	3	J. H. Brown	1
L. Vincent	1	M. Dwyer	3
G. Carter	1	T. Williams	1
C. Grant	3	G. Duffield	1
L. Wyer	1		

Appendix I - Full Circle Winners

G. Armytage   2   A. Farrell   1

There were 2 Successful Trainers
Nigel Tinkler - 175   Bill Harney (Ireland) - 1